HOW TO USE

Microsoft®

Outlook 97

F13
F14
F15
Num Lock
Page Up
Home
Insert
Backspace
Delete
End
Page Down
Enter
Shift
Ctrl
Alt
Enter

HOW TO USE

Microsoft® Outlook 97

Deborah Lewites

ZD Press
An Imprint of Que®

Ziff-Davis Press
An imprint of Macmillan Computer Publishing USA
Emeryville, California

Publisher	Joe Wikert
Associate Publisher	Juliet Langley
Acquisitions Editor	Lysa Lewallen
Development Editor	Margo Hill
Copy Editor	Margo Hill
Technical Reviewer	Mark Hall
Production Editor	Ami Knox
Proofreader	Timothy Loughman
Book Design	Dan Armstrong
Page Layout	Janet Piercy and Bruce Lundquist
Indexer	Carol Burbo

Ziff-Davis Press imprint books are produced on a Macintosh computer system with the following applications: FrameMaker®, Microsoft® Word, QuarkXPress®, Adobe Illustrator®, Adobe Photoshop®, Adobe Streamline™, MacLink®Plus, Aldus® FreeHand™, Collage Plus™.

Ziff-Davis Press, an imprint of
Macmillan Computer Publishing USA
5903 Christie Avenue
Emeryville, CA 94608

PART OF A CONTINUING SERIES

ISBN 1-56276-550-7

Manufactured in the United States of America
10 9 8 7 6 5 4 3 2 1

This book is dedicated to my mother and to E.T. for providing so much help and support during its writing.

DEBORAH LEWITES has been working with computers and training new users most of her adult life. Writing books that let her use those same skills is a new career that lets her stay home to play with her daughter.

GUSHING AND FERVENT thanks are due to David Madison of Microsoft Corporation for his help, his humor, and his general all-around "nice-guyness."

I owe an enormous debt of gratitude to Nancy Warner, who brought her abundant talents to this book in a variety of ways. You wouldn't be holding this book in your hands without her help.

Working with the people at Ziff-Davis Press is a joy. Lysa Lewallen's support and encouragement are responsible for the very existence of this book. She's more fun to work with than almost anybody else I know. Margo Hill and Ami Knox did the work of at least four people to push the manuscript out the door and into the hands of the printer in perfect shape. Pipi Diamond faced the impossible job of coordinating all the details and managed it without a single slip, which is a remarkable feat. The good fortune of having Mark Hall and Scott Warner as technical editors was an unbelievable stroke of luck which probably means I did something worthy in an earlier life.

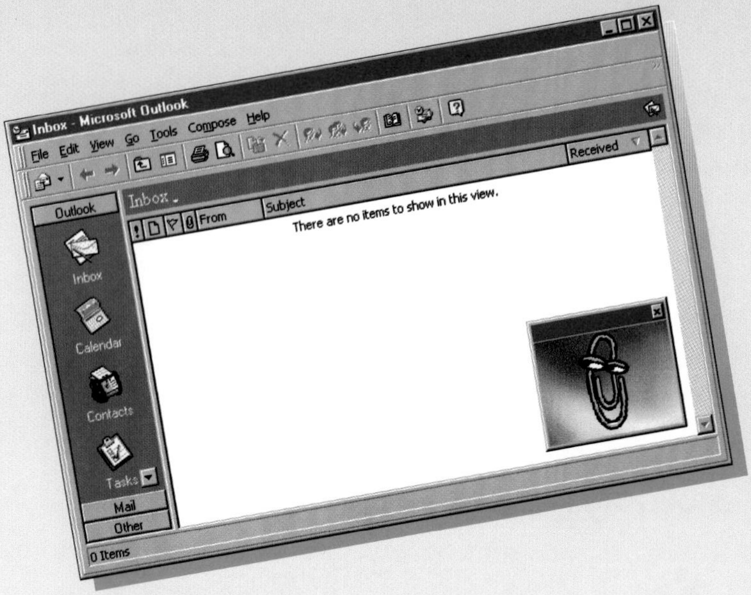
Inbox - Microsoft Outlook
File Edit View Go Tools Compose Help
Received
Inbox
From
Subject
There are no items to show in this view.
Outlook
Inbox
Calendar
Contacts
Tasks
Mail
Other
0 Items

T A B L E

Inbox - Microsoft Outlook
File Edit View Go Tools Compose Help
Outlook
Inbox
From
Subject
Received
There are no items to show in this view.
Inbox
Calendar
Contacts
Tasks
Mail
Other
0 Items

INTRODUCTION

HOW TO USE MICROSOFT OFFICE 97 is an illustrated guide through all the features and functions of this new software from Microsoft Corp. With a step-by-step approach, this book walks you through all the things you can accomplish when you use the software.

As you follow along, the illustrations for each step match what you'll see on your own computer screen. The steps are presented in a logical order so you can work along with us and end up in the same place.

There are some tips about how you can be more productive along the way as you travel through all the different parts of Outlook. And there's some advice to help you make some of the decisions you'll face about handling files and using features.

As you move through the chapters, you'll find that even though you primarily use Outlook for e-mail, there is plenty of power in the other parts of this software. This book makes it easy to use that power with confidence.

Ctrl + Shift + I=
Inbox
Ctrl + Shift + O=
Outbox

PART 1

Getting Started with Outlook

YOU'RE ABOUT TO LOOK at a new, powerful way to handle and organize your e-mail and other communication software. Microsoft Outlook 97 gives you control over the way you keep records as you contact people in your company, send e-mail over the Internet, or write letters.

In this chapter, you'll learn how to open Outlook, and you'll also get a peek at the Outlook software window. Then, of course, you'll learn how to correctly exit the software.

Once we finish with these preliminary necessities, we'll move onward and upward until you've learned how to use this powerful software to increase your productivity and efficiency, and we'll show you how much fun it is to use.

IN THIS SECTION YOU'LL LEARN

How to Start and Exit Outlook

I'm assuming that Outlook has been installed on your computer, either as part of your installation of Microsoft Office 97, or as a stand-alone software application that connects you to your company's e-mail system (such as Microsoft Exchange Server). While starting Outlook isn't difficult, the actual steps you'll follow will depend upon the way the software was installed.

1. If you're working in Windows 95 or Windows NT 4, there is probably a Microsoft Outlook icon on your desktop. Double-click it to launch the software.

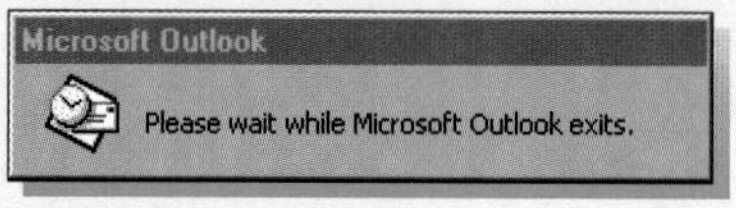

6. The software has an internal exit routine and asks you to wait until the program is totally shut down before proceeding with your next computer task (especially if the next thing you're planning to do is shut down your computer). After a few seconds, the message disappears to indicate that all the files are in order and Outlook has shut itself down properly.

FYI

- **If there is no Outlook icon on your Windows 95 or Windows NT 4 desktop and you'd like one, you can create one by finding the file named OUTLOOK.EXE in Explorer and using the right mouse button to drag the file's icon to the desktop. Release the mouse button and then choose Create Shortcut(s) Here. A shortcut is created automatically (move it anywhere that's convenient on your desktop) and you can double-click it to start Outlook.**
- **If you're logged onto a network message service, you can also choose Exit and Log off from the File menu when you close Outlook. This not only shuts down the software, it disconnects you from the message service. There are times when this is a good idea, and other times when it isn't, so check with your system administrator to learn what the consequences are on your particular network setup.**

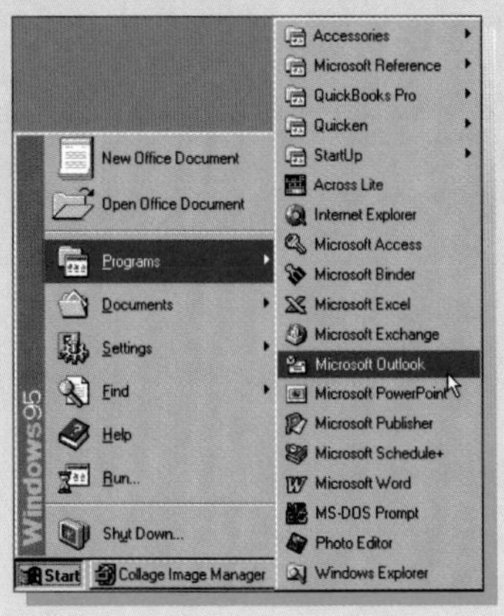

2 If your Windows 95 or Windows NT 4 desktop doesn't have an Outlook icon, click Start, then point to Programs on the Start menu. Choose Microsoft Outlook from the Programs group.

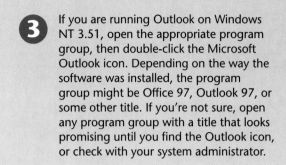

3 If you are running Outlook on Windows NT 3.51, open the appropriate program group, then double-click the Microsoft Outlook icon. Depending on the way the software was installed, the program group might be Office 97, Outlook 97, or some other title. If you're not sure, open any program group with a title that looks promising until you find the Outlook icon, or check with your system administrator.

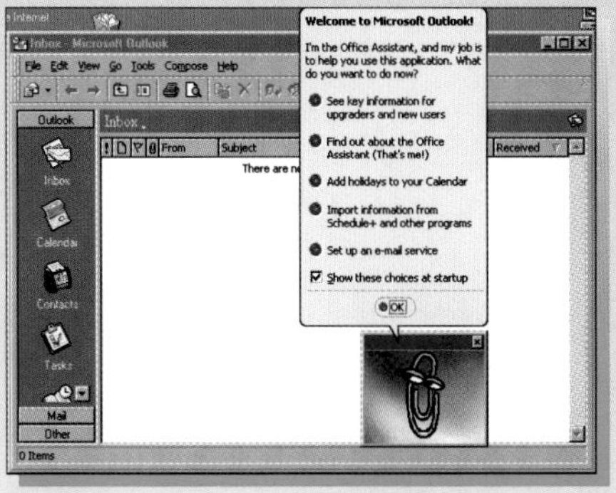

4 Whatever method you use to launch Outlook, the program opens with the Inbox in the software window. The Microsoft Office Assistant sits on top of the software window, waiting for a chance to help you (we'll learn more about this opening window in the following pages). Your opening window may not look exactly like the one in the illustration, but the Inbox and the Office Assistant should be there.

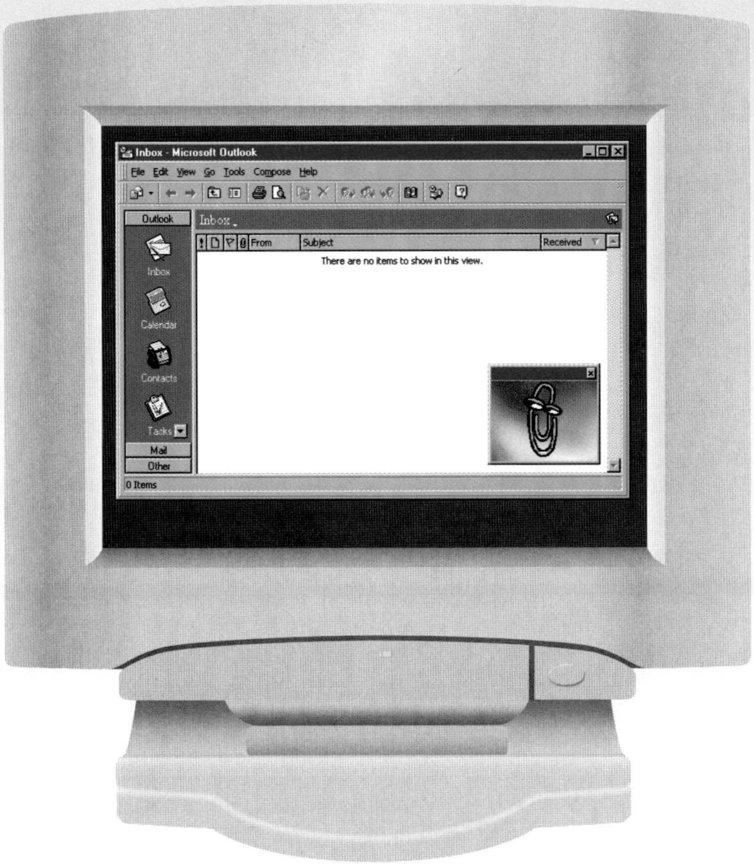

5 You can't do anything until you clear the Office Assistant's message, so click OK to make it go away. Then you can access the Outlook window. To close Microsoft Outlook, choose File, Exit. Or, in Windows 95 or Windows NT 4, click the close button (the X) in the upper right corner of the software window.

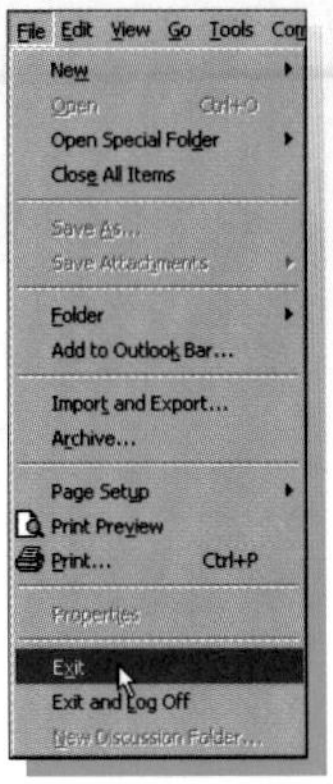

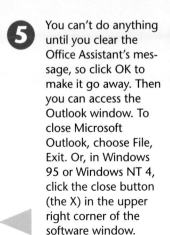

How to Navigate the Opening Window

Your first view of Outlook may be a bit confusing, because there are quite a few things on the software window that display on your screen. You have control over the window's elements and appearance. As you continue to use Outlook and grow more proficient at it, you'll probably change the opening window's appearance to suit your needs.

One of the most noticeable things about the opening window is the bright yellow message that appears over the icon for the Office Assistant. While the message offers to help, the fact is that most of the choices actually lead you to some decision-making process about various parts of your Outlook system. This can be confusing, so you may want to wait until you have to use those features and make your setup decisions at that time (we'll discuss them throughout this book, of course).

1 Click the OK button at the bottom of the Office Assistant's message to get rid of this message. The Office Assistant stays behind (he'll remind you he's there by wiggling occasionally) and you can move him away by placing your mouse pointer on the blue bar at the top of the box that contains the paper clip and dragging the box off to one side until it's on the desktop. After you move the Office Assistant box, Outlook remembers where you parked him and he'll be in his new parking place the next time you open the software.

FYI

- **If you don't want to see the opening message from the Office Assistant when you open the software, click the checkbox that says Show These Choices At Startup. The checkmark disappears and the next time you open Outlook the Office Assistant doesn't show the welcoming message.**
- **The Help menu also contains links to Microsoft on the World Wide Web. If you have an Internet browser installed, it opens and heads for the appropriate Microsoft Web page.**
- **There may be other Help system listings on your Help menu, depending on the services you've installed with Outlook. For example, if you're using Internet Mail services, there is a help system for that.**

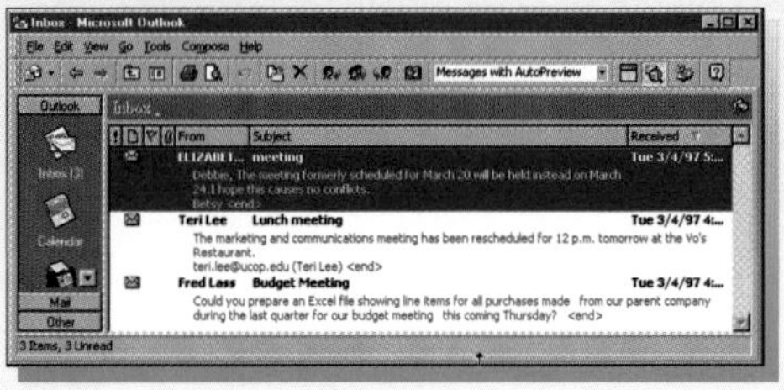

6 To change the size of the Outlook window, move your mouse pointer to one of the edges of the window. When the pointer turns into a double-headed arrow, press and hold the left mouse button while you drag the arrow in the appropriate direction. You can make the Outlook window large enough to fill your screen by clicking the Maximize button on the Title Bar. Outlook remembers the size of the window when you exit and presents it in the same size the next time you launch the software.

2 The Office Assistant shows up when you click the Help icon on the toolbar (the question mark) or choose Help, Microsoft Outlook Help from the menu bar. You can change the persona of the Office Assistant if you don't like paper clips winking at you and making metallic noises. First, make sure your Office 97 CD-ROM is in the CD-ROM drive (that's where the other Assistants hang out while they wait for you to bring them over to your computer). Click the Options button on the Office Assistant message (click the blue bar at the top of the Office Assistant to display a message if there isn't one at the moment). When the Office Assistant dialog box displays, click the Gallery tab. Then continue clicking Next until you see all the choices for the Office Assistant character. Pick the one that appeals to you. When you change the Office Assistant character, it changes for all the software in Microsoft Office 97.

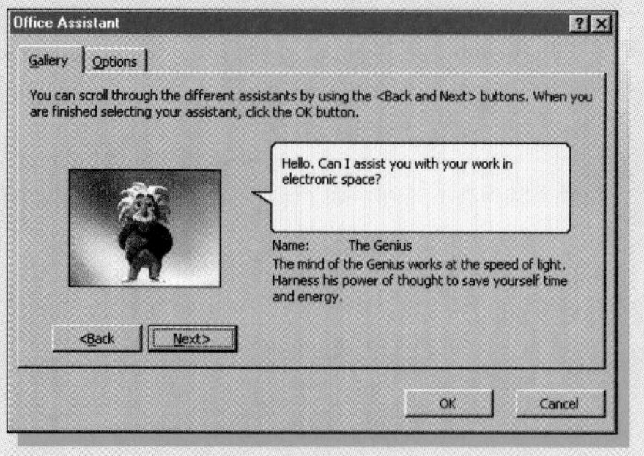

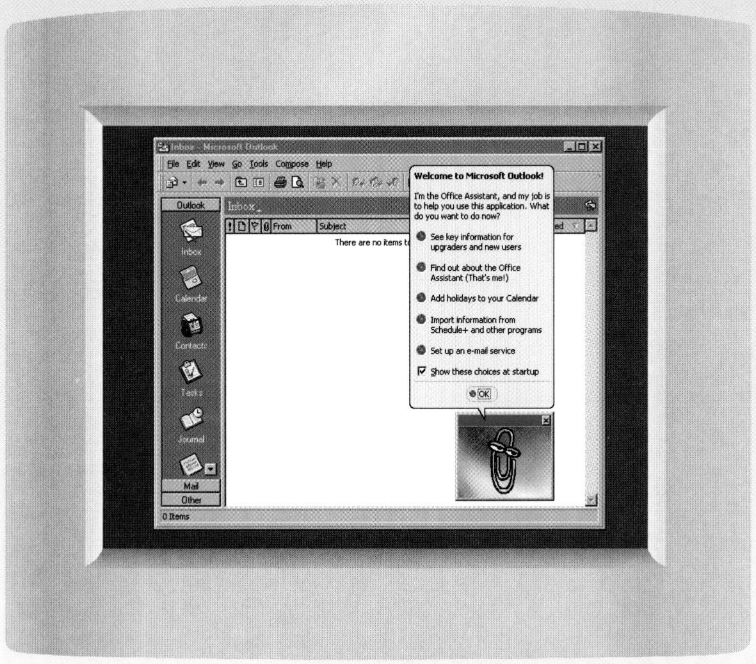

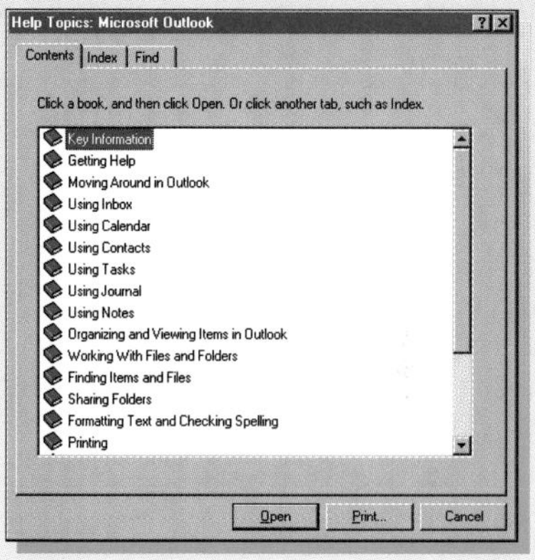

3 Choose Help, Contents and Index from the menu bar to bring up the full Outlook help system.

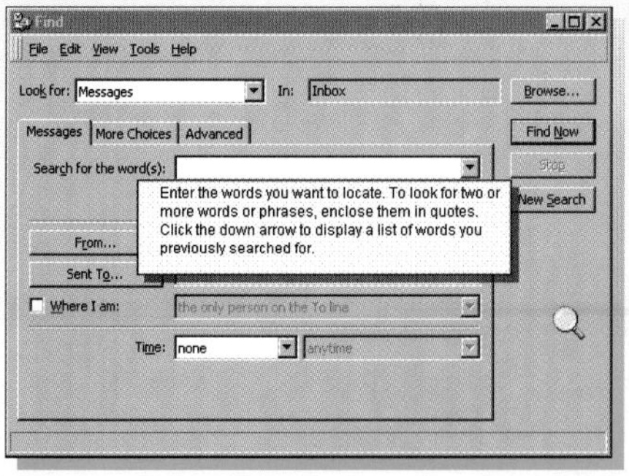

4 When you want to know about a specific item in an Outlook Information Viewer or dialog box, point to the item and press Shift+F1. The What's This? feature kicks in to explain the item. (In this illustration I asked what the "Search for the Words" box was and how it works). Click anywhere on the explanation to make it go away.

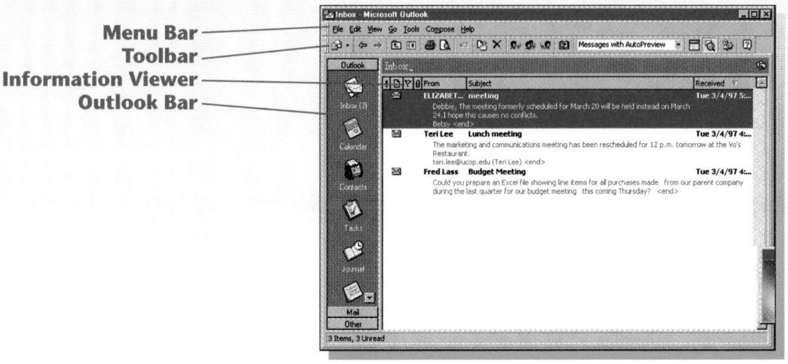

5 By default, when you start Outlook, the Inbox is the Information Viewer that displays in the Outlook window. This is because the Inbox holds the e-mail you've received and most people use the e-mail features in Outlook more than they use any other feature. The title of the current Information Viewer displays atop its window, and a menu bar and a toolbar are above that. The Outlook Bar, which contains icons that move you to other Outlook features, is on the left side of the window.

How to Use the Mail Windows

When Outlook first opens, the Inbox displays—it is the current Information Viewer in the Outlook window. The Inbox is actually a folder, and it is one part of your e-mail system. There are a number of other folders in the Outlook mail system. Each folder has a role to play in the overall handling and manipulation of e-mail that you send and receive.

The folders act much like folders in a physical filing cabinet: they hold items (in the mail system, of course, the items are e-mail messages).

1 A quick way to move to a specific Outlook folder or feature is to use the icons in the Outlook Bar. To see the folders in the mail system, click the horizontal bar labeled Mail. Now, the icons for the Outlook mail system will display on the Outlook Bar.

Folder List icon

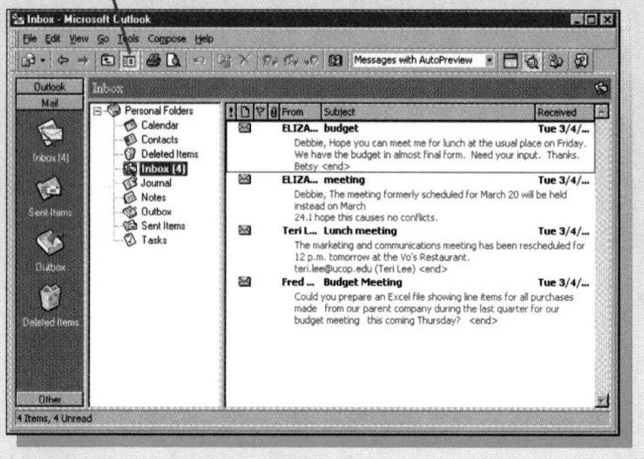

6 Since each icon on the Outlook Bar for Mail represents a folder, it might be nice (or more productive) to see those folders. Once you see them, you can click the folder you want to move to (which is handy if the Outlook Bar isn't displaying the set of folders you need at the moment). Click the Folder List icon on the toolbar (to the left of the Printer icon) or choose View, Folder List from the menu bar.

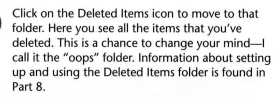

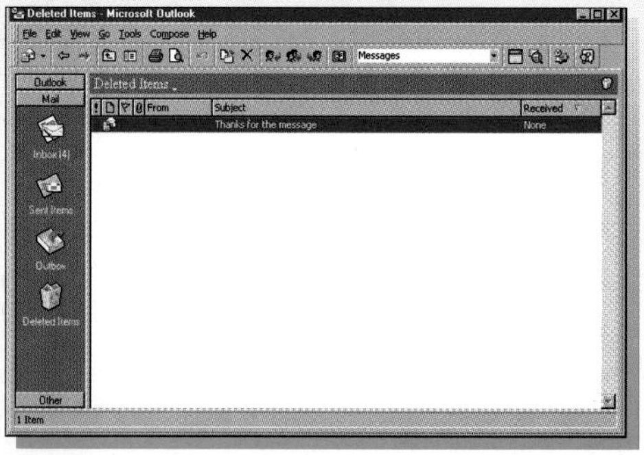

5 Click on the Deleted Items icon to move to that folder. Here you see all the items that you've deleted. This is a chance to change your mind—I call it the "oops" folder. Information about setting up and using the Deleted Items folder is found in Part 8.

FYI

- **The Folder List option is a toggle switch, and you make the same selection (the Folder List icon or the menu option) to get rid of the folder list and use all the space in the Information Viewer for the items in that folder.**
- **You can change the width of the folder pane if you need to. Move your mouse pointer to the vertical bar between the folder pane and the items listing. When your pointer changes to a double-headed arrow, drag the pane in the appropriate direction.**

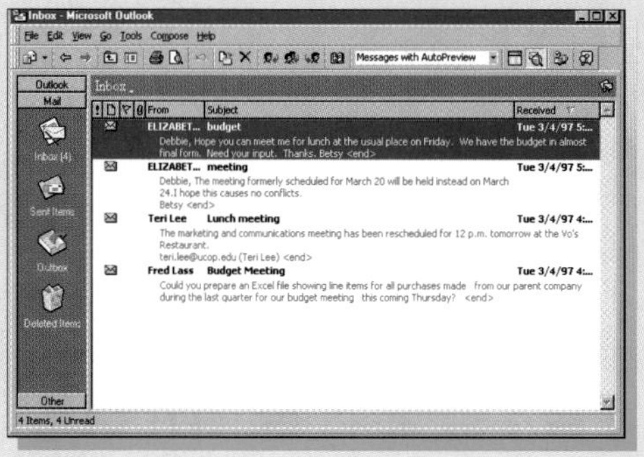

2 The Inbox, which is already in the Information Viewer, displays received e-mail. Mail that you haven't read yet is listed in bold type. By default, the mail is listed in the order in which it was received (the most recent message is on top), and the first couple of lines of the message are shown. You can change the display in the Inbox, and information about making changes is found in Part 2.

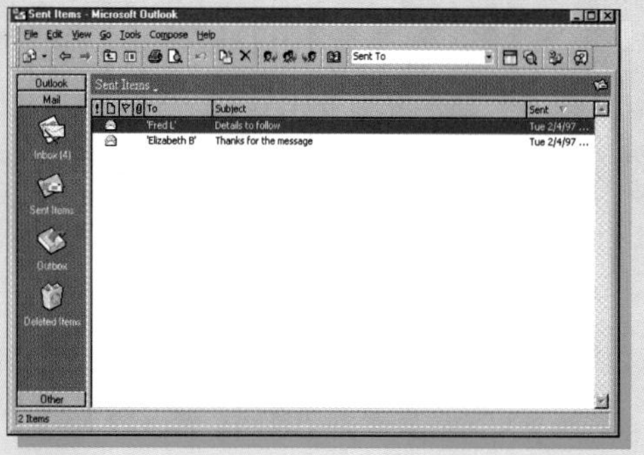

3 Click the Sent Items icon on the Outlook Bar to move to that folder. This folder holds messages you have sent. The fact that a message is in the Sent Items folder indicates that the process of shipping the message to the recipient has been completed. If you are connected to a network mailbox, it means the message was sent to the network post office. If you use your modem and an Internet service provider to send mail, these items were sent to the ISP when you dialed in and uploaded messages.

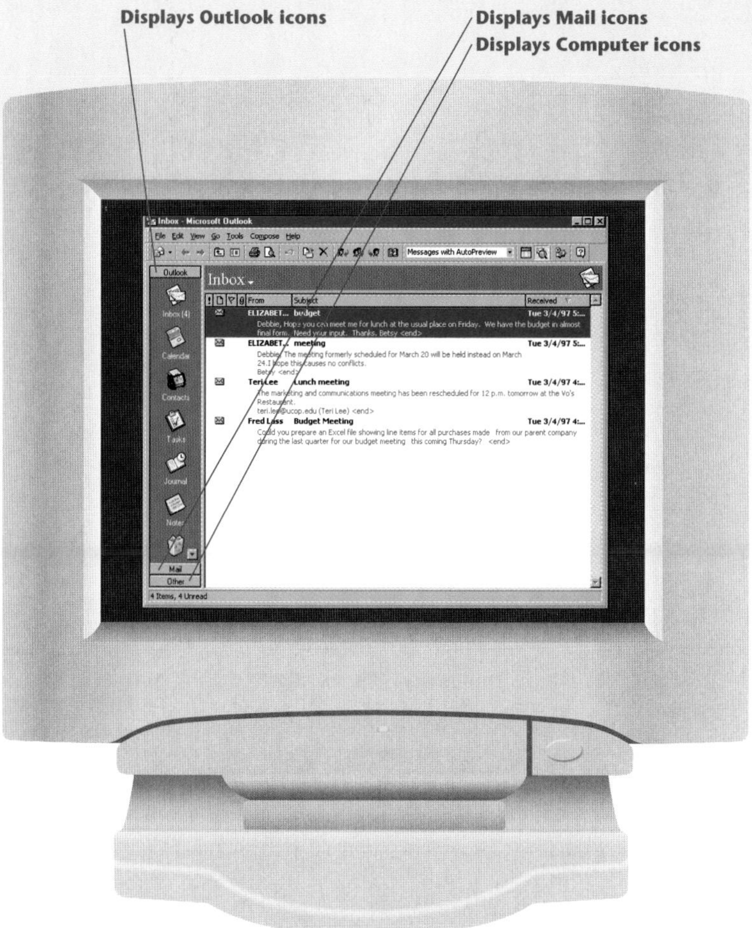

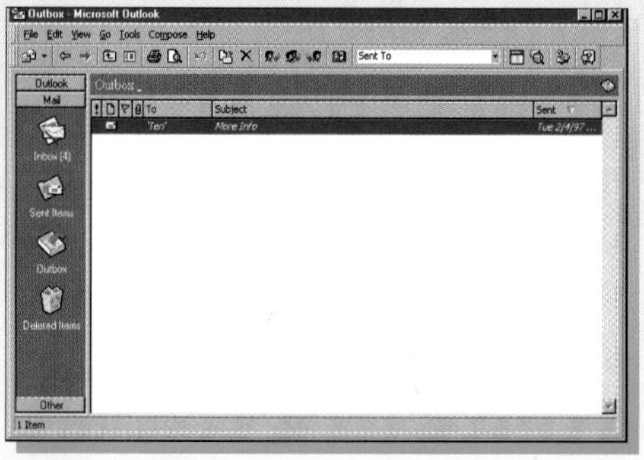

4 Click the Outbox icon on the Outlook Bar to see the items in the Outbox folder. Any messages listed are waiting to be sent to their recipients. Their presence in the Outbox indicates that you composed the message and sent it. However, they haven't been picked up yet. If you're on a network mail system you probably will never see anything in the Outbox folder, because when you choose Send after composing a message, it's sent to the network post office immediately. (See Part 2 for all the details about composing and sending messages). If you dial in to an ISP to get and send mail, however, this Outbox is checked and any item in it is sent to the mail server of the ISP. The message then moves to the Sent Items folder.

How to Use the Calendar Windows

The Outlook calendar features will provide more than just the answer to "What's today's date?" A robust appointment system helps you keep your life in order.

Information about using the features in the calendar system can be found in Part 3. Here we'll take a brief view of the windows that display as you work in Outlook.

To move to the Calendar features, click the Outlook horizontal bar on the Outlook Bar to display the Outlook icons. Then click the Calendar icon.

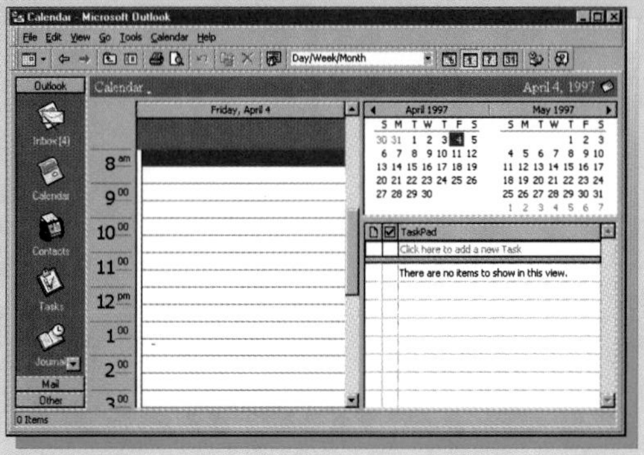

1 The Day view of the Information Viewer for the Calendar shows a detailed view of the current date, monthly calendars for the current and next months (the monthly calendars are called the Date Navigators), and a view of the TaskPad (which displays any current tasks). It's really a Day/Week/Month view. While this view can be a productive way to approach your time management, it can sometimes look a bit busy.

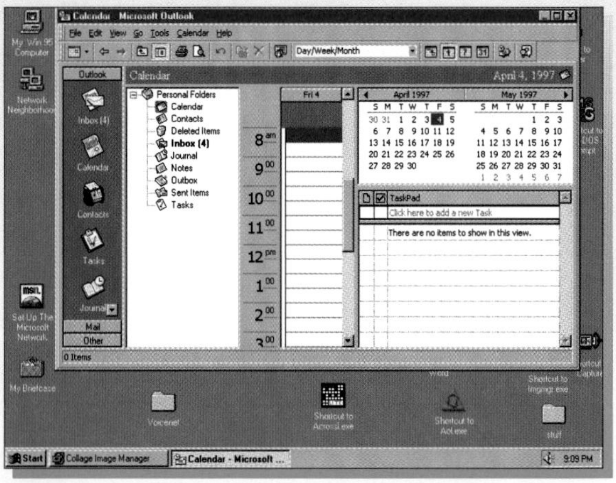

6 Use the Folder list icon on the toolbar to turn the folder display on (and off) for quick access to other Outlook features and folders.

FYI

- **Notice that when you move to the Calendar window, the menu bar changes to include a Calendar menu.**
- **If you are on a network that uses Exchange Server, there are additional functions available in Calendar. You can view free and busy times for users throughout your organization (you're looking at their calendars, which are marked as "busy" when an appointment is scheduled). This makes it possible to set up meetings in such a way that you can plan a time when everyone you need is free.**

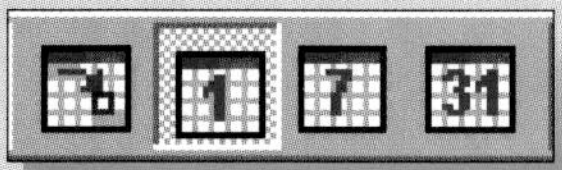

2 The toolbar on the Calendar window holds icons for changing the view. Choose among Today, Day, Week, and Month.

3 Use the Today icon to move back to the current date when you've been entering information in other months. It's a fast way to get back without scrolling through the calendars when you've been entering appointments for dates three or four months away.

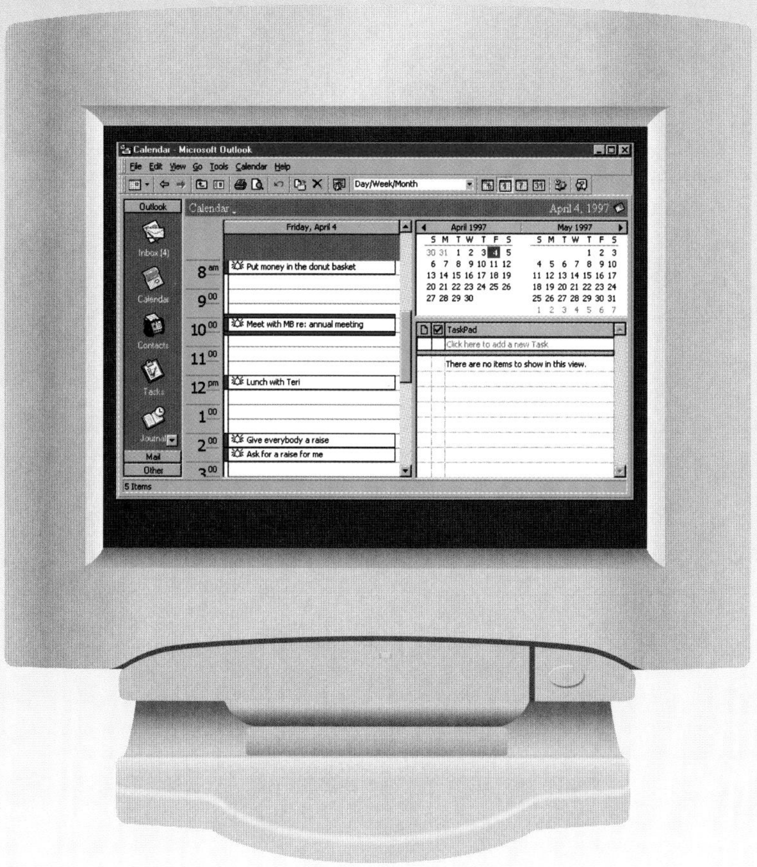

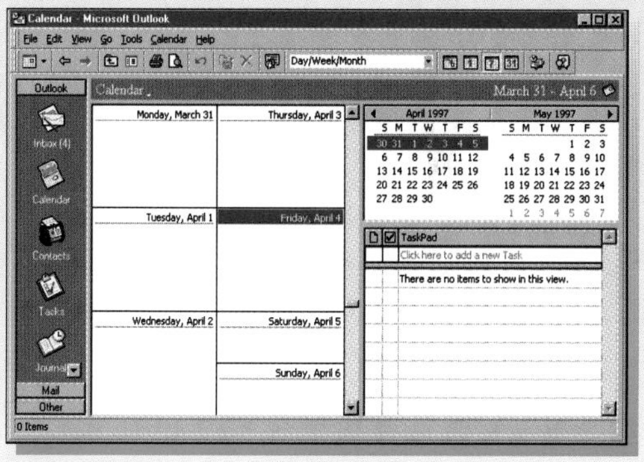

4 Click the Week icon to see the current week along with the Date Navigator and the TaskPad. The current date is highlighted for you in case you have trouble remembering what day it is.

5 Click the Month icon to view the current month. You can use the scroll bar to move up and down through past and future months.

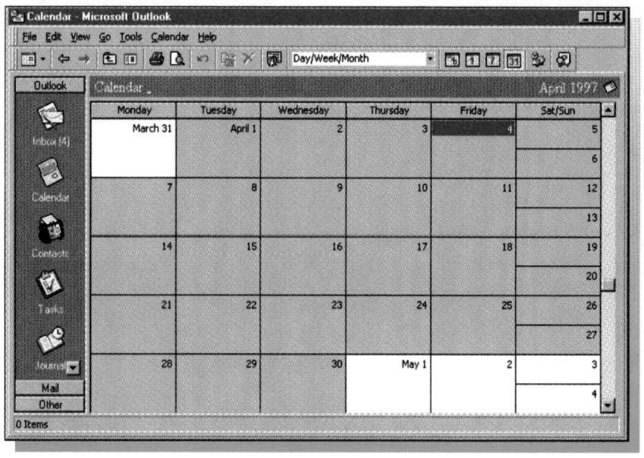

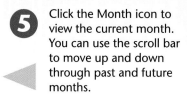

How to Use the Contact Database Windows

Outlook includes a powerful personal information manager with a system for tracking contacts. Not only can you keep a list of contacts, along with all sorts of detailed information about each person, but you can also use the list with other Outlook features. In fact, you can use it with other Microsoft Office products. For example, you can create a mailing with Microsoft Word's mailmerge feature, using your contact database as the data file.

Detailed information about using the Contact database is in Part 5. In this section we'll take a brief look at the ways you can view the Contact database so you can get comfortable with it. Click the Contacts icon on the Outlook Bar to see the Contacts Information Viewer.

FYI

- **Creating filters and changing the sort scheme by selecting a column heading works for all the Outlook Information Viewers, not just Contacts.**
- **To AutoDial, you need to have a phone (instrument) connected to your modem. Otherwise, when the contact answers your call, all those screechy modem noises will annoy her.**
- **The Web Page access that's available on the toolbar of the Contact card is handy for all the hardware, software, and other company contacts. Going to the Web page is usually faster than calling that contact when you need information or support.**

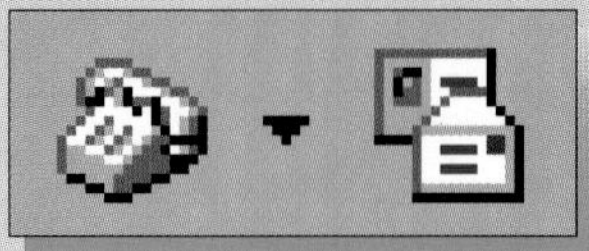

1 When you choose Contacts from the Outlook Bar, the toolbar changes a bit to give you quick access to Contact features. Two handy tools are AutoDial, which automatically dials the selected contact's phone number, and New Message to Contact, which opens an e-mail message form so you don't have to switch to the Mail window when you need to drop a note to this contact.

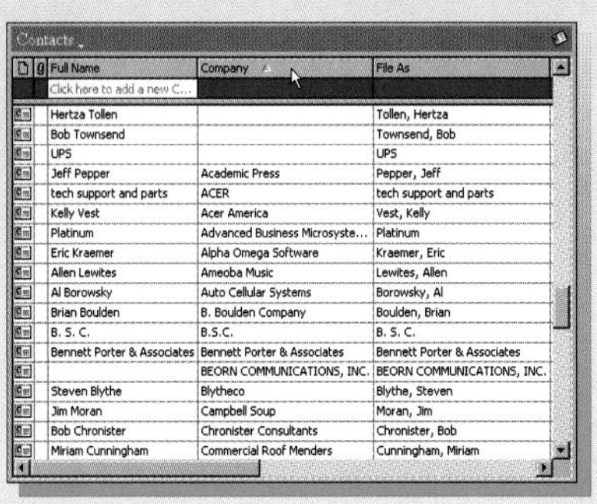

Full Name	Company	File As
Click here to add a new C...		
Hertza Tollen		Tollen, Hertza
Bob Townsend		Townsend, Bob
UPS		UPS
Jeff Pepper	Academic Press	Pepper, Jeff
tech support and parts	ACER	tech support and parts
Kelly Vest	Acer America	Vest, Kelly
Platinum	Advanced Business Microsyste...	Platinum
Eric Kraemer	Alpha Omega Software	Kraemer, Eric
Allen Lewites	Ameoba Music	Lewites, Allen
Al Borowsky	Auto Cellular Systems	Borowsky, Al
Brian Boulden	B. Boulden Company	Boulden, Brian
B. S. C.	B.S.C.	B. S. C.
Bennett Porter & Associates	Bennett Porter & Associates	Bennett Porter & Associates
	BEORN COMMUNICATIONS, INC.	BEORN COMMUNICATIONS, INC.
Steven Blythe	Blytheco	Blythe, Steven
Jim Moran	Campbell Soup	Moran, Jim
Bob Chronister	Chronister Consultants	Chronister, Bob
Miriam Cunningham	Commercial Roof Menders	Cunningham, Miriam

6 You can change the way a listing displays by altering the way the listing is sorted. The quickest way to do that is to choose the column you want to sort on, and click the column heading. A little arrow appears on the column heading to tell you that this is the way the list is sorted. Click the column heading again to reverse the sorting scheme (from ascending to descending).

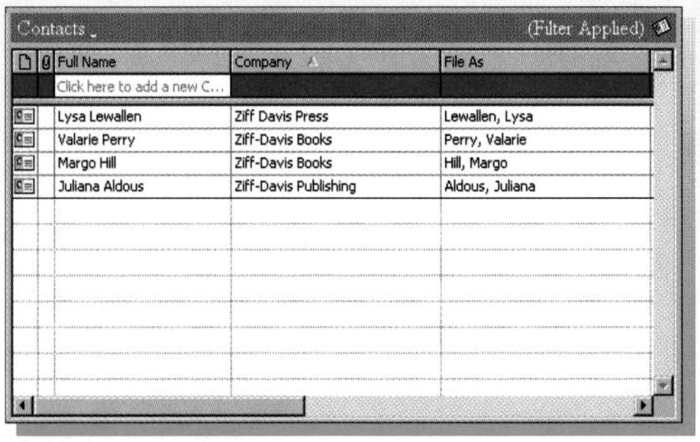

Full Name	Company	File As
Click here to add a new C...		
Lysa Lewallen	Ziff Davis Press	Lewallen, Lysa
Valarie Perry	Ziff-Davis Books	Perry, Valarie
Margo Hill	Ziff-Davis Books	Hill, Margo
Juliana Aldous	Ziff-Davis Publishing	Aldous, Juliana

5 Click OK on the Filter dialog box and the listing in the Information Viewer matches the filter. To eliminate the filter, return to the Filter dialog box and choose Clear All, then click OK.

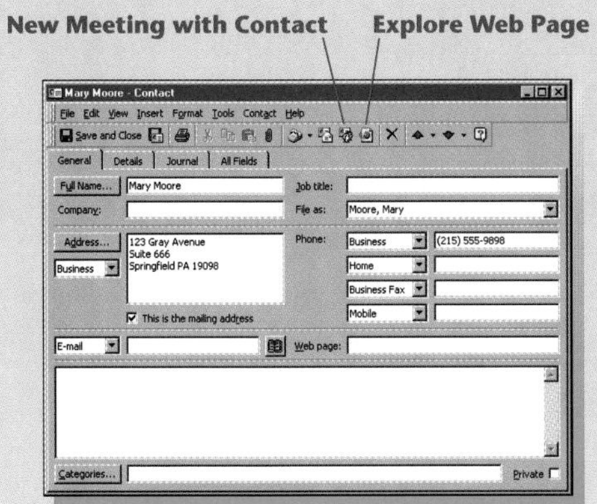

2 When you double-click a contact listing, that Contact Card opens, displaying all the information you've previously entered. The toolbar on the Contact Card window adds two more handy icons: New Meeting with Contact, to let you set up an appointment without switching to the Calendar window; and Explore Web Page, which opens your Internet browser and heads for the contact's Web page.

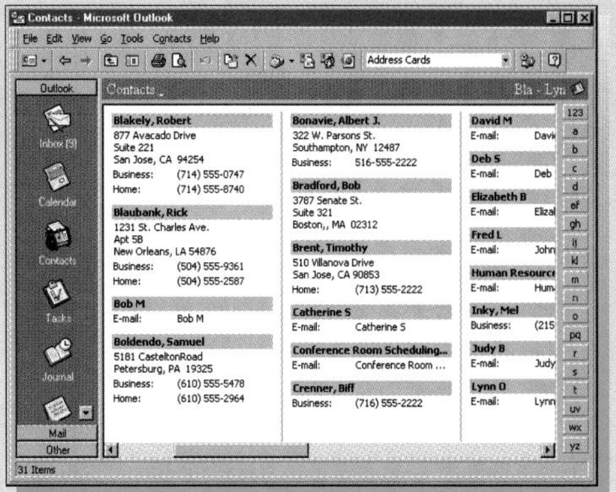

3 The Current View box on the toolbar lets you change the display of your contact list. The Address Cards view is nifty because you see more information about each contact, and you can get to any contact quickly. The alphabetical column on the right side of the Information Viewer provides a quick way to move to a specific part of your contact list. Above the alphabet display is the alphabetical description of the current view—it's rather like a telephone book.

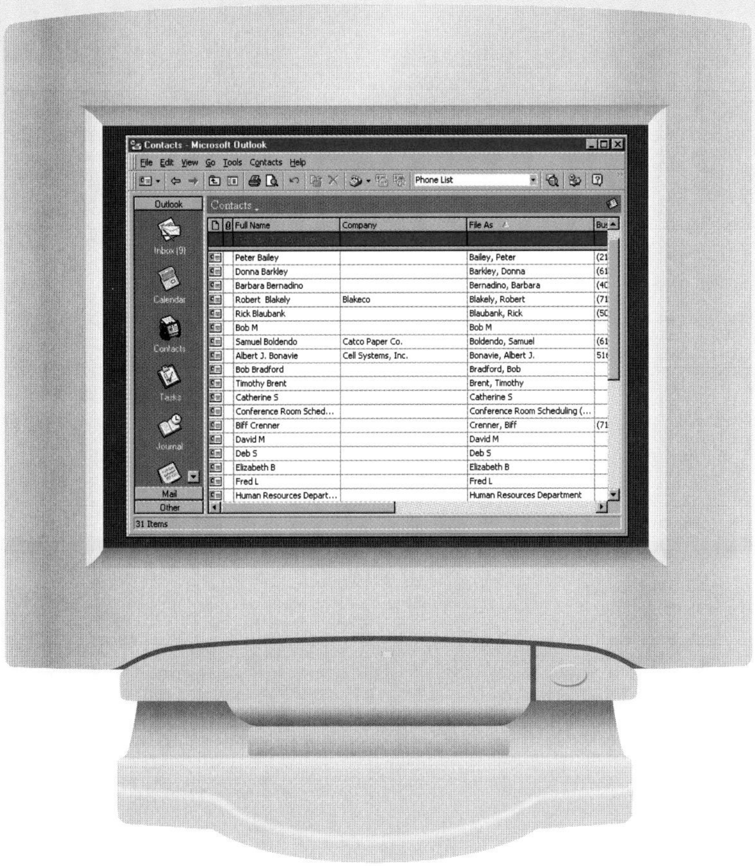

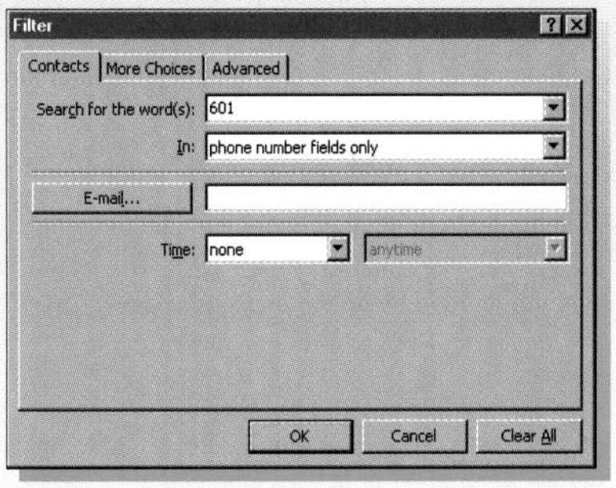

4 One of the more clever and powerful features in the contact database is the ability to filter the listing so that you see only specific items that match your criteria. For instance, I have trouble remembering names, and when I need to call an editor I use a filter so I can search by some item I do remember. Ziff-Davis (the publisher of this book) has a telephone number that starts with 601 (Isn't it strange that I can remember that and not the names of my editors?), so I apply that filter. Get to the Filter dialog box by choosing View, Filter from the menu bar.

How to Use the Tasks Window

Outlook provides a robust task tracking system that you'll find useful for everything from a simple to-do reminder to a complicated project. (Full coverage of Outlook tasks is found in Part 4). To get to the Tasks Information Viewer, click the Tasks icon on the Outlook Bar.

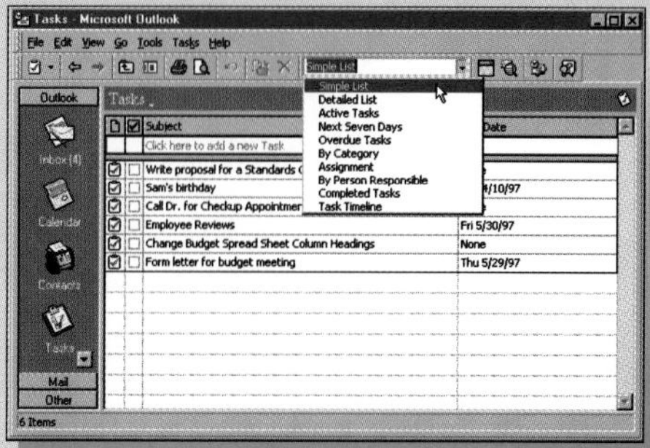

1 The default Information Viewer for tasks displays the tasks as a simple list. There are a number of other schemes for displaying tasks and you can choose one from the Current View box on the toolbar.

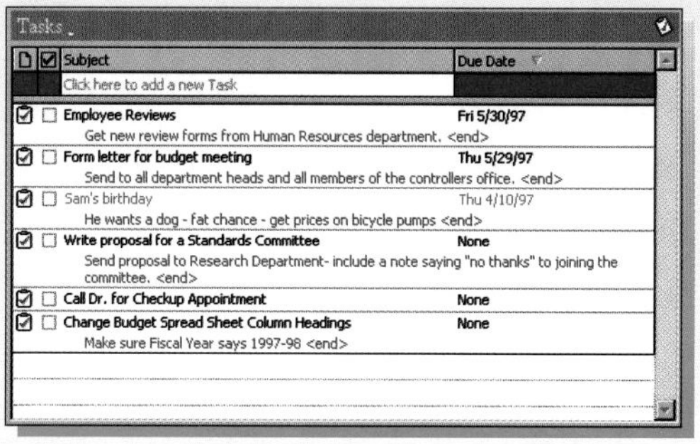

6 Another clever nagging technique Outlook uses is highlighting overdue tasks in red.

FYI

- **You can drag a task to a folder instead of an Outlook Bar icon if you have the folder pane displayed in your Tasks window.**
- **The Monthly view of the Calendar Information Viewer does not contain a TaskPad.**

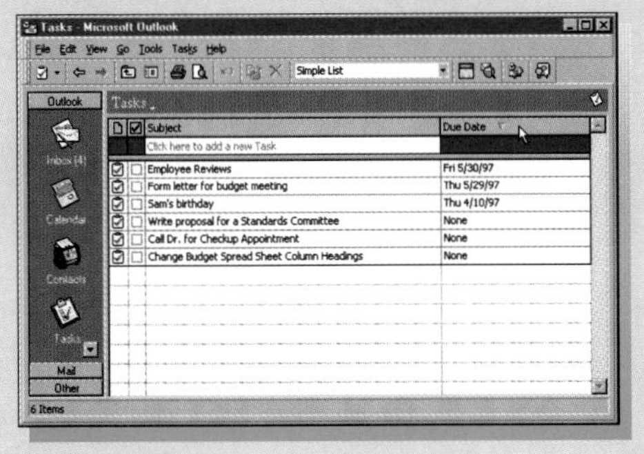

2 While it seems reasonable to want to list your tasks in the order in which they're due, there's no choice for that on the Current View drop-down list. That's because you can sort the list by due date easily—click the Due Date column heading on the Information Viewer. To reverse the sort (from ascending dates to descending dates), click the column heading again.

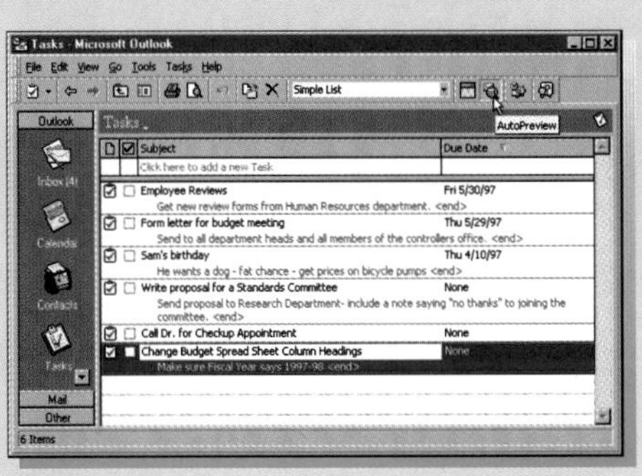

3 Click the AutoPreview icon on the Tasks toolbar to reveal any comments you entered when you created the tasks. Up to three lines of comments display, which is enough to jog your memory about the task.

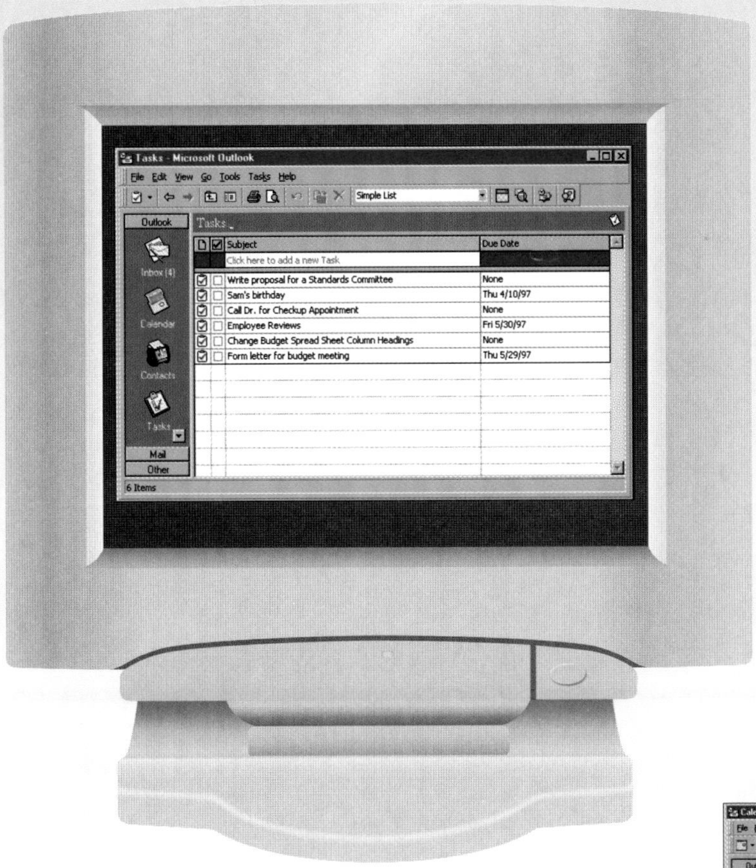

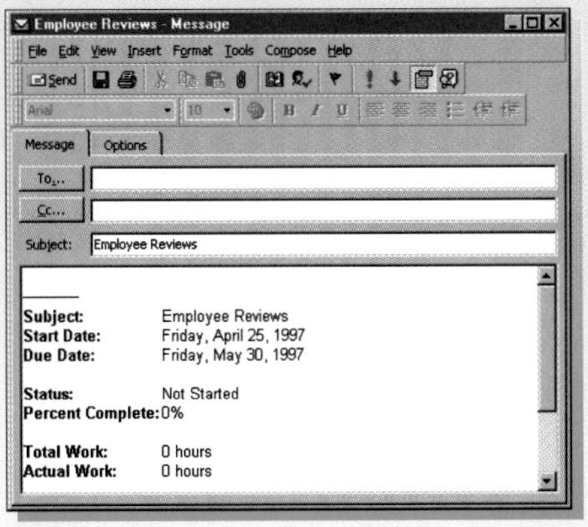

4 If you need to send a status report on a task, drag the task to the Inbox icon on the Outlook Bar. A message form opens and so much information is entered automatically that there's practically nothing left to do (except fill in the recipient's name, of course).

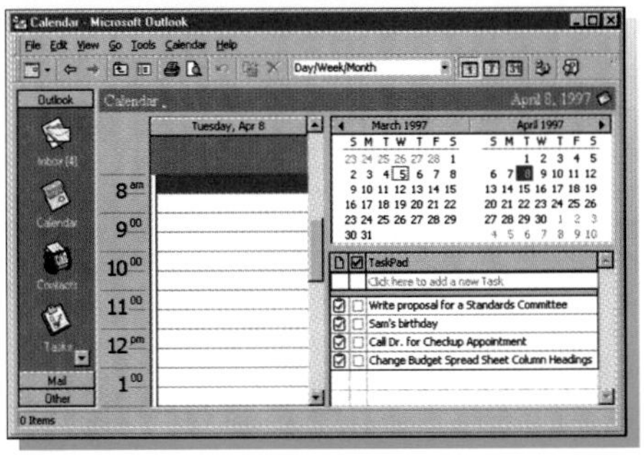

5 Since tasks are always hanging over your head, Outlook makes sure you are reminded about them, especially when you are planning your time. The Calendar windows display your tasks on the TaskPad—it's a form of nagging that Outlook uses to make sure you get your work done.

How to Use the Mail Group Icons

The Mail group consists of the Inbox, Sent Items, Outbox, and Deleted Items icons. This is where you can receive, send, delete, and read e-mail messages. When you send a message, it is placed in the Outbox. This is where the message remains until you decide whether to send it or delete it.

You can review outgoing e-mail messages in the Outbox folder before the message is sent. This allows you to make changes or add new information to a message. After a message is sent, it will appear in the Sent Items folder. Message can be deleted at any time. Deleted messages are placed in the Deleted Items folder.

This page will show you how to view messages that have been sent and messages that are waiting to be sent.

1. Click on the button labeled Mail on the Outlook Bar to open the mail group.

FYI

- **In addition to altering the content of a message in the Outbox, you can change the list of people that will receive the message. You can also change options such as the Importance or Sensitivity of a message.**
- **Keep messages that you have sent as a record of correspondence with others. If you need to recall the contents of a message or resend a message, you have the original.**

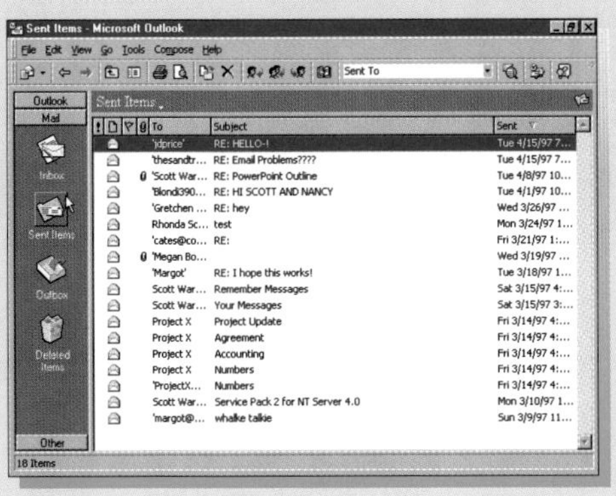

2 Click on the Sent Items icon on the Outlook Bar. It looks like a manila folder with a stamped envelope speeding past it. The contents of the Sent Items folder will be displayed.

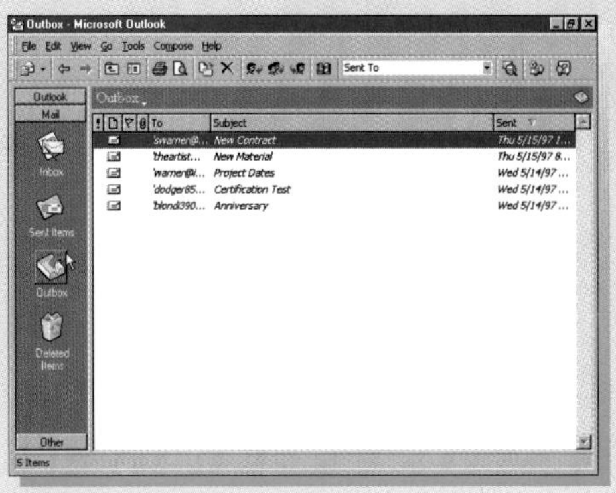

3 Click on the Outbox icon on the Outlook Bar. It looks like a gray outbox with a green arrow pointing out of it. The contents of the Outbox folder will be displayed. To delete a message, click on a message in the Outbox that you do not want to send and press the delete key.

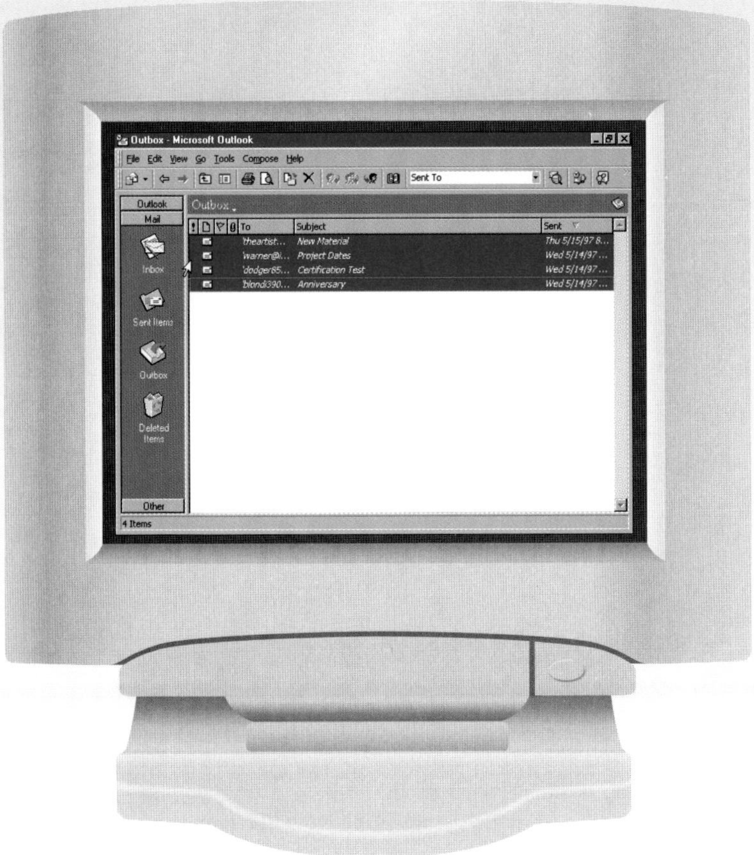

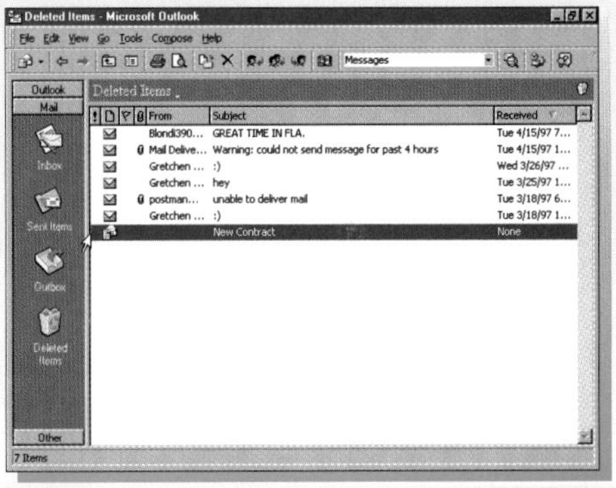

4 Click on the Deleted Items icon in the Outlook Bar. It looks like a trash can with a recycle symbol on the side. The message you just deleted will be displayed with the other contents of the Deleted Items folder.

5 Click on the Outbox icon to view the messages remaining in the Outbox folder.

How to Use the Other Group Icons

Outlook also provides some icons on the Outlook Bar that are there for your convenience. They don't have any direct connection to the Outlook functions or features. My guess is that the programmers figured you'd have the Outlook window up on your screen all the time because you'd find it so invaluable, and just in case you had to take care of something outside of Outlook, they'd let you do it without closing down the software. Pretty clever. Very handy if you run Outlook in a maximized window.

These icons are available when you click the horizontal bar with the title Other on the Outlook Bar.

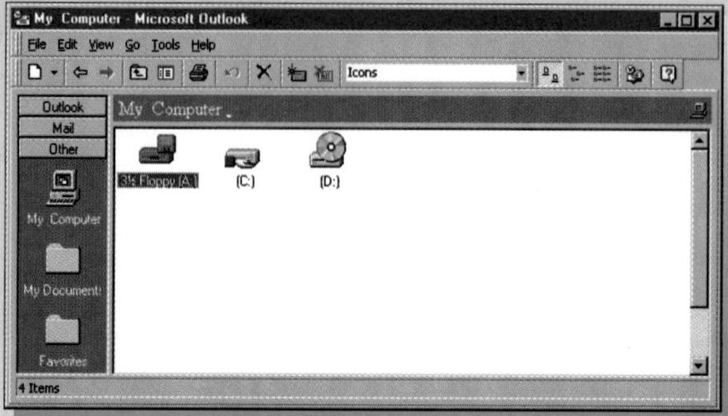

1 Click the My Computer icon to open the My Computer folder. It opens in the Outlook window in the same format as any other Outlook Information viewer. You can use all the features of My Computer right from here, manipulating drives and folders the same way you do when you open My Computer from your desktop.

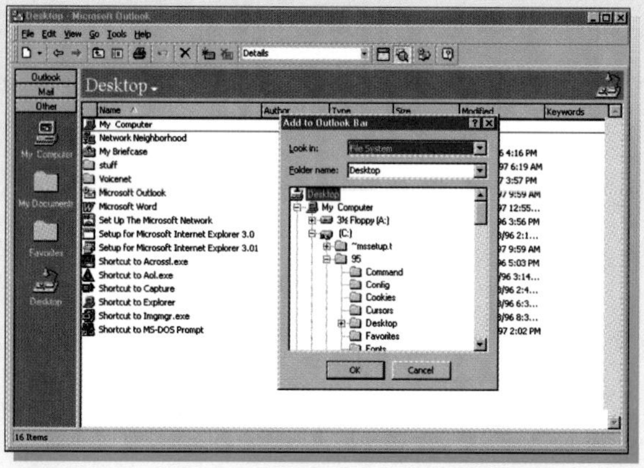

6 Does your desktop have a lot of shortcuts for quick access to your favorite programs? Do you have to move the Outlook window around to find and use those shortcuts? Here's a nifty trick (and it's not in any help file, so it's really a secret tip). Follow step 5, but when the Add to Outlook dialog box appears, click the arrow to the right of the Folder name box. Then use the scroll bar to move up to the top listing, which is Desktop. Select the Desktop and click OK. An icon for your desktop is on the Outlook Bar. Click on it to see all of your familiar shortcuts. Double-click on a shortcut as if you were on the real desktop. In this illustration, although you see the dialog box, I've already transferred my desktop to the Outlook Bar.

FYI

- **When you have the contents of My Documents in the Information Viewer, you can delete, move, copy, and otherwise manipulate the files just as if you were working in Explorer. In fact, that's true for all the Outlook Bar system folders.**
- **To remove an icon from the Outlook Bar, right-click it and choose Remove from Outlook Bar.**

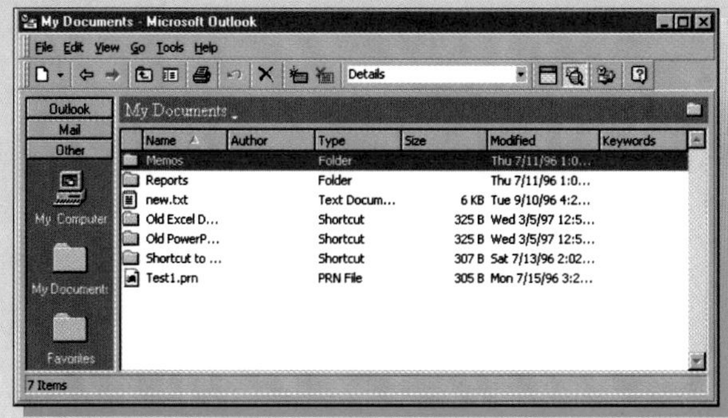

2 Click My Documents to open the My Documents folder on your system. By default, Microsoft Office 97 installs a folder called My Documents to hold the work you do in Office. The folder is placed here, available and convenient in case you need to place anything in it or take anything from it (you might want to attach one of those files to a message, for instance).

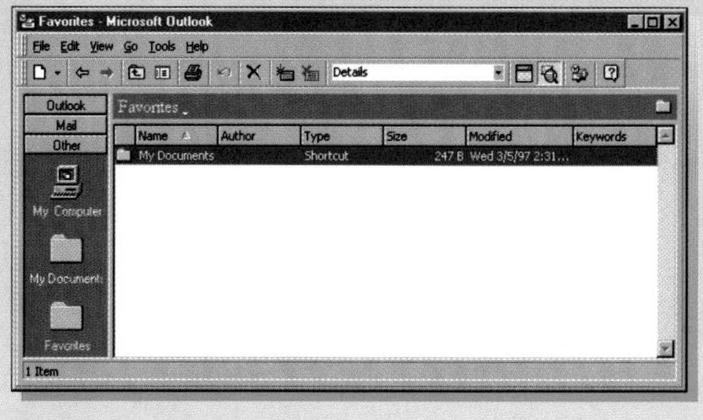

3 The Favorites folder is on the Outlook Bar to act as a container for any folders or files you think you might want to work with while you're working in Outlook. By default, Outlook places a shortcut to My Documents in Favorites. If you double-click it, Explorer opens with My Documents selected.

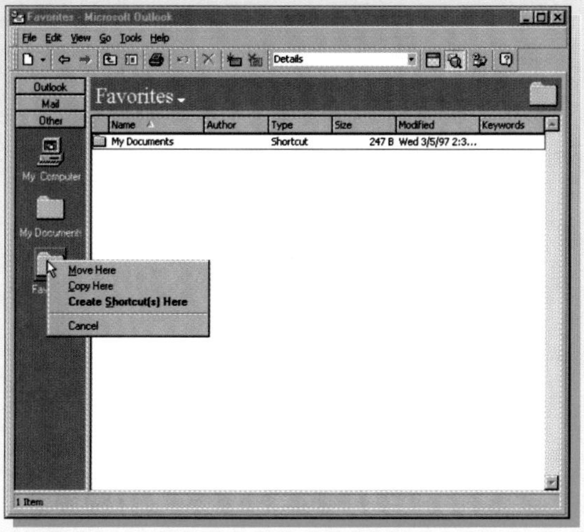

4 You can add shortcuts to frequently used software to the Favorites folder. Click My Computer on the Outlook Bar, then open the drive and folder that has the executable file for the software you want to launch from the Favorites folder while you're working in Outlook. Using the right mouse button, drag the file's icon to the Favorites folder icon. Release the mouse button and choose Create Shortcut(s) Here. In this example, I've just made it possible to open QuickBooks while I'm working in Outlook.

5 You can add folders to the Outlook Bar itself, if you think that opening Favorites to get to them is too much trouble. Right-click on a blank spot on the Outlook Bar and choose Add to Outlook Bar from the menu that displays. When the Add to Outlook Bar dialog box appears, select the folder you want to place on the Outlook Bar, then choose OK.

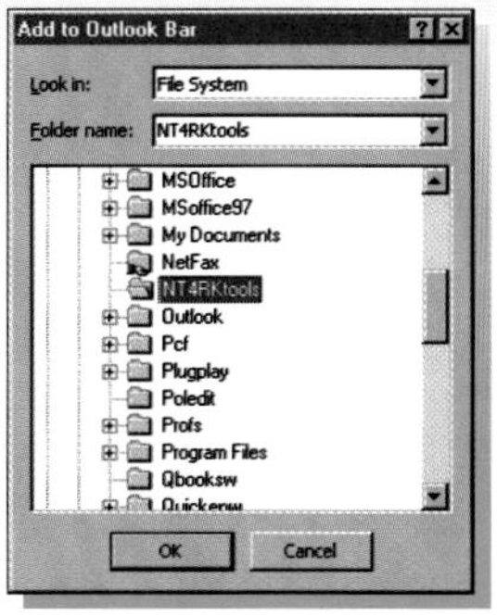

How to Customize the Outlook Bar

The Outlook Bar is designed to give you quick access to your computer's resources in the same way that toolbars make application features quickly accessible. The Outlook Bar can be customized for an individual's particular needs, just as a toolbar.

The Outlook Bar consists of groups. These groups are the equivalent of a single toolbar. Groups can be added or removed as needed. If the Outlook Bar is not needed, it can be hidden, and displayed again when you need it.

This page will teach you how to create new groups, add new items to groups, and customize the icons used to represent a group's items.

1 Click on the button labeled Other in the Outlook Bar to open the Other group.

7 Choose Hide Outlook Bar from the Outlook Bar Quick Menu and the Outlook Bar will no longer be visible.

(Continues on next page)

FYI

- **The default groups created for the Outlook Bar are there to get you started. Create new groups that will help you work better and faster.**
- **Outlook Bar groups can be named and renamed. Use a name that best describes the group. If the group's contents or role change significantly, the name of the group should reflect that change too.**

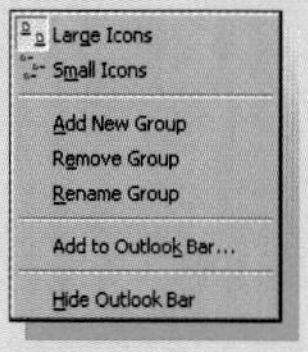

2 Right-click on the Other group button or on any unused portion of the Other group. The Outlook Bar Quick Menu appears, which allows you to perform several functions on the Outlook Bar. Choose Small Icons from the menu.

3 The icons displayed in the Other group are now smaller and their caption is displayed to the right.

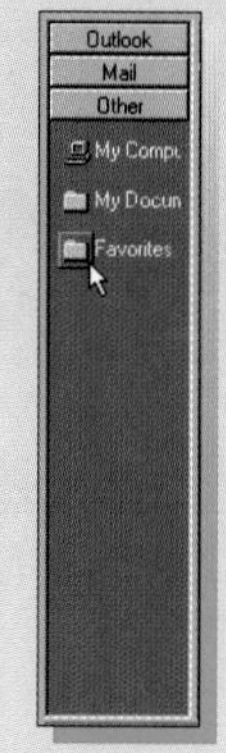

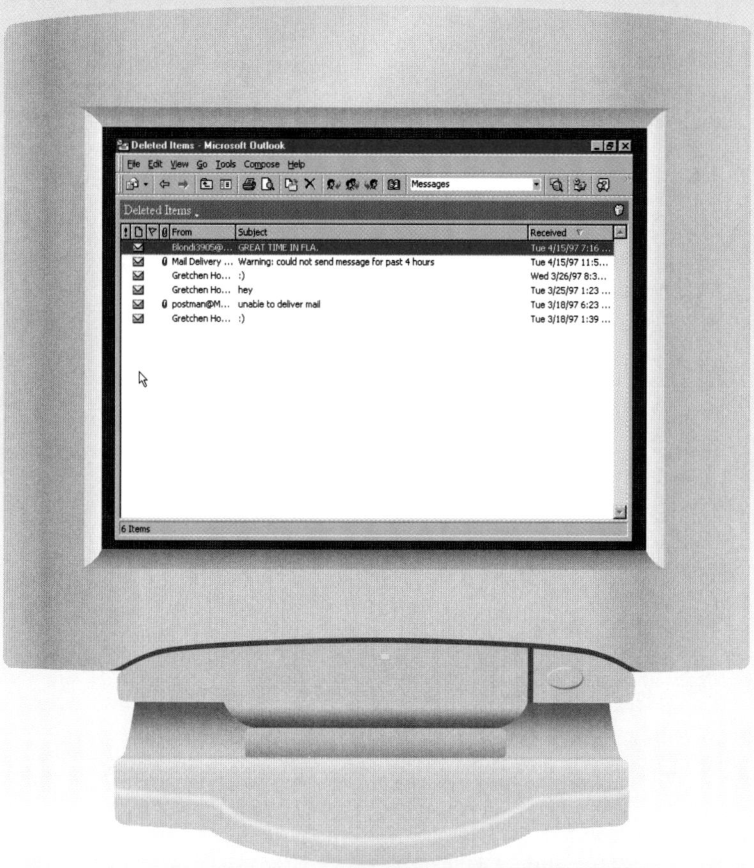

4 Right-click again to open the Outlook Bar Quick Menu and choose Large Icons. Then open the Outlook Bar Quick Menu and choose Add New Group. A new group is added to the bottom of the Outlook Bar. The default name, New Group, is highlighted. Change the name to Test and press the Enter key. Click on the Test group to open it.

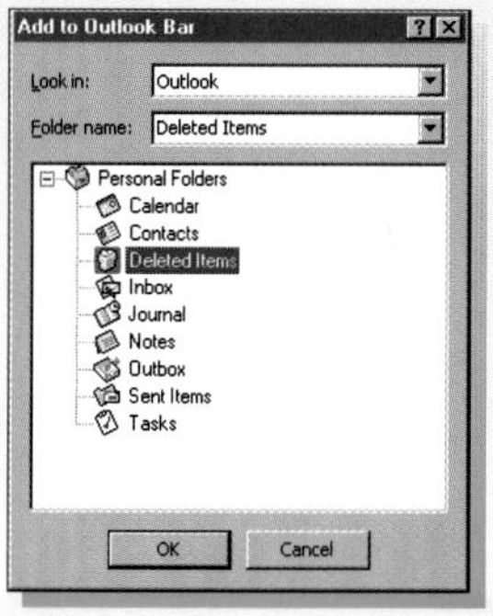

5 Open the Outlook Bar Quick Menu and choose Add to Outlook Bar to display the Add to Outlook Bar dialog box. The Look In list box allows you to look for an Outlook folder or one on your computer or network. You can choose a folder in the Folder Name list box or highlight a folder in the middle of the dialog box. Choose the Deleted Items folder and click the OK button.

6 The Deleted Items icon is added to the Test group. Click this icon to display the contents of the Deleted Items folder.

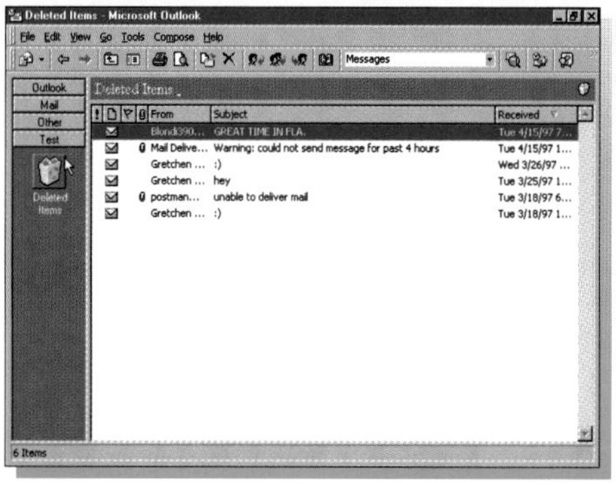

How to Customize the Outlook Bar (Continued)

The Outlook Bar is separated into groups to make it easier to access related information stored in different locations. The Outlook Bar groups contain any number of items. Each item represents either an Outlook folder or a resource contained within a computer's file system. A file system resource could be a folder on your computer or another computer on your network.

This page will show you how to add and remove items from the Outlook Bar and how to remove entire groups.

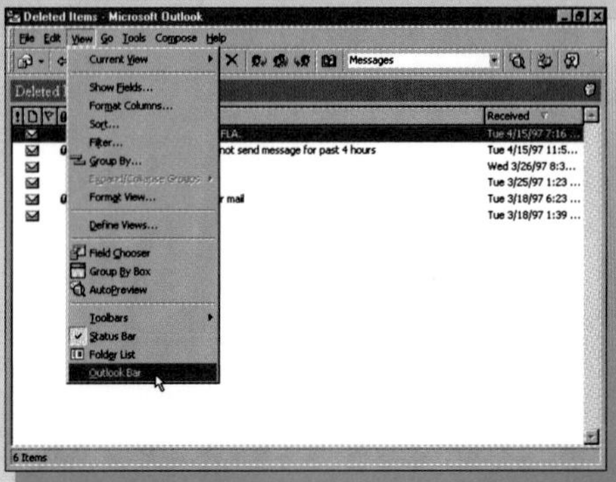

8 Choose Outlook Bar from the View menu to display the Outlook Bar. The Outlook Bar can also be hidden again by choosing Outlook Bar from the View menu.

14 Open the Outlook Bar Quick Menu and choose Remove Group. The Delete Me group is removed and the top group in the Outlook Bar is opened.

FYI

- **If you don't like the order of items in a group, click on an item and drag it to the location you would prefer.**
- **Just because an item is displayed in one group on the Outlook Bar does not mean that it cannot be displayed in another. Place a folder in as many different groups as necessary.**
- **Use the groups in the Outlook Bar to group resources for specific needs, such as projects or clients. Such groups will be helpful when searching for information specific to a project or client.**

9 Open the Outlook Bar Quick Menu and choose Add to Outlook Bar to display the Add to Outlook Bar dialog box. Change the Look In section of the dialog box to File System to display the resources available on your computer's file system. Choose the Desktop in the Folder Name list box and click the OK button.

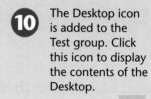

10 The Desktop icon is added to the Test group. Click this icon to display the contents of the Desktop.

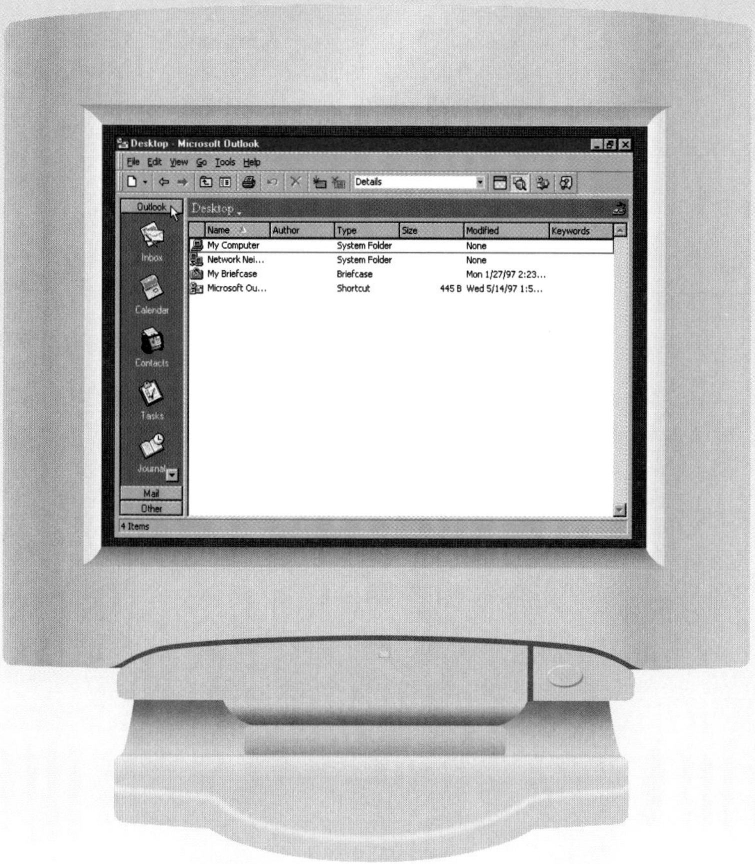

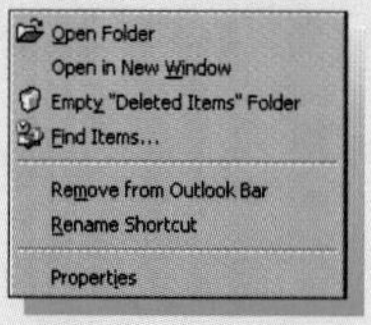

11 Right-click on the Deleted Items icon. The Outlook Bar Item Quick Menu appears. This menu displays actions specific to items displayed in the Outlook Bar. Choose Remove from Outlook Bar.

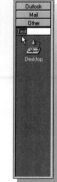

12 The icon is removed, leaving only the Desktop icon. Open the Outlook Bar Quick Menu and choose Rename Group. The Group button's caption becomes highlighted and can now be changed.

13 Change the name to Delete Me and press Enter. The button's name has now been changed.

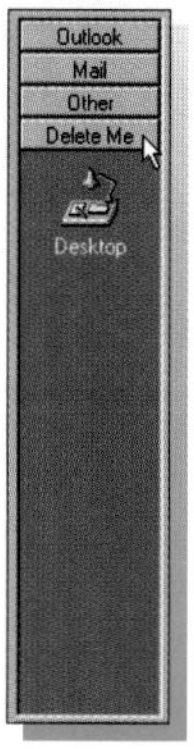

How to Enter an Address in Your Address Book

The first thing you have to do is open your PAB. Then you have to begin entering data into it. If you're connected to a network Exchange Server mail system, you can copy addresses from the Global Address Book (GAB) instead of entering them from the keyboard. There are a couple of rules about entering addresses, and there are lots of optional entries. We'll go over all of these items in this section.

1 The easiest way to open your PAB is to click its icon on the toolbar. If you opened any Information Viewer from the Mail bar in the Outlook Bar (Inbox, Sent Items, Outbox, or Deleted Items), the icon is there. Otherwise, choose Tools, Address Book from the menu bar (or press Ctrl+Shift+B).

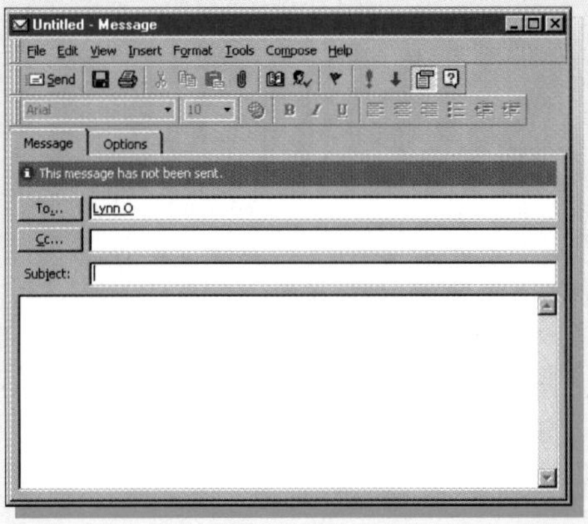

6 Most of the time you'll use the PAB when you are composing a new message—you start a new message, then call up the PAB to select a recipient (composing and sending e-mail messages is discussed in the next chapter). However, you can perform those steps in the opposite way, calling up a new message form from the PAB. Select the listing in your PAB that you want to send a message to, then click the New Message icon on the toolbar. A message form appears, the recipient's name is filled in, and your cursor is waiting in the Subject field.

FYI

- **The Add to Personal Address Book icon on the PAB toolbar may be inaccessible to you. This is used when the Global Address Book is displayed and you want to copy a name from it into your PAB. If you're not on a network mail system, it's never available. If you are on a network mail system, it's only available when you select the GAB in the box named Show Names From The.**
- **If you get e-mail from someone who is not in your address book, right-click on the sender's name when the message is open (it's the From field). Then choose Add to Address Book from the menu that displays.**
- **If you're adding an entry for someone on AOL or CompuServe, that's an Internet Address. For AOL, use the screen name followed by @aol.com. For a CompuServe address that is a number (for example, 74222,4120), substitute a period for the comma in the identification number, then add @compuserve.com.**

2 The PAB opens, and it looks like a mini-software window. It has a menu bar, a toolbar, and entry boxes.

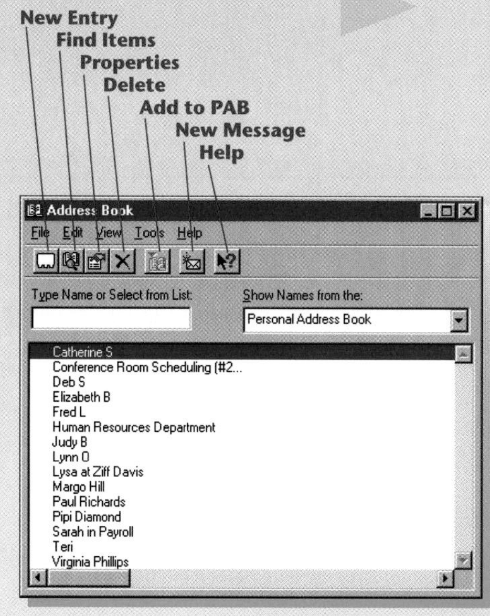

3 To add an entry to the PAB, click the New Entry icon on the toolbar (or, if you like doing things the long way, choose File, New Entry from the menu bar). The New Entry dialog box appears, and the first step is to indicate the address type for this entry. Your choices may look different from this illustration, and may include entry types such as cc:Mail, Microsoft Mail, or X.400, depending upon the setup of the network you're connected to. Most of the time, since this is a personal entry instead of a company entry, you should select Internet Mail. Click OK when you have selected the address type.

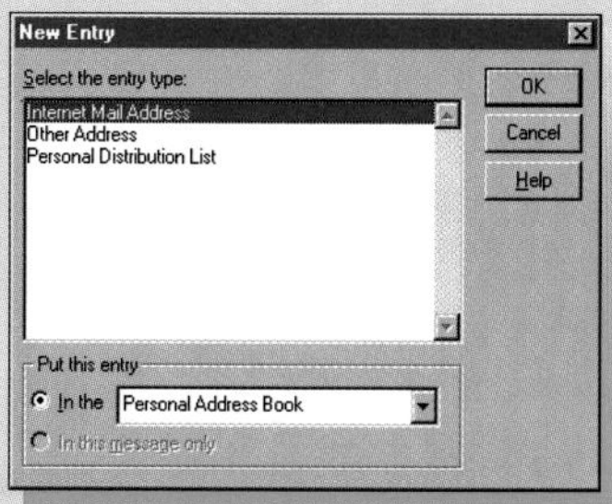

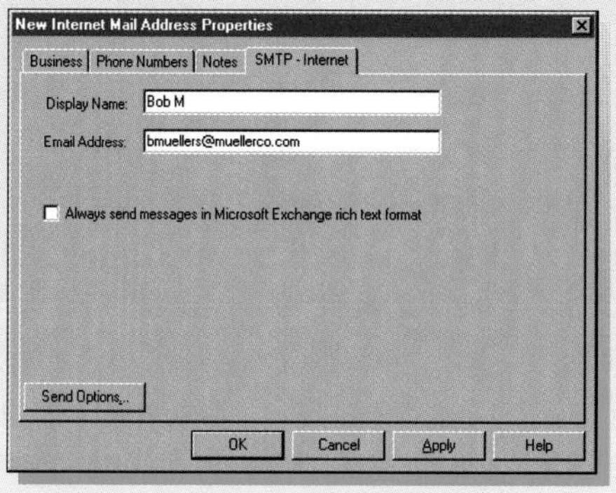

4 Enter a Display Name for this entry. This is the name or phrase that appears in your PAB. There's nothing official or technical about it, it's your own way of referring to this person. You can use "Mom," or "Aunt Tessie," or "the good looking guy in accounting." However, when you send this person e-mail this display name appears in the To box of the message, so don't use anything you wouldn't want the recipient to see. In the Email address box, enter the official, technical, e-mail address for this recipient. The checkbox about Rich Text Format is available so that if you know that this recipient has a mail system that can handle RTF, you can format message text with fancy attributes. If it can't handle RTF, your formatted message could arrive as hard-to-read garbage. (We'll discuss the other tabs on this dialog box later in this chapter.) When you have filled out the dialog box, click OK.

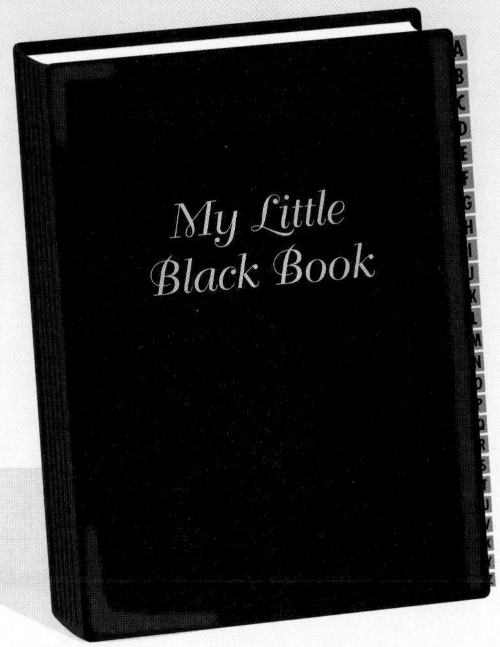

5 When you return to your PAB window, the new entry is on the list. You can scroll through the list to find it, but if you have a long list that can be inefficient or even annoying. A quick way to get to a name on your list is to enter characters in the Type Name or Select from List text box. As you type each character, you move to the entry that matches the characters you're entering.

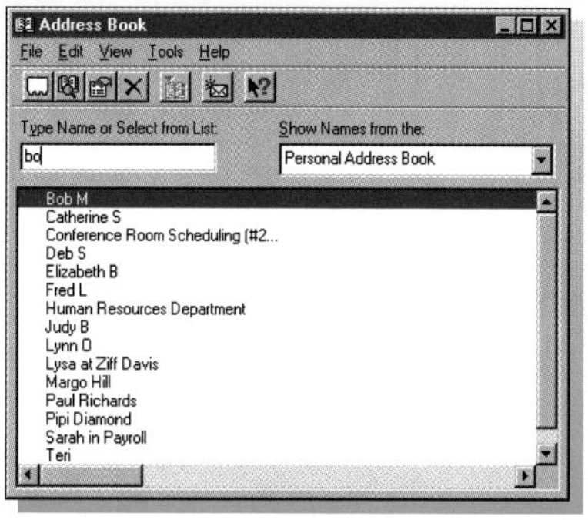

How to Create a Distribution List

There are tons of reasons for sending the same message to an entire group of people. At work, there are messages that go to all the members of your department, or all the department heads, or all the members of some committee or project group. For personal mail, there's that annual Christmas note that fills everyone in on the family gossip.

Sending a note to multiple recipients isn't terribly difficult, but it is time consuming. You have to select each person from your PAB by clicking on each name. Okay, so clicking 10 or 20 times isn't the hardest thing you ever did, but it is annoyingly time consuming, especially the fifth time you do it for the same group of recipients. And, of course, there is always that nagging worry that you may have forgotten someone, or included someone who shouldn't have been on the list.

All these problems go away when you discover how to create distribution lists. This is a way to take a group of entries from your PAB and turn them into one entry. Send a message to that entry, and every person on the list gets a copy. It's a real time and trouble saver.

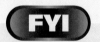

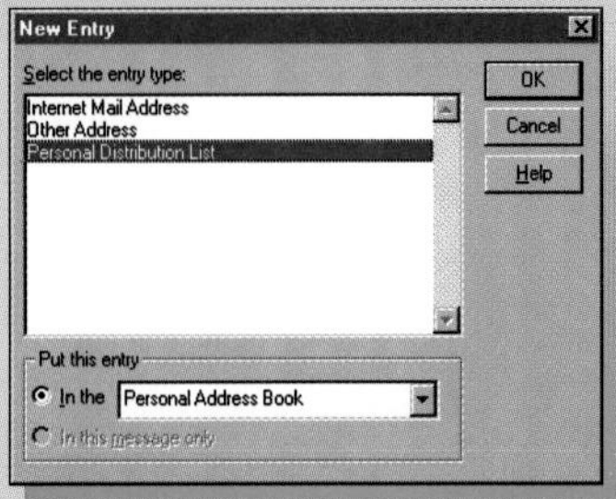

1 To create a distribution list, open the PAB and click the New Entry icon on the toolbar. When the New Entry dialog box appears, select Personal Distribution List. Then choose OK.

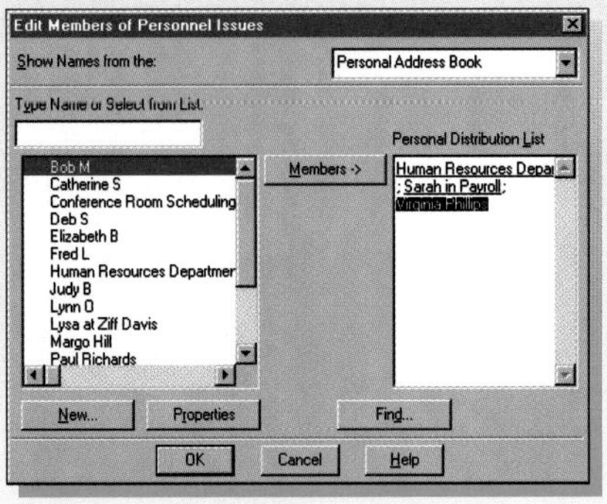

6 If you want to add or remove any members from this distribution list, double-click its listing in the address book and when the Properties dialog box opens, choose Add/Remove Members. To add members to the list, use the same steps we just used. To remove a member from the list, click anywhere on that member's name (which highlights the name) and press the Delete key.

FYI

- **When you choose a distribution list as the recipient while you are composing a message, only the name of the distribution list appears in the message form. When you send the message, the individual members on the list receive it.**
- **You can create a new entry for your address book while you are adding members to a distribution list. Choose New on the distribution list dialog box and fill out the entry information. When you click OK the new entry is added to the list and also added to your address book.**

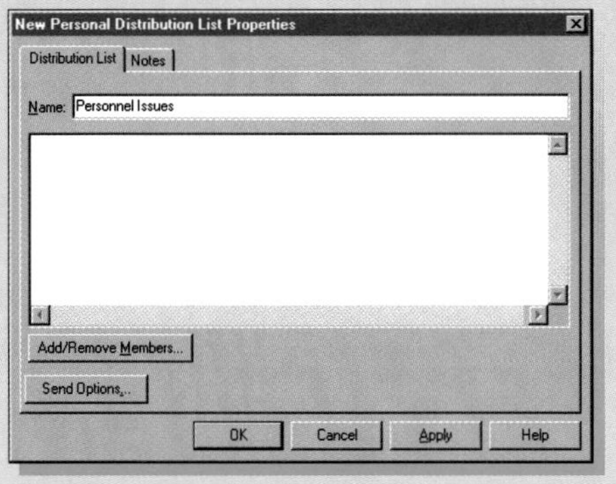

2 The New Personal Distribution List Properties dialog box appears and the first thing you have to do is give this list a name. Choose a name that reminds you of the reason for this list. Remember that eventually you'll probably develop a number of distribution lists and each will have its own function. The more exact the name, the easier it is to pick the right list when you have to send e-mail to the members on the list.

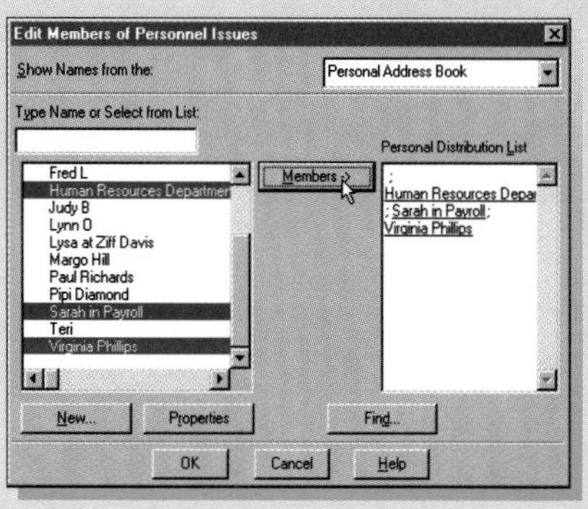

3 After you enter the name, click Add/Remove Members to display the Edit Members dialog box so you can begin to add recipients to the list. This is a simple process, because all you have to do is click. The left pane of the dialog box displays the names in your PAB. The right pane displays the names on this distribution list. To move a name from left to right, double-click it (or click once, then click Members). To move multiple names in one fell swoop, click the first name and then hold down the Ctrl key while you click all the other names. When all the names you want to add are highlighted, click Members. Then click OK to return to the Distribution List dialog box.

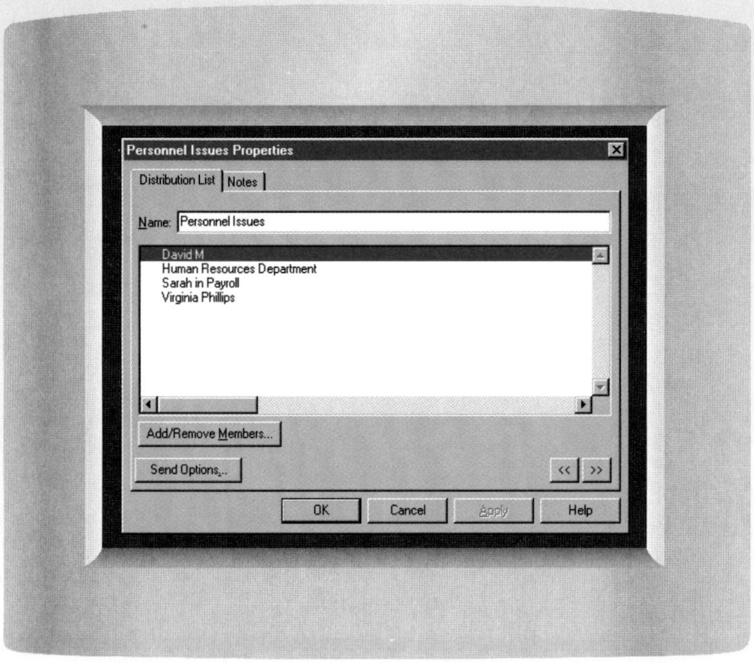

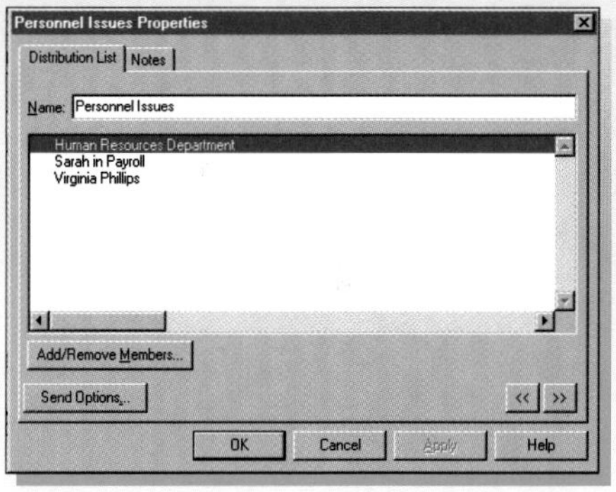

4 The current members on the list display in the dialog box, and if you wish you can click the Notes tab to enter notes or comments about this list. These are notes to yourself and have no bearing on the way the list works. Click OK to return to your address book.

5 The distribution list appears in your address book along with all the other entries. To remind you that it's a list instead of a person, an icon (two people) is placed next to the listing.

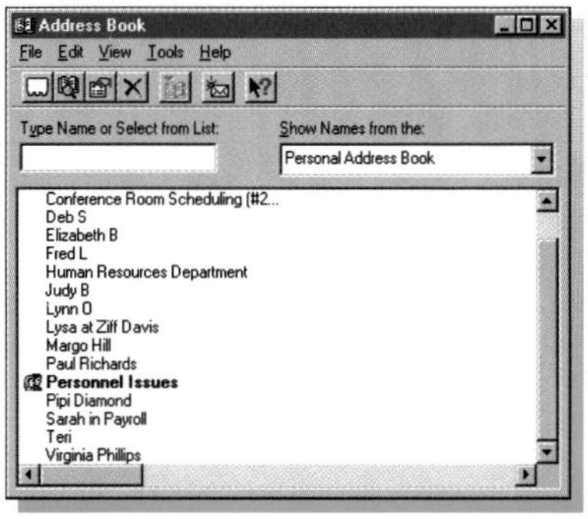

How to Edit and Delete Addresses

People change jobs, move, change their on-line service providers, go into witness protection programs, or do any of a zillion things to make sure there's always at least one entry in your address book that's obsolete. One day you'll get an e-mail message bounced back to you with a note attached saying it couldn't be delivered.

It's important to keep the entries in your address book current and accurate, and luckily it's not difficult to do.

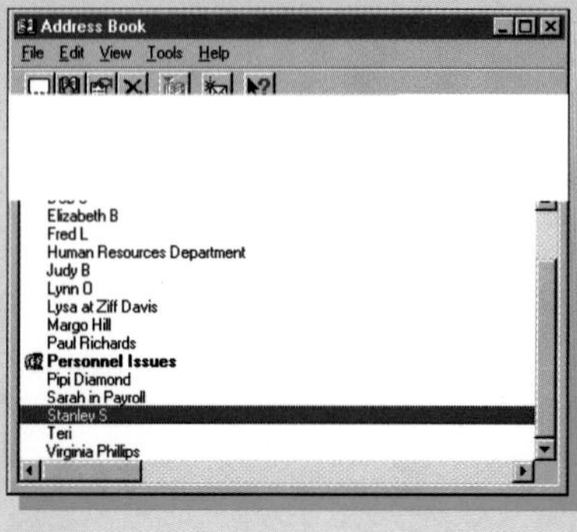

1 To delete an address book entry, open your PAB and select (highlight) the entry you want to delete. Click the Delete icon on the toolbar (or press the Delete key, or choose File, Delete from the menu bar). Outlook flashes a message asking if you're sure you want to remove this entry. Click Yes (unless you made a mistake, in which case you should click No).

FYI

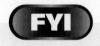

- **When you delete an address book entry, it is a permanent deletion. The entry is not placed in the Deleted Items folder.**
- **If you delete a distribution list, only the list's entry is deleted, not the members of the list.**
- **You can delete multiple entries at the same time by selecting each entry while you hold down the Ctrl key. When you click the Delete icon (or press the Delete key) and answer Yes to the confirmation query, all the entries are deleted.**

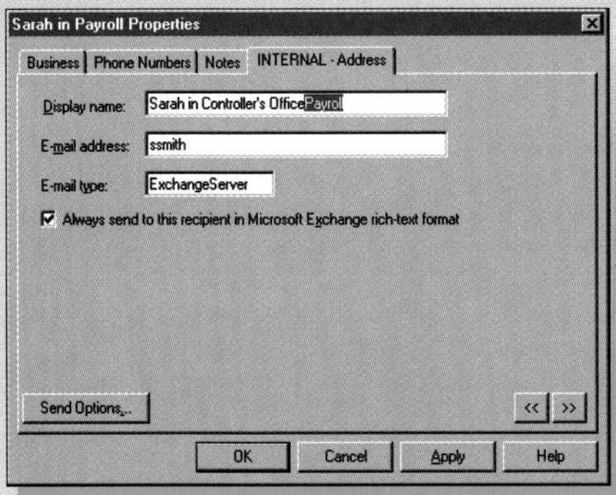

2 To edit an address book entry, open your PAB and select the entry you want to change. Double-click it to bring up the entry dialog box. Make the changes you need by adding data, deleting data, or both. You can change the data for any field in the entry's dialog box. Click OK when you are finished making changes.

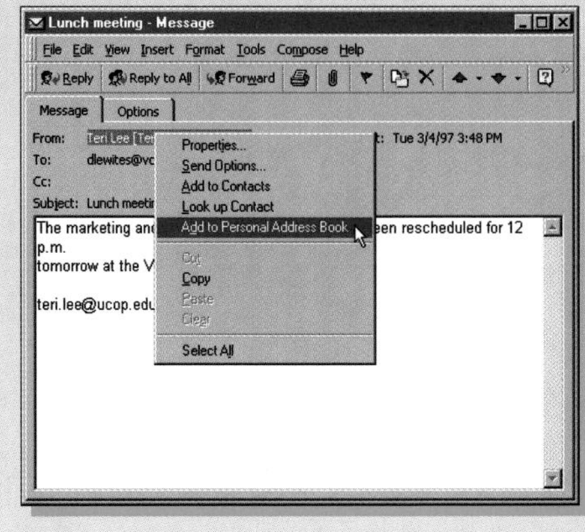

3 You can also correct an address when you receive mail from that entry. If you notice that the sender's address differs from the address in your PAB, right click on the data in the From field when the message is open. Then select Add to Address Book.

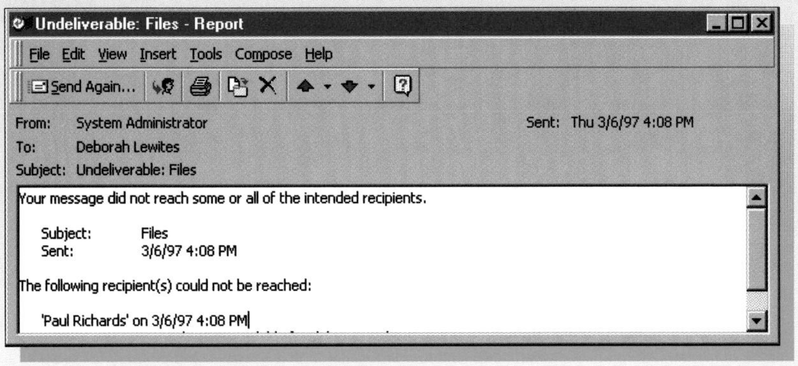

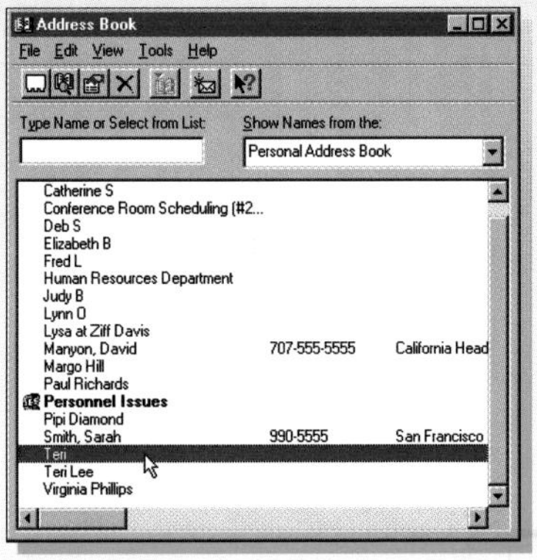

4 Close the message and open the address book. The sender is listed twice. If the sender's name doesn't match your original display name for this entry, the two names won't be adjacent to each other in the list and you'll have to find the original entry. Delete the original entry.

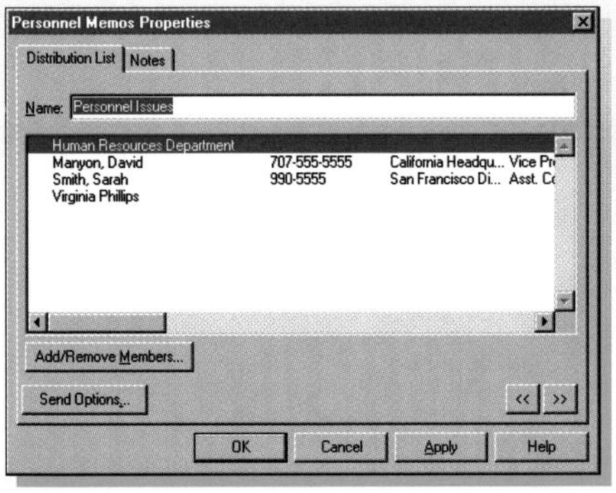

5 You can also edit the name of a distribution list. This changes only the name, the members on the list are not changed.

How to Use Other Information

There's much more information about an address entry that you can store besides the e-mail address. After all, information is power (or is that knowledge?). You can turn your address book into a reference book, accumulating a lot of useful information.

Outlook provides some structured forms for compiling information, and also gives you free-form text boxes to keep information that you feel is important.

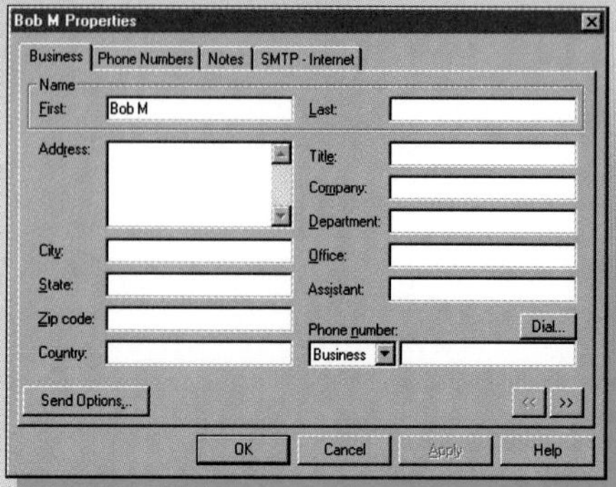

1 To see the variety of information you can amass, open the address book, then double-click on an entry to see the Properties dialog box. Click the Business tab. This form provides a way to keep basic business information about an entry. The display name pops into the First Name field, and you'll have to change that, then fill in the rest of the information. For internal entries you won't need to enter a company name, of course.

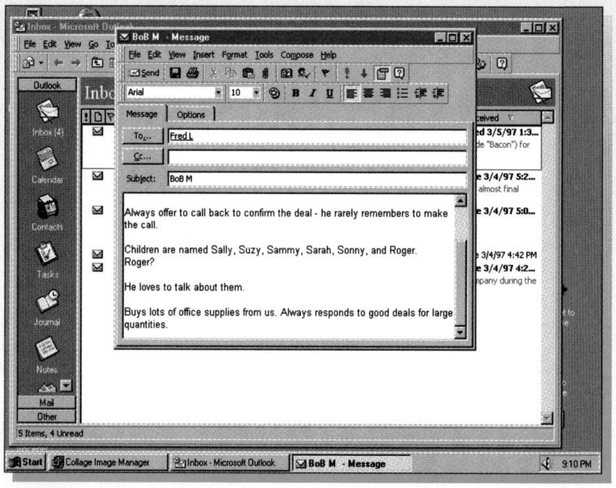

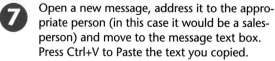

7 Open a new message, address it to the appropriate person (in this case it would be a salesperson) and move to the message text box. Press Ctrl+V to Paste the text you copied.

FYI

- **You can use the Copy and Paste technique to move text anywhere, not just into a message. Try it with a word processing document, a Contact card, or a Note.**

2 Use the Phone Number field for the primary number you'd dial if you wanted to reach this person by telephone. There's even a Dial button to click in order to dial this person automatically. Of course, you need a telephone attached to your modem to do this.

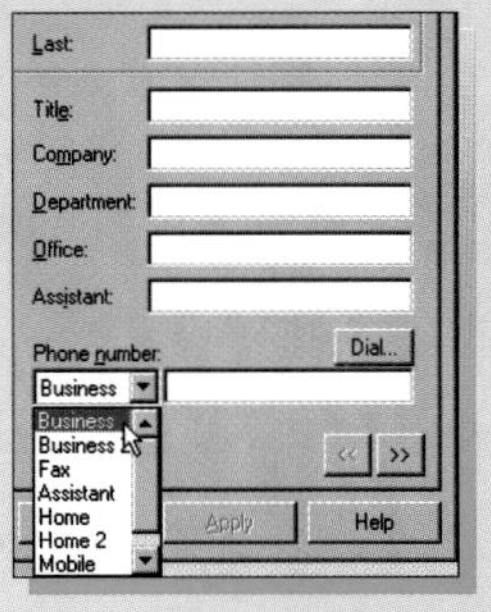

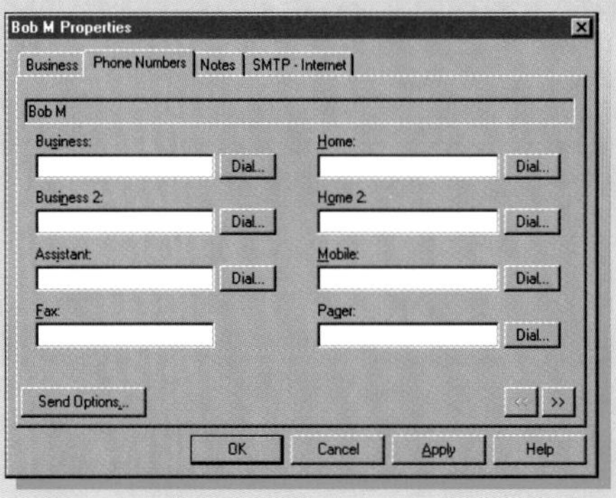

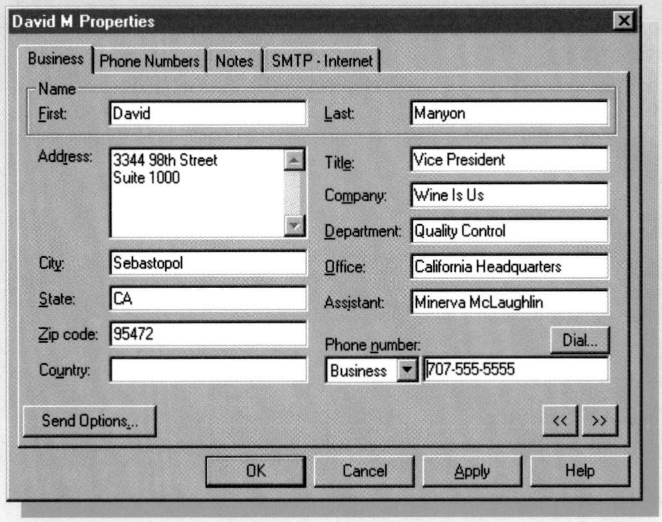

3 Click the Phone Numbers tab and start typing. There are enough options here to track this person down no matter where he or she is. Notice that every one of the numbers except the fax number can be autodialed. At this point you should be thinking about putting a telephone instrument on your modem (just plug the phone cord into the other modem jack—all modems have a second jack for this purpose).

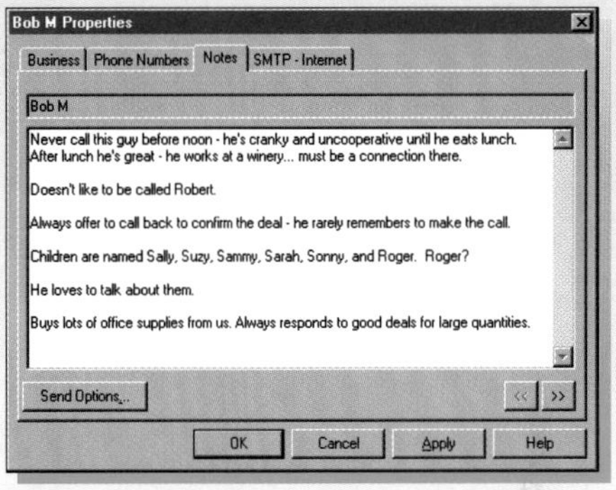

4 The Notes tab is for you to use as you see fit. You can write notes, reminders, personality analysis, whatever you need.

5 When you finish entering information, click OK. You return to the address book and some of the data you entered in the Business tab is now showing in the window. Use the scroll bar at the bottom of the window to see all the information.

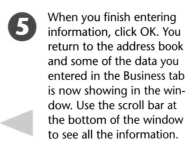

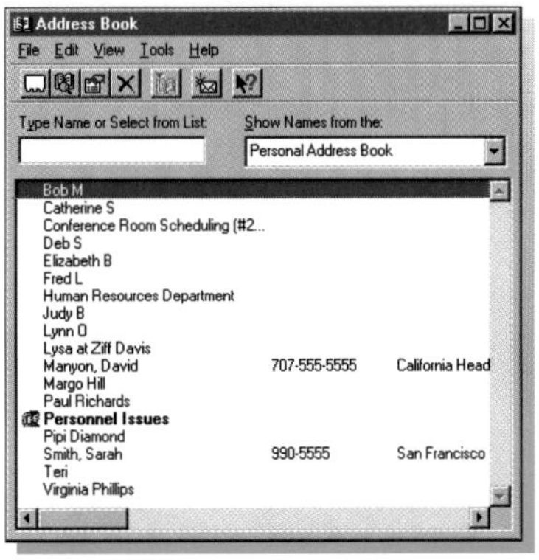

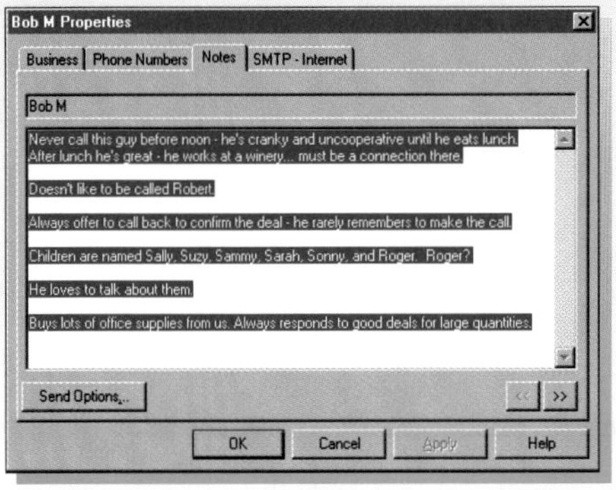

6 What isn't documented in the Help files is the fact that you can cut and paste information from the tabs in the entry Properties dialog box. For example, you may want to send some information about this address book entry to somebody in your office through an e-mail message. Select (highlight) the relevant text. Then press Ctrl+C (the shortcut key for Copy). Then close the dialog box and the address book.

How to Use Outlook Help

Windows applications are built to take advantage of a set of standard features that Microsoft Windows uses. These features include menus, toolbars, and, of course, windows. Once the basic functions of Windows are mastered, applications become easier to use.

In an effort to standardize the method for using an applications Help system, Microsoft created a standard for Windows Help files. This standard made it easier to find help by making all Windows applications use the same method to search for and display Help information.

This page will illustrate the use of the Contents and Index sections of Outlook's Help file.

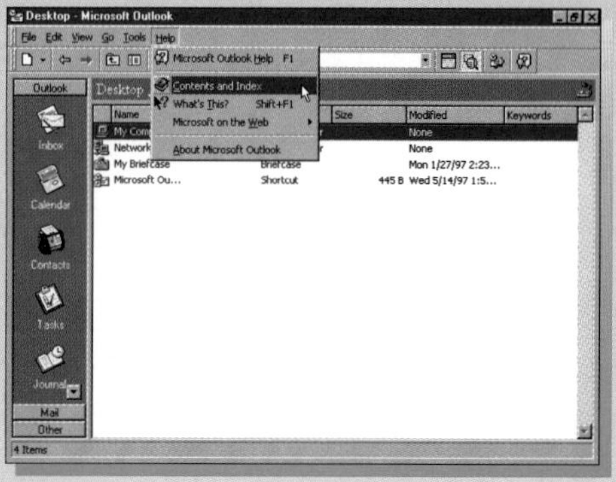

1 Click Help on the Menu bar to bring down the list of Help topics. Choose Contents and Index from the Help menu.

6 Double-click on a topic to display the Help file information for that topic.

FYI

- **You may not have time or want to view a Help topic on your computer monitor. Instead, you can click the Print button to send the Help topic directly to the printer.**
- **The Contents and Index sections of a Help file can contain errors or suffer from omissions. If you have trouble finding a Help topic, try a different approach. For instance, you could try to think of a different word to search for.**

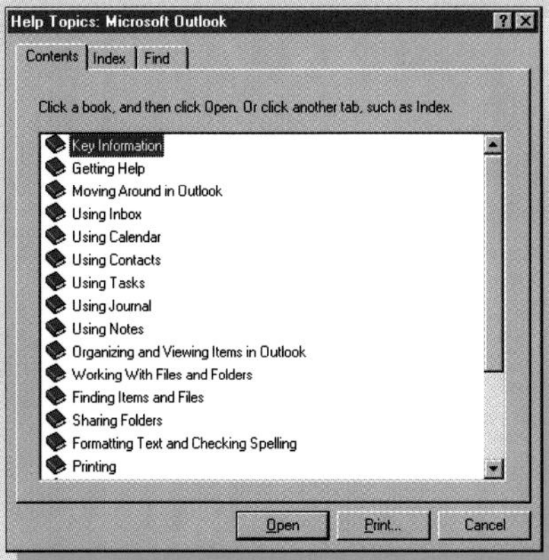

2 Click the Contents tab of the Help Topics window to display the categories of information in the Help file.

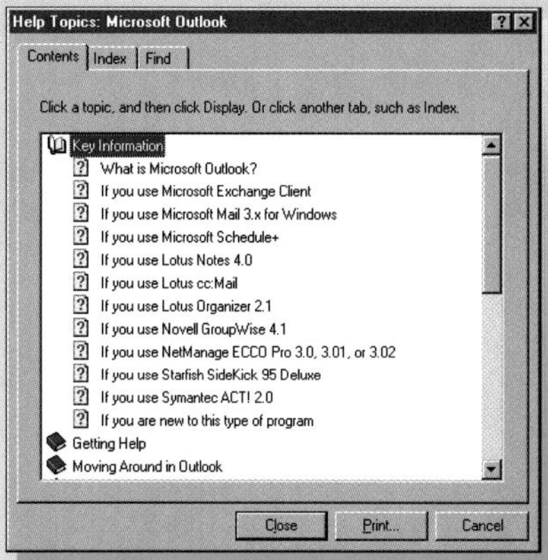

3 Double-click a category, which is represented by a book icon, to see what Help topics are contained within that category. Individual Help topics are viewed by double-clicking on the topic, which is represented with a question mark on a page icon.

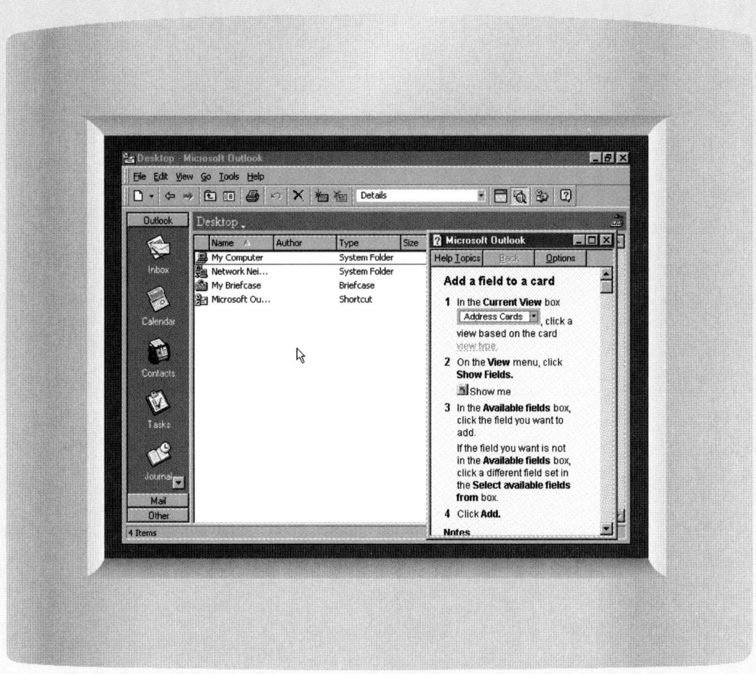

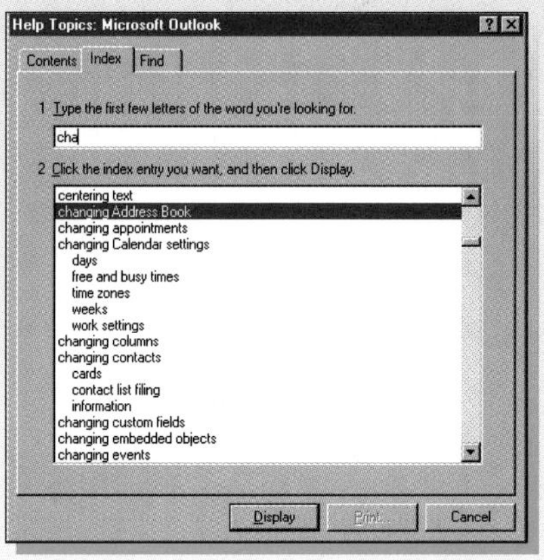

4 Click the Index tab to display a list of words that the Help file is indexed on. The creators of the Help file placed words in the index that they felt most people would search for. It does not contain all of the words in the Help file. Type cha in the dialog box at the top of the window. The list of indexed words goes to the first word that starts with cha. You do not have to choose the topic that your search has led you to, which is "Changing Address Book." Double-click on "changing contacts" instead.

5 There are several Help topics associated with the changing contacts phrase. They are displayed in the Topics Found dialog box.

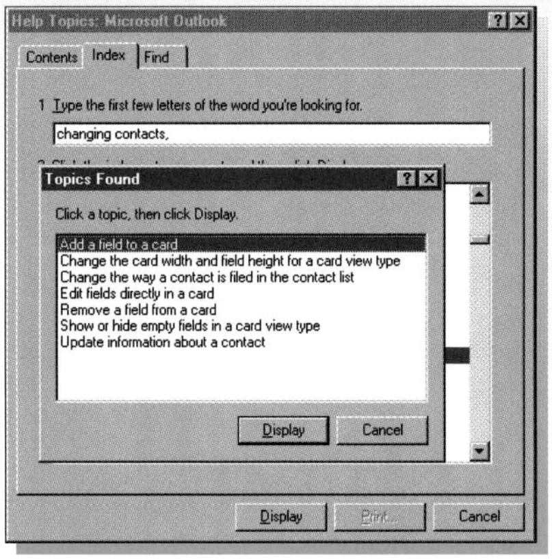

How to Use the Office Assistant

The Office Assistant takes Help file information and makes it interactive. You can ask questions in plain English or you can be *asked* questions. The interactive nature of the Office Assistant makes it easy and even fun to use.

Though information is displayed using the Windows Help System, it is the interactive ability of the Office Assistant that makes it unique. You may find it easier to ask a question than to try to think of a single word that describes your task.

On this page, you will learn how to interact with the Office Assistant to receive help in completing tasks.

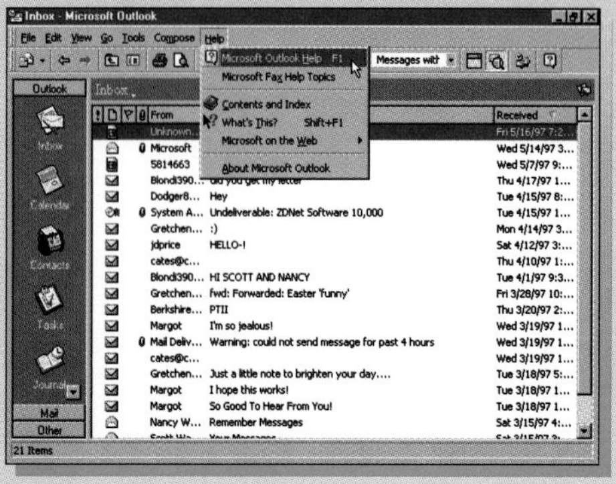

1 Choose Microsoft Outlook Help from the Help menu or click the Help button on the toolbar.

6 The Gallery is where you can change the appearance of the Office Assistant. It can be a paper clip, dot, Einstein, robot, office logo, planet Earth, dog, cat, or even Shakespeare. You can open directly to the Gallery page of the dialog box by choosing Choose Office Assistant from the Office Assistant Quick Menu.

FYI

- **In addition to using the menu and the toolbar, you can receive help at any time by pressing the F1 key.**
- **Let the Office Assistant give you a tip of the day when first learning an application. Skip to the next tip if you already know it. This way you will learn something new every day.**
- **You can see the animation of the Office Assistant by choosing Animate from the Office Assistant Quick Menu.**

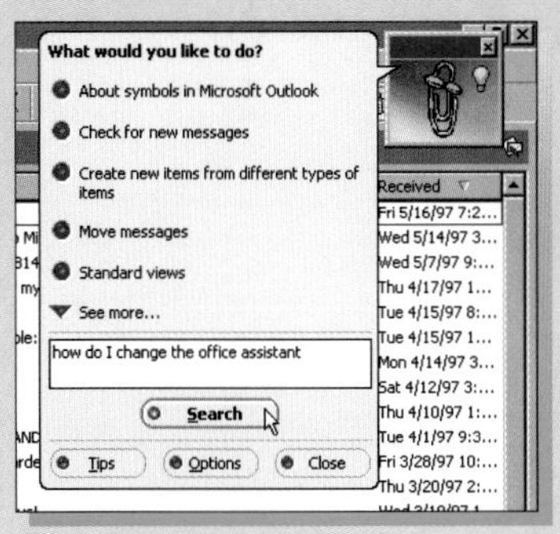

2 The Office Assistant appears. It asks, "What would you like to do?" and gives you a list of tasks that can be completed from the part of the application that you are using. You can choose one of the tasks listed or ask a question to find the help that you need. Type "how do I change the office assistant" and click the search button.

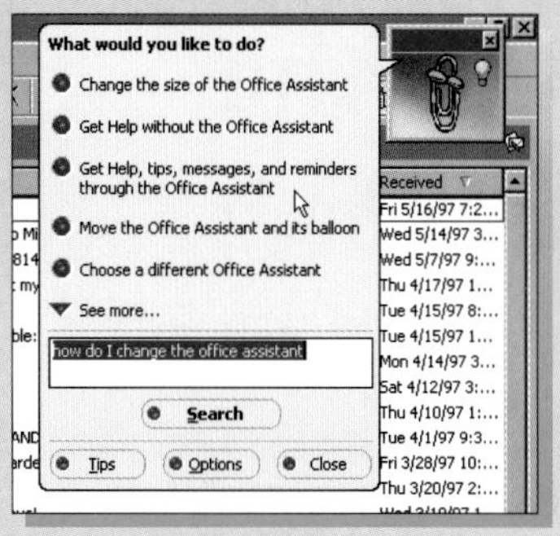

3 A new list of options appears that pertains to changing the Office Assistant. Select from the list to get help on any of the tasks listed. When you are finished, click the Close button. Then, right-click on the Office Assistant to open the Quick Menu.

4 Choose Options from the Office Assistant Quick Menu.

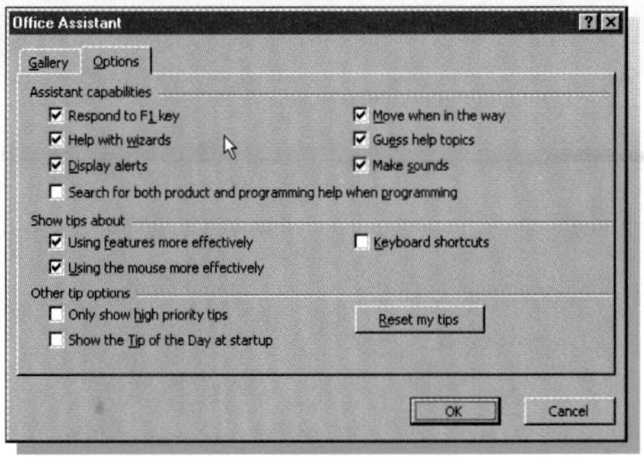

5 The Office Assistant dialog box appears. It is open to the Options page. This is where you can change the behavior of the Office Assistant. Click on the Gallery tab.

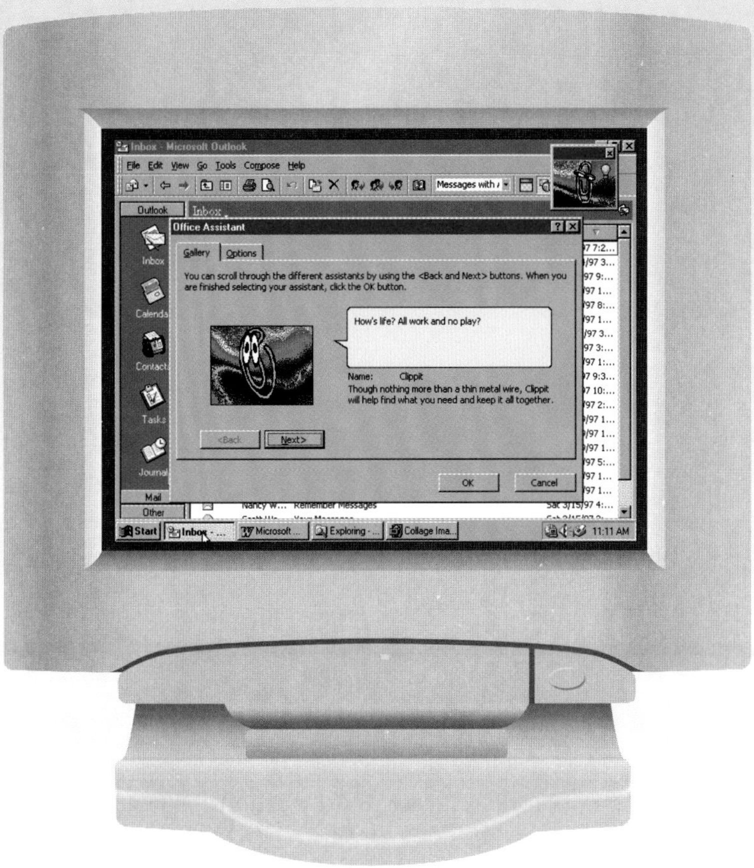

How to Use the Find Feature

In addition to the Contents and Index sections of the Windows Help system, there is a third section called Find. This is a special feature that must be individually configured by the user. It uses the same Help file that is used by the other two sections and the Office Assistant, but it can conduct more customized searches.

The Find tool builds a database of the words used in the Help file. It uses this database to show you every Help topic that contains any phrase, word, or word fragment that you supply.

This page will teach you how to create the database used by the Find tool and conduct a customized search.

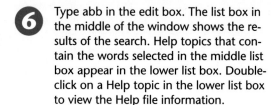

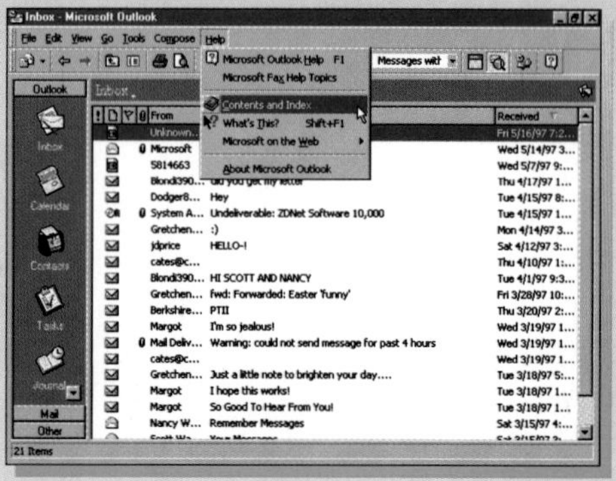

1. Choose Contents and Index from the Help menu.

6. Type abb in the edit box. The list box in the middle of the window shows the results of the search. Help topics that contain the words selected in the middle list box appear in the lower list box. Double-click on a Help topic in the lower list box to view the Help file information.

FYI

• Databases for the Find tool that were created using the Maximize Search Capabilities option will contain a large amount of data. While this marginally improves your ability to find Help topics, it takes longer to build and requires more storage space than the other options.

• The Find feature is case-sensitive. If you type capital letters, only words that contain those same capital letters will be returned by your search.

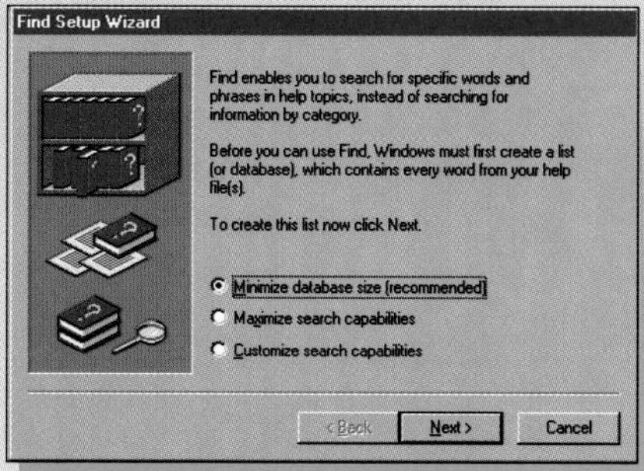

2 Click on the Find tab. The Find Setup Wizard dialog box should appear. If it does not, your Find database has already been set up and you can skip to step 4. Choose Minimize Database Size, which is the recommended option, and click the Next button.

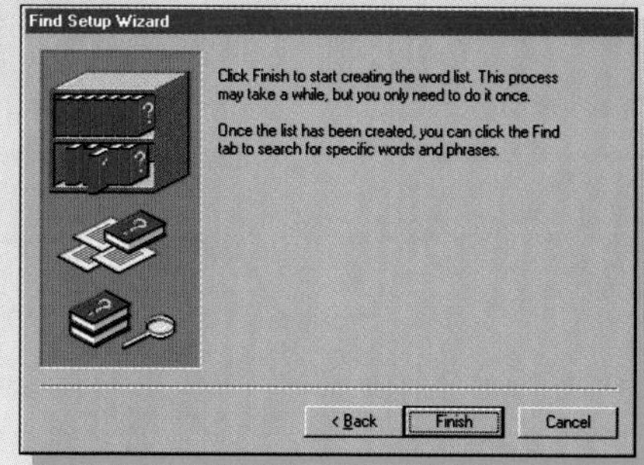

3 Click the Finish button to build the database.

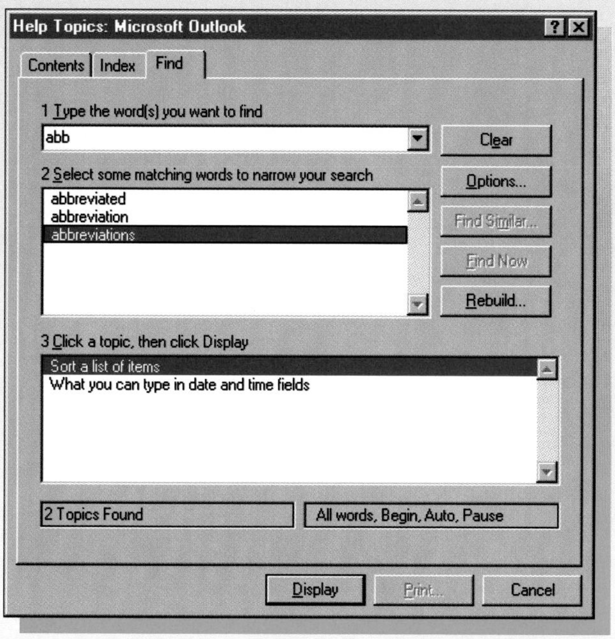

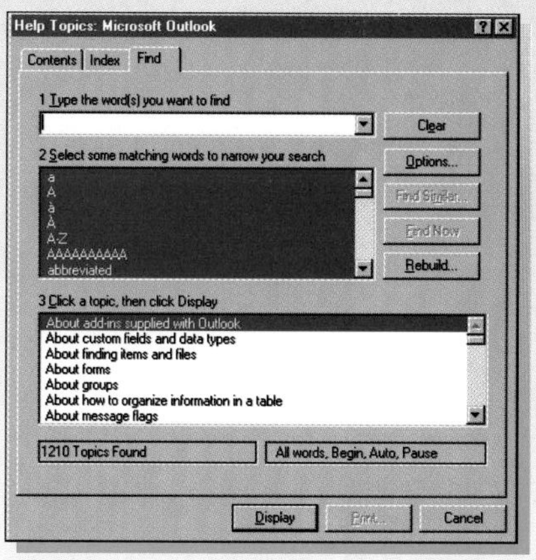

4 The Find section appears after the database has been built. Click the Options button to customize the method used to match words.

5 The Find Options dialog box lets you specify how your search should be conducted. Normally the default settings are best. Click the OK button to close the Find Options dialog box.

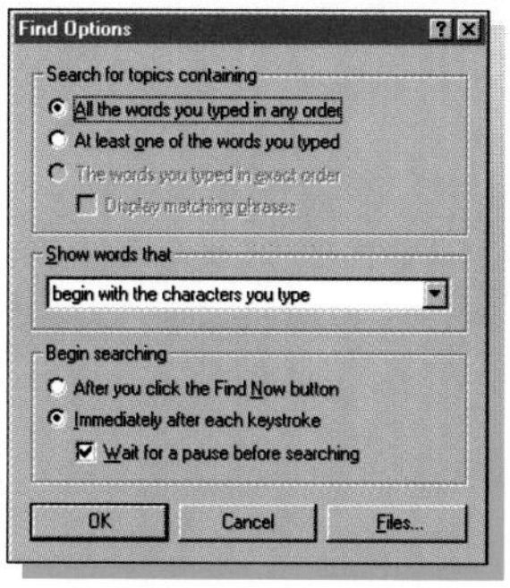

Ctrl + N=
New Mail
Message
F5= Check
for New Mail

P A R T 2

How to Use E-Mail

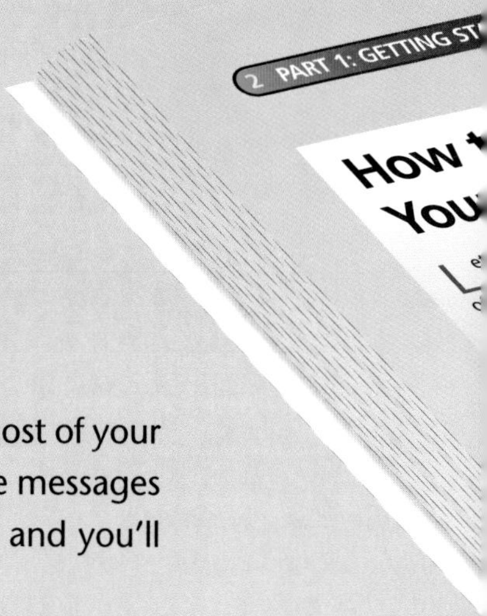

E-MAIL is the heart of your Outlook system. It's where you'll probably spend most of your time, it's the easiest part of Outlook, and it's fun. The ability to send and receive messages electronically is one of the most important developments in communications, and you'll wonder how you ever lived without it.

Using e-mail changes the way you think about time, and time zones. Have a thought, write a note, send it. If the recipient is in your time zone (or a time zone close to yours) it could be a matter of moments before your message is read (and replied to), which is almost as good as making a phone call to transmit the information in the note. If the recipient is on the other side of the world, you don't wake him or her with a ringing phone, yet you know your message won't take a week or so to get there (even with airmail).

In Part 2 you'll learn all the basic information you need in order to send messages electronically. It's easy, there are only three steps: fill out the header, write the message, and click Send. Outlook takes care of the rest. Additionally, we'll explain how to format your messages and add an autosignature to your messages.

IN THIS SECTION YOU'LL LEARN

How to Set Basic E-Mail Options

Outlook has a set of basic e-mail options that control the way you send and receive e-mail. For example, if you want a notification message to appear to alert you that you have received a new message, you can set that option. This would be useful if you were working in Microsoft Word and waiting for an important e-mail message. It's more efficient than continually checking your Inbox.

There is another set of options that allows you to change the appearance of new messages you are sending. You might want to change your font or set the sensitivity of your message as confidential. You can also set options for replying, forwarding, and commenting on messages. This page will show you how to set the basic e-mail options for Microsoft Outlook.

FYI

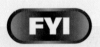

- **Within the E-Mail tab of the Options dialog box, it is likely that you will have multiple locations to check for mail. If you want to check only a single source, make that source the only one that is selected. This can also be accomplished by choosing Check for New Mail On from the Tools menu.**
- **If most of your messages do not need to be marked as important or sensitive, leave them both set to Normal. If you want to mark a specific message as High importance, you can do that from within the Options tab while creating a new message.**
- **Click the Apply button to apply the changes you make in the Options dialog box before you go on to alter other settings. The new options will go into effect immediately and you can continue to change other options.**

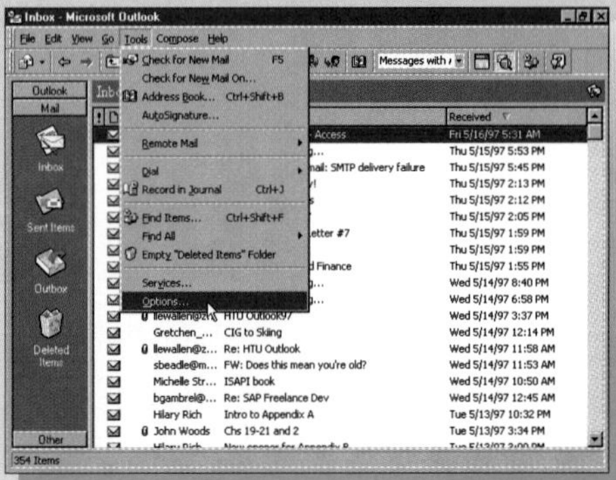

1 Choose the Mail group button on the Outlook Bar and click the Inbox icon. Choose Options from the Tools menu.

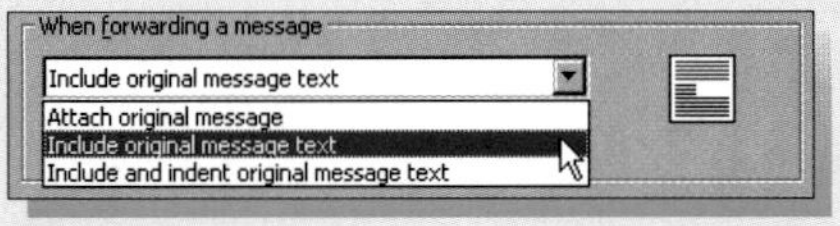

7 When forwarding a message, you can include the original text, include the text with an indent, or include the original message text as an attachment. Click the OK button when you have finished selecting your options.

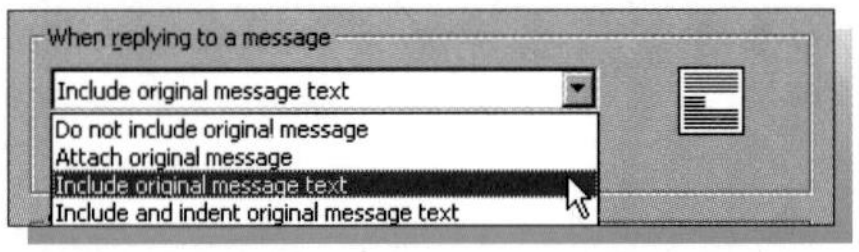

6 When replying to a message, you can include the original text, include the text with an indent (to differentiate the text), include the text as an attachment, or not include the original message at all.

2 The Options dialog box will appear with multiple tabs that will allow you to set defaults and options for your electronic mail. You will automatically be in the E-Mail tab. You can select where you want to check for new mail and how you are notified when new mail arrives. In addition, you can choose how your mail is processed and determine whether you want to use Word as your e-mail editor. Click the Sending tab to view more options.

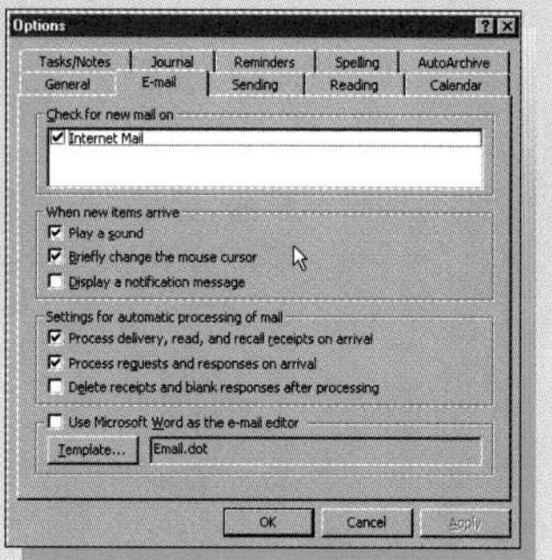

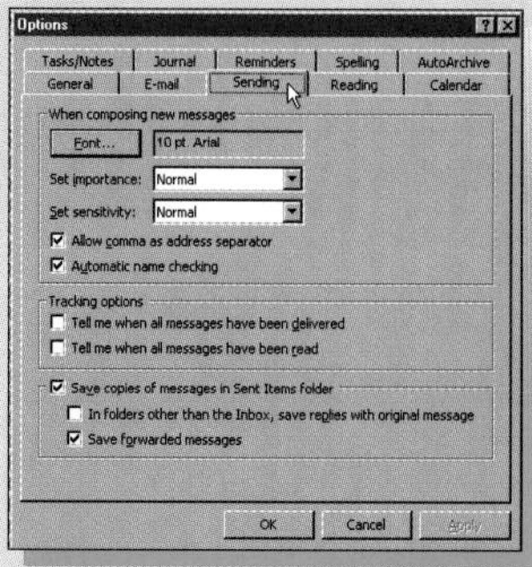

3 The Sending tab on the Options dialog box is where you set options for messages that you compose. In addition, you can choose your default options for setting importance and sensitivity levels, tracking options, and indicating where you want to save copies of your sent messages. Click the Font button to see all the font choices.

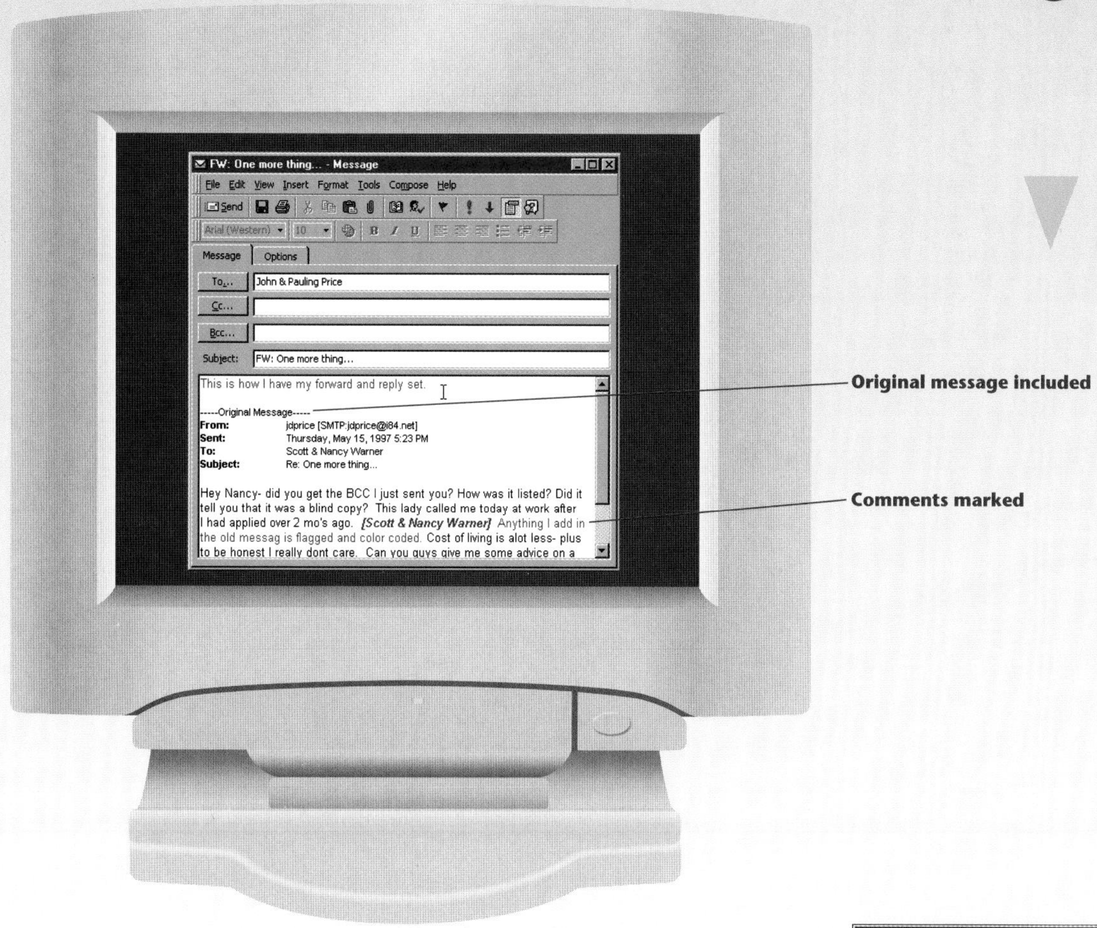

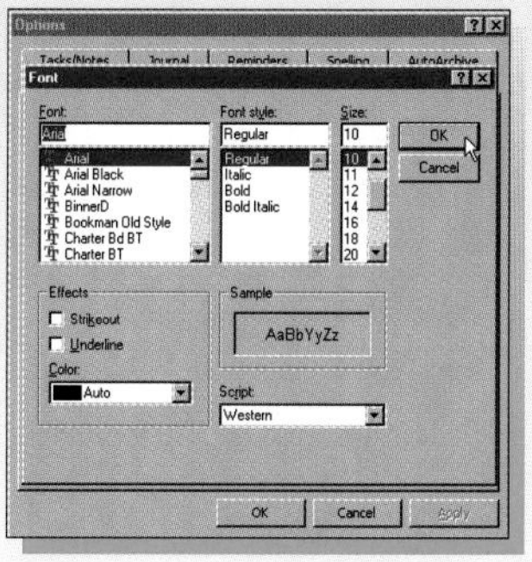

4 The Font dialog box will appear. The font you select displays how the text will appear while you type the message. Click the OK button to return to the Options dialog box, then click the Reading tab.

5 The Reading tab on the Options dialog box is where you set options for messages that you read, reply to, and forward. The most important options to set are what you want to do with the original message when you reply or forward a message. An example message shows how the selected option will appear. As with the Sending tab, you can select different fonts for replying and forwarding. You can also have your comments in the original message identified with your name or other text.

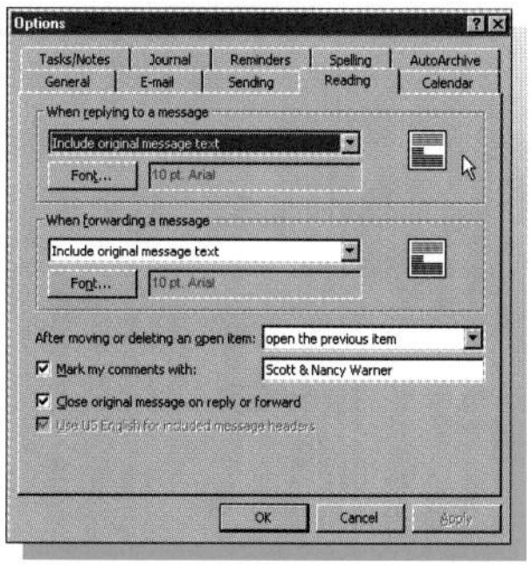

How to Fill Out the Message Header

The header of an e-mail message contains the information about the sender, receiver(s), subject, and any additional options that are attached to the message. It's actually everything except the text of the message. When you view a list of messages in an Information Viewer, it is the header information you see.

Some of the header information is required, and other information is optional. In this section, we'll go over all the parts of the header.

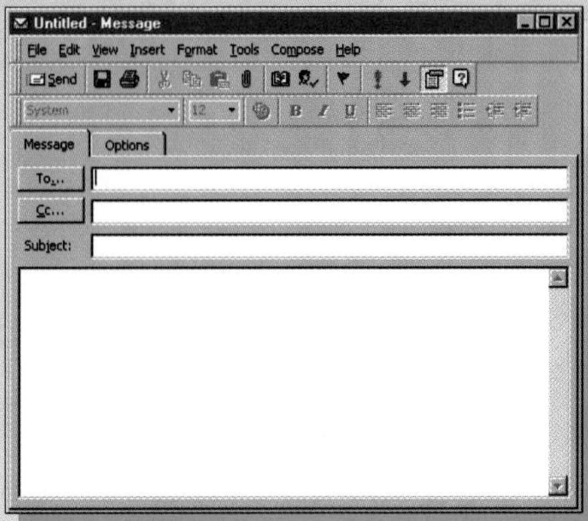

1 To compose a message, click the New Message icon on the toolbar (if you're working in one of the Information Viewers for the Mail section of the Outlook Bar), or choose File, New, Mail Message from the menu bar. A blank message form displays.

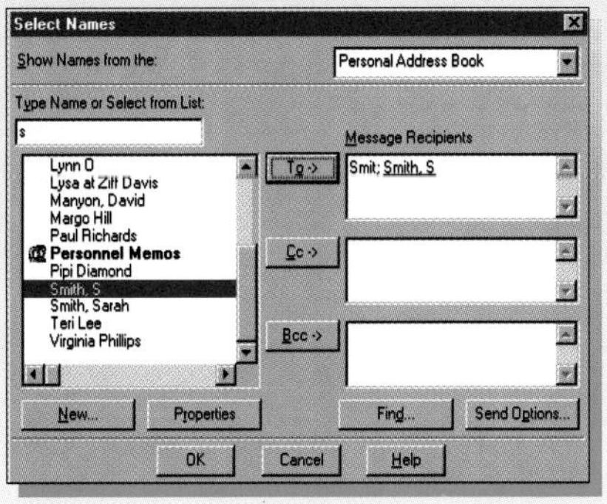

6 To fix the problem, click the To button on the message form, which brings up the Select Names dialog box with all your address book entries. Find the name you want (remember that you can move to the right alphabetical section of the list by entering characters in the Type Name box at the top of the address book) and double-click. Then delete the partial name, including the semi-colon, and click OK to go back to the message. (If you're not really sure which name you meant to use, highlight the entry and click Properties to see detailed information about the entry).

(Continues on next page)

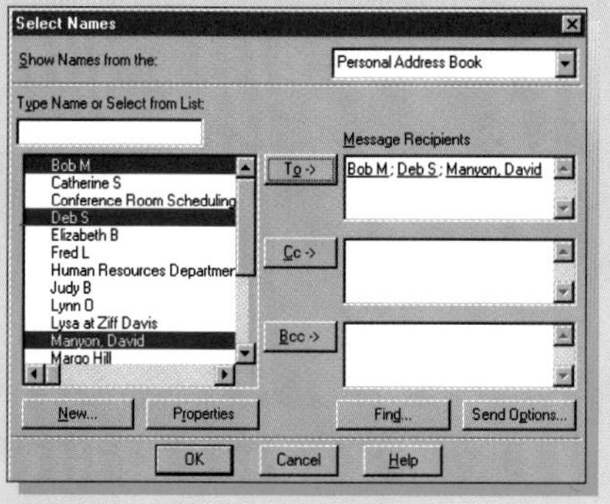

2 A recipient's name must appear in the To field, it is a required field. Click the To button to bring up the Select Names dialog box, which contains all the entries in your address book. Select a name and then click To (or double-click on the name) to move that name into the Message Recipients pane. You can select more than one recipient for the To field, and the fastest way to do that is to hold down the Ctrl key as you click on each entry. Then click To to move all the selected names into the Message Recipients pane.

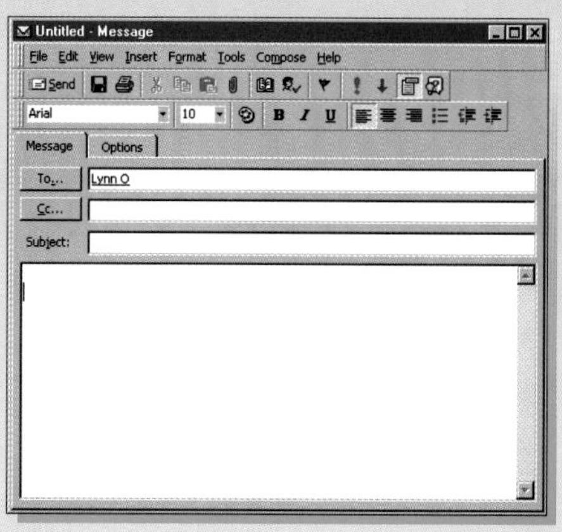

3 You don't have to press To and use the address book, you can enter a name into the To field directly. Outlook checks the address book and if it finds the name, it underlines it. You can even enter a name that isn't in your address book, but you can't use a display name, you must enter a valid e-mail address. Outlook checks the address book and if it doesn't find the name, it then checks your typing to make sure you entered a valid e-mail address format. If so, it underlines it. (Of course that doesn't mean you have the address right, it just means you typed it in a valid format). If you enter multiple names directly, put a semi-colon between them.

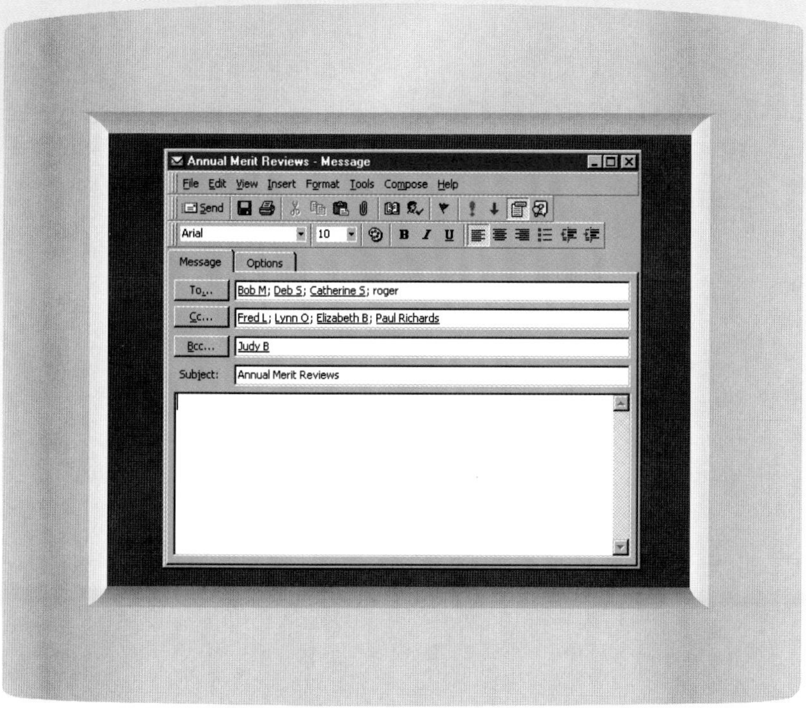

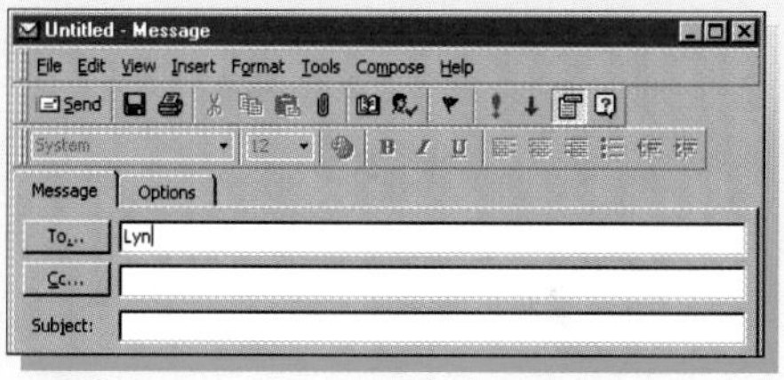

4 You can even enter a partial name in the To field if the full name is in your address book. Outlook will peek into the address book and fill out the full name for you.

5 If you enter a partial name and there are multiple names that contain the letters you typed, Outlook tells you that it couldn't read your mind and wants you to decide which name you meant. It signals this message to you by putting a wavy red line under the characters you typed.

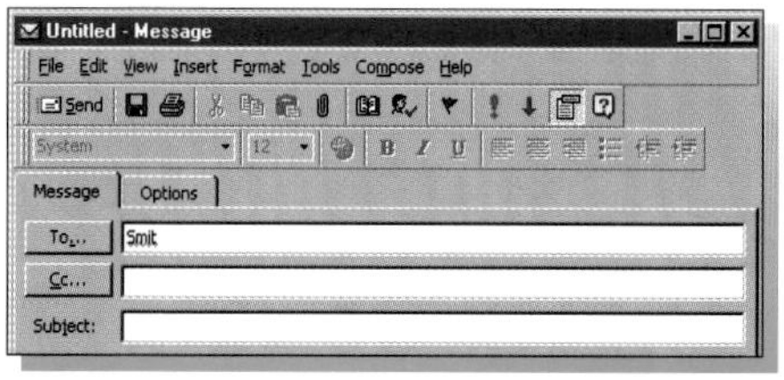

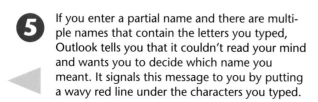

How to Fill Out the Message Header
(Continued)

The recipient, or multiple recipients, you place in the To field are the only required entries for the header. However, there are times when you want to send courtesy copies of a message to another recipient, and there are times you'll want to send a copy to somebody else without letting the recipient know that you did. The last field in the header, the Subject, should always be filled out because it gives a clue about the contents to the recipient. That clue is helpful to people who get a great deal of e-mail and have to prioritize which messages to read first.

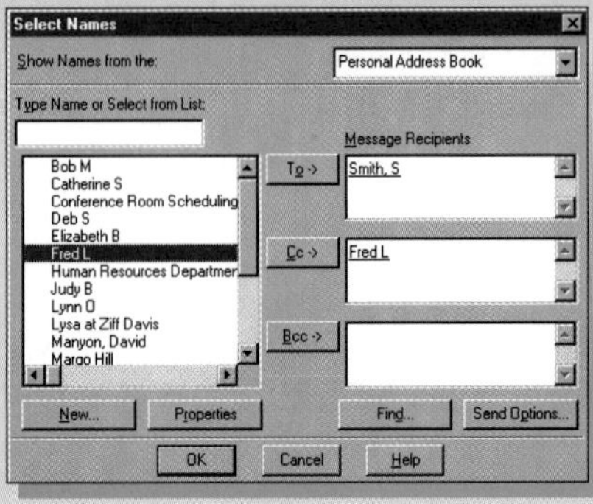

7 If you want to send a copy of the message to another recipient, or multiple recipients, you have to enter the name in the Cc field. Click on the Cc button to bring up the Select Names dialog box, then double-click on the entry you want. Because you clicked the Cc button, double-clicking automatically places the name in the Cc portion of the Message Recipients pane. Click OK to return to the message. The names in the Cc field are visible to the recipient of the message.

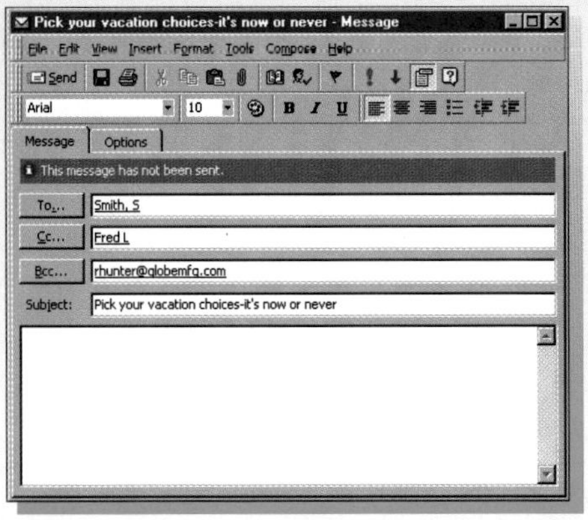

12 Press Tab to move to the message text section (or click anywhere in the text box). We'll discuss the message text in the next section. In the meantime, notice that the title bar of the message now carries the text of the Subject box. In effect, you've named this message file with the text of the Subject box.

FYI

- **If you enter an e-mail address directly into a recipient field, you can right-click it and choose Add to Address Book if it isn't in there already.**
- **If you click the To button on the message in order to use the Select Names dialog box to enter the recipient name, you can enter the Cc and Bcc names at the same time. Just click an entry to highlight it, then click Cc or Bcc to place that entry into the right part of the Message Recipients pane. This eliminates all the steps involved in returning to the message, and then entering the recipients for the Cc field and the Bcc field.**
- **You can enter names directly, including partial names, in the fields for copies, the same way you do for the To field.**

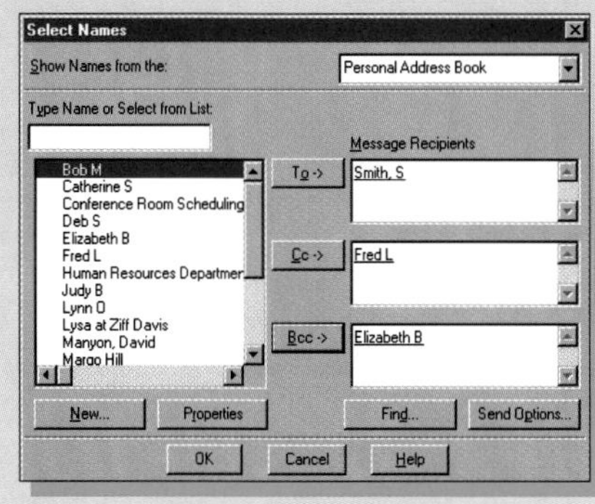

8 If you want to send a copy to someone and you want it to be a secret, that's called a blind carbon copy. The recipient will not see any indication of this copy on the message. You can add a name to the Bcc field by clicking either the To or Cc button in order to bring up the Select Names dialog box (there is no Bcc button on the message form until you use the Bcc feature). Select the entry that you want to send a blind copy to, then click Bcc. The display name for the entry is placed in the Bcc section of the Message Recipients pane.

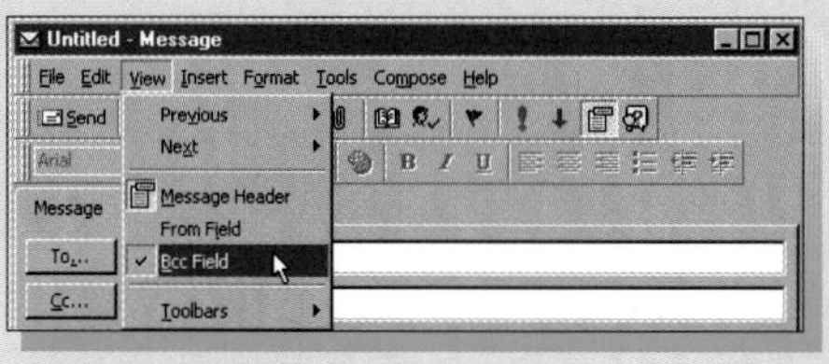

9 You can add the Bcc field to the message without using the Select Names dialog box. This is handy if you're entering an e-mail address directly into the Bcc field because that recipient isn't in your address book. To place a Bcc field in a message form so you can enter an e-mail address in it, choose View, Bcc Field from the menu bar of the message form. A checkmark indicates the field is available on this message.

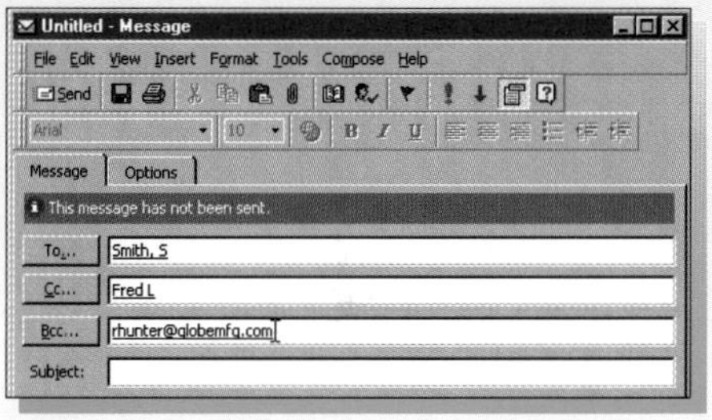

10 The message form now has a Bcc box in the header. Enter a recipient (if the recipient is not in your PAB, enter a valid e-mail address).

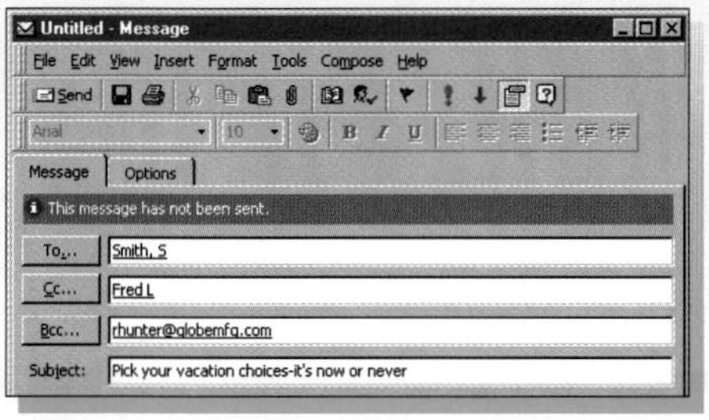

11 Move to the Subject box, either by pressing Tab or clicking in the Subject box. Enter a short phrase that describes what this message is about. Remember that when the recipient looks at his or her received messages, it may be only the header that's seen, so this phrase becomes a clue that helps determine whether the message gets read now or sits in the Inbox until the recipient gets around to reading it. Many Internet recipients use software that cannot reveal any of the message, so the text in the Subject box is the only clue to the message contents.

How to Enter and Format the Message

Once you've taken care of the header, the real work (and the real fun) begins. Now you have to write a message. You have plenty of tools to help you, except, of course, there's no tool that invents the words for you—you'll have to do that all by yourself.

In this section we'll look at all the Outlook tools for message writing. You'll find you're really working with a mini-word processor.

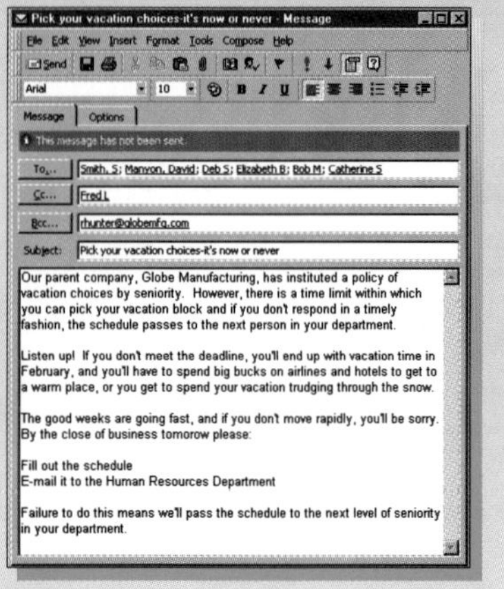
Pick your vacation choices-it's now or never - Message
File Edit View Insert Format Tools Compose Help
Send
Arial
10
Message
Options
This message has not been sent.
To...
Smith, S; Manyon, David; Deb S; Elizabeth B; Bob M; Catherine S
Cc...
Fred L
Bcc...
rhunter@globemfg.com
Subject:
Pick your vacation choices-it's now or never
Our parent company, Globe Manufacturing, has instituted a policy of vacation choices by seniority. However, there is a time limit within which you can pick your vacation block and if you don't respond in a timely fashion, the schedule passes to the next person in your department.
Listen up! If you don't meet the deadline, you'll end up with vacation time in February, and you'll have to spend big bucks on airlines and hotels to get to a warm place, or you get to spend your vacation trudging through the snow.
The good weeks are going fast, and if you don't move rapidly, you'll be sorry. By the close of business tomorrow please:
Fill out the schedule
E-mail it to the Human Resources Department
Failure to do this means we'll pass the schedule to the next level of seniority in your department.

1 The first step is to enter text for the message. I'll do mine and you do yours.

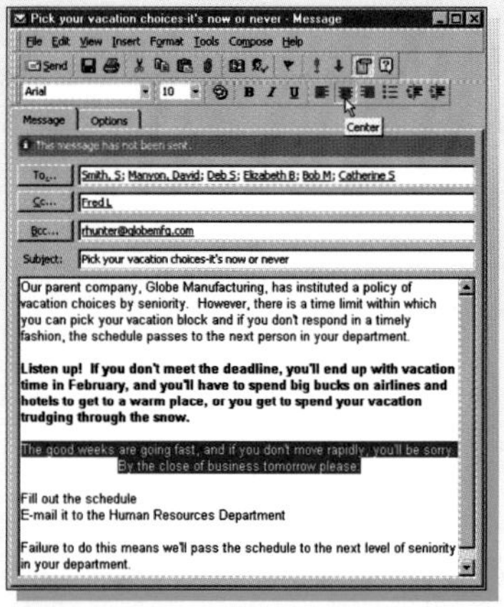
Pick your vacation choices-it's now or never - Message
File Edit View Insert Format Tools Compose Help
Send
Arial
10
Center
Message
Options
This message has not been sent.
To...
Smith, S; Manyon, David; Deb S; Elizabeth B; Bob M; Catherine S
Cc...
Fred L
Bcc...
rhunter@globemfg.com
Subject:
Pick your vacation choices-it's now or never
Our parent company, Globe Manufacturing, has instituted a policy of vacation choices by seniority. However, there is a time limit within which you can pick your vacation block and if you don't respond in a timely fashion, the schedule passes to the next person in your department.
Listen up! If you don't meet the deadline, you'll end up with vacation time in February, and you'll have to spend big bucks on airlines and hotels to get to a warm place, or you get to spend your vacation trudging through the snow.
The good weeks are going fast, and if you don't move rapidly, you'll be sorry.
By the close of business tomorrow please:
Fill out the schedule
E-mail it to the Human Resources Department
Failure to do this means we'll pass the schedule to the next level of seniority in your department.

6 To change the alignment of text (by default it is lined up on the left margin) to Centered or Aligned Right, select the text you want to change and click the appropriate icon on the Format toolbar.

(Continues on next page)

2 Before applying any fancy formatting schemes, you should really check all your spelling. Otherwise, your co-workers may be tempted to return your message with the spelling errors pointed out, making you feel as if you're back in third grade. To use the Outlook Spell Check feature, choose Tools, Spelling.

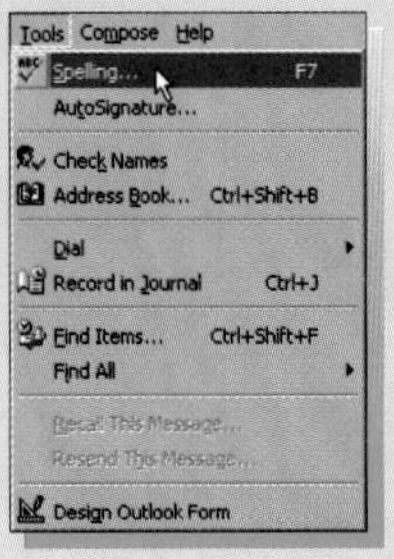
Tools Compose Help
Spelling... F7
AutoSignature...
Check Names
Address Book... Ctrl+Shift+B
Dial
Record in Journal Ctrl+J
Find Items... Ctrl+Shift+F
Find All
Recall This Message...
Resend This Message...
Design Outlook Form

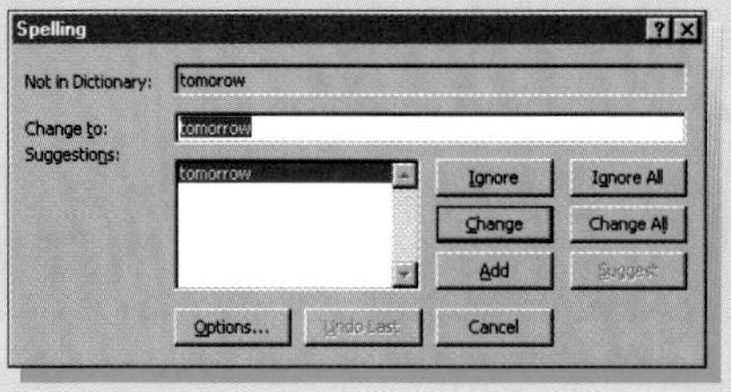
Spelling
Not in Dictionary: tomorow
Change to: tomorrow
Suggestions: tomorrow
Ignore
Ignore All
Change
Change All
Add
Suggest
Options...
Undo Last
Cancel

3 When the spelling checker finds a word that isn't in its dictionary, it notifies you. If there's a word close to your misspelled word, it's offered as a suggestion. To accept the suggestion for this word, choose Change. To tell Outlook to correct this word every time it appears misspelled in your text, choose Change All. If the word is a proper name or a technical term, choose Ignore to tell Outlook to leave it alone (or Ignore All to leave it alone every time it appears in the message). If you want to add that proper name or technical term to the dictionary so it's not flagged as a misspelling in future messages, choose Add.

Pick your vacation choices-it's now or never - Message
Smith, S; Manyon, David; Deb S; Elizabeth B; Bob M; Catherine S
Fred L
rhunter@globemfg.com
Subject: Pick your vacation choices-it's now or never
Our parent company, Globe Manufacturing, has instituted a policy of vacation choices by seniority. However, there is a time limit within which you can pick your vacation block and if you don't respond in a timely fashion, the schedule passes to the next person in your department.
Listen up! If you don't meet the deadline, you'll end up with vacation time in February, and you'll have to spend big bucks on airlines and hotels to get to a warm place, or you get to spend your vacation trudging through the snow.
The good weeks are going fast, and if you don't move rapidly, you'll be sorry. By the close of business tomorrow please:
Fill out the schedule
E-mail it to the Human Resources Department
Failure to do this means we'll pass the schedule to the next level of seniority in your department.

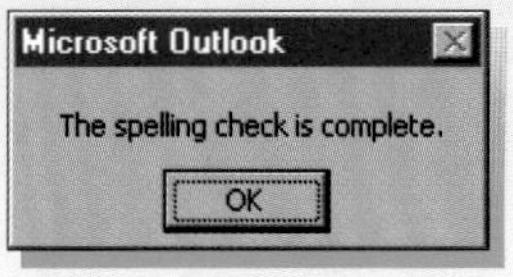
Microsoft Outlook
The spelling check is complete.
OK

4 Outlook moves on to the next misspelled word. When the entire message is checked, an informational dialog box displays to notify you. Click OK.

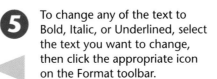

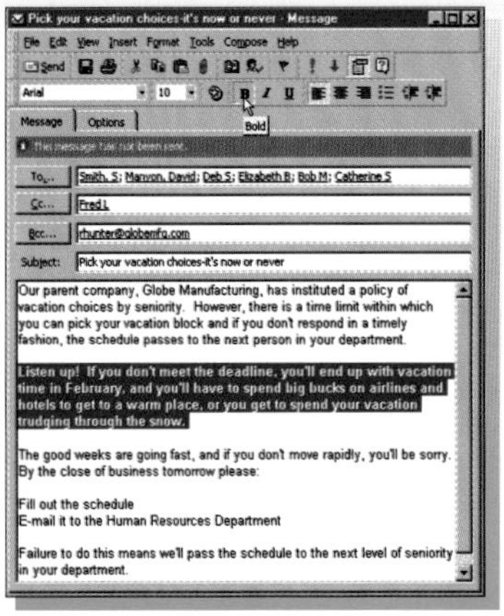
Pick your vacation choices-it's now or never - Message
Bold
Subject: Pick your vacation choices-it's now or never

5 To change any of the text to Bold, Italic, or Underlined, select the text you want to change, then click the appropriate icon on the Format toolbar.

How to Enter and Format the Message (Continued)

You can see how changing the formatting helps you emphasize text, making it stand out. There are many times when this becomes important, so recipients understand when you really mean business, as opposed to those times you're merely passing along information.

There are also many times when formatting just becomes a way to make messages look interesting or pretty. And, of course, formatting a message in an interesting way makes the process of writing e-mail a little more fun and a little more creative.

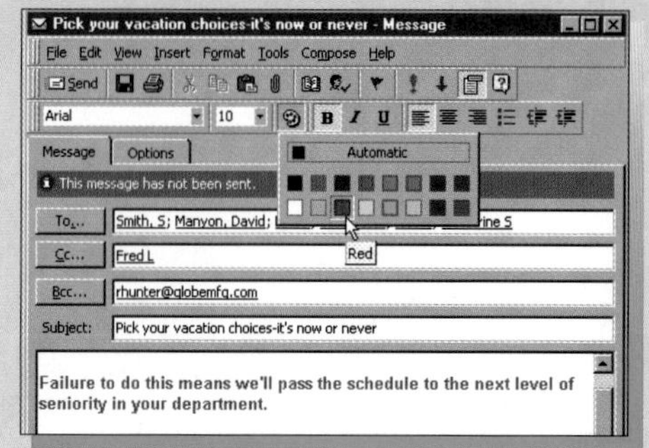

7 To add color to a section of text, select the text and click the Color icon on the Format toolbar. Then pick whatever color tickles your fancy. Don't panic if the selected text seems unchanged, you have to deselect it in order to see the color (press an arrow key or click anywhere else in the message box).

FYI

- When you select text, you can cut, copy, and paste in the same way you perform those tasks in all other Windows software.
- If you want to apply formatting to the entire message, press Ctrl+A to select all the text in the message.
- When you are searching for a specific font, instead of scrolling through the whole font list, begin typing the name of the font in the font box. As you enter characters, you move to the part of the alphabetical list of fonts that matches your typing.
- Not all fonts have a large number of font sizes available, and some offer only one size.

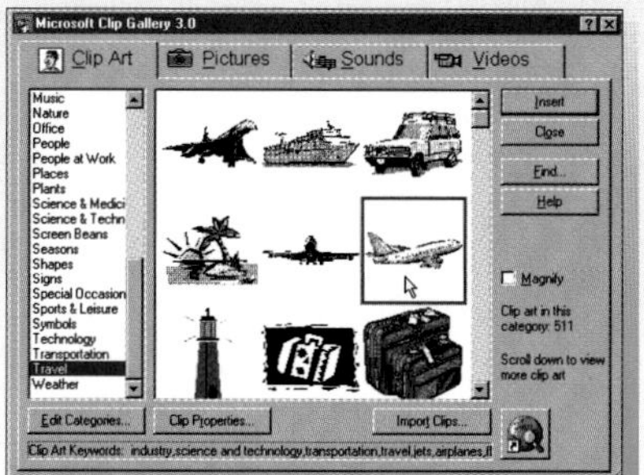

12 Select the picture you want, then click Insert. You're done! What a great message! Everyone will love it! Click that Send button!

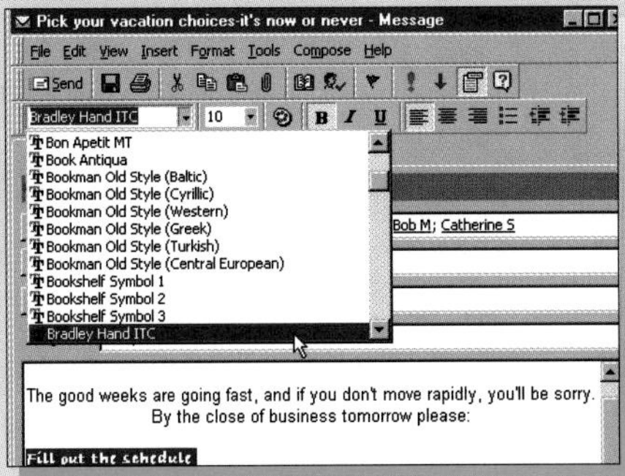

8 To change the font, select the text you want to change and click the arrow to the right of the font selection box. Pick a new font that has a "personality" to match your words.

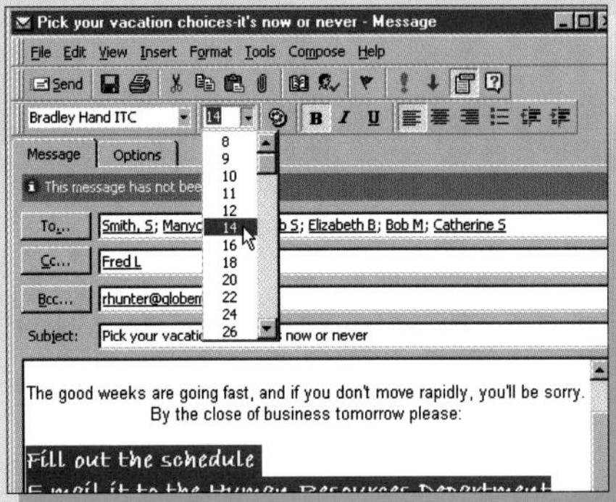

9 To change the font size, select the text you want to change and click the arrow to the right of the font size selection box. Pick a new size.

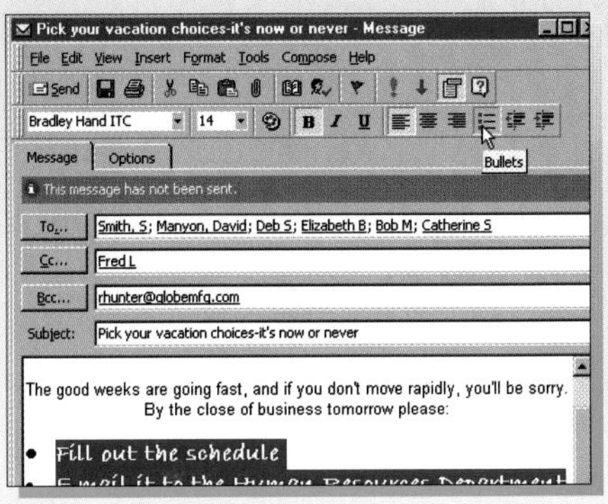

10 To create a bulleted list, select the text you want to turn into a list and click the Bullets icon on the Format toolbar.

11 To put some pizzazz in your message, add a graphic. Place your pointer at the point in the message where you want to place the artwork (you should press Enter a few times to clear some space), then choose Insert, Object from the menu bar. The Insert Object dialog box appears. Pick an object type (Hint: go for the Microsoft Clip Gallery to keep things uncomplicated—make sure your Office 97 CD-ROM is in the drive because that's where the files are kept, unless you know you copied them to your computer's hard drive). Click OK to see the Clip Gallery.

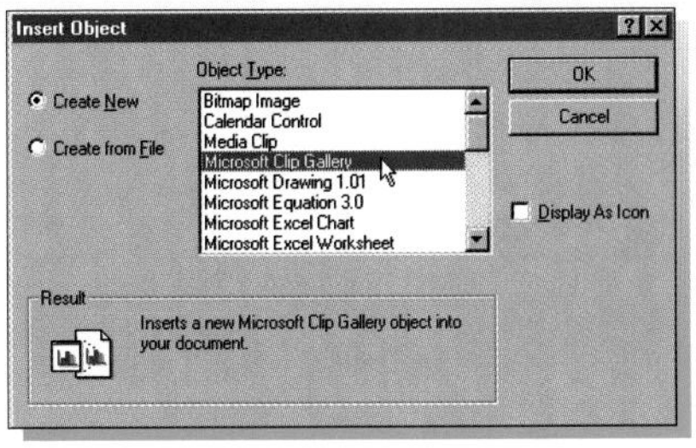

How to Create an AutoSignature

An AutoSignature is a phrase you invent that is automatically appended to every message your write. But don't let the word "signature" limit your imagination. You can do a lot more with an AutoSignature than sign messages. You can include information about yourself, a commercial (about yourself or your company), even an amusing anecdote if you wish. In fact, some people have AutoSignatures that are so long, they're sometimes longer than the message they're attached to.

Most people use AutoSignatures to sign their names, titles, and any other information they feel is important, and they don't want to bother typing it in every time they send a message.

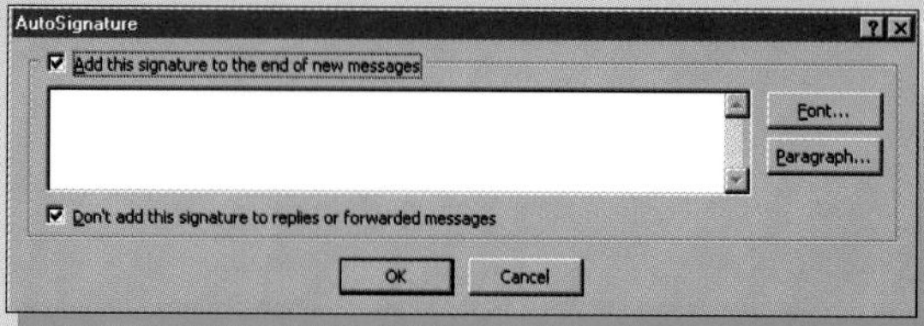

1 To create an AutoSignature, choose Tools, AutoSignature from the menu bar. The AutoSignature dialog box opens so you can begin. If you want this AutoSignature to appear at the end of every message you send, click the box that says Add this signature to the end of new messages (when you open this dialog box, there's no checkmark in that box—I selected it). If you don't select this option, you can add your AutoSignature to individual messages when the mood strikes you (explained later in this section). If you do not want your AutoSignature added to message that are replies to the sender, or messages you receive that you are forwarding to others, check that box.

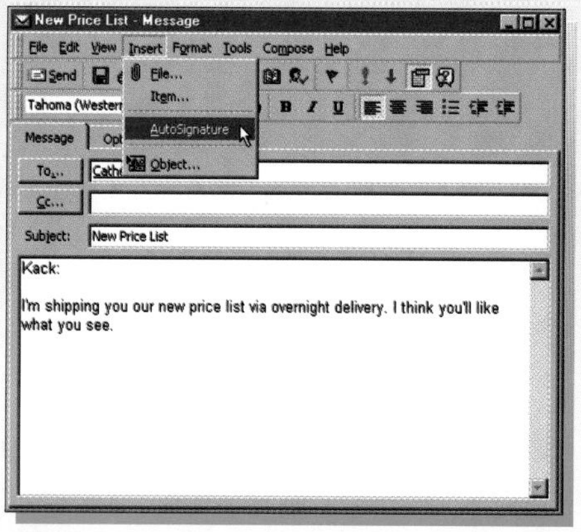

6 If you did not select the automatic insertion of an AutoSignature, you can add the AutoSignature you designed to any message you wish. After you compose the message, place your pointer where you want the AutoSignature to be, then choose Insert, AutoSignature from the menu bar.

FYI

- **If you opted to add an AutoSignature automatically and don't want it on a particular message, select the text and press Del.**
- **If you don't want the entire AutoSignature to appear, select the text you want to remove, then press Del.**
- **Not all the fonts available have all the attributes (bold, italic, and so on). Some fonts have very limited size choices.**

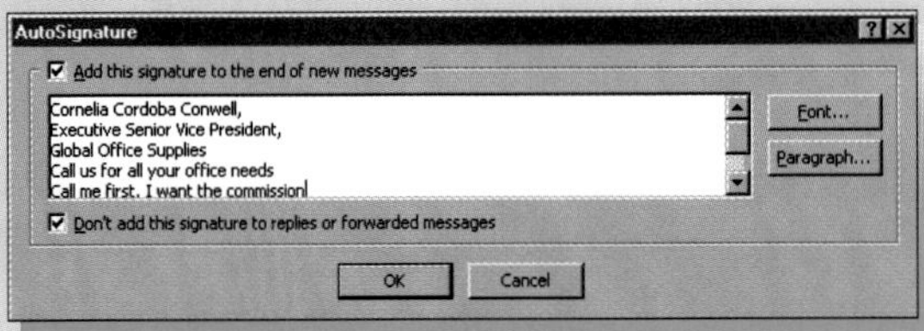

2 Type the text you want to use for your AutoSignature. Don't worry about formatting the text at this point, just enter the information. You can enter just your name, your name and title, or even enter a little marketing plug. If you wish, you can add a clever or humorous line, or a favorite quote.

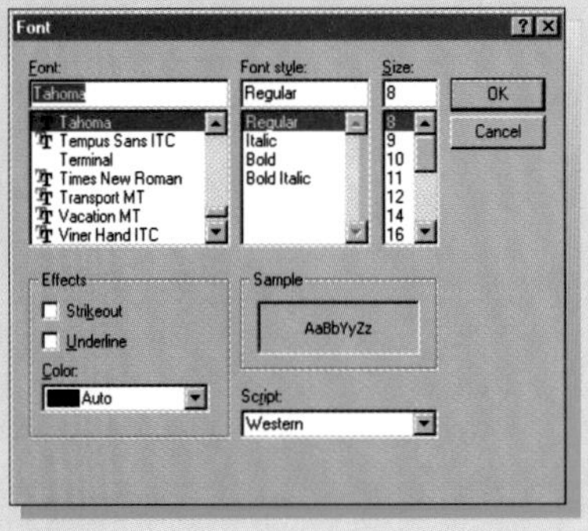

3 To change the font, select the text you want to change (or press Ctrl+A to select all the text), then click Font. The Font dialog box opens with plenty of options for changing the appearance of the text.

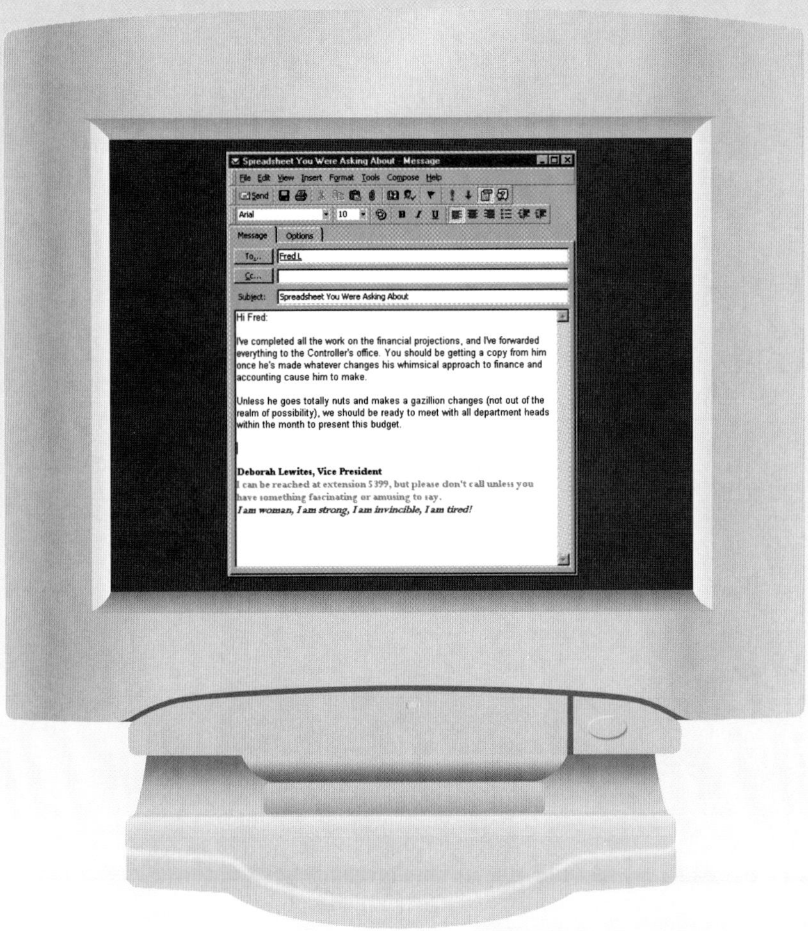

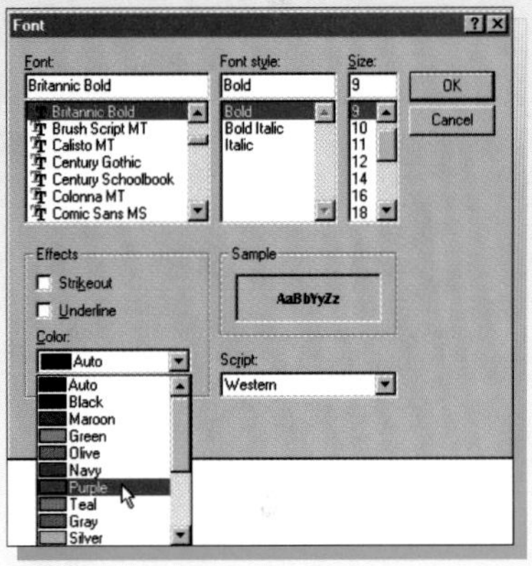

4 Select a different font. Then choose a Font style (regular, italic, bold, or bold italic), and a size. You can also choose a different color. Keep an eye on the Sample box, it shows you what your selections look like. Click OK to return to the AutoSignature dialog box. If you don't like the appearance, go back and change your selections. When your AutoSignature is all set, click OK.

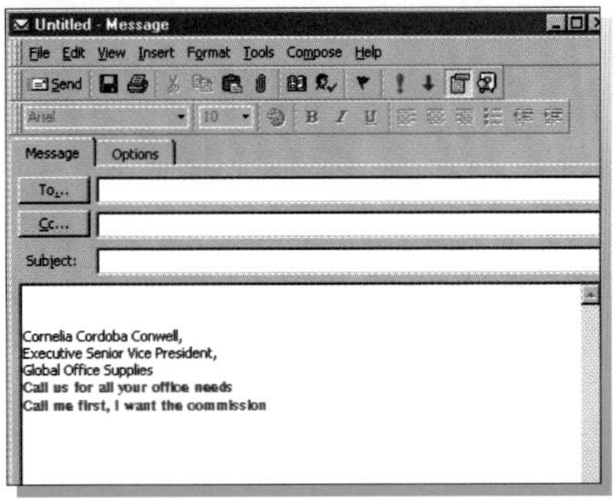

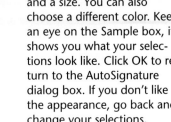

5 The next time you open a new message form to begin composing a message, your AutoSignature is right there.

How to Set Up WordMail

WordMail isn't automatic, you have to set it up. Once you do, you can turn it on and off as you need it. When you decide to use MS Word for composing e-mail, you have to realize that only other WordMail users will see the full effect of your formatting and special features. However, those recipients who can't see the features unique to WordMail won't miss a word of your text, because the message contents are converted to plain text.

In this section we'll turn on WordMail and go over the features you'll have available.

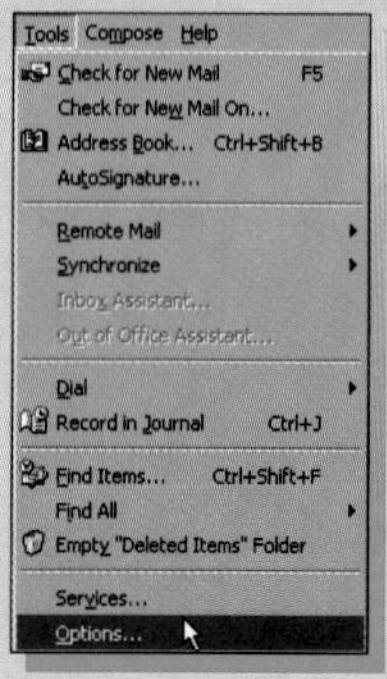

1 Turning WordMail on (and off) starts with the Options dialog box. To see it, choose Tools, Options from the menu bar.

5 There is another difference that's important, and that's the Help system. You're working in Outlook and Word at the same time, so help is available for both.

FYI

- **Most of the icons on the toolbars are grayed out (inaccessible) while you're entering information in the header. When you move to the message text box, they'll light up for you.**
- **The Contents and Index choice on the Help menu is for Microsoft Word. Choose Outlook Help to see the full Contents and Index help system for Outlook.**

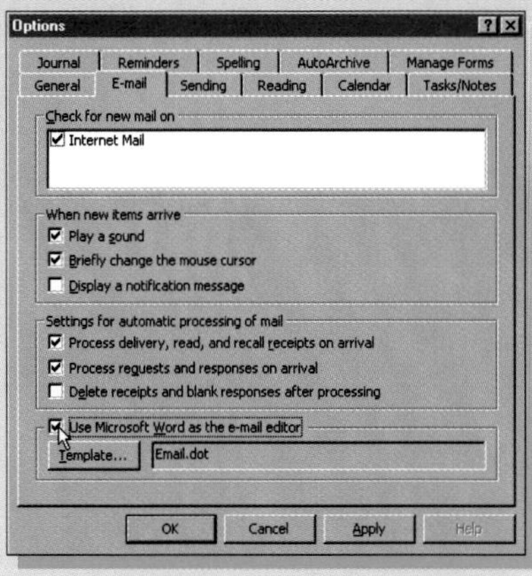

2 When the Options dialog box displays, click the E-mail tab. Near the bottom of the page is an option named Use Microsoft Word as the E-mail Editor. Click the box next to that option, which places a checkmark in the box. Then click OK.

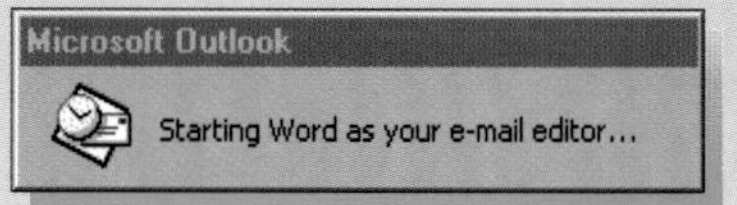

3 Click the New Mail Message icon on the toolbar, or choose File, New, Mail Message from the menu bar to compose a new e-mail message. Outlook reminds you that you'll be using WordMail.

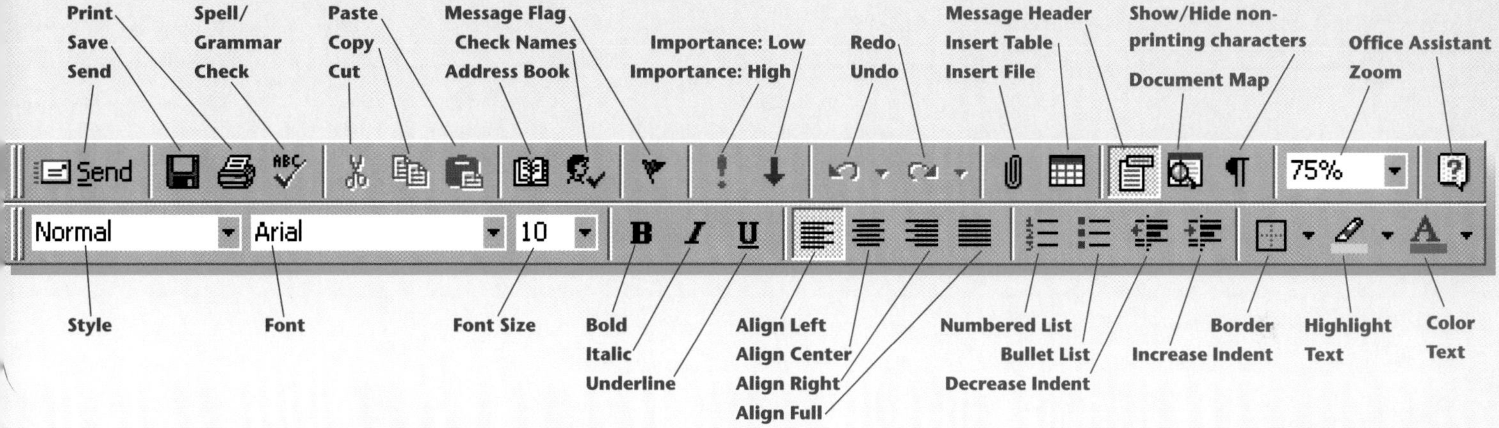

4 When the Message window opens, it doesn't look all that different from the Outlook message window you're used to. There are, however, a larger number of icons on the toolbars. Most people have to widen the message window to see the entire toolbar. If your window doesn't have all the elements you see in this illustration, you'll have to make the window wider. To do that, move your pointer to the right edge of the window until the pointer turns into a double-headed arrow. Then press and hold the left mouse button and drag to the right. When the toolbars are totally displayed, release the mouse button.

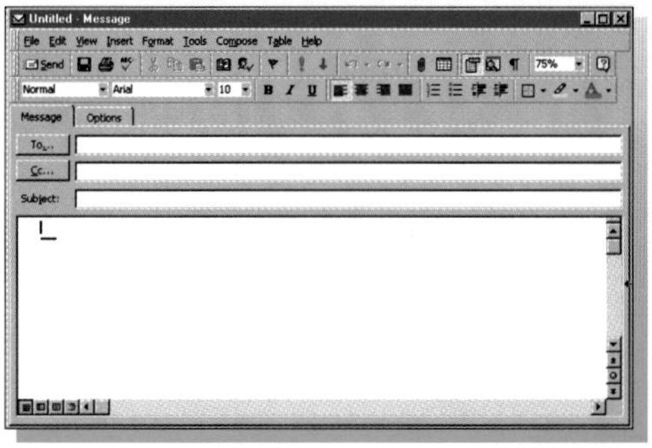

How to Use WordMail Features

Let's take a look at some of the additional power you gain when you opt to use WordMail for composing e-mail messages. We'll go over some of the options that are missing from the basic Outlook e-mail features. Of course, if you're an expert Word user, some of these will be familiar, but the features specific to e-mail might not be.

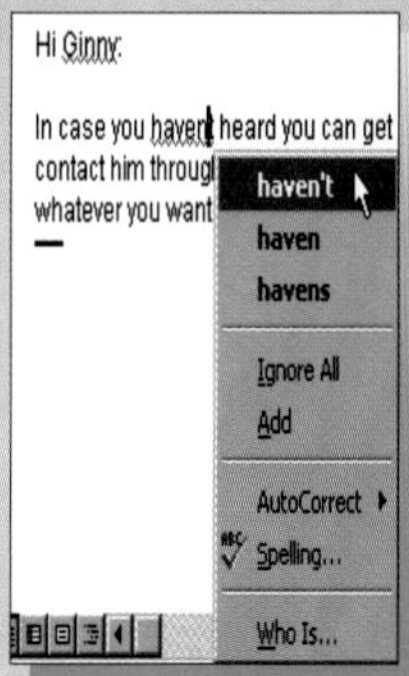

1 As you enter text, you might see a little red squiggly line beneath words. This is the WordMail instant spell checker at work (Microsoft's official name for it is "check spelling as you type"). The wavy red line indicates that WordMail cannot find that word in its dictionary. Right-click the word to see suggestions for correcting the problem.

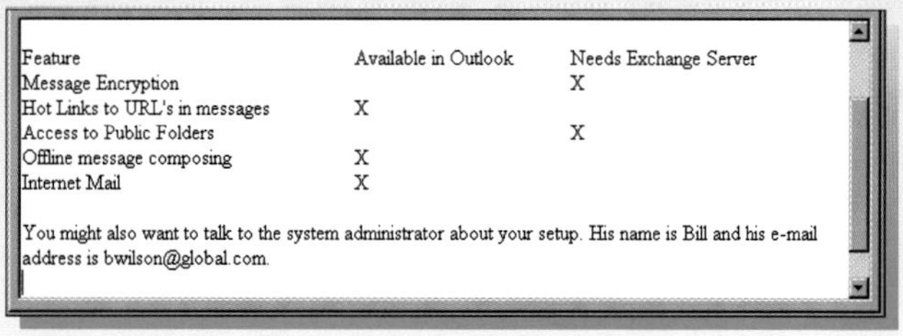

Feature	Available in Outlook	Needs Exchange Server
Message Encryption		X
Hot Links to URL's in messages	X	
Access to Public Folders		X
Offline message composing	X	
Internet Mail	X	

You might also want to talk to the system administrator about your setup. His name is Bill and his e-mail address is bwilson@global.com.

6 When the recipient receives your message, if he or she isn't using a mail reader that supports the formatting in your WordMail message, all is not lost. Tables, for example, will convert to tabular columns. Text won't be highlighted, but it's still readable.

FYI

- **One of the other useful tools in WordMail that isn't available when you use Outlook for e-mail is the Thesaurus. Choose Tools, Language, Thesaurus (or press Shift+F7) to see synonyms for a word.**
- **If the red wavy lines are driving you crazy and you'd rather just run a spell check when you want to, you can turn them off. Choose Tools, Options. When the Options dialog box opens, move to the Spelling & Grammar tab, then click Check spelling as you type to remove the check mark and deselect this option. Click OK to close the dialog box.**

2 If you refer to a mail recipient in a message, you can ask Outlook to check the name you entered, to make sure you're giving the recipient the proper name. Select (highlight) the name and right-click. Then choose Who Is from the menu.

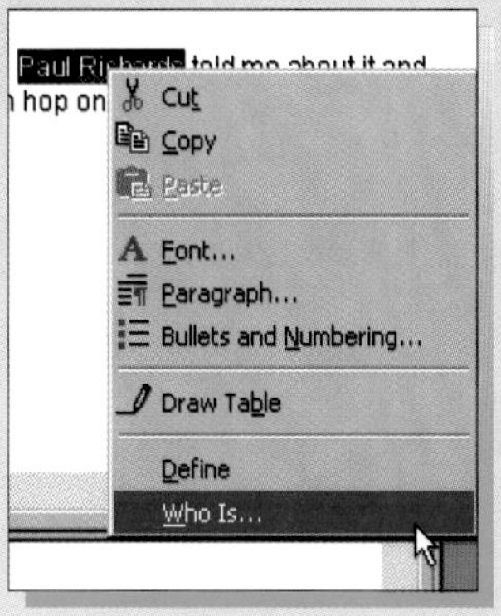

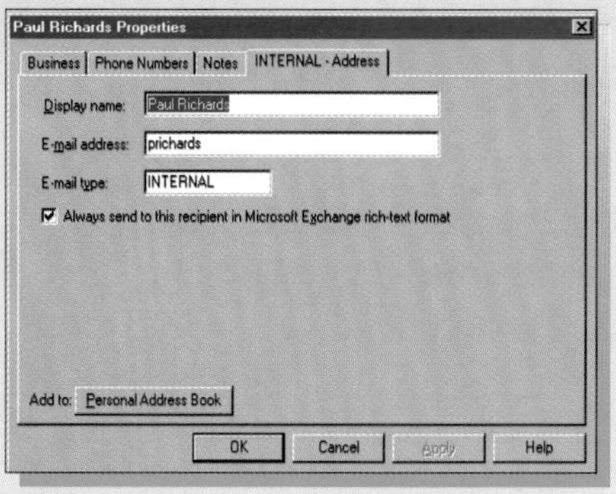

3 Outlook opens your address book and finds this display name. Now you're sure you gave the right information. In fact, since you have the entry's Properties dialog box in front of you, it might be nice to click the Business tab or the Phone Numbers tab and put additional information (like a telephone number or extension) into your message. Click Cancel or OK to close the dialog box.

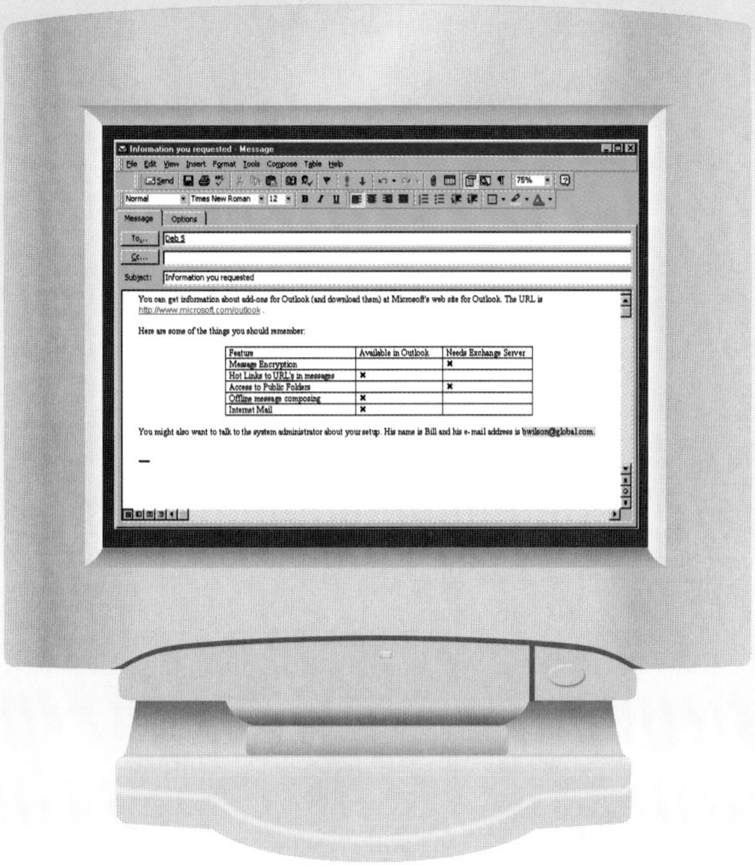

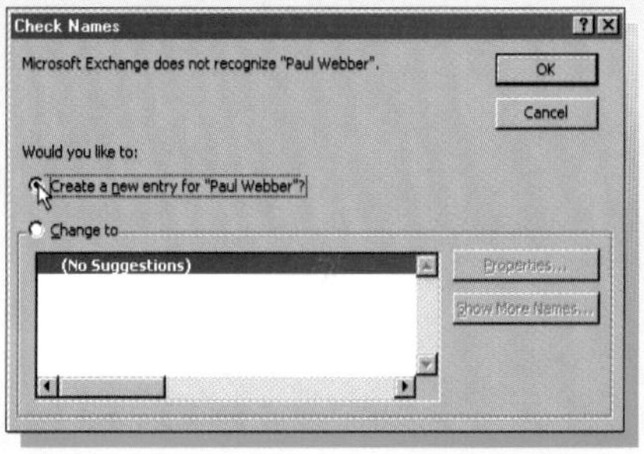

4 If the name in your message is not found in the address book, but it is a valid e-mail display name for an internal system, or a valid e-mail address for an Internet recipient, you can add this name to the address book. Select Create a new entry and click OK, then fill out the New Entry dialog boxes.

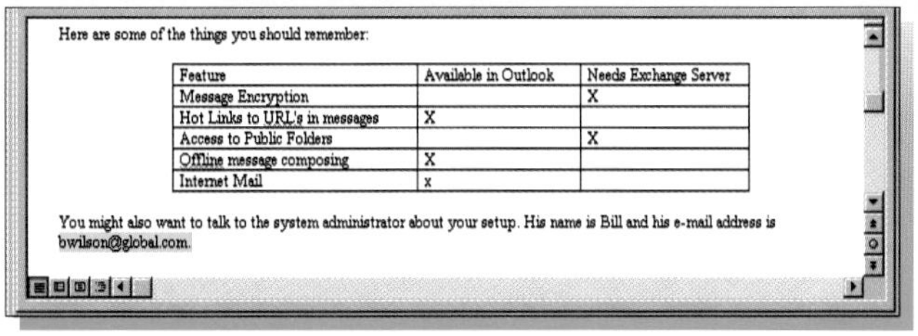

Here are some of the things you should remember:

Feature	Available in Outlook	Needs Exchange Server
Message Encryption		X
Hot Links to URL's in messages	X	
Access to Public Folders		X
Offline message composing	X	
Internet Mail	x	

You might also want to talk to the system administrator about your setup. His name is Bill and his e-mail address is bwilson@global.com.

5 You can use tables and text highlighting in your e-mail messages when you use WordMail. Use the Insert Table icon on the toolbar to create a table. To highlight text, select it and then click the Highlight icon on the toolbar (you can click the arrow to the right of the icon to select a different color).

How to Create Hot Links in a Message

Besides all the neat word processing features you have available when you use WordMail, there are some special features directly related to the Internet. If your recipient has Internet access (access to an Internet browser and a modem), you can send her or him to an Internet site from within your message.

In fact, you can provide a hot link to a specific document, or part of a document, either on the Web or on a computer in your office.

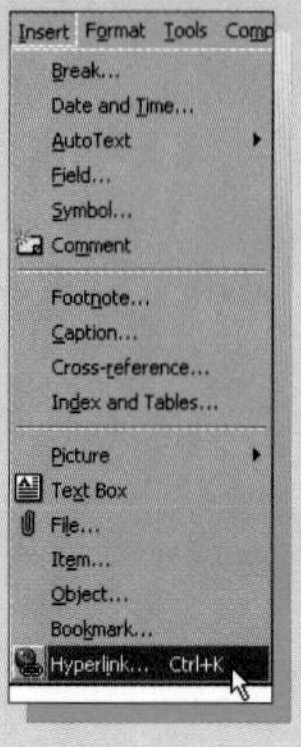
Insert Format Tools
Break...
Date and Time...
AutoText
Field...
Symbol...
Comment
Footnote...
Caption...
Cross-reference...
Index and Tables...
Picture
Text Box
File...
Item...
Object...
Bookmark...
Hyperlink... Ctrl+K

1 If you're sending e-mail within your network, you can point the recipient to a document on the network server (or on any computer on the network to which that recipient has access). This is handy if you want somebody to look at a work in progress. It's easier than attaching a file, and takes up much less room on the hard drive. To put a hyperlink to a document into an e-mail message, choose Insert Hyperlink from the menu bar (or press Ctrl+K).

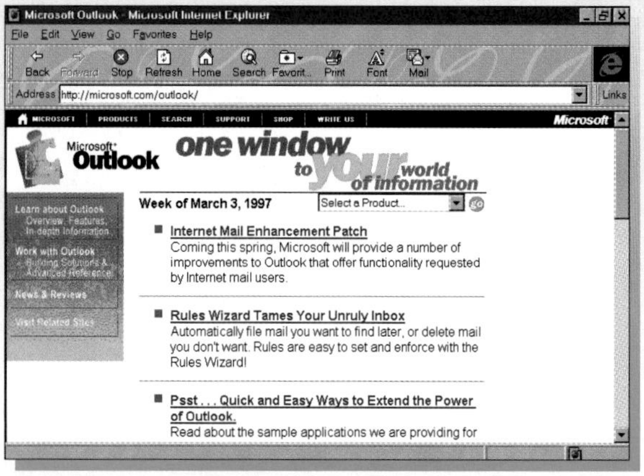
Microsoft Outlook - Microsoft Internet Explorer
File Edit View Go Favorites Help
Back Forward Stop Refresh Home Search Favorit... Print Font Mail
Address http://microsoft.com/outlook/
Microsoft Outlook
one window to your world of information
Week of March 3, 1997
Select a Product...
Internet Mail Enhancement Patch
Coming this spring, Microsoft will provide a number of improvements to Outlook that offer functionality requested by Internet mail users.
Rules Wizard Tames Your Unruly Inbox
Automatically file mail you want to find later, or delete mail you don't want. Rules are easy to set and enforce with the Rules Wizard!
Psst . . . Quick and Easy Ways to Extend the Power of Outlook.
Read about the sample applications we are providing for

6 When the recipient gets the message, clicking anywhere on the hyperlink opens a browser and loads the page indicated on the hyperlink. You can test it by clicking it while you're composing the message. Your browser opens and you head for the Web. Go ahead, test it, and I'll test mine at the same time.

FYI

- **To make sure that a file you're using for a hyperlink is available to the recipient, put it on a network server.**
- **If Internet access is obtained through a dial-up service, when you (or a recipient) click a hyperlink, the browser will launch the dial-up connection. After you log on to the dial-up connection (using the steps needed by your Internet service provider), the browser heads for the Web page indicated in the hyperlink.**

2 The Insert Hyperlink dialog box appears and you can enter the location and name of the file you want to link in the Link box at the top of the dialog box. If you don't have it memorized, choose Browse, and when you find the folder and file you want, double-click its icon. If the document has a bookmark that you want to use as the link, insert that in the optional Named location in file box (you can also enter an object that's inserted in the file, or a slide number if the file is from PowerPoint). When the dialog box is filled in, choose OK.

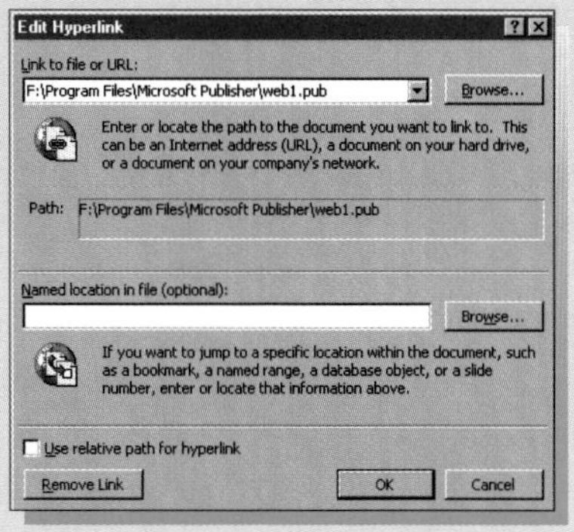
Edit Hyperlink
Link to file or URL:
F:\Program Files\Microsoft Publisher\web1.pub
Browse...
Enter or locate the path to the document you want to link to. This can be an Internet address (URL), a document on your hard drive, or a document on your company's network.
Path: F:\Program Files\Microsoft Publisher\web1.pub
Named location in file (optional):
Browse...
If you want to jump to a specific location within the document, such as a bookmark, a named range, a database object, or a slide number, enter or locate that information above.
Use relative path for hyperlink
Remove Link
OK
Cancel

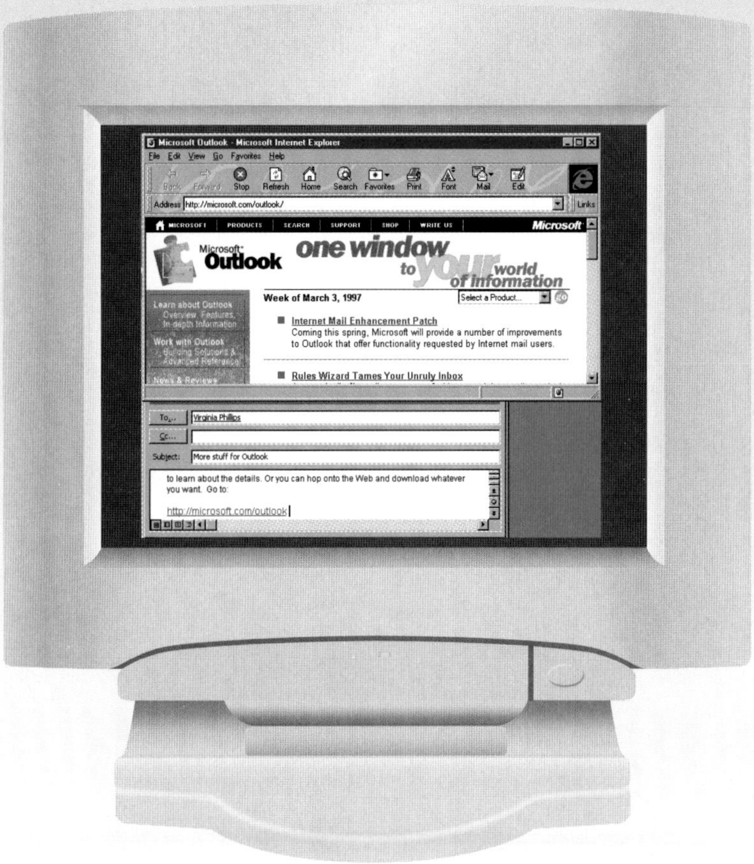
Microsoft Outlook - Microsoft Internet Explorer
Address http://microsoft.com/outlook/
Microsoft Outlook
one window to your world of information
Week of March 3, 1997
Internet Mail Enhancement Patch
Coming this spring, Microsoft will provide a number of improvements to Outlook that offer functionality requested by Internet mail users.
Rules Wizard Tames Your Unruly Inbox
Virginia Phillips
Subject: More stuff for Outlook
to learn about the details. Or you can hop onto the Web and download whatever you want. Go to:
http://microsoft.com/outlook

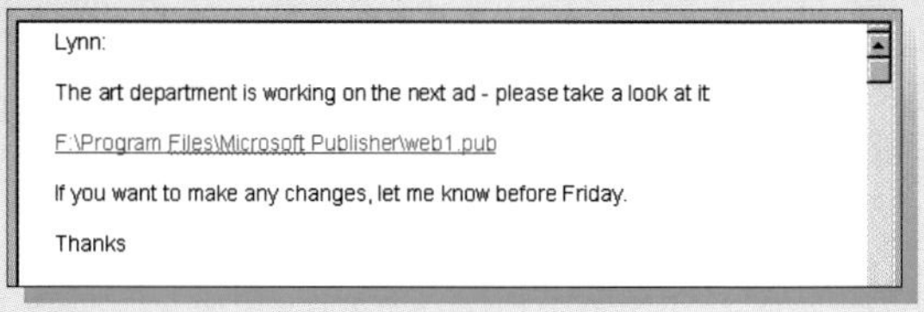
Lynn:
The art department is working on the next ad - please take a look at it
F:\Program Files\Microsoft Publisher\web1.pub
If you want to make any changes, let me know before Friday.
Thanks

3 The hyperlink appears in your message. It is blue and underlined. When the recipient receives this message and puts a mouse pointer on the hyperlink, the pointer changes to a hand.

web1.pub - Microsoft Publisher
File Edit View Insert Format Tools Arrange Table Mail Merge Help
Global Office Supplies, Inc.
We'll beat anyone's prices!
Call for our catalog.

4 Clicking anywhere on the hyperlink opens the software associated with the file and displays the file. Closing the software brings you back to the message.

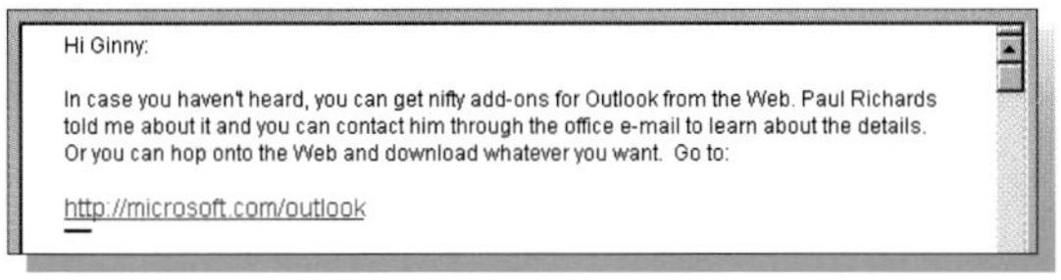
Hi Ginny:
In case you haven't heard, you can get nifty add-ons for Outlook from the Web. Paul Richards told me about it and you can contact him through the office e-mail to learn about the details. Or you can hop onto the Web and download whatever you want. Go to:
http://microsoft.com/outlook

5 In both the standard Outlook message form and the WordMail message form, inserting Web links is a simple matter of typing. If you enter the characters http://, everything you type after that, until the next space, becomes a hyperlink automatically.

How to Use WordMail Templates

Microsoft Word has become a very popular tool for creating and viewing documents. It has many formatting features that can be used to create distinctive and attractive documents.

While Outlook comes with a very capable editor that is used to create and view e-mail messages, it also has the option to use Word as its e-mail editor. This allows e-mail messages to use the powerful features of Microsoft Word. Document Templates is one of those features. Templates allow a document to start with some of the formatting work already completed. The default formatting provided by templates can range from a font color to an entire skeleton document with graphics.

On this page, you will learn how to set the default template to be used with the WordMail editor.

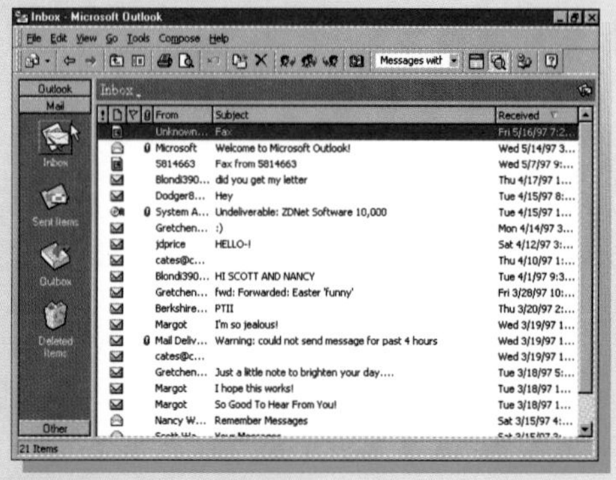

1 Go to the Mail group on the Outlook Bar and click the Inbox icon.

FYI

- **Select Choose Template from the Compose menu and click the Outlook tab for a list of available WordMail templates. Double-click the template you would like to use to create an e-mail message. This does not change your default template and will work even if you do not use Word as your e-mail editor.**
- **You can design your own templates that will cut down on the amount of busy work when creating an e-mail message. The same type of information appears in numerous messages. Placing this information into a template makes creating a message quicker and easier.**

2 Choose Options from the Tools menu.

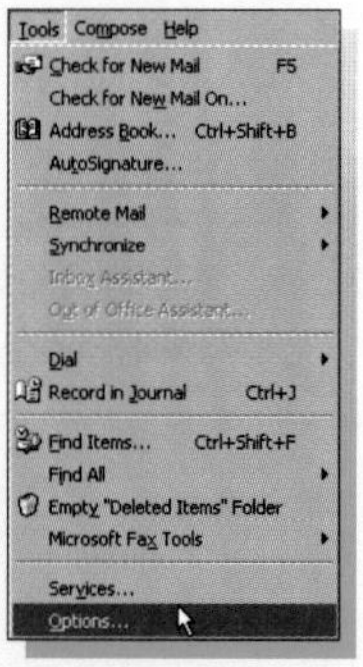

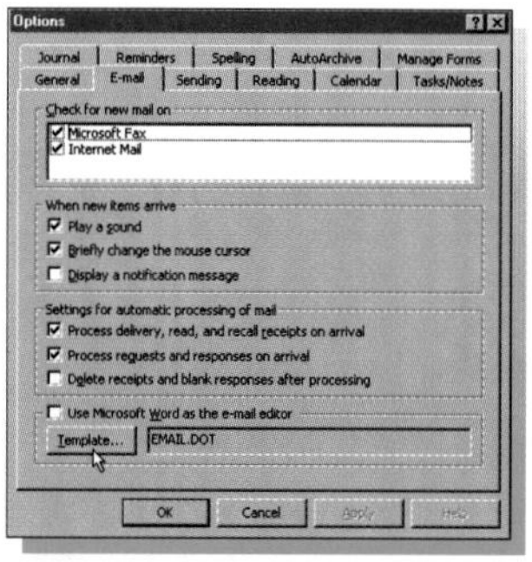

3 The Options dialog box will open to the E-mail tab. Click the Template button in the Use Microsoft Word as the e-mail Editor section. Notice that EMAIL.DOT is the current template.

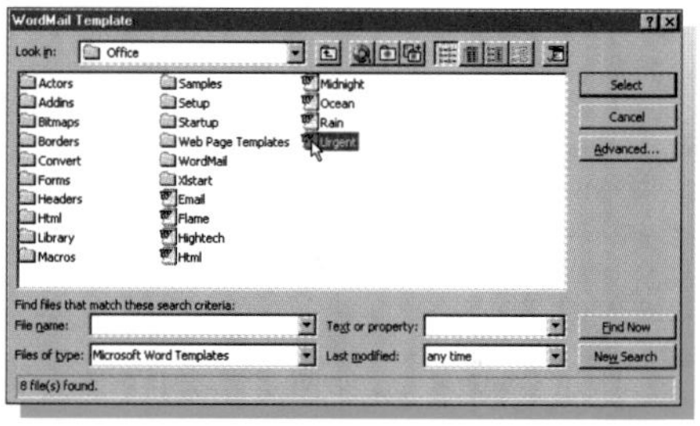

4 In the WordMail Template dialog box, choose the Urgent template to be the default and click the Select button.

5 URGENT.DOT is now listed in the Options dialog box as the template to be used when creating an e-mail message using Microsoft Word as the e-mail editor.

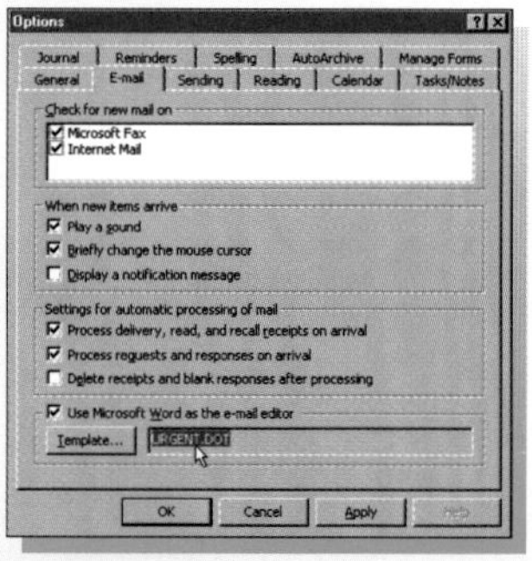

How to Attach Software Files

When you want to attach or insert something into an e-mail message, most of the time you'll find that it's an existing file that was created in a software application you use. For example, you may have created a letter or report in a word processor. Or perhaps you created a presentation in PowerPoint or Microsoft Publisher. When you need to share the information in those files with others, you can send them an e-mail message with the appropriate file attached to the message.

In order to view or open the file, the recipient has to have the software associated with the file, or software that can convert the file and then use it.

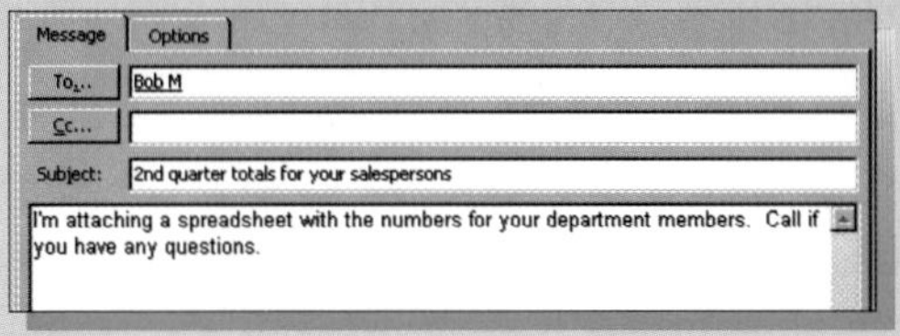

1 Start by writing an e-mail message as you usually do. That means you fill out a header, subject, and message text. It's polite to tell the recipient what file it is you're sending, and why.

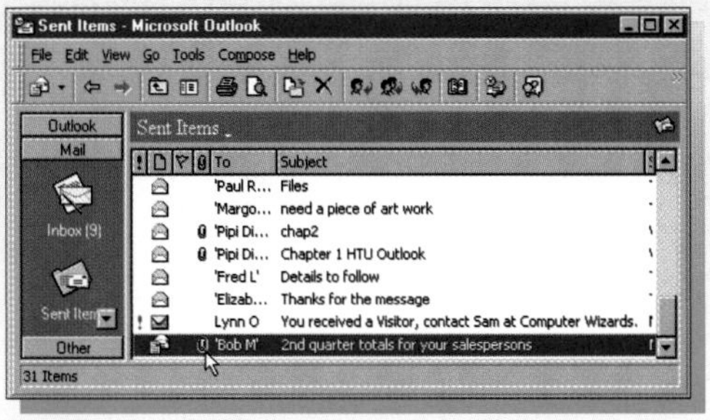

6 After the file is sent, when you see its listing in the Sent Items folder, a paper clip icon appears in the listing to remind you that you attached a file to this message.

FYI

- **If you dial out to an Internet service provider to send and receive messages, you should be aware that messages with files attached take longer to send. Remember, the icon isn't being sent, the entire file is. Most software files are quite large and take time to transfer over telephone lines.**
- **You can attach multiple files to a message by repeating steps 2 through 5 as often as you need to.**
- **If you do send multiple files, it's better to use a compression program such as WinZip to pack the files together. Not only are they sent as one file, but each file is compressed to make it much smaller. The recipient unzips the file at the other end.**

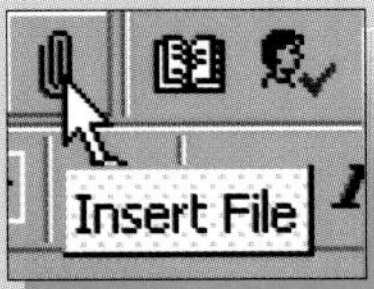

2 Click the Insert File icon on the message toolbar.

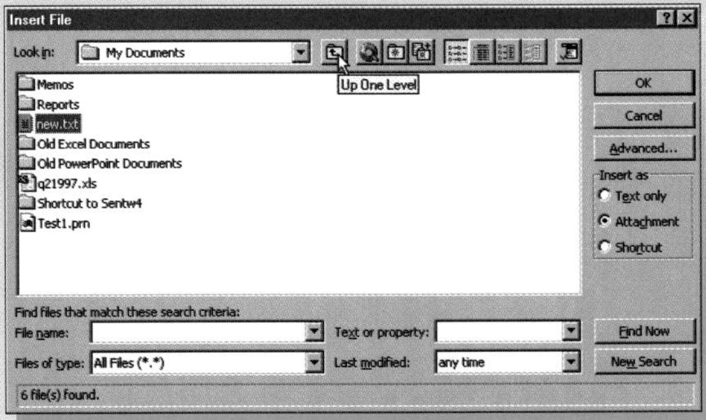

3 The Insert File dialog box opens. By default, Outlook searches the folder named My Documents. If the file you need isn't in this folder (or its subfolders), use the Up One Level icon to begin navigating around your hard drive so you can locate the file.

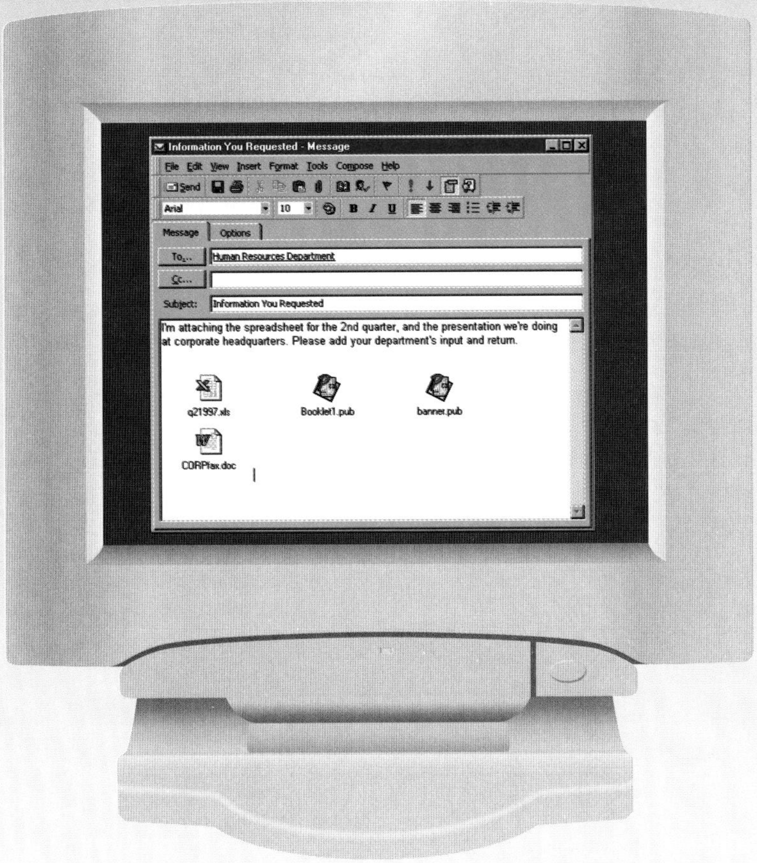

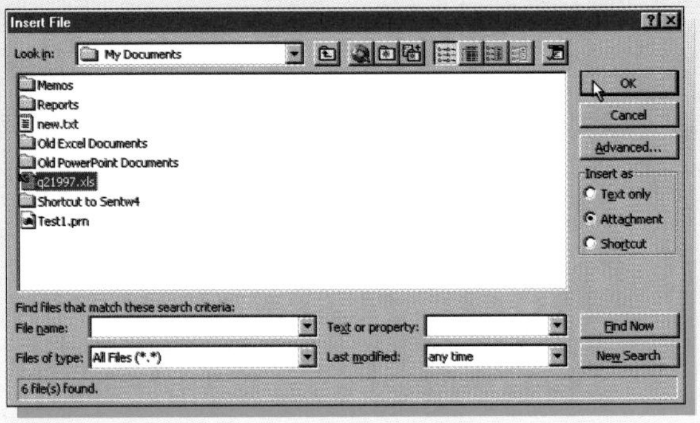

4 When you find the file you need, select it and choose OK (or double-click on it).

5 The dialog box closes and an icon representing the file is in the message. Click Send to ship the message, together with the file, to the recipient.

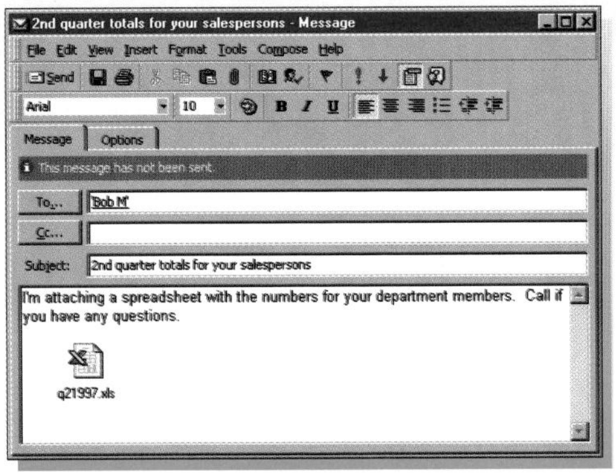

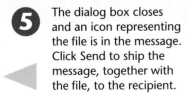

How to Insert Text Files

Sometimes you just want to take the information that's contained in a file and insert it right into your message. Perhaps there is some part of a message you received that you want to send to another recipient. Or there may be text in a word processing file that your recipient can't view as a file because he or she doesn't own the appropriate software. And it may be that you want to send a recipient a portion of the file, instead of the entire file.

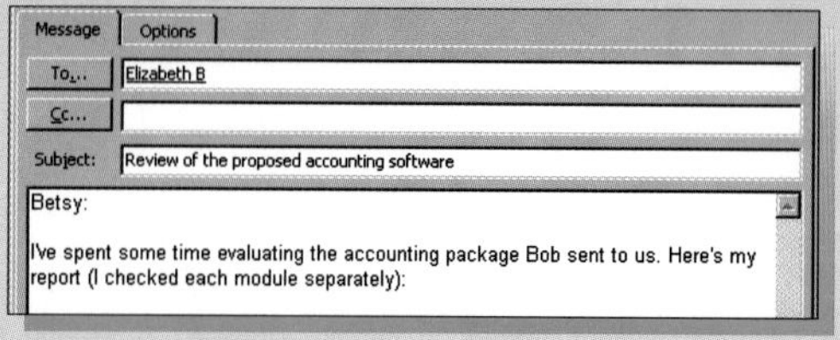

1 To begin, fill out the header and the message text for this e-mail message.

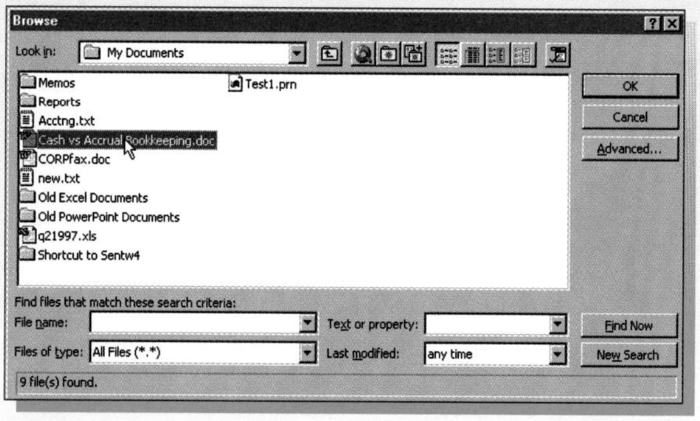

6 If you don't know the full path and name of the file (a path is the folder and subfolder names and the file name, separated by a backward slash), click Browse and find the folder and file.

(Continues on next page)

FYI

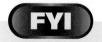

- **You cannot insert a graphics file or a sound file as text, you must attach them.**

2 If the file you want to insert is a plain text file (saved in a text editor), click the Insert File icon on the toolbar. In the Insert File dialog box, move to the folder that contains the file. Select the file and then select Text Only from the Insert As section of the dialog box. Click OK.

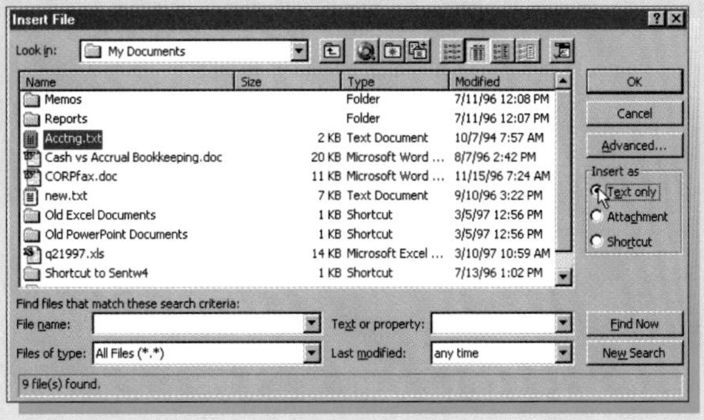

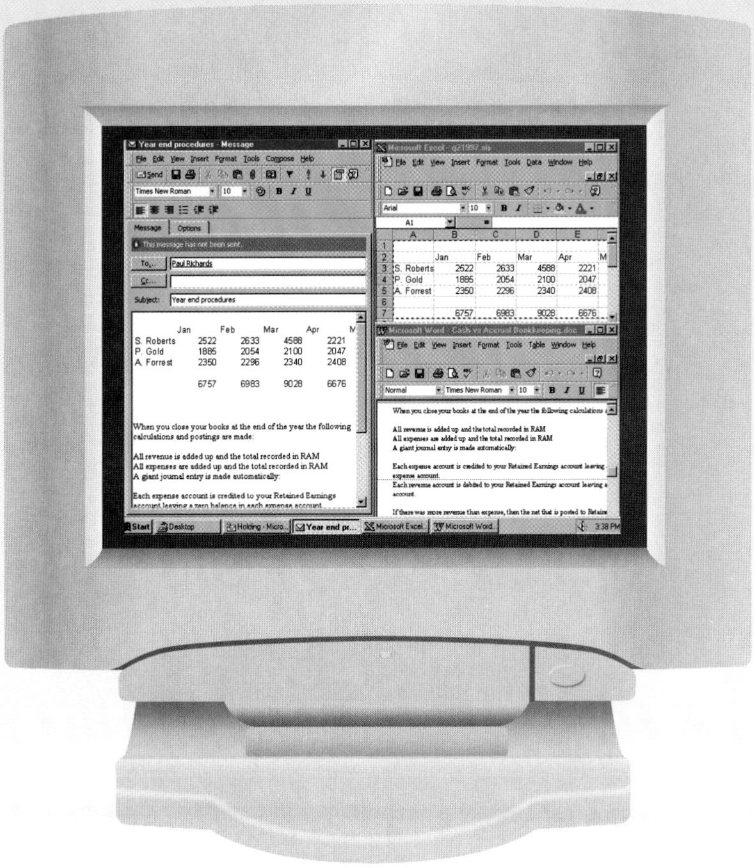

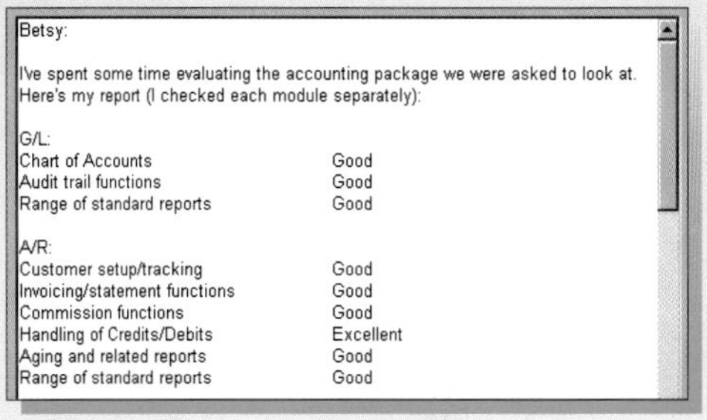

3 The text is placed in your message. You can edit it and format it as if you had typed it.

4 If you want to send the contents of a word processing file, but the recipient cannot accept an attachment because he or she does not have the software in which the file was created, you can convert the contents of the file to text and insert that text in the message. To do this, select Insert, Object from the menu bar.

5 When the Insert Object dialog box opens, Select Create from File (the default selection is Create New). The original list of object types that displayed in the dialog box goes away and is replaced with a box in which you can enter the name of the file you want to use.

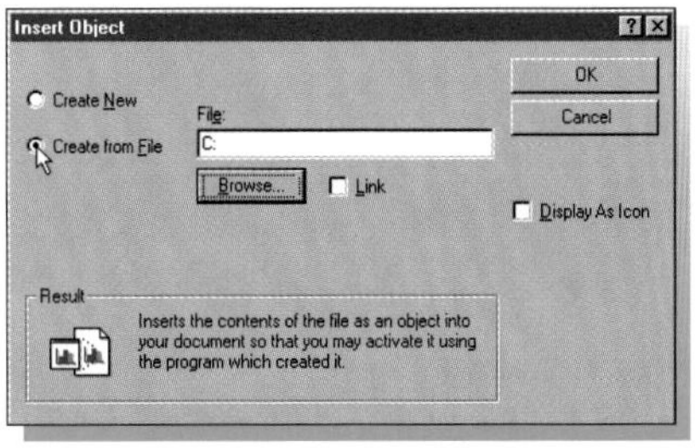

How to Insert Text Files
(Continued)

Now that you've found the word processing file you want to insert into your message (instead of attaching it to the message), you have to finish all the steps. Then we'll discuss other ways to get text into messages without typing.

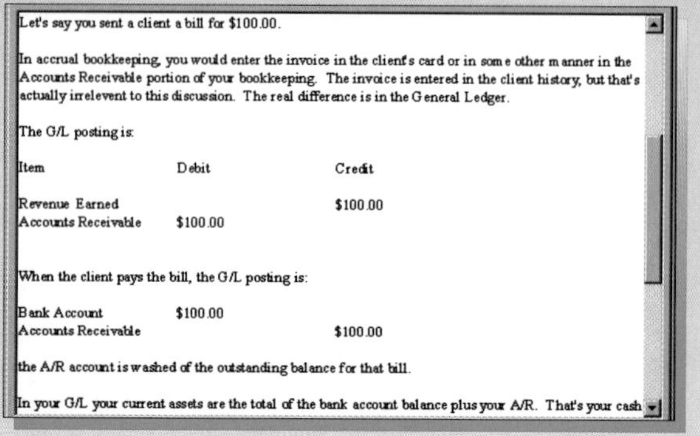
Let's say you sent a client a bill for $100.00.

In accrual bookkeeping, you would enter the invoice in the client's card or in some other manner in the Accounts Receivable portion of your bookkeeping. The invoice is entered in the client history, but that's actually irrelevent to this discussion. The real difference is in the General Ledger.

The G/L posting is:

Item	Debit	Credit
Revenue Earned		$100.00
Accounts Receivable	$100.00	

When the client pays the bill, the G/L posting is:

Bank Account	$100.00	
Accounts Receivable		$100.00

the A/R account is washed of the outstanding balance for that bill.

In your G/L your current assets are the total of the bank account balance plus your A/R. That's your cash

7 With the file selected, click OK on the Browse dialog box (or double-click the file). The file name is placed in the Insert Object dialog box. Click OK. There's a short delay (well, maybe not too short if the file is very large or your computer isn't terribly fast) and then the text from the file pops into the message. Since this is not really text, but is a representation of the contents of a word processing file, you cannot edit the text in the message.

Subject: FYI

Here's the information you wanted:

Full Name: Margo Hill
Company: Ziff-Davis Books

Business: 555-9660

12 The entire item is placed in the message text box of your new message. You can edit it as if you'd typed it in.

FYI

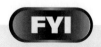

- **If the item you want to send in your message is an e-mail message from another user, it's easier to forward the original message.**

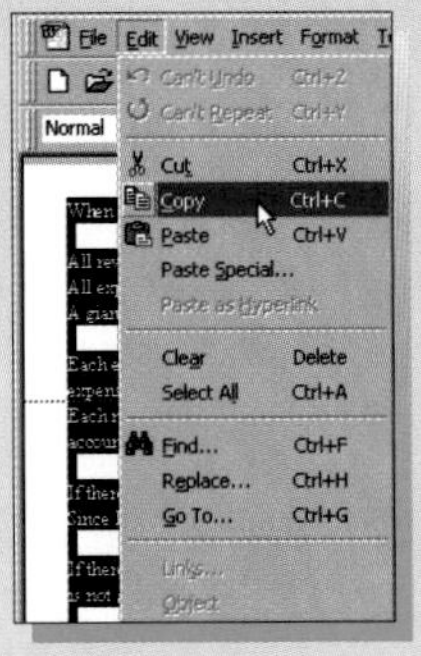

8 If you want to place only part of the contents of a file from a word processor, open the word processor software and then open the file. Select the portion of the file you want to place into your message by highlighting it. Choose Edit, Copy from the menu bar (or press Ctrl+C). Then close the software.

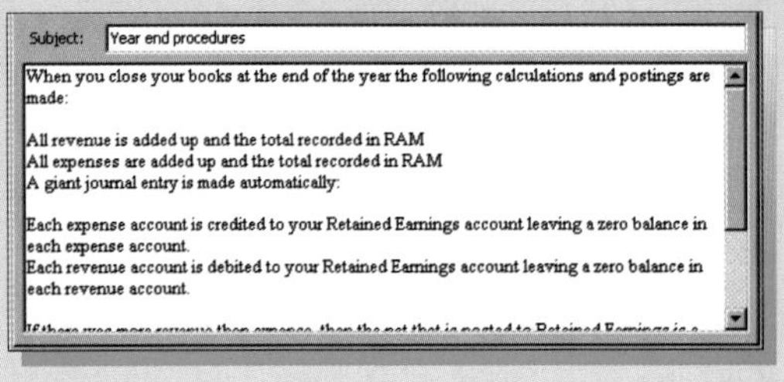

9 Move to your message window (or open a new message window if one isn't waiting) and click in the message text area where you want to insert this information. Choose Edit, Paste from the menu bar (or press Ctrl+V). The text appears in the message. Since this is text that has been copied (instead of a file that has been converted to text), you can edit this text as if you had typed it into the message.

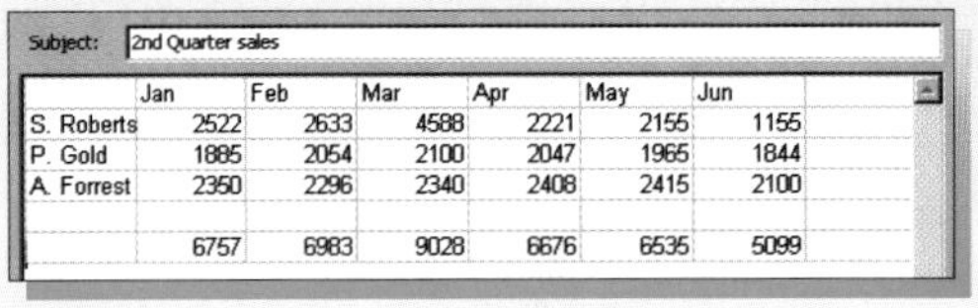

10 If the file that has the information is a spreadsheet file, perform the same steps. The cells of the spreadsheet are inserted into the message. The information cannot be edited.

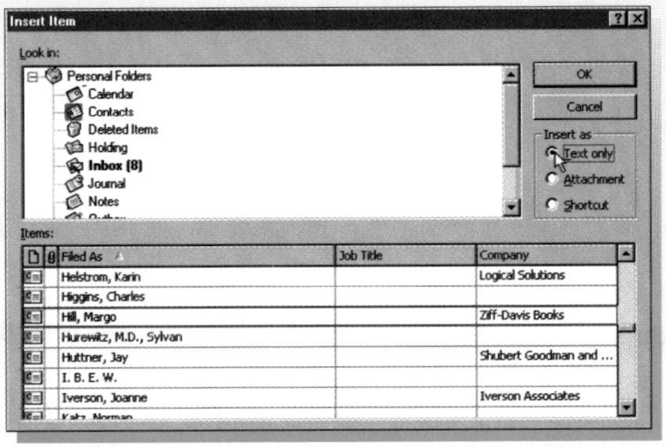

11 To insert the contents of another Outlook item, from the message text box choose Insert, Item. The Insert Item dialog box opens, with your Outlook folders displayed on the top and the contents of the selected folder displayed on the bottom. Select a folder and an item. Then select Text only from the Insert As section of the dialog box. Click OK when you have finished making these selections.

How to Drag Files into Messages

If you're comfortable with a mouse, and you're used to having more than one software window open at a time, you should think about dragging items to place them in e-mail messages. It's quick, it's easy, and it's more fun than using dialog boxes.

Once you get used to dragging items in order to turn them into messages, you'll learn to keep Outlook open all the time. Then, no matter what you're doing, when the thought occurs to you that somebody might want to see the information you're creating in a software package, it's easy to turn that thought into a deed.

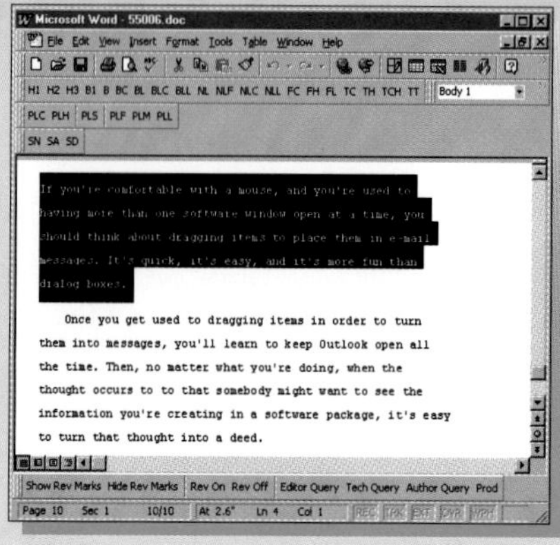
Microsoft Word - 55006.doc
File Edit View Insert Format Tools Table Window Help
Once you get used to dragging items in order to turn them into messages, you'll learn to keep Outlook open all the time. Then, no matter what you're doing, when the thought occurs to to that somebody might want to see the information you're creating in a software package, it's easy to turn that thought into a deed.
Show Rev Marks Hide Rev Marks Rev On Rev Off Editor Query Tech Query Author Query Prod

1 If you're working in word processing software, select the text you want to put into a message.

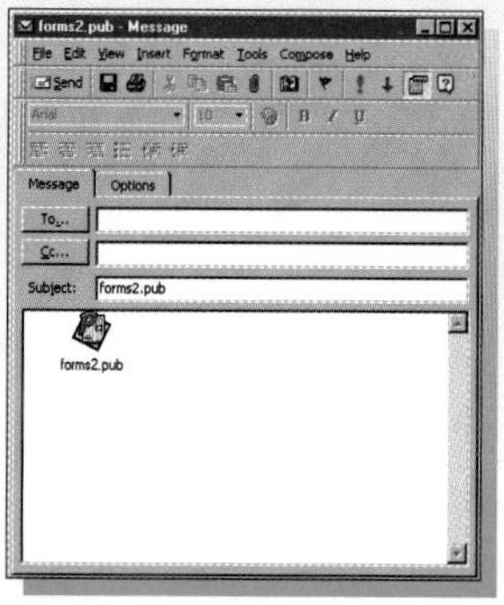
forms2.pub - Message
File Edit View Insert Format Tools Compose Help
Send
Message
Options
To...
Cc...
Subject: forms2.pub
forms2.pub

5 A new message form opens with an icon for an attached file indicating that the file is attached to this message. The Subject field contains the name of that file. You can change the text in the Subject field if you wish. Enter the name of a recipient, enter any text you want to add to the message box, and Send the file.

FYI

- **You can also drag a file onto an open message form.**
- **You can select multiple files and drag them to the Inbox icon or an open message form.**

Inbox (9)

2 Place your pointer anywhere in the selected text and drag it to the Outlook Bar, and drop it on the Inbox icon.

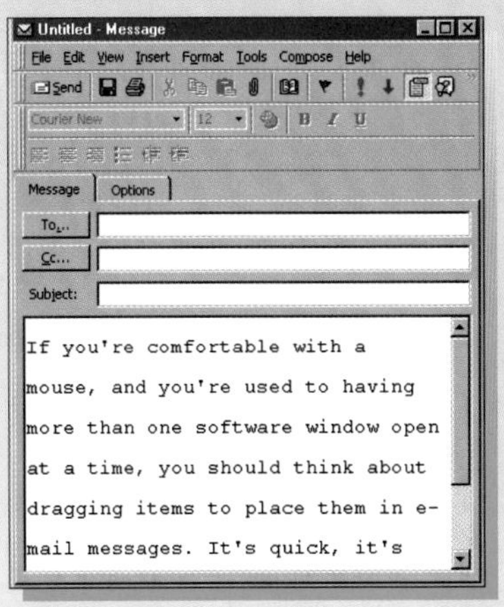
Untitled - Message
File Edit View Insert Format Tools Compose Help
Send
Message
Options
To...
Cc...
Subject:
If you're comfortable with a mouse, and you're used to having more than one software window open at a time, you should think about dragging items to place them in e-mail messages. It's quick, it's

3 Immediately a new message form opens with the selected text in the message box. If you wish, you can edit it. Then enter a recipient name into the header (along with a subject) and click Send. The information is on its way.

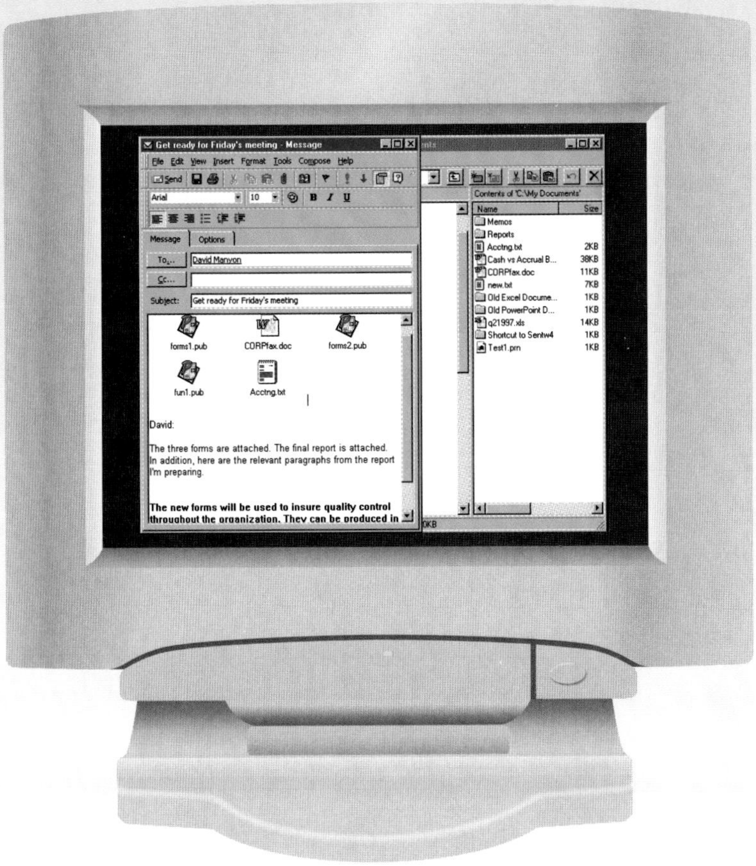
Get ready for Friday's meeting - Message
To... David Manyon
Subject: Get ready for Friday's meeting
forms1.pub
CORPfax.doc
forms2.pub
fun1.pub
Acctng.txt
David:
The three forms are attached. The final report is attached. In addition, here are the relevant paragraphs from the report I'm preparing.
The new forms will be used to insure quality control throughout the organization. They can be produced in
Contents of 'C:\My Documents'

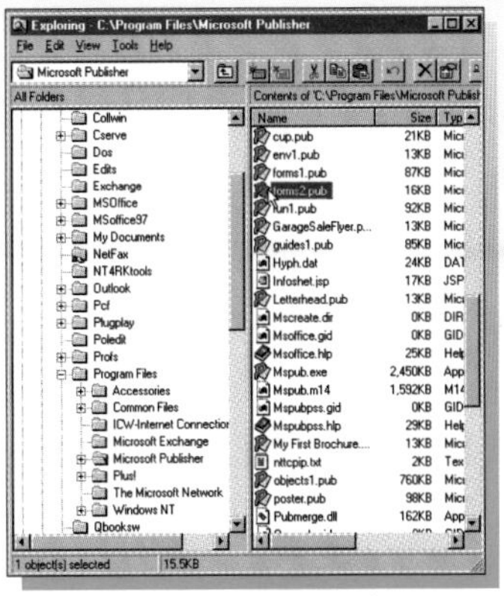
Exploring - C:\Program Files\Microsoft Publisher
All Folders
Contents of 'C:\Program Files\Microsoft Publisher'

4 With Explorer open, find a file you want to attach to a message and drag it onto the Inbox icon on the Outlook Bar.

How to Create E-Mail from a Contact or a Task

There are other ways to send e-mail messages aside from simply creating a new message. Outlook allows you to send e-mail messages from the Contacts and Tasks folders.

You might be viewing your contact from the contact cards view; or you might have just entered contact information for an individual and you now want to send them an e-mail message. Wherever you are in Contacts, you can quickly and easily send an e-mail message.

If you are viewing your assigned tasks and decide that you want to send a task status report message to your main contact (or anyone else), you can do so within Tasks.

On this page, you will learn how to create an e-mail message from a contact or a task.

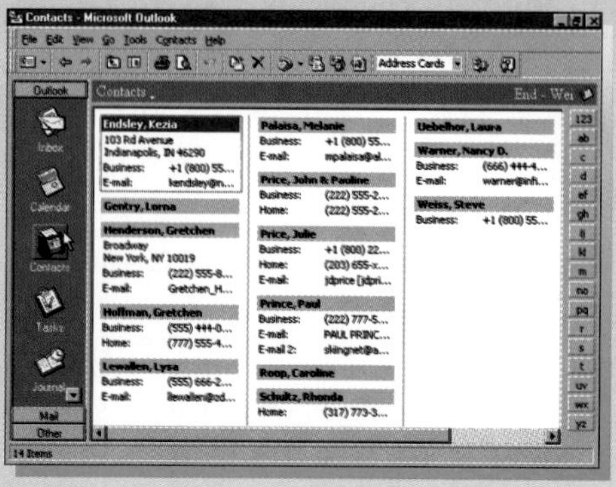

1 Go to the Outlook group on the Outlook Bar and click the Contacts icon. You will see all the contacts that you have listed in your contact database.

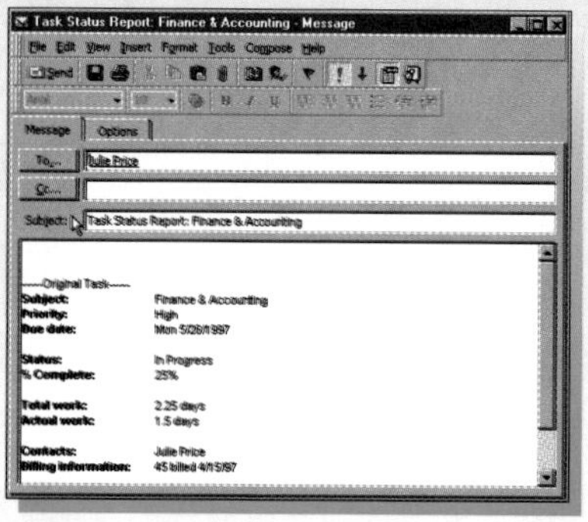

6 A Task Status Report e-mail will be created with the task's name as the Subject. You will need to specify to whom you want to send this message. Notice all the status report information that has been automatically pasted into the bottom of the message. You can delete this if you wish, by highlighting the information and pressing the Delete key.

FYI

- **When you decide to send an e-mail message to a contact, it doesn't matter what the current view is. We are in the Address Cards view.**
- **Most likely the person you are sending a task status report to is the contact listed as the Contact on the Status tab. However, you can send a status report e-mail message to anyone you want.**
- **When you are ready to send the e-mail you create from a contact or task, simply click on the Send button in the toolbar.**

2 Click on the name of the person you want to send an e-mail message to. Then, click on the New Message to Contact button on the toolbar. An Untitled e-mail message window will appear with the contact's name in the To area. (The center graphic is an example.)

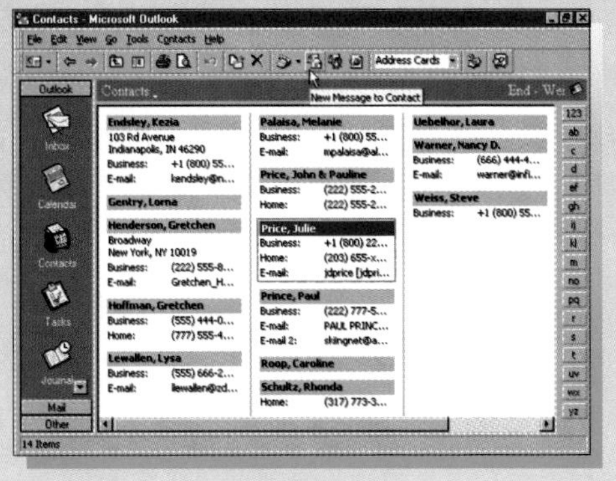

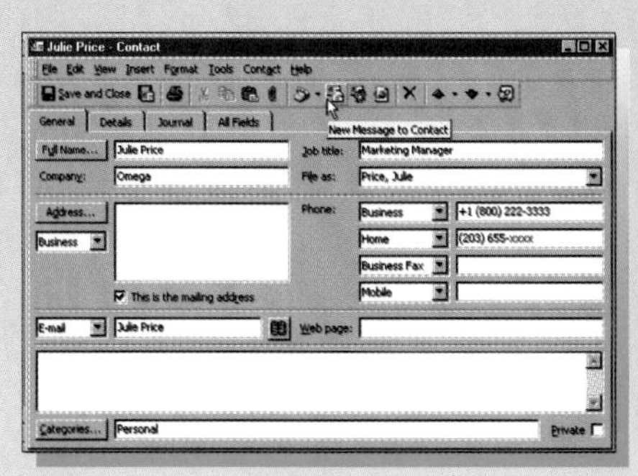

3 Another option when sending a contact a message is to double-click on the contact name. The contact information dialog box will appear. Then click on the New Message to Contact button on the toolbar. An Untitled e-mail message window will appear with the contact's name in the To area. (The center graphic is an example.)

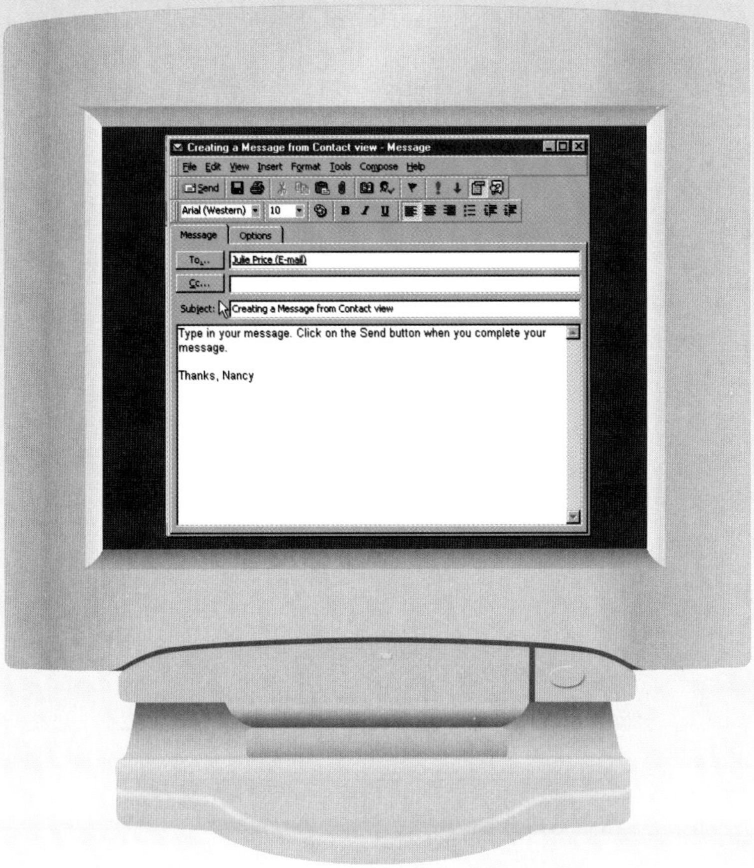

4 Click the Tasks icon on the Outlook Bar. You will see all the tasks you have created. Double-click on the task that you are interested in writing an e-mail message about.

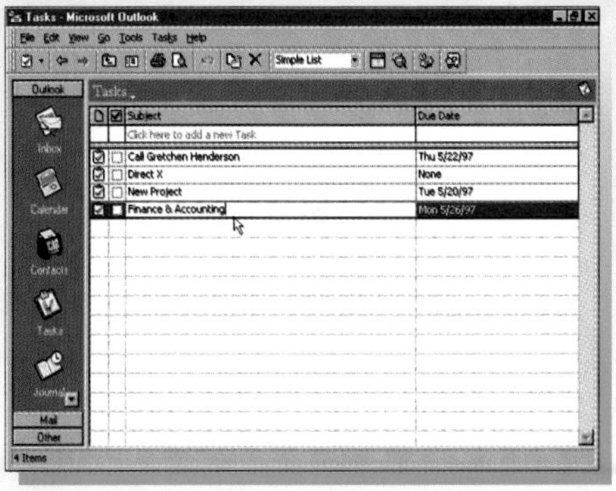

5 The Task dialog box will appear with all the information regarding that specific task. Click on the Send Status Report button on the toolbar. A Task Status Report e-mail message will appear.

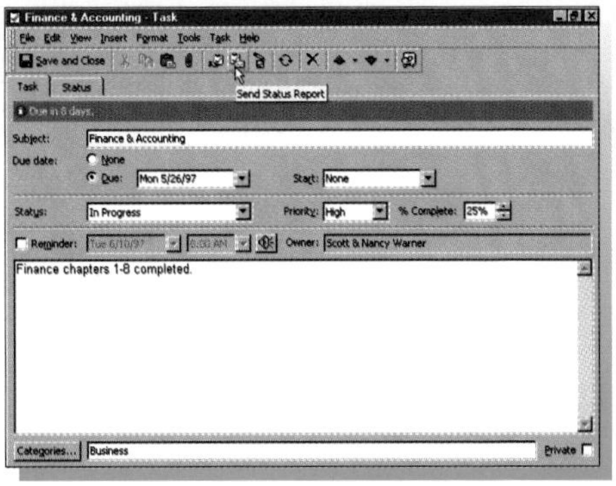

How to Get Your Mail

The most important thing about receiving e-mail is making sure everything is set up properly so that your messages are put into your mailbox—actually it's the Inbox that collects the mail (to be technical, the Inbox is a folder in your mailbox).

There are two different methods for putting messages into Inboxes. If you're on a network with an e-mail system, mail just shows up in your Inbox. In this section we'll discuss Microsoft Exchange Server as the e-mail system, but if your company uses another e-mail program, the procedures are similar. You don't have to do anything to make that happen. The second method is the one in which you have to go fetch your mail from a holding place. The good part is that you don't have to walk or drive to the nearest post office, your modem does the work for you. The holding place is an Internet service provider (ISP), to whom you pay money every month for this "hold my mail until I fetch it" service.

FYI

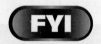

- **Actually, if you use an Internet service provider, you have a mailbox on the ISP computer. Most ISP's let you change your options so that mail is saved in the ISP mailbox, making that mailbox an Inbox. It's not a good idea, because you don't have access to your mail at all times (and there are certain times of the day when it is difficult to get through to your ISP because half the world is trying at the same time).**
- **To set up the Dial Up Networking connection to an ISP, contact the ISP for instructions.**
- **If you use an ISP system that requires a post-dial window in which you enter your name, password, and other information, you can write a script that automates all of those entries. Check the documentation that came with your Windows operating system to learn how to do this.**

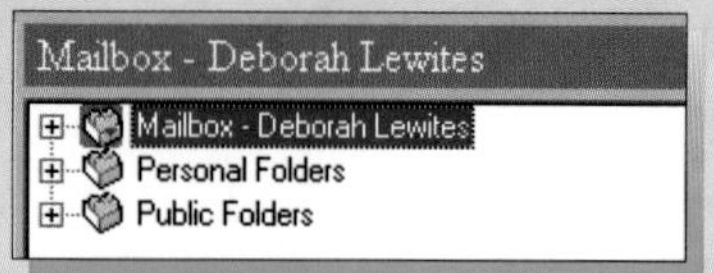

1 If you're on a network with a mail service, your mailbox is probably on the network server. When you look at your Inbox, however, you can't tell that you're looking at a folder that's residing on the server instead of residing on your own computer. In this illustration, the mailbox and the set of public folders both reside on the computer that acts as the server for Microsoft Exchange Server. The personal folders are stored on the local computer. The mailbox receives mail automatically—Exchange Server collects the mail and deposits it in the Inbox folder of the server-based mailbox.

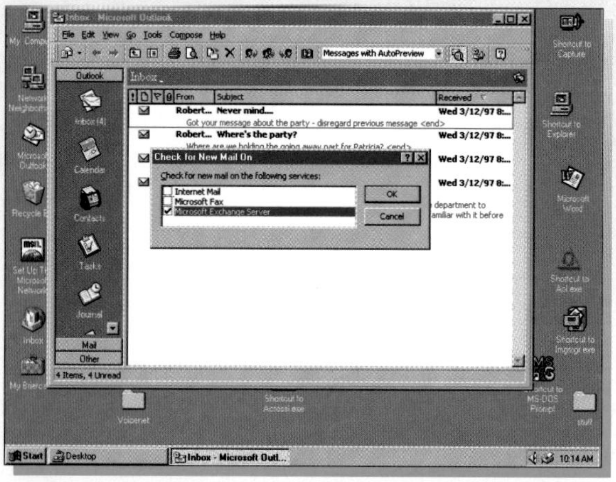

6 If you dial in to a network server to get mail from other employees, and use an ISP for Internet mail (or if you have more than one ISP for some reason), you have to tell Outlook which mailbox service you want to check. Choose Tools, Check for New Mail On, and then select the service you want to contact.

2 The server-based mailbox has an Inbox, an Outbox, and a Sent Items folder (all provided by Microsoft Exchange Server and displayed in the Outlook software window). Mail shows up automatically and constantly (there isn't a mail carrier making rounds once a day—when mail arrives on the server it's placed in the Inbox within seconds). If Outlook is open, a chime sounds every time a piece of mail is dropped into the Inbox. The Personal Folders listed below the mailbox have an Inbox, an Outbox, and a Sent Items folder (all provided by Outlook). The Inbox that is part of the Personal Folders does not receive mail and is always empty.

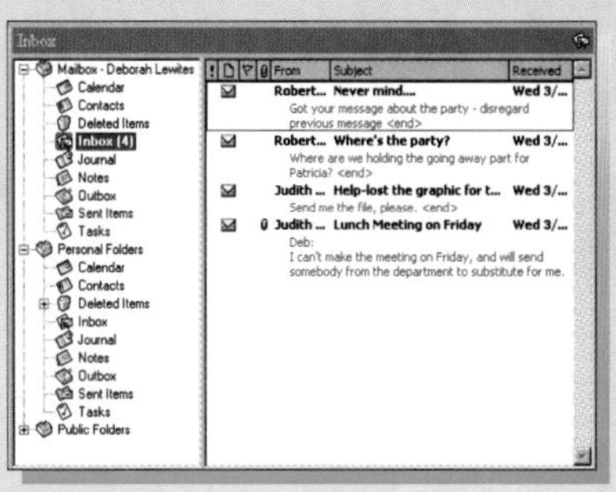

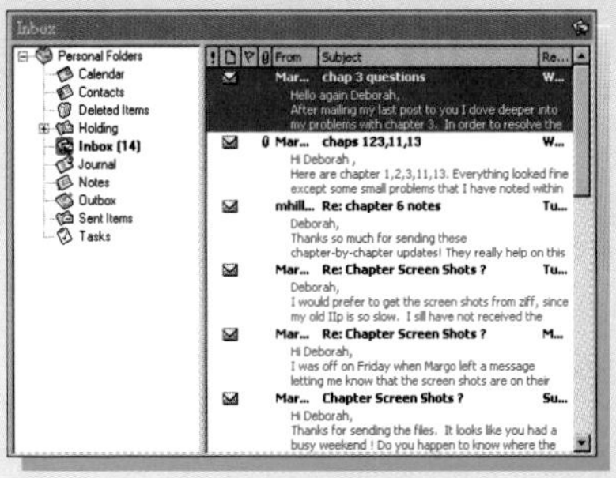

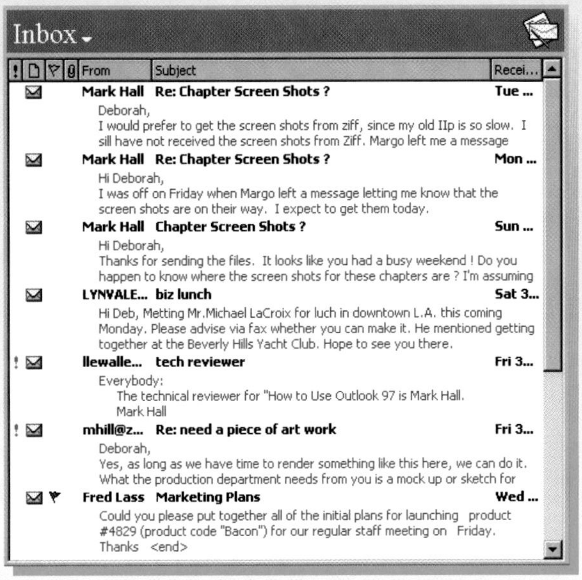

3 If you are not connected to a server-based e-mail system, only the Personal Folders display in Outlook. There is no server-based mailbox, and there are no public folders. The Inbox in the personal folders container is the only Inbox available, so it holds your received mail. Most of the time you won't be viewing the Inbox with the folders displaying—we did this to make it clear what the differences are between a network system and a stand-alone system. If you want to see the folders in your Outlook system, click the Folder List icon on the toolbar or choose View, Folder List from the menu bar. This option is a toggle switch, each time you choose Folder List you reverse the option.

4 If you don't have a network mailbox with instant, automatic delivery, you have to fetch your own mail. This requires a modem and a preconfigured Dial Up Networking connection to an Internet service provider (ISP). That service provider could be a Microsoft Exchange Server network that you dial into because you work in a different building (and the cable won't stretch that far), but most of the time it's an independent ISP you pay monthly. To connect to the ISP, choose Tools, Check for New Mail (or press F5).

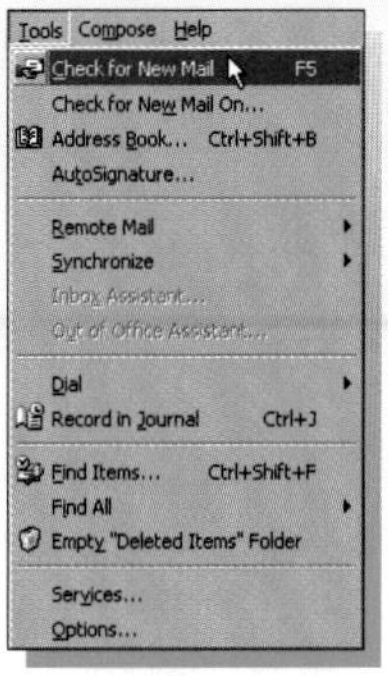

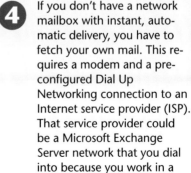

5 A number of things happen automatically. The Dial Up Networking connection dials the number for your ISP. When it connects, you may have to enter a name, password, and a few other items (depending upon the protocols needed for your ISP). Then Outlook checks the Outbox to see if there is mail waiting to be sent. If there is, it's delivered to the ISP mail server. Then Outlook checks your mailbox on the ISP mail server to see if there is any new mail for you. If there is, it's transferred to your Inbox.

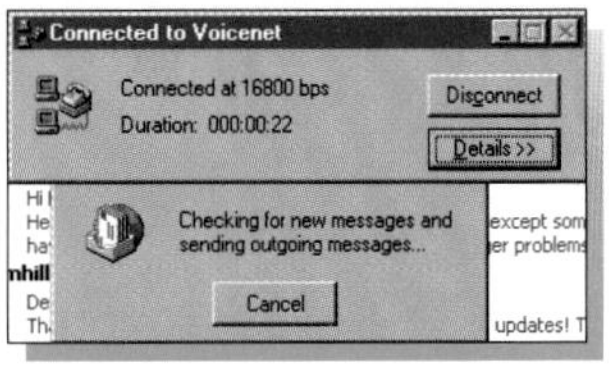

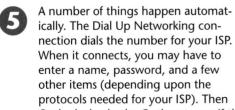

How to Open Messages

Okay, the mail carrier has been here or you've dialed out to get your mail from a remote mailbox. Now it's time to open and read the messages. There's nothing difficult about opening and reading messages, you could probably figure it out without my help. But I'm assuming you get tons of messages, that all those interoffice memos, all those questions from other employees, all those directives and assignments from the bosses, whew... they pile up every day.

You have other things to do, deadlines to meet, places to go, people to see, you have a life—so sometimes there just isn't time to read and take care of all the e-mail. This section helps you to figure out what to read right away, and what to do about messages that require follow-up.

FYI

- In this section, the Inbox was shown both with AutoPreview and without it (an easier way to see a large number of messages).
- You can make a message that's been read look as if it wasn't read (put its listing back to bold and take advantage of the AutoPreview feature) by right-clicking its listing and choosing Mark as Unread.

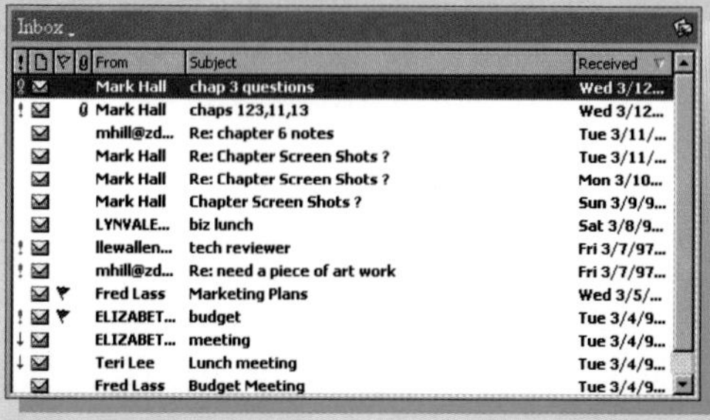

1 Before you start opening and reading messages, you should decide which messages to read first. There are a couple of clues in the Inbox listing that help you make this decision. The text in the Subject column is always a big clue (or should be, but some people don't know how to write good subject lines). In addition, senders can mark messages to draw attention to special features about them. A red exclamation point means important; a blue down arrow means not important, a red flag means the message requires some follow-up action by you, and a paper clip indicates there's a file attached to the message.

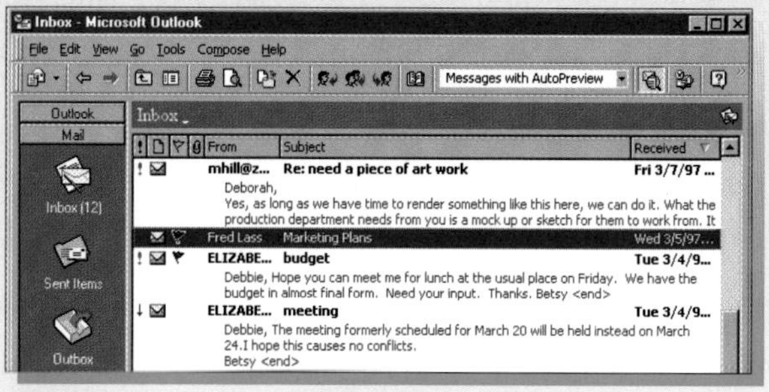

7 To close the file, click the close button on the message window, or press Alt+F4, or choose File, Close from the menu bar. The message closes and its listing changes so that it is no longer bold. If your Inbox listing is set up for AutoPreview (some of the message text displays), no text displays for this message because AutoPreview only acts on unread messages.

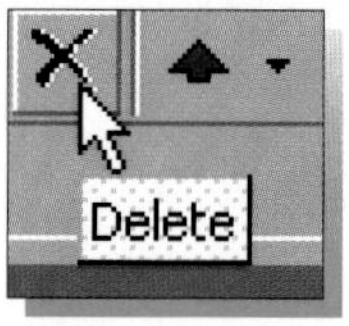

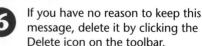

6 If you have no reason to keep this message, delete it by clicking the Delete icon on the toolbar.

2 After you decide which messages require your immediate attention, open them and read them. To open a message, double-click its listing. The message opens and there's lots of stuff on the top part of the message (we'll discuss that in this section), but the important part is the text in the message box. Read it, if you're following along with messages in your own Inbox, I'll wait...okay, ready to move on?

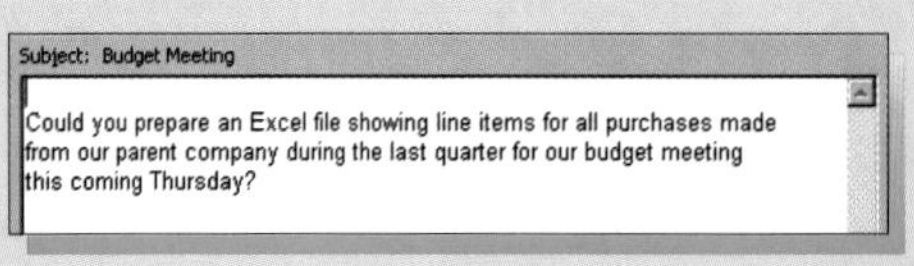

3 If this message requires some follow-up action by you (besides replying to the message, which you learn about later in Part 2), you can give yourself a reminder by flagging it so a red flag is next to its listing when you look at the Inbox. Click the Flag icon on the toolbar of the message window to display the Flag Message dialog box. Click the arrow to the right of the Flag box and choose a Flag message from the drop-down list, or enter your own reminder message. If appropriate, click the arrow to the right of the By text box and click on a date on the calendar that shows up to set a deadline for yourself. Click OK to close the dialog box.

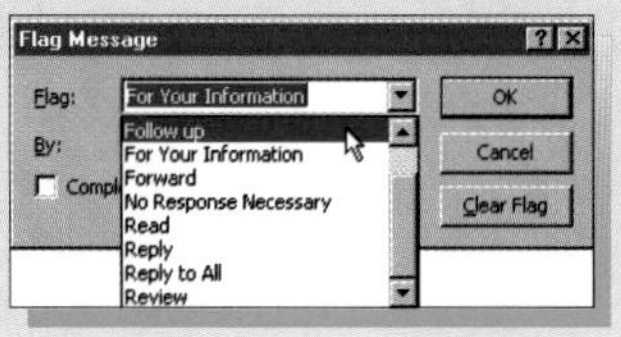

4 If you want to print the message, click the Print icon on the toolbar. The message prints immediately. If you have to set up a printer, or pick a printer, or need the printer dialog box for any reason, press Ctrl+P (or choose File, Print from the menu bar).

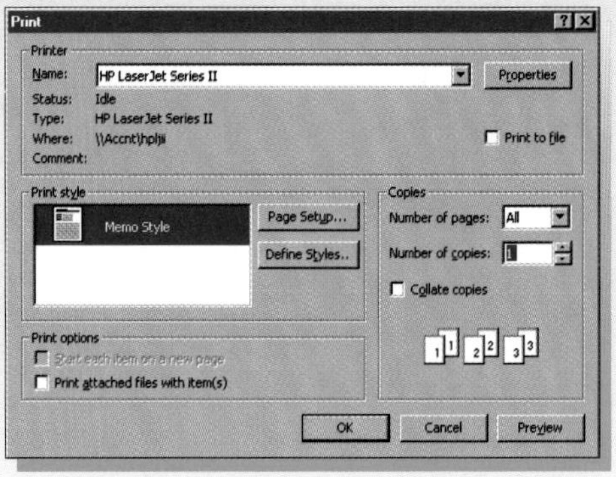

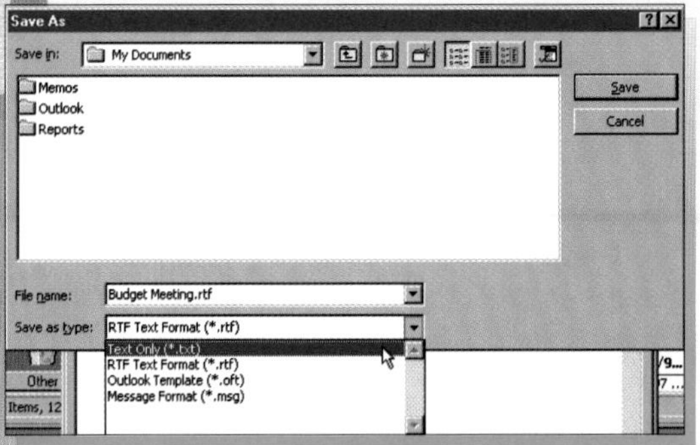

5 If you want to save the message as a file, choose File, Save As from the menu bar. The Subject of the message becomes the file name, but you can change that if you wish. By default, Outlook saves the message as a Rich Text Format file (some word processors, including Microsoft Word, can handle RTF files), but you can click the arrow to the right of the Save As type box and choose another file type. You can also change the folder in which you save the message.

How to Handle Attachments

If somebody wants to send you all the important information in a report, it's easier to send the report than it is to type in all the text of the report. For that and many other reasons, people attach documents to e-mail messages. These attachments are handled separately from the message, since you can't see the contents when you open the message.

You know before you open a message that it contains an attachment because a paper clip icon appears in the attachment column to the left of the message listing in your Inbox. You have several options for handling attachments and this section covers them.

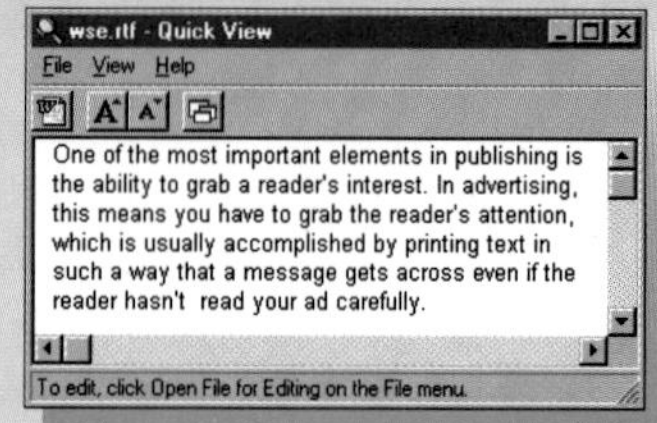

1 Some attachments can be viewed quickly without opening them or otherwise manipulating them by using the Windows Quick View program. This is a software application that is installed with your Windows operating system, and it has the ability to display the contents of certain kinds of files (the specific file types are dependent upon the way Quick View was installed). Right-click the attachment's icon and choose Quick View to open the Quick View window. The contents display but you won't see any formatting or other special effects. If there is no Quick View viewer for the file type, an error message will inform you of that fact.

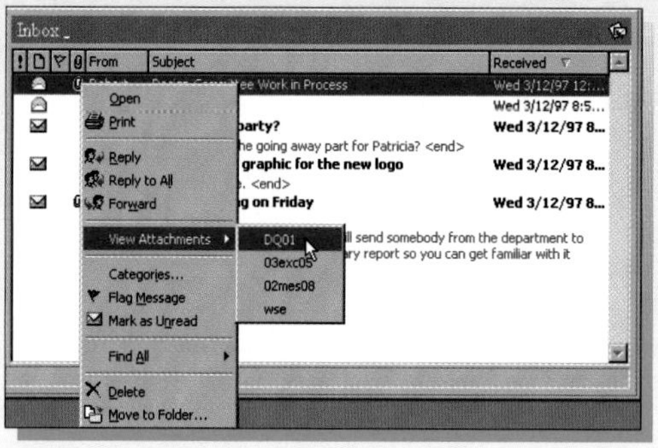

6 For a really quick look, using Quick View, you don't even have to open the message. Right-click the listing in the Inbox and choose View Attachments. If there are multiple attachments, they're listed in a submenu and you can click the one you want to view.

FYI

- **If you open an attachment and make changes and save the file, when you close the associated software and return to the message the attachment icon represents the new, changed file.**
- **If you select an attachment icon and click the Print icon on the message toolbar, the message prints, not the attachment. You must use the right-click menu to print the attachment without opening it.**
- **If you don't have the appropriate software to open an attachment, copy it to a floppy disk. Then take the disk to a computer that does have the right software.**

2 You can open the attached file by double-clicking it. Open means that the software application that can handle this file (usually the same application that created it) opens, and the attached file is then opened in the software window. If you don't have the associated software, the file won't open. People should check with you before attaching files to messages they send you, just to make sure you have the software needed to open the files they want to send. Once the software is open and the attachment is loaded in the software window, you can use all the tools the software offers to manipulate the file. That means, for example, you can edit it, save it, print it, and so on. When you exit the software, you return to the message.

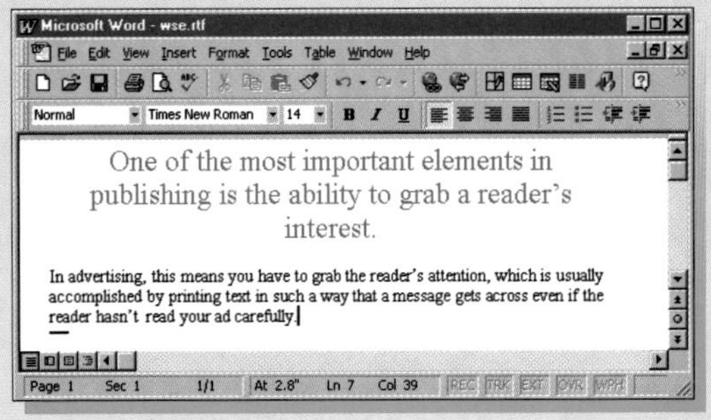

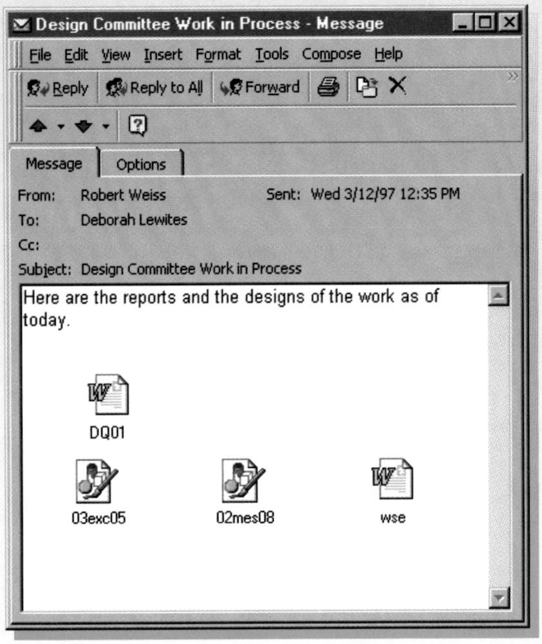

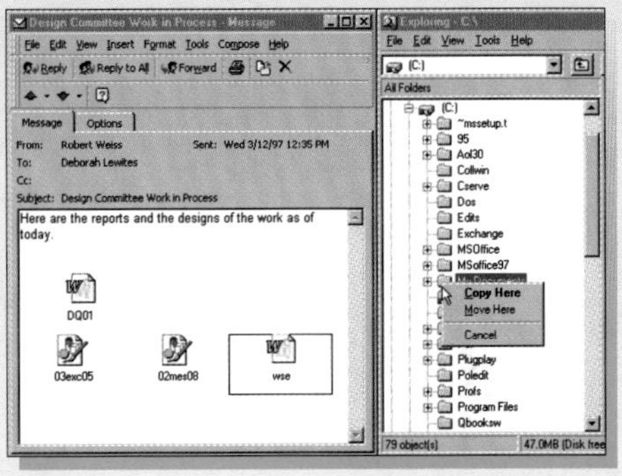

3 You can move or copy the attachment to a folder for later attention. Open Explorer or My Computer, then drag the attachment to the appropriate folder. If you right-drag, a menu is offered when you release the mouse button so you can choose to move or copy the file. If you left-drag, the attachment is copied.

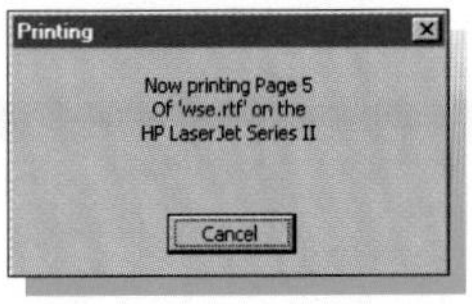

4 You can print the document by right-clicking it and choosing Print. The associated software opens, loads the file in its software window, prints the file, and then closes.

5 You can choose Cut or Copy from the right-click menu, then paste the attachment into a folder or even into a message you're sending to someone else.

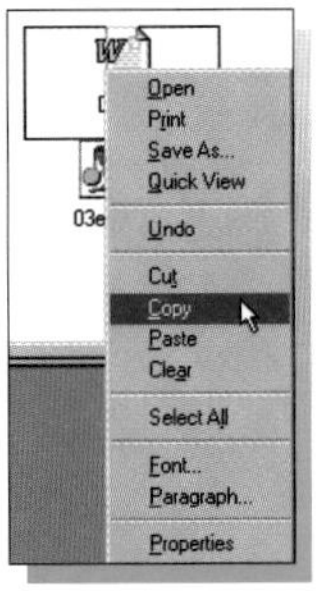

How to Reply To and Forward Messages

Replying to a message means sending a message back to the person who sent you e-mail. Forwarding a message is sending that message on to a different person, because you believe there's some reason that third party has an interest in the message contents.

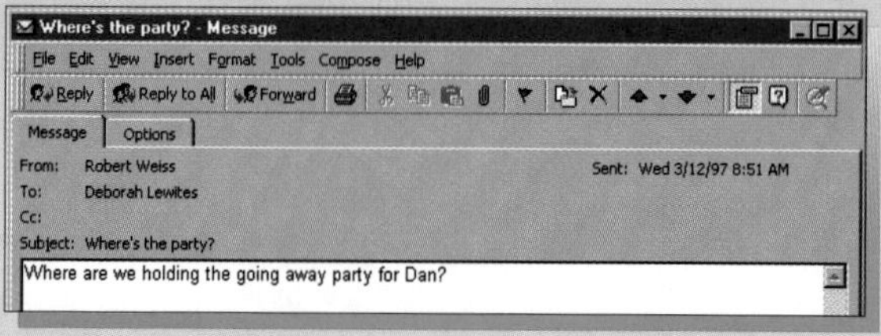

1 When you open a message, the message window contains all the tools you need to make responding to the sender quick and easy. To reply to the sender, click the Reply button on the toolbar.

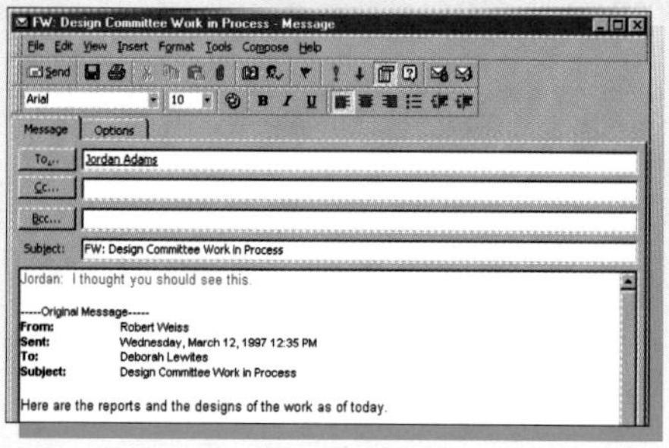

6 Enter the name of the recipient and add any comments of your own above the message text (usually something like "I thought this would be of interest to you"). If there are attachments on the original message, they are forwarded also. If you don't want to forward any or all of the attachments, delete them by selecting them and pressing Del. Click Send to forward the message, then close the original message.

FYI

- **If you don't want to include the original header or message (or either) in your reply, select the text and delete it.**
- **When you are replying (either to the recipient or to all recipients), you can add any additional recipients you wish. The new recipients can be direct recipients (in the To field) or copied recipients (in either the Cc or Bcc field).**
- **If you choose to reply to all recipients, you can delete any of the multiple recipients you wish to.**

2 A message form opens with a lot of information filled in automatically. The recipient is there, and of course, it's the sender (that's why we call it a reply). The subject is the same as the original subject, except it has RE: before the subject text. The original message header and message text are in the message area, and your insertion point is waiting just above that. All you have to do is enter your response. You can delete all or some of the original message, in fact it's probably a good idea to do that.

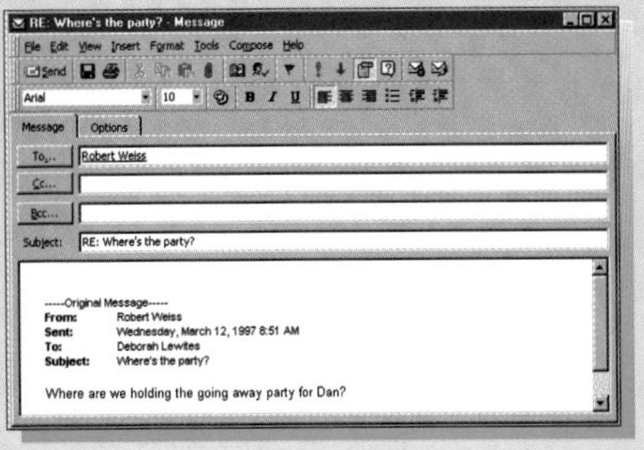
RE: Where's the party? - Message
To...
Robert Weiss
Subject:
RE: Where's the party?
-----Original Message-----
From: Robert Weiss
Sent: Wednesday, March 12, 1997 8:51 AM
To: Deborah Lewites
Subject: Where's the party?
Where are we holding the going away party for Dan?

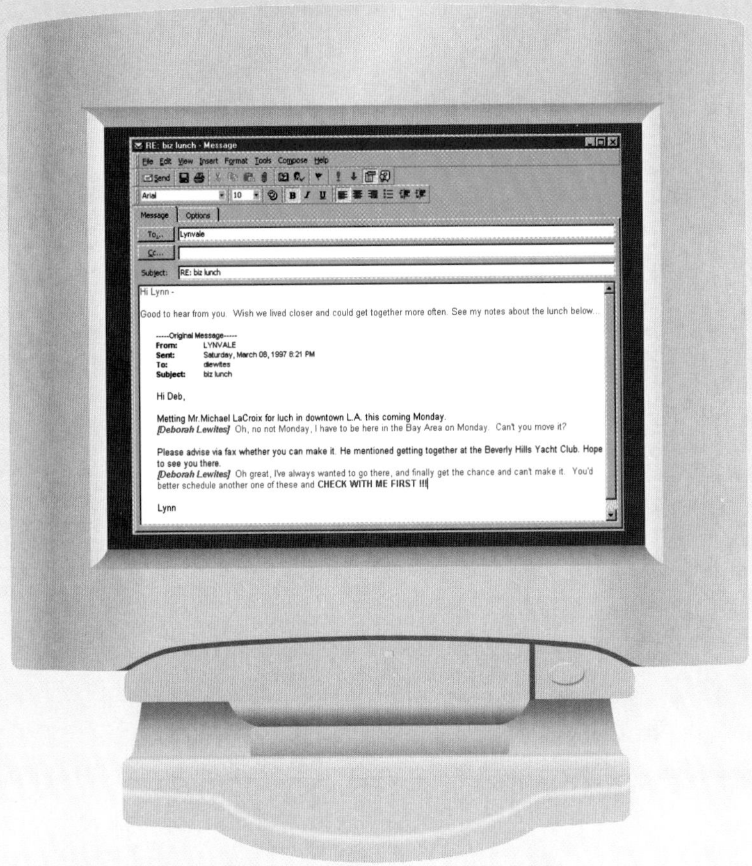
RE: biz lunch - Message
To...
Lynvale
Subject:
RE: biz lunch
Hi Lynn -
Good to hear from you. Wish we lived closer and could get together more often. See my notes about the lunch below.
-----Original Message-----
From: LYNVALE
Sent: Saturday, March 08, 1997 8:21 PM
To: dlewites
Subject: biz lunch
Hi Deb,
Metting Mr.Michael LaCroix for luch in downtown L.A. this coming Monday.
[Deborah Lewites] Oh, no not Monday, I have to be here in the Bay Area on Monday. Can't you move it?
Please advise via fax whether you can make it. He mentioned getting together at the Beverly Hills Yacht Club. Hope to see you there.
[Deborah Lewites] Oh great, I've always wanted to go there, and finally get the chance and can't make it. You'd better schedule another one of these and CHECK WITH ME FIRST !!!
Lynn

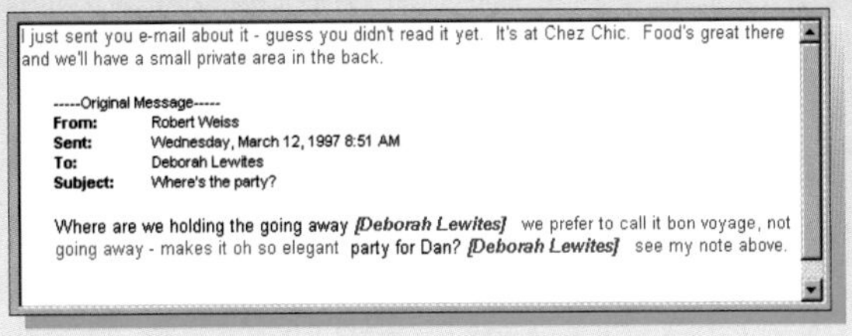
I just sent you e-mail about it - guess you didn't read it yet. It's at Chez Chic. Food's great there and we'll have a small private area in the back.
-----Original Message-----
From: Robert Weiss
Sent: Wednesday, March 12, 1997 8:51 AM
To: Deborah Lewites
Subject: Where's the party?
Where are we holding the going away [Deborah Lewites] we prefer to call it bon voyage, not going away - makes it oh so elegant party for Dan? [Deborah Lewites] see my note above.

3 Notice that when you enter your response, the characters on the screen are blue (if you are using Outlook in Exchange Server, and the recipient is on your Exchange Server system, the recipient will see your entry in blue). You can also enter comments directly in the original message. To draw attention to the fact that you're entering text inside an existing message, each time you enter text Outlook inserts your name. It's a good idea to delete the parts of the original message you're not writing responses to, otherwise this message could be extremely long. Click Send when you are finished writing your reply. Then close the original message.

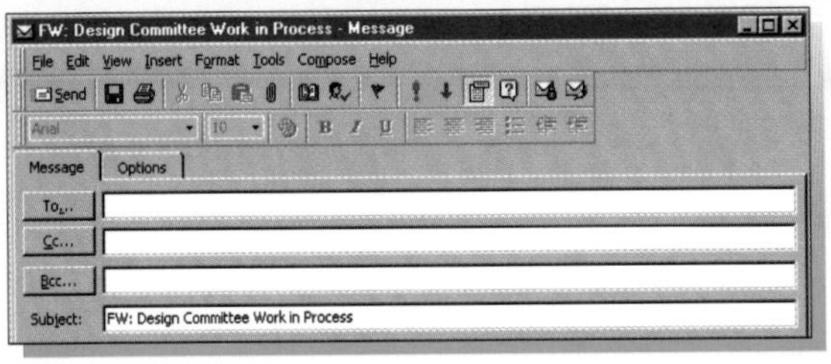
FW: Design Committee Work in Process - Message
File Edit View Insert Format Tools Compose Help
Send
Message
Options
To...
Cc...
Bcc...
Subject:
FW: Design Committee Work in Process

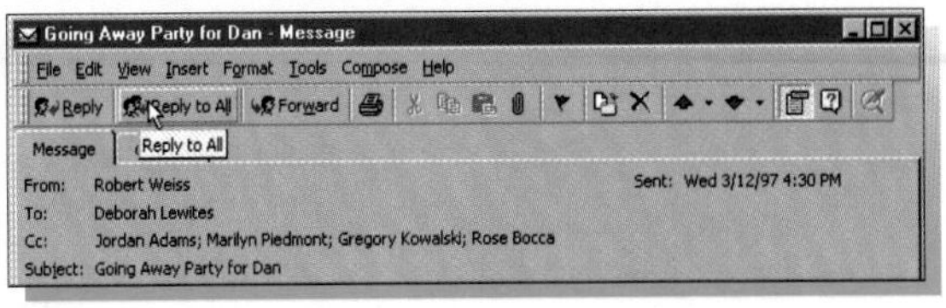
Going Away Party for Dan - Message
File Edit View Insert Format Tools Compose Help
Reply
Reply to All
Forward
Message
Reply to All
From: Robert Weiss
Sent: Wed 3/12/97 4:30 PM
To: Deborah Lewites
Cc: Jordan Adams; Marilyn Piedmont; Gregory Kowalski; Rose Bocca
Subject: Going Away Party for Dan

4 If you receive a message that displays a number of additional recipients in the Cc box, you can choose to reply to every recipient. Click Reply to All and then proceed as described in the previous steps.

5 Sometimes you'll receive a message you think would be of interest to another person. You don't have to write that person a note detailing the information in the message you received, you can just forward the message. To do so, click Forward on the toolbar. A new message form opens with the Subject filled in, preceded by FW: to indicate that this is a forwarded message.

How to Change the Reply Options

The original message is inserted in a reply because Outlook is configured to behave that way. You can, however, change the way replies are handled. After you've been using Outlook for a while you'll figure out which options for replying and forwarding you don't like (and have to change every time you go through the procedure). This is a definite signal that it's time to change the default options.

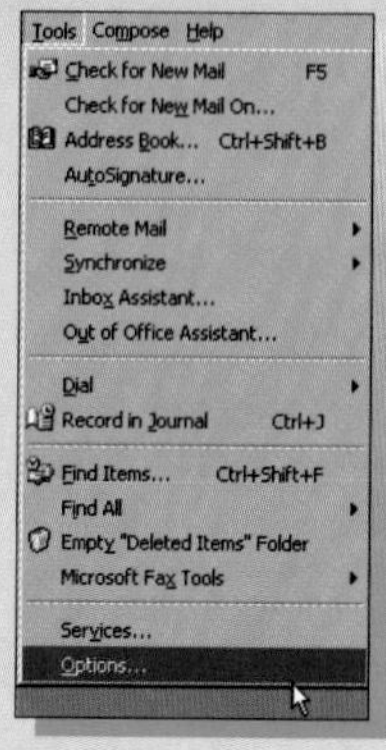

1 To change the options for replying to and forwarding e-mail, choose Tools, Options from the Outlook menu bar.

7 Click the checkbox marked Close Original Message on Reply or Forward to save yourself that step whenever you reply to or forward a received message. When you are finished selecting the options you want, click OK to close the dialog box.

6 In the bottom section of the dialog box you can change the text that marks your comments within the original text. By default, it is your name that is entered, but you can change that to any text you wish (keep it very brief). You can also click the checkbox to remove the checkmark and deselect the option of having your comments marked at all.

FYI

- **The indented original text is handy because it offsets your additional comments from the original message. Remember that unless you and your recipients are working on an Exchange Server mail system, your text will not show in color. In fact, if you use bold for your text, it may not translate to other e-mail software applications.**

2 When the Options dialog box opens, click the Reading tab to see the options.

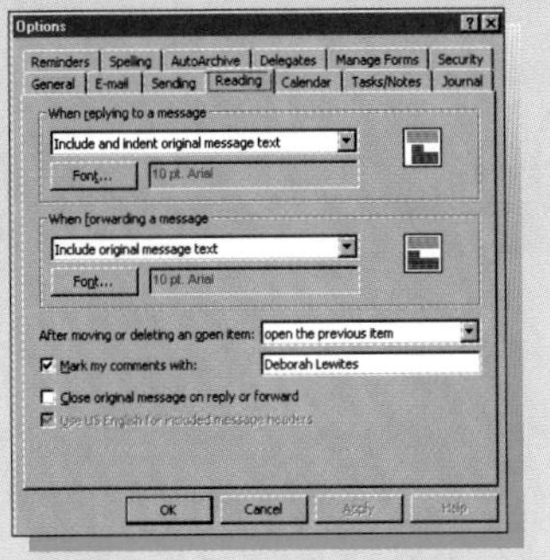

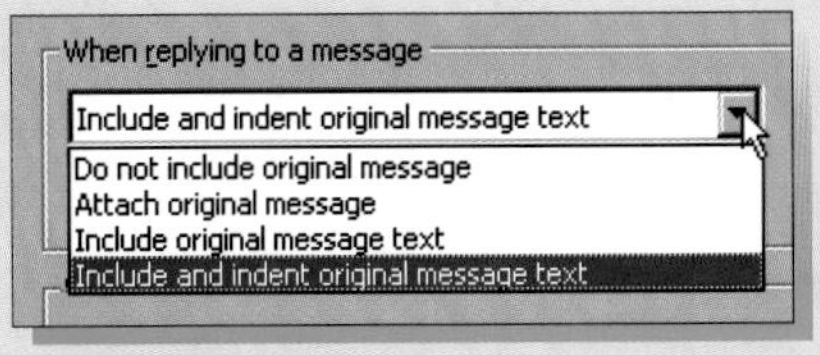

3 By default, the original message text is included and indented from the left margin (your additional text above the original text started at the left margin). Click the arrow to the right of that option to see the choices. You can omit the original message, include it as an attachment, or include it without indenting it.

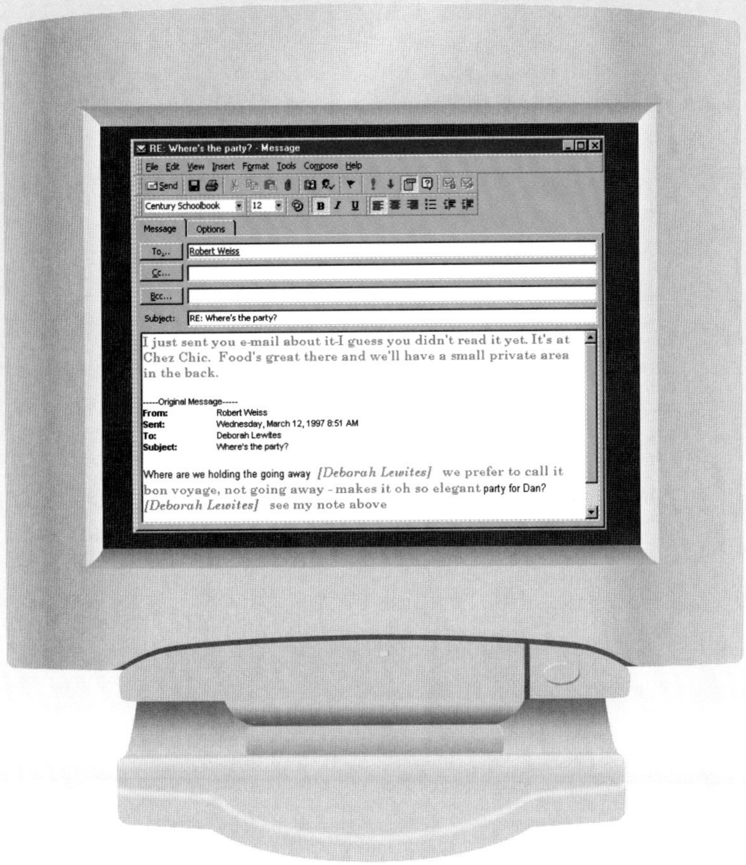

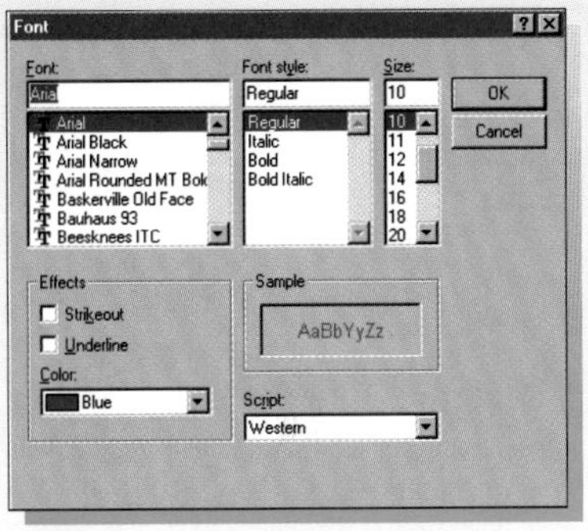

4 Click the Font button to open the Font dialog box and pick a font, style, size, and color for your response text. Click OK when you have made your selections, and you return to the Options dialog box.

5 In the next option box, choose the way you want to handle forwarded messages. In this case, of course, there is no option to omit the original text. Then click Font to make font selections for your text in a forwarded message.

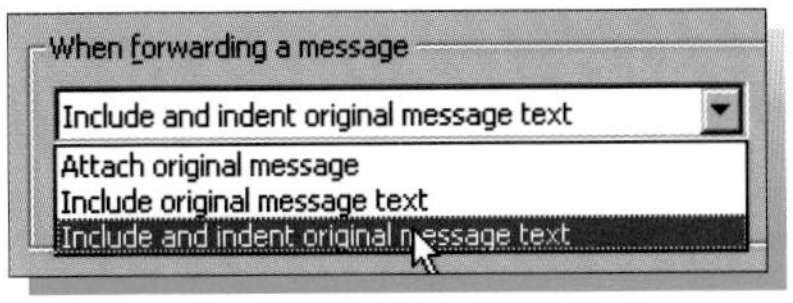

How to Create Folders to Hold Mail

The first step in managing any significant volume of data is organization. Steps two and three of the procedure for managing files are organization and organization. There's a theme here. And creating folders for the purpose of organizing all the items you want to save is good organization scheme.

In this section we'll create a folder. The steps we use can be repeated for any additional folders you need to create.

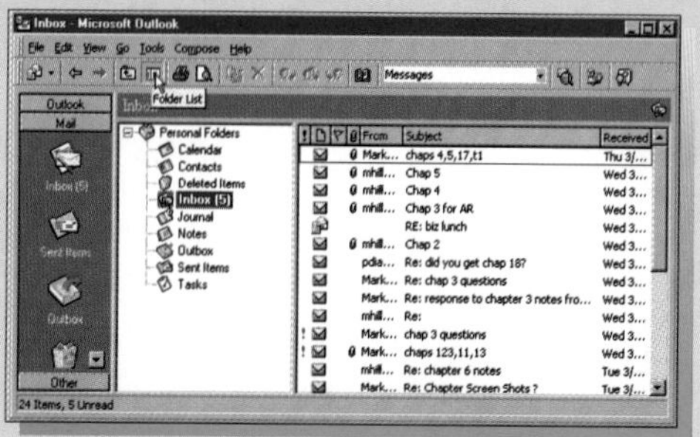

1 We start by viewing Outlook as a series of folders, and that's accomplished by displaying the Outlook folders in the Outlook window. To do so, click the Folder List icon on the toolbar. The folders appear in their own pane, between the Outlook Bar and whatever Information Viewer you currently have in your window. Notice that there's a folder for each Outlook feature (matching the icons on the Outlook Bar).

FYI

- **The Folder List icon is a toggle switch, so click it again to remove the folder display. Outlook remembers the state of the folder toggle when you exit the software and presents the same window when you launch the software the next time.**
- **If you have a lot of saved messages in your Sent Items folder, you may want to create additional child folders for it. However, you could move items from the Sent Items folder into the folders you create under the Inbox if you're saving messages by category (and you don't care if you mix received messages with sent messages for the particular category).**
- **You can, of course, create your new folders at the same hierarchical level as the Inbox or Sent Items folders. To do so, just right-click Personal Folders and create the subfolder from that parent folder.**

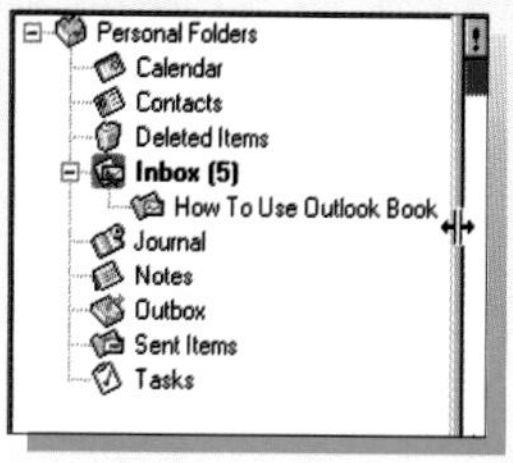

6 You could also widen the folder pane to make sure you see the complete names of all folders. Place your pointer over the vertical border line on the right side of the folder pane. When the pointer turns into a double-headed arrow, press and hold the left mouse button while you drag the border line to the right. Outlook remembers the width of the folder pane the next time you launch Outlook and display the folders.

2 When you create a folder, you really create a subfolder of an existing folder. All the Outlook folders are subfolders of your Personal Folder (the personal folder has no items in it except other folders). If you want to create a folder to store certain categories of received mail, it makes sense to make that folder a subfolder of the Inbox (which is the folder that holds all your received mail). (When you create a subfolder of a folder, the computer jargon for that is a parent-child relationship. The subfolder is called a child folder, the folder above the child is the parent folder.) To perform this task, right-click the Inbox and choose Create Subfolder.

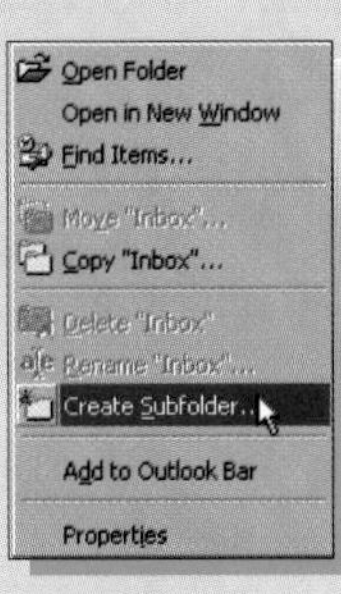

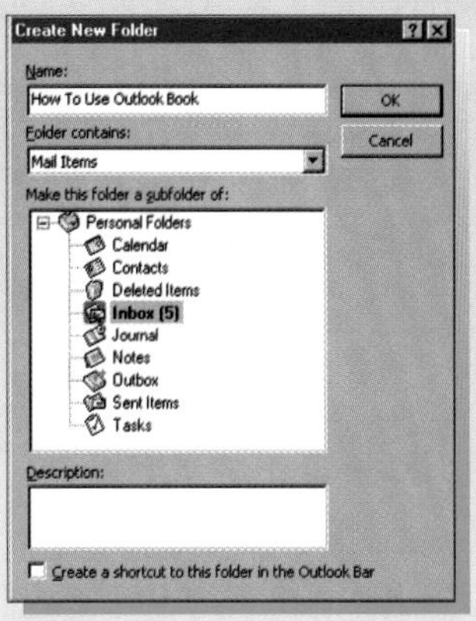

3 When the Create New Folder dialog box appears, enter a Name for this new folder. The name should describe the items you're planning to store in the folder. Because we started by creating a subfolder of the Inbox, the field for the type of item is already filled out properly (Mail Items) and the parent folder (the Inbox) is already highlighted. If you also want to put an icon for this folder on the Outlook Bar (so you can click it to move into this folder), select Create a shortcut to this folder in the Outlook Bar (at the bottom of the dialog box). Then click OK to close the dialog box and save your entries.

4 The new folder displays below its parent folder. The parent folder has a minus sign (-) to the left of its icon and if you click the minus sign the subfolder no longer displays and the minus sign turns into a plus sign (+). Clicking the plus sign expands the folder's hierarchy so you can see any child folders. Notice that each level of folders is indented and little lines appear to display all the parent and child relationships. The lines on your screen may be dotted (mine are) or solid, depending on the capacities of your video equipment.

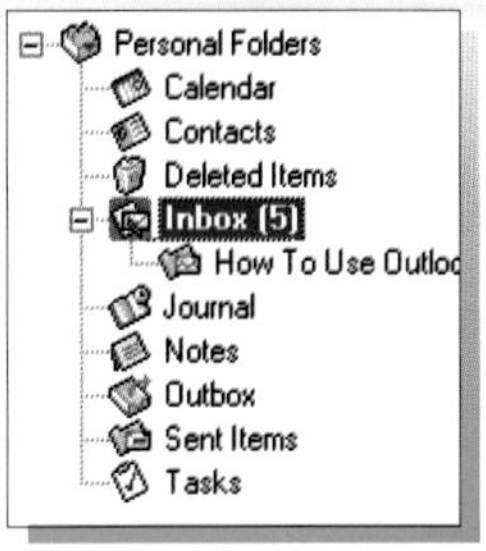

5 If you create child folders with long names, you may not be able to see the entire name of the folder. You can use the horizontal scrollbar at the bottom of the pane to move the display, or you can place your mouse pointer over the folder name that's truncated (don't click, just hold it there). Outlook displays the full name of the folder under your pointer.

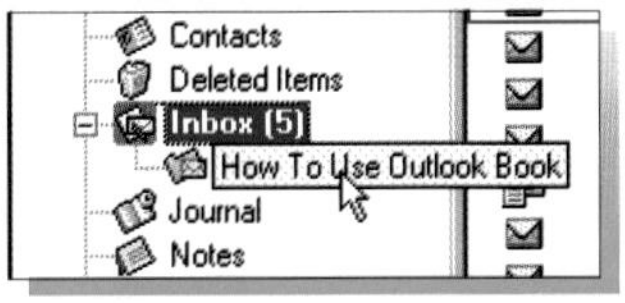

How to Move Items into Folders

You're all set. Since reading the previous section you've created lots of subfolders so you can organize all those items in your Outlook system. No? Okay, then read this section so you'll know what to do when you do find the time to create the folders you need. While you were turning the page, I was busy creating folders for my system. We can use them as examples for this section.

FYI

- The next time you click the Move to Folder icon on the toolbar, this folder's name will appear on the list and you can click it to avoid going through all the steps using the dialog box. Each time you move items to a folder, that folder appears on the Move to Folder icon list.
- When you're moving messages from the Inbox, be careful not to move unread messages. You can tell unread messages because they're listed with bold type.
- You are not limited to just creating categories for projects, you might want to think about creating folders to hold all the messages that are flagged for follow up so all your "things to do" are in one place. Then, as you complete the appropriate tasks, you can move the item to another category folder or delete it.

1 To move an item or a group of items, the first thing to do is select the item you want to put into a different folder. I've found the quickest and easiest way to do this is to display items in a simple, easy-to-read way. For the Inbox, that means getting rid of the folder pane and displaying messages as simply as possible. To accomplish this, click the Folder List icon on the toolbar so it toggles the folder display off, then click the arrow to the right of the Current View box and select Messages (instead of the default Messages with AutoPreview). Now those unread messages won't display message text and you can see more messages in the Information Viewer. You can still tell which messages aren't yet read because their listing is bold.

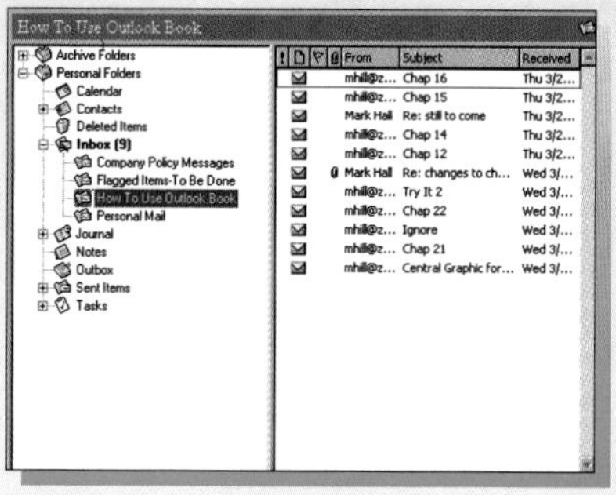

7 To reassure yourself, click the Folder List icon to display the folder pane and then click on the folder you just used as the target of your moving maneuver. All the messages display in the rightmost pane. Notice the Information Viewer bar above the display shows the name of the folder.

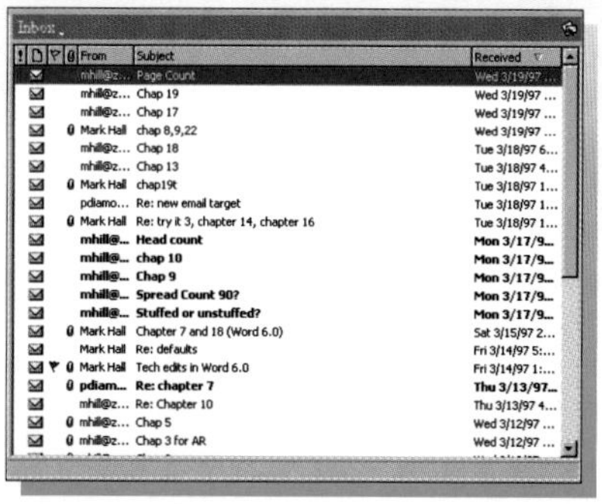

6 When you return to the Inbox Information Viewer, the messages you moved are gone.

2 Select the message you want to move to a subfolder. To select multiple messages, hold down the Ctrl key while you click each message. Then click the Move to Folder icon on the toolbar.

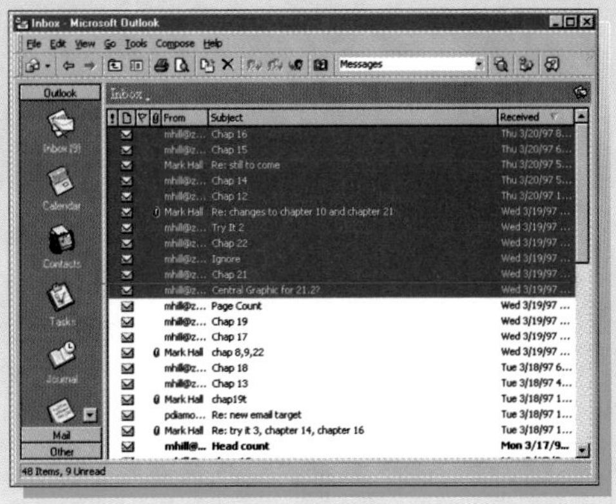

3 The Move to Folder drop-down list displays. It shows any folders you've previously chosen when you performed this step. If the folder you want to use isn't listed (in this case, it's not), choose Move to Folder.

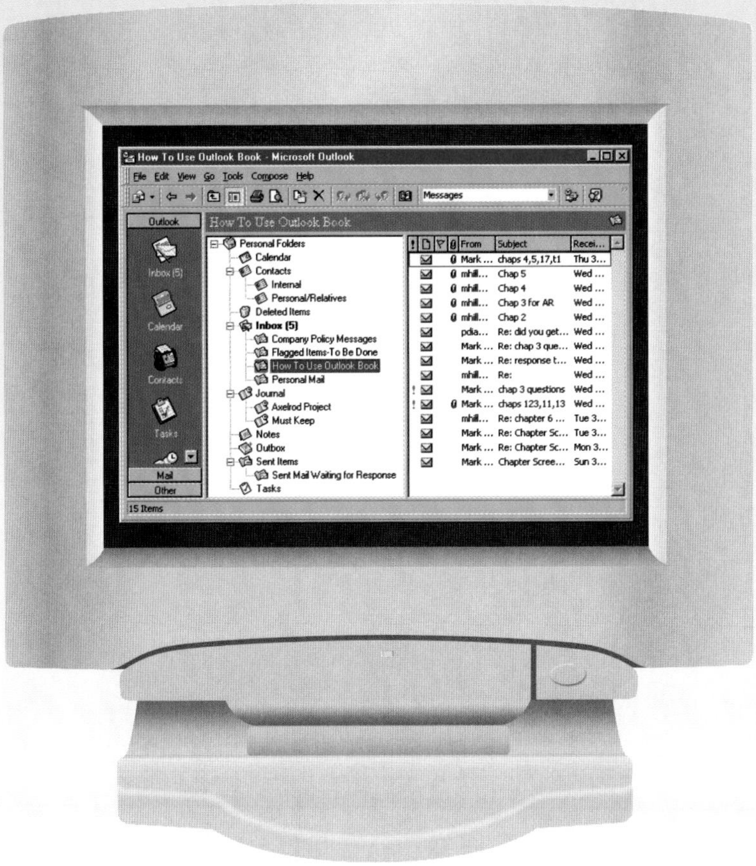

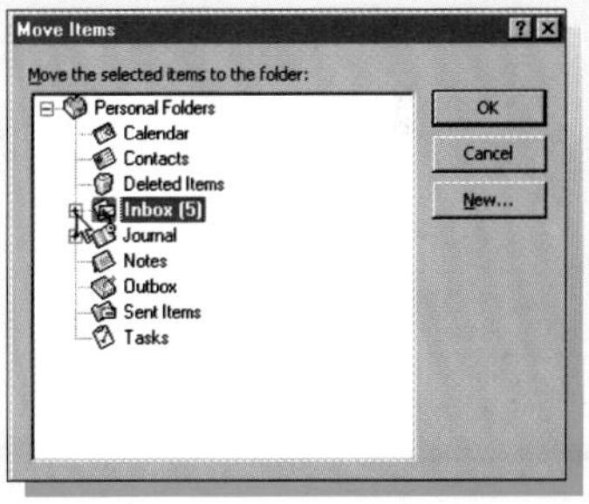

4 The Move Items dialog box displays. Click the plus sign next to the parent folder that holds the child folder you want to use as the container for the messages you're moving.

5 When the child folders can be seen, click the one you want to use, then click OK.

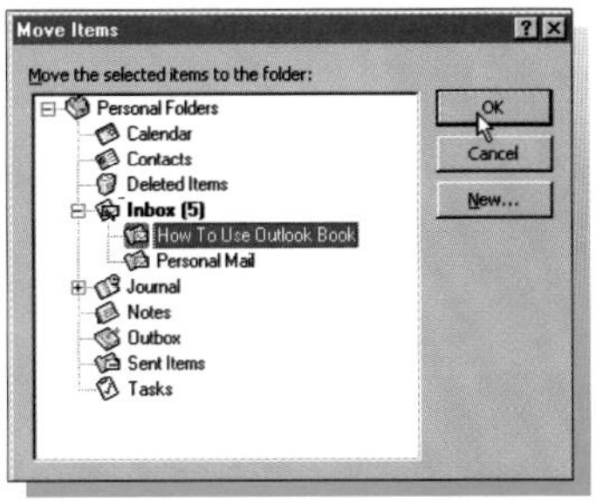

How to Change the View

View, in Outlook, refers to the way you see things in an Information Window. Outlook provides a slew of options for viewing items, and each section of Outlook (mail, contacts, and so on) has specially designed views. Changing the view changes the arrangement of the items you're looking at. In this section we'll examine all the ways you can look at your messages, which should make it easier to get an at-a-glance idea of what's what in your Inbox.

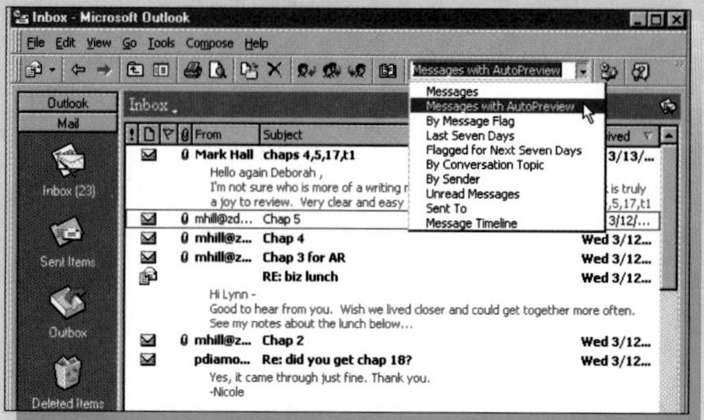

1 By default, Outlook chooses Messages with AutoPreview as the view for new messages in the Inbox. While it's handy to see the first three lines of message text below the header, it means you don't see a lot of messages at one time in the Information Viewer. And, there's an awful lot of text to read through when you just want a quick look at the messages. You can change the view by choosing a different view option in the Current View box on the toolbar.

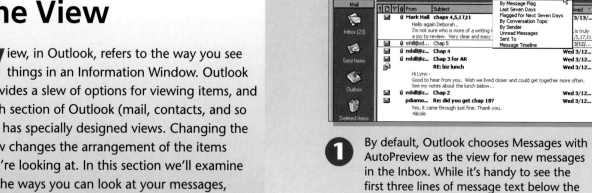

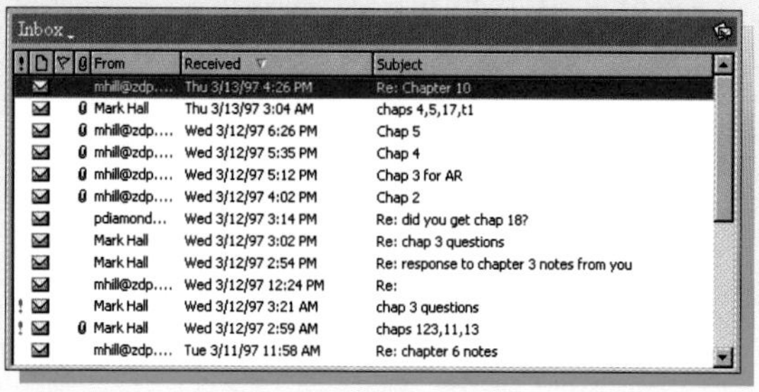

6 The column now occupies its new space and the information about each message is rearranged to match the new column arrangement. Stay tuned, in the next section we're going to Name That View (sounds like a good title for a TV show).

(Continues on next page)

FYI

- **Most of the available views for the Inbox are table views. That means the items display in columns, with each column displaying some specific information. There are other types of views available, such as Timeline Views, which present items in a calendar format, but these usually aren't useful for messages (although they're quite handy for appointments).**
- **The icon columns can provide a useful sort scheme, because you can bring all the flagged messages to the top of the listing, or all the messages marked for high priority (the red exclamation point).**

15 When the Format Table View dialog box appears you can see there are fonts defined for the elements of the view.

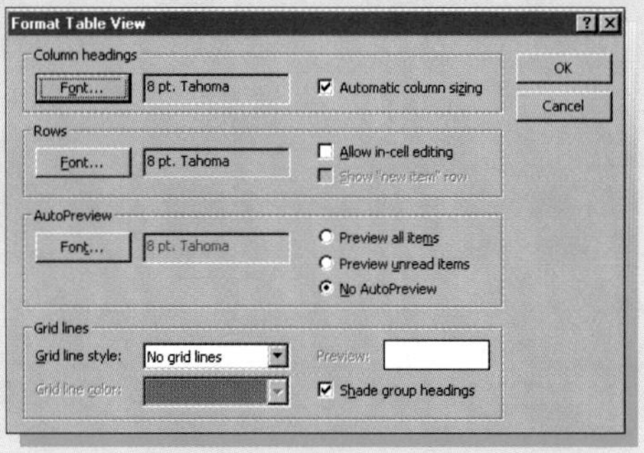

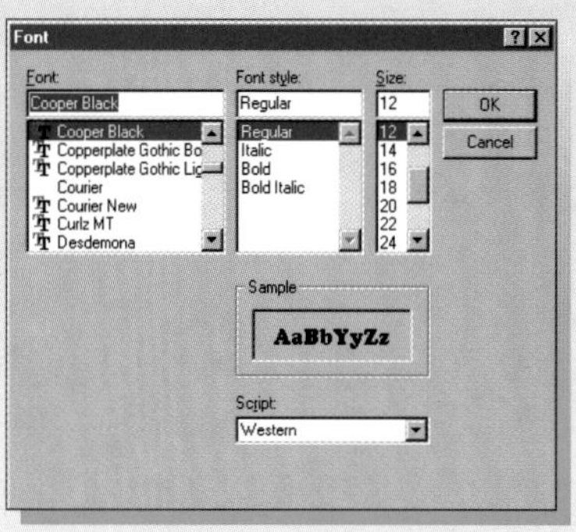

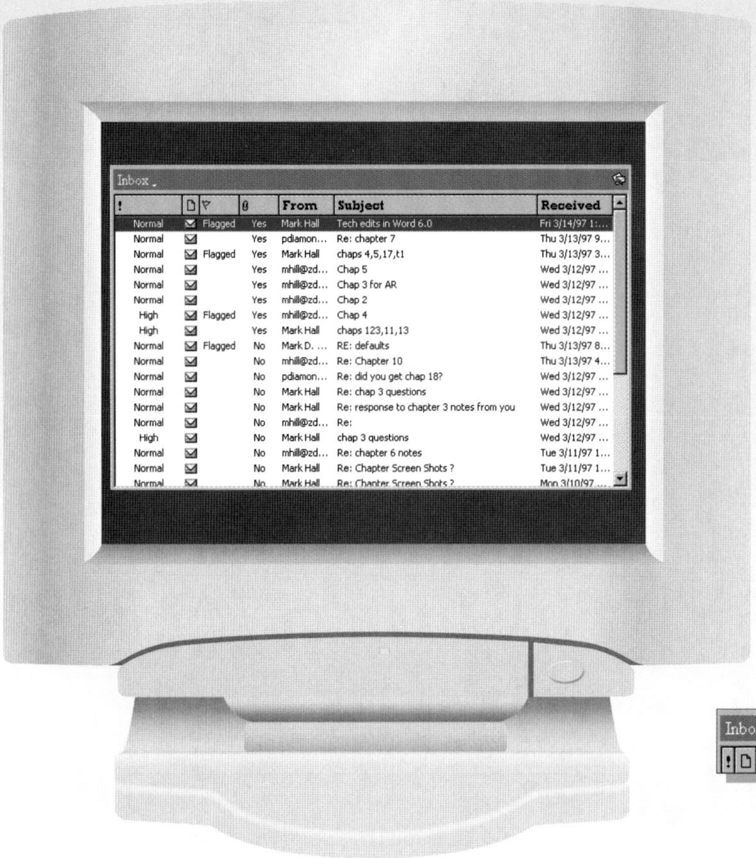

16 To change the look of any element, click the appropriate Font button (in this example, I chose the font for column headings). You can change the font, the style, and the size of the font. For the font that displays AutoPreview, you can also change the color. When you finish making changes, press OK to return to the Format Table View dialog box. Then press OK when you're ready to close that dialog box.

17 Your window reflects your changes. If you decide you don't like it, repeat the steps and make additional changes, or put everything back the way it was.

18 If you don't remember the way it was, don't worry. Outlook remembers. You can reset the view with the Define Views feature. First change to another view (Outlook won't reset a current view). Choose View, Define Views to open the Define Views dialog box. Choose the name of the view you changed, then choose Reset. You'll be asked to confirm the fact that you want to reset the view to its original settings. Then choose Close to leave the dialog box. To make sure you accomplished your deed, switch to the view you reset and breathe a sigh of relief—it looks the way it did when you first started using Outlook.

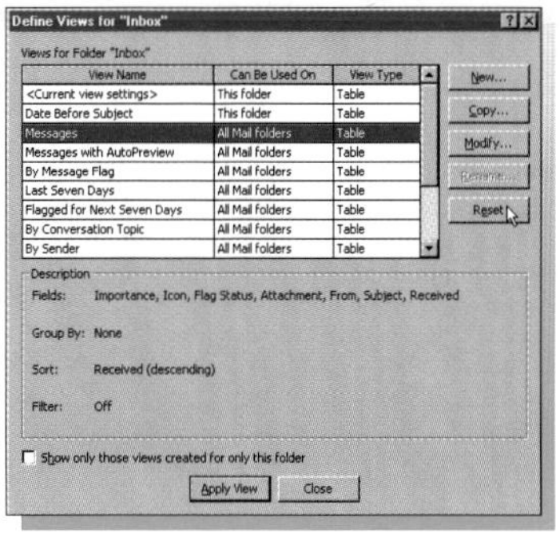

How to Sort the View

Finding a message or a group of messages is much easier when you have control over the way the listing is displayed. Sorting gives you those controls.

Sorting is arranging items in a way that displays them in the order in which you need to see them, and this section covers some of the easy ways to sort the items in the Information Viewer. Although we'll be using the Inbox for this discussion, the features you'll learn about work throughout all the Outlook folders.

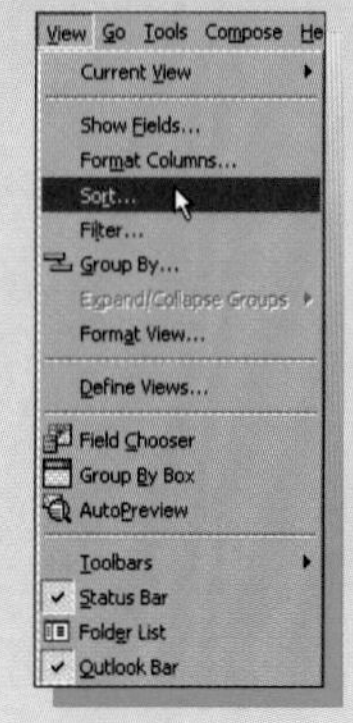

1 To sort the listing in the Information Viewer, select View, Sort from the menu bar.

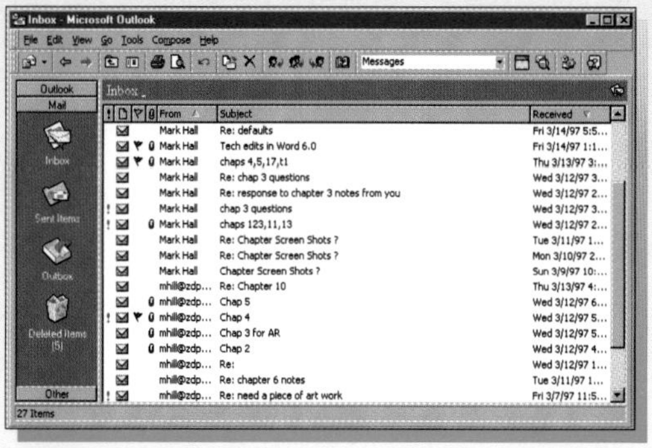

6 If you want to sort only by the columns in the view, there's a short cut. We've already covered the fact that you can sort your list of messages by any column heading, just by clicking that heading. If you hold down the Shift key and continue to click column headings, each time you do so you're creating a subsort on that column heading. In this example the primary sort is the sender and the secondary sort is the received date.

FYI

- **If you do add a field as a result of a sort selection, when you change the view in the Current View box, you're asked if you want to update the view, create a view, or discard the settings. If this new column is important and you'll be sorting on it a lot, create a new view.**
- **If you sort and subsort by clicking multiple columns, to return to one sort scheme, click any column heading without using the Shift key.**

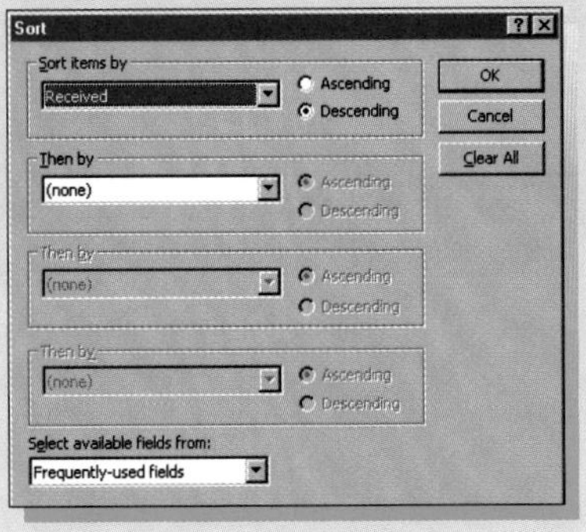

2 The Sort dialog box appears and the currently selected sort column is already established as the primary sort.

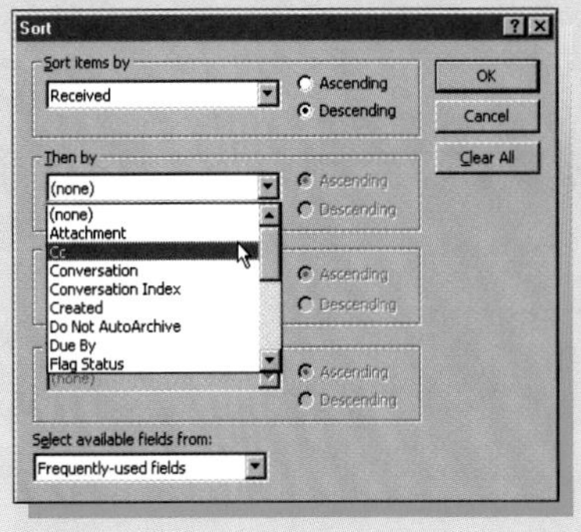

3 Select a primary sort (or keep the current one), then select each secondary sort by using the boxes named Then By. Click the down arrow to the right of each sort level to choose a field. You are not restricted to the fields that are currently represented by columns in the Information Viewer. You can choose any field available for this item.

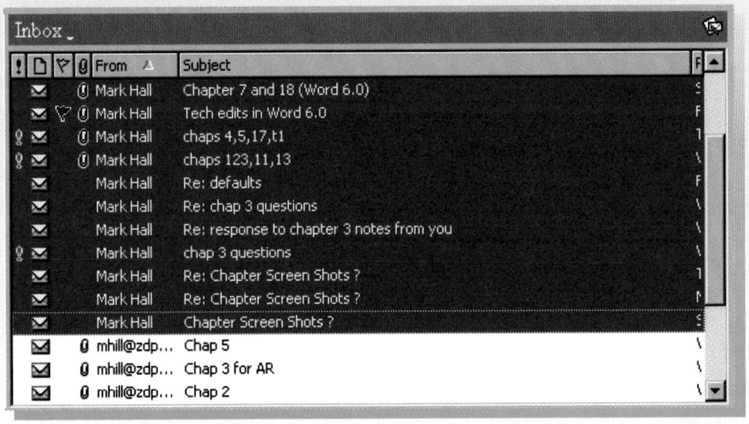

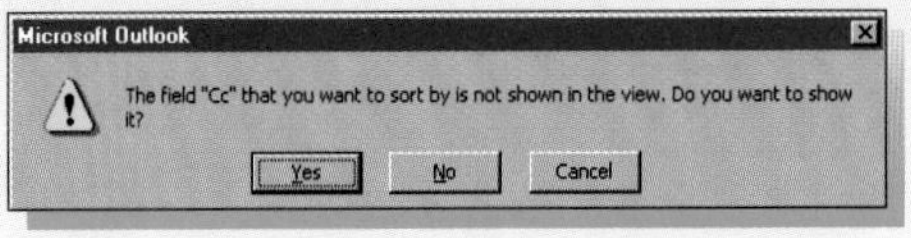

4 If you choose a field not represented by a column, you're asked if you want to show the field.

5 Answer yes to display a column for the field. It will be on the right side of the view and will have an arrow on the column heading indicating it's part of the sort scheme. If you answer No, the field is still used for the sort, but you don't see the information in a column.

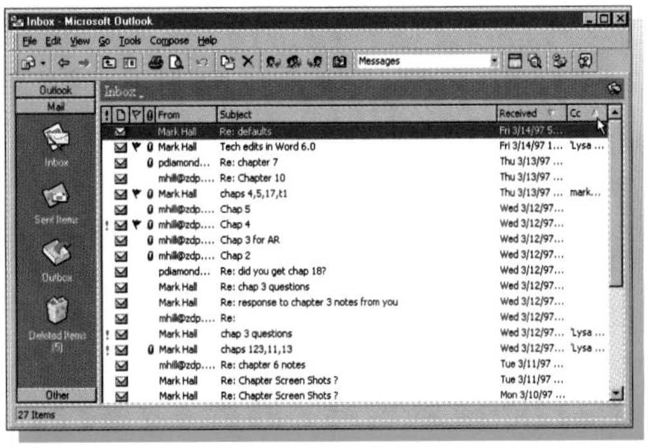

How to Filter the View

Filtering is setting up criteria that describes the items you want to view. Items that meet your criteria get through the filter and are displayed. Items that don't meet your criteria don't get through the filter.

There are all sorts of reasons to filter the items in an Outlook folder. We'll use the Inbox in this section, but the theory and practice of filters is the same throughout the Outlook folders.

FYI

- **You'll probably find that most of the time you can set your filter with the first tab and not have to use the More Choices and Advanced tabs.**
- **In the first tab you can enter partial words or names, since the Filter searches for characters, not specific items.**
- **If you click on From or Sent To, your Personal Address Book displays so you can pick an entry (or you can just enter a name or part of a name directly into the field).**

1. To build the criteria for a filter, choose View, Filter from the menu bar.

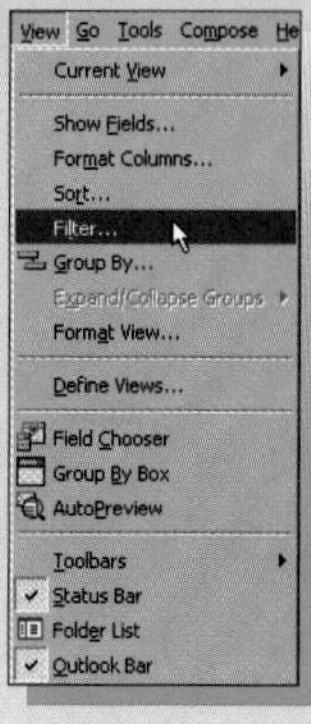

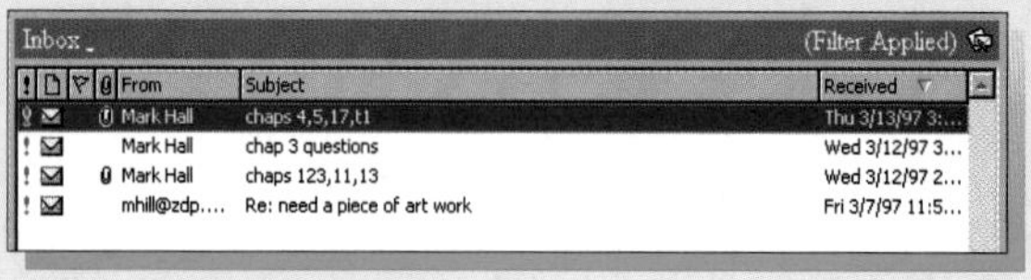

7. The Information Viewer displays the items that match the criteria you set throughout all the tabs of the Filter dialog box. Notice that the Inbox bar above the column headings indicates that a filter is being applied to the list. To remove the filter, select a different view from the Current View box on the toolbar (you'll be asked about saving or updating the view, and you should select Discard the current view settings).

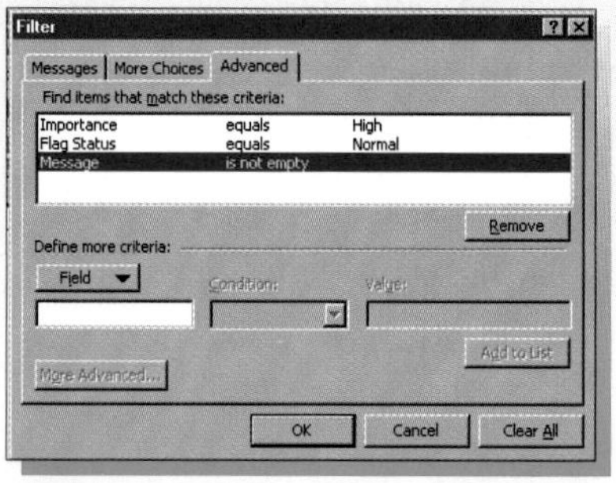

6. Continue to select fields, conditions, and values, and add them to the list until you've designed exactly the filter you need to find the items you need. Click OK when you are finished with all the tabs on the Filter dialog box.

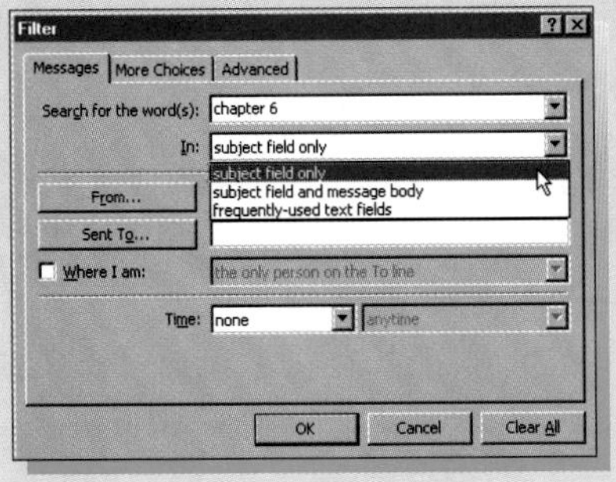

2 When the Filter dialog box appears, you start with the Messages tab. For other Outlook folders, the first tab relates to the specific folder (for instance, meetings for the Calendar folder, and so on). You can enter criteria for as many fields as you wish. The more you enter, the narrower the search (however, the search takes much longer). Here, I'm looking for a specific set of characters and I used the drop-down box next to the selection box named In to choose the subject field.

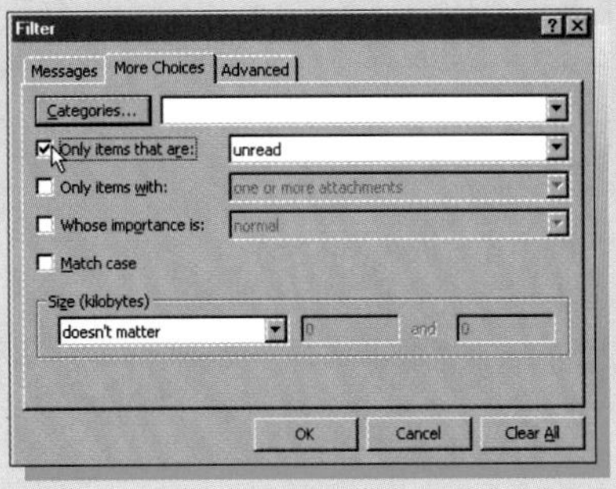

3 Move to the More Choices tab for criteria that you can set only if you want to narrow them. The choices are grayed out (inaccessible) until you click the checkbox. Then you must choose one of the options in the selection box. Omitting the checkbox omits the filter. You can choose only items that are read or only items that are unread; only items with an attachment or only items that don't have an attachment; or only items of a specific importance level.

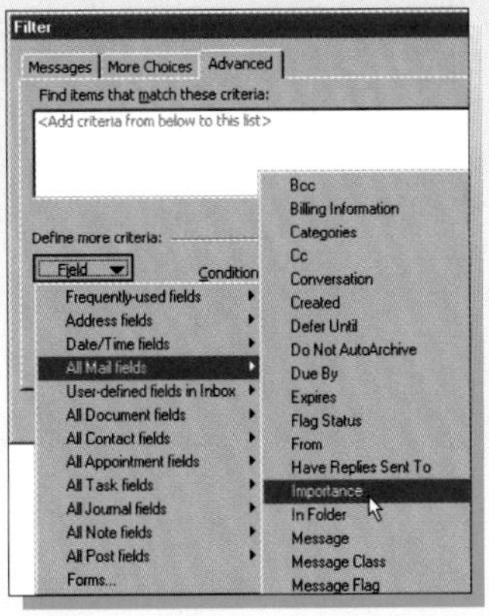

4 The Advanced tab gives you an opportunity to design very specific criteria for your filter. The box at the top of the sheet fills up with your choices as you add them. You begin by clicking the arrow to the right of the field box to choose a category of fields. Then click the field you want in that category.

5 When the field is in place, select a condition and a value for that condition. Then click Add to List.

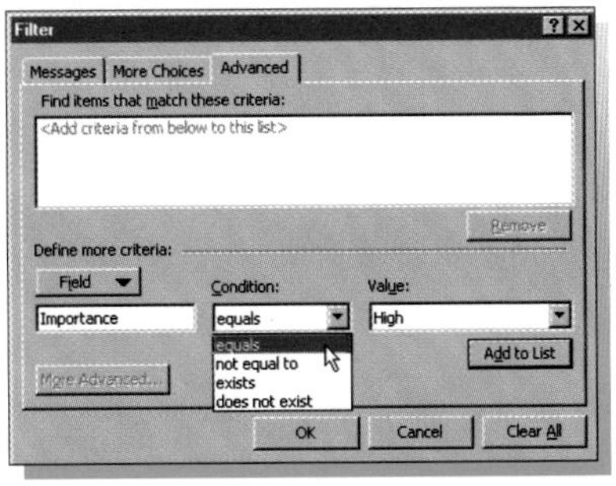

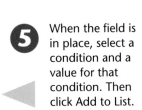

How to Group the View

Outlook has a really nifty way of arranging a crowded display so you can access the items you need in a hurry. It's called grouping, and it's like sorting except that each group in the sort scheme is represented in the Information Viewer by a gray bar with a title representing the sort criteria. You just have to look for the title you want, making it easy to head right for the group you need without scrolling through a lot of individual items.

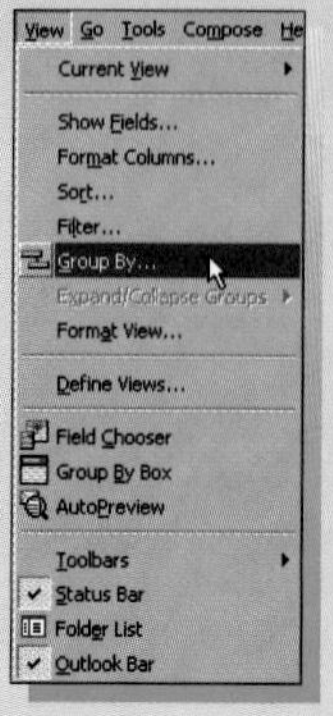

1 To group items, choose View, Group By from the menu bar.

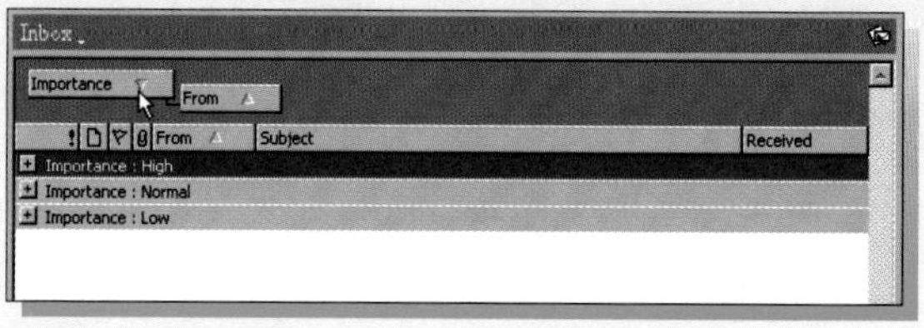

6 Notice that the bar above the column headings has icons representing the sort and subsort groups. An arrow displays on each icon, indicating whether the sorting scheme is ascending or descending. Click the icon to change the order of the sort.

FYI

- **Just as in sorting without grouping, you can sort by a field that does not appear in a column heading on the Information Viewer.**
- **To ungroup, pick a new view from the Current View box (answer Discard to the question about saving the view). When you return to this view, all the items are displayed as usual.**

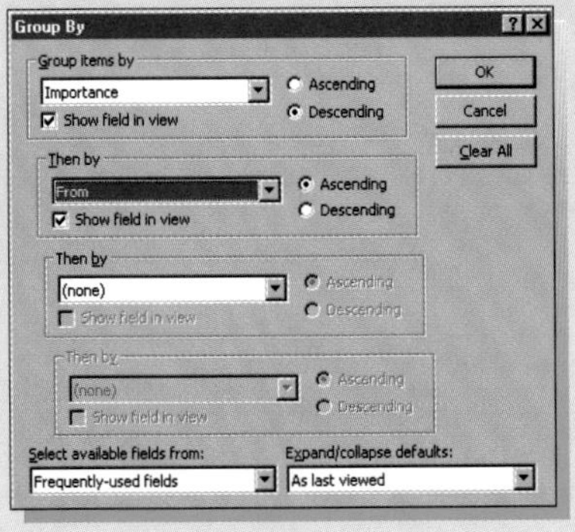

2 The Group By dialog box appears and you fill in the fields you want to use to group and sub-group the listing. This is just like sorting. Click OK when you have finished making your selections.

3 The Inbox is grouped by the fields you chose. Hiding behind each of those titles are the items that match your sorting criteria.

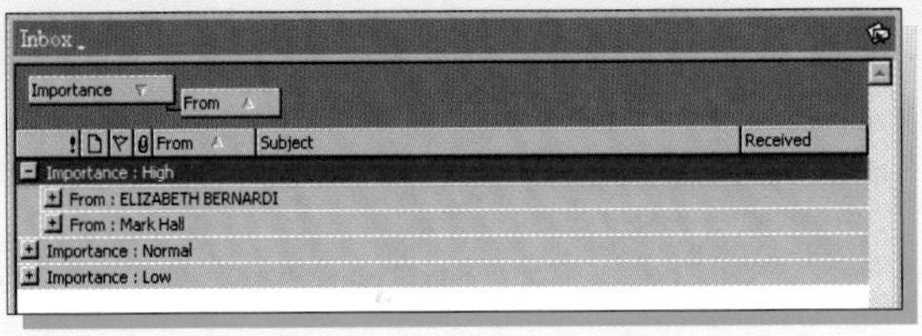

4 Click the plus sign (+) to expand any group. If you chose a secondary sort field, there's a group for that subsort. (If you didn't choose a secondary sort, the items that belong in the group are displayed.)

5 Click the plus sign of the group you're interested in to expand the subsort group. Now you can see the items (unless you have a third subsort, in which case you have to click the plus sign of the group you want to look at).

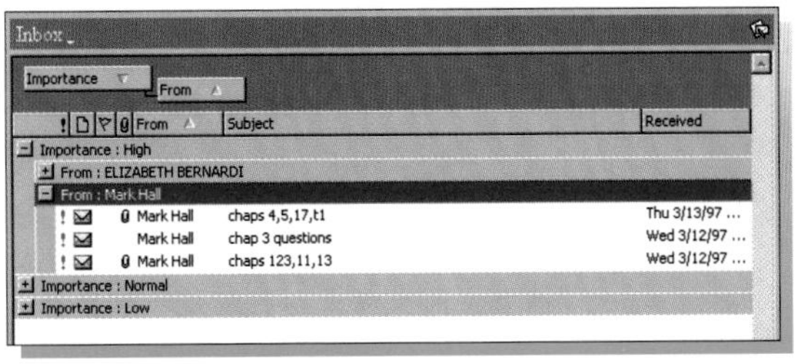

Ctrl + Shift + Q= New Meeting Request
Ctrl + N= New Appointment

PART 3

Using Calendar

THE Calendar feature in Outlook provides the tools you need to gain mastery over your time by putting you in control of your calendar. Scheduling and tracking appointments is a vital part of time management and the tools in Calendar are powerful enough to keep you on track and on time.

To work in the Calendar, click the Calendar icon on the Outlook Bar.

IN THIS SECTION YOU'LL LEARN

How to Create an Appointment

Whether you're using a date book, a wall calendar, or post-it notes to keep track of your appointments (you are keeping track of them, aren't you?), you have to record certain basic information, like who, what, when, and where. In that respect Outlook is no different than any manual system you've been using all along.

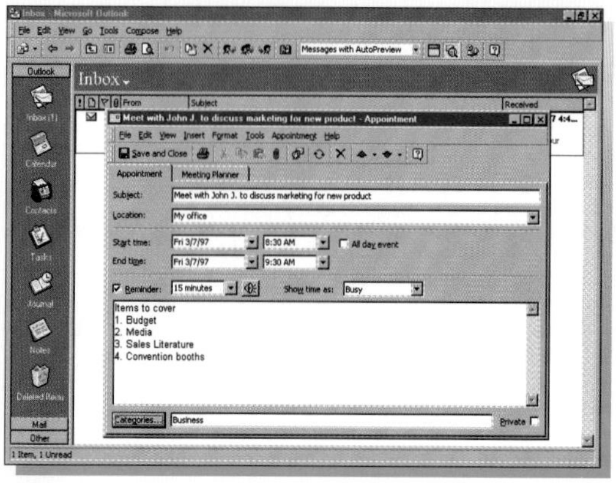

1. To create an appointment, click the New Appointment icon on the toolbar to open a blank appointment form.

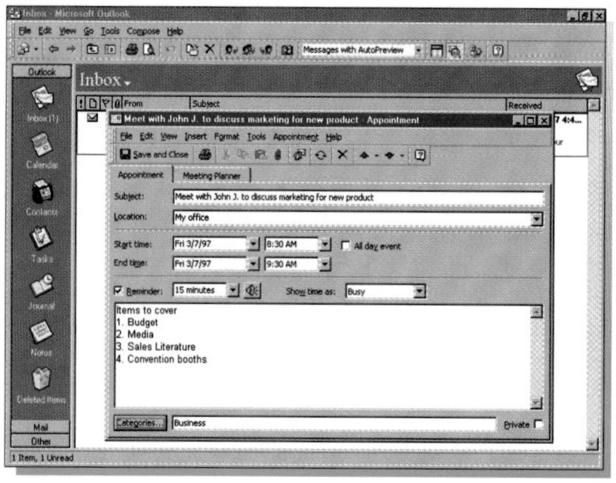

6. Click the Save and Close icon to save the new appointment and return to the Calendar window.

FYI

- To open a new appointment form with the correct date and time already entered, select a date from the Date Navigator and double-click the appropriate time slot in the daily calendar.
- An easy way to enter dates without having to look them up is to use plain English commands. You can enter such phrases as **next Tuesday**, **a week from Thursday**, or **two weeks from tomorrow**.

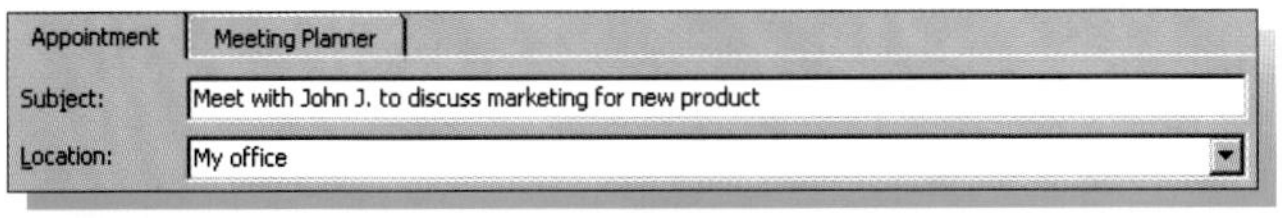

2 Complete the Subject field with a brief description that explains the reason for this appointment (one that will jog your memory). Then fill in the Location field so you know where to go.

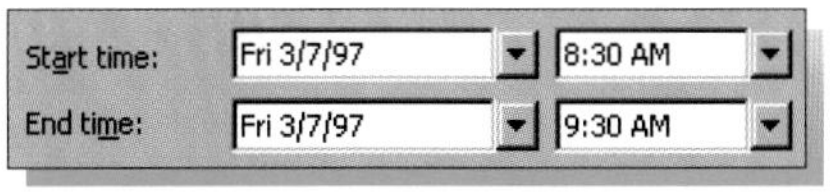

3 Press Tab to move to the Start Time field and enter the date and time for this appointment. You can use the drop-down list (click the down arrow at the right of the field) or type the information directly.

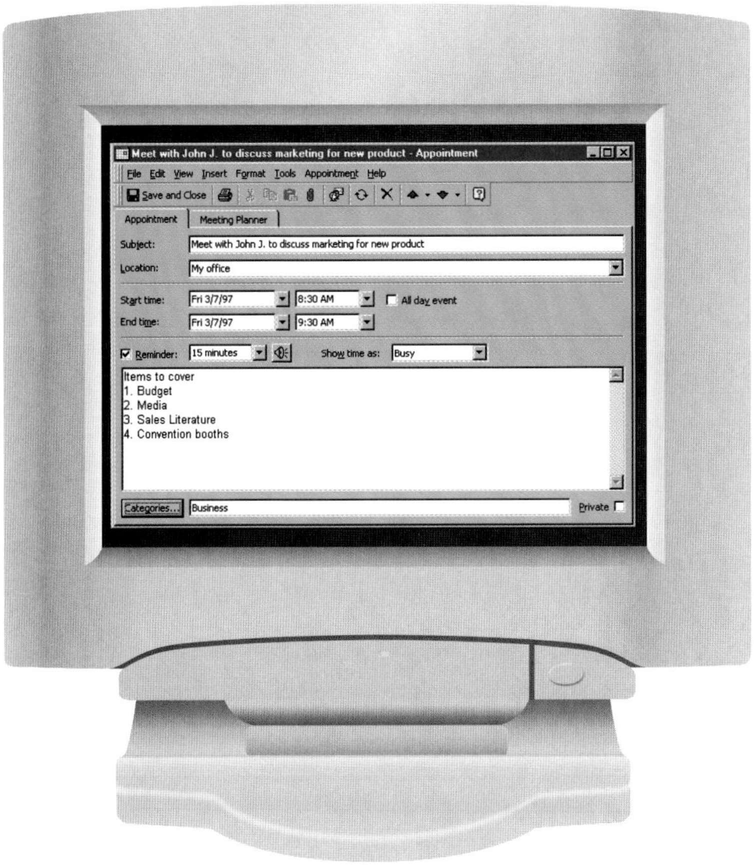

4 Press Tab to move to the Reminder field and click the Reminder checkbox to enable a reminder for this appointment. From the Reminder Time drop-down list, select the amount of advance warning you want the reminder to give you. By default, Outlook plays a chime sound when the reminder displays. To change the sound that plays, click the speaker icon next to the reminder time and select a different file (sounds are really files).

5 Press the Tab key to get to the text box and type in any notes or comments you want to have on record (for yourself) about this appointment.

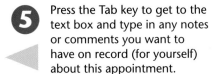

How to Create a Recurring Appointment

Recurring appointments are those appointments that just won't seem to go away. You know the ones I mean, the weekly strategy meeting, the monthly sales meeting, and the daily session with your therapist. Rather than create a separate appointment for each occurrence, Outlook allows you to create one appointment that automatically occurs at regular intervals.

1 To create a recurring appointment, choose Calendar, New Recurring Appointment from the menu bar.

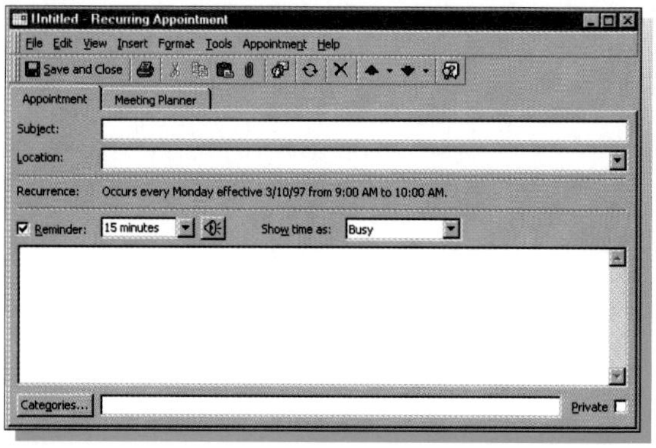

6 Click OK to go to the new appointment form for this recurring appointment. The steps for filling out the recurring appointment form are the same as those for creating a non-recurring appointment, except that the dates and times are already set for the recurring appointment. When you have filled out the Subject, Location, and other fields, click Save and Close.

FYI

- **As with a non-recurring appointment you can select a date from the Date Navigator and double-click the appropriate time slot to open a new recurring appointment form.**
- **Right-clicking on the daily calendar in any of the time slots activates a pop-up menu that offers a number of choices, including a New Recurring Appointment form.**

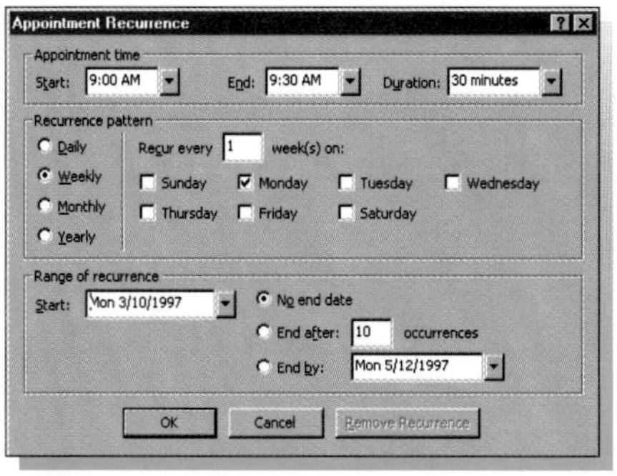

2 The Appointment Recurrence dialog box that is now displayed provides three sets of options. You can set the Appointment time, the Recurrence pattern, and the Range of recurrence.

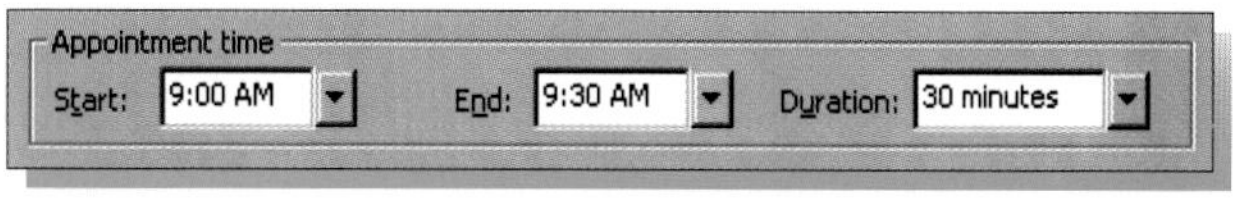

3 Enter the Start time for the appointment. Notice that the End time is automatically set depending on the Duration setting. You can reset the End time or the Duration time by clicking the arrow at the right of each field and making your selection from the drop-down list.

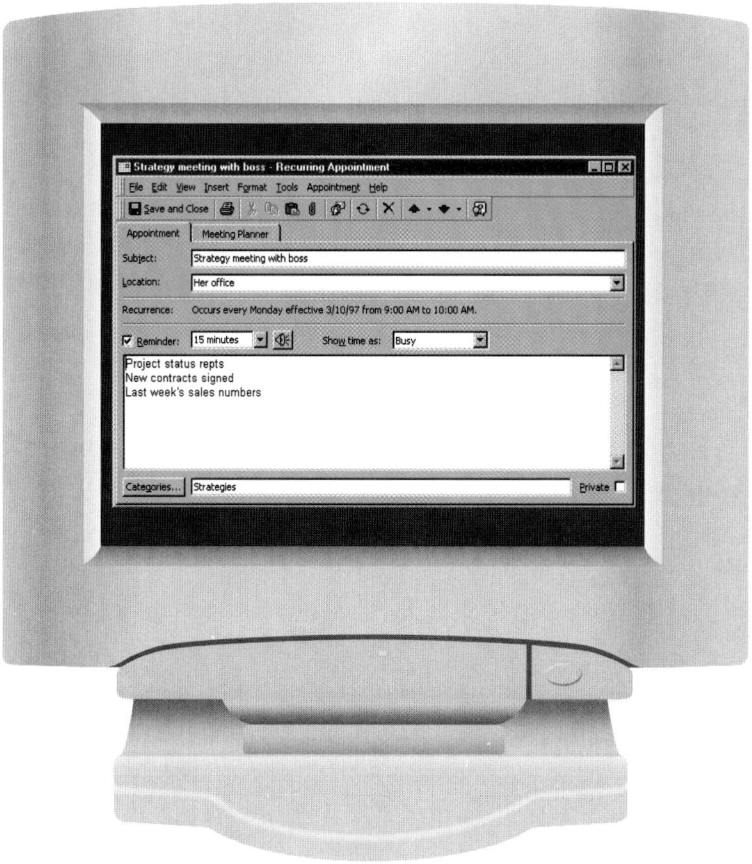

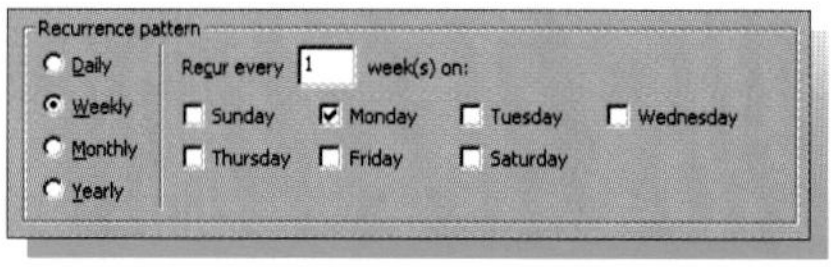

4 Select the frequency with which you want the appointment to occur from the Recurrence Pattern options. Depending on the selection of Daily, Weekly, Monthly, or Yearly, the other Recurrence pattern options vary. Choose the number of recurrences per time period and the specific days for each occurrence.

5 Choose the Start date and the end date from the Range of Recurrence options. You can elect to set no end date, limit the appointment to a specific number of occurrences, or set a fixed end date.

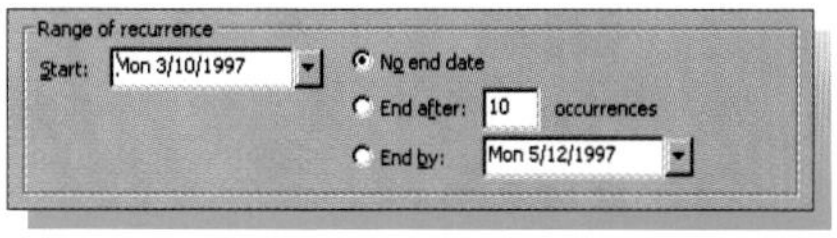

How to Edit Appointment Forms

Editing an appointment form is a simple matter of opening the appointment form and making the desired changes. Recurring appointments are a little more complex in that you have a choice of changing only one appointment or the entire series of appointments.

Editing an appointment can mean changing the location, the date, the time, the reminder, or even the note you wrote to yourself about the appointment.

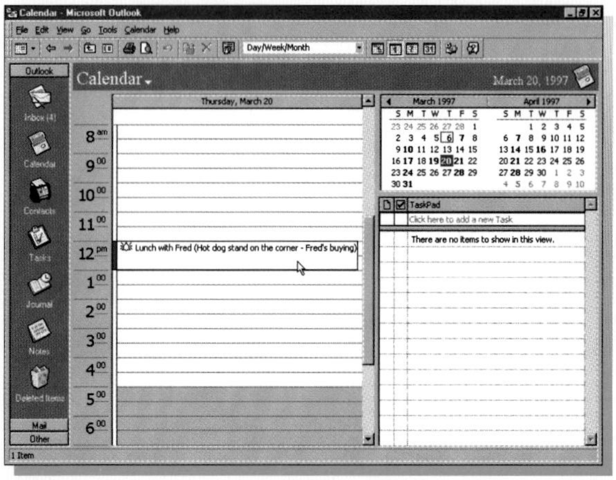

1 To edit an appointment, double-click on it. This opens the appointment form so you can review and edit it. Go to the field you want to change and make the necessary adjustment. Sometimes you might need to change more than one item in the appointment. Make all the changes you need, then choose Close and Save to make those changes permanent.

FYI

- **For a quick way to open an appointment, highlight the appointment entry in the daily calendar and press Ctrl+O.**
- **A quick and easy way to change the time of an appointment is to drag the appointment from one time slot to another in the daily calendar view.**
- **If you want to delete an appointment rather than reschedule it, you can do so from the daily calendar without opening the appointment. Simply click (highlight) the appointment you want to eliminate, and click the Delete icon (the black X) on the Calendar window toolbar. This applies to both recurring and non-recurring appointments. When deleting a recurring appointment, Outlook offers the option to delete a single occurrence or the entire series of occurrences.**

2 Editing a recurring appointment is just as easy, except that you have to specify whether you are changing one occurrence of the appointment or the entire series of occurrences. To edit one occurrence, double-click the recurring appointment, and select Open This Occurrence from the Open Recurring Item dialog box. Make the necessary changes and click Save and Close.

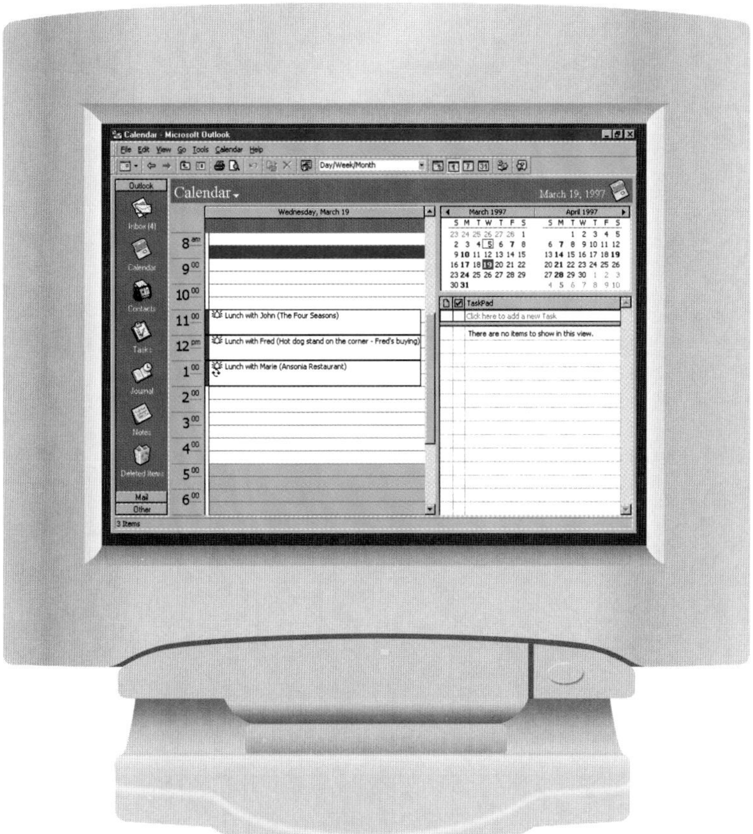

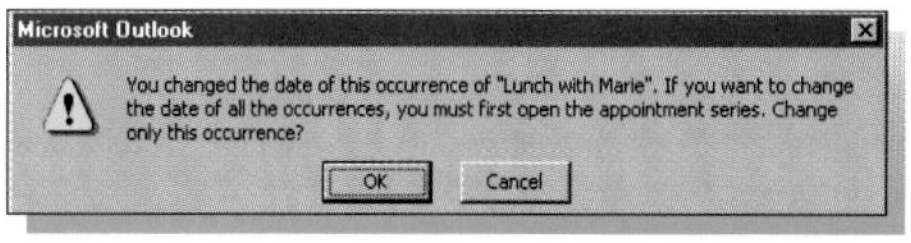

3 An informational dialog box appears, confirming your changes for either this occurrence or for all occurrences. If it matches what you meant to do, click OK. Otherwise, make the appropriate change and then click OK.

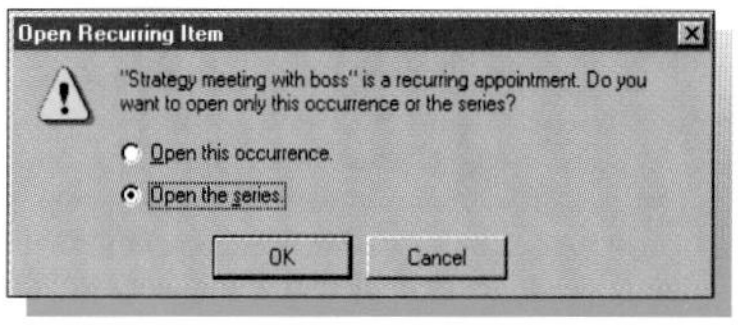

4 To edit the entire series of a recurring appointment, double-click the appointment, and select Open the Series from the Open Recurring Item dialog box. Make the appropriate changes to the basic form.

5 To edit the recurrence time, pattern, or range, click the Recurrence icon on the appointment form toolbar. Make the necessary edits in the Appointment Recurrence dialog box and click OK to return to the appointment form. Click Close and Save to save your changes and return to the Calendar window.

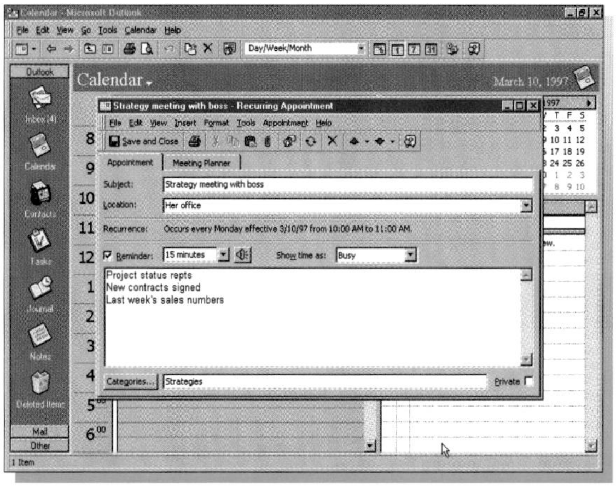

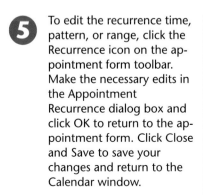

How to Create an Event

An event in Outlook's calendar is any activity that lasts 24 hours or longer. Examples of events include a seminar, a vacation, or a trade show. An event occurs once and may last for one or multiple days. Another type of event is an annual event. Examples of annual events are birthdays and holidays because they occur yearly on a specific date. Events and annual events appear as banners on your calendar because they occupy blocks of time that only you can see. If you are connected to other people's calendars on a network, they will not see your blocked-out time for an event or annual event, nor will you see theirs.

On this page you'll learn how to create events and view your scheduled events.

1 Choose New Event from the Calendar menu.

6 To see a list of all your scheduled events, choose Events from the drop-down list box on the toolbar.

FYI

● Notice the down arrow ellipse button that is visible on your calendar's scheduled event. If you click that button, the Calendar view changes so that you can enter and schedule appointments on the first day of the event. Also, the Date Navigator displays the event dates in bold.

● When viewing your scheduled events, notice that the (Filter Applied) message is in the right corner of the Folder Banner. This is because when the Calendar shows only your scheduled events, it is actually filtering by recurrence (none).

2 An Event dialog box will appear with the current title as "Untitled." In the Appointment tab, type a subject in the list box. As soon as you move to another field in the dialog box, the subject you entered will become part of the title.

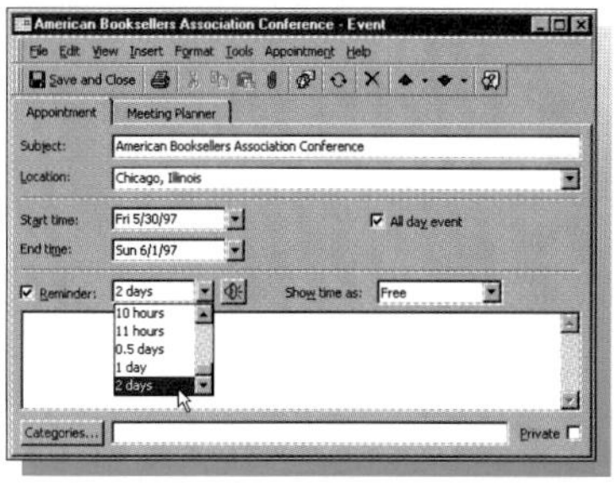

3 Type in the location of the event, the startttime, and the end time. There is also a checkbox to note whether the event lasts all day or not. If you would like to have a reminder about the event—possibly several days in advance—select the Reminder checkbox and select the time for the reminder in the drop-down list box.

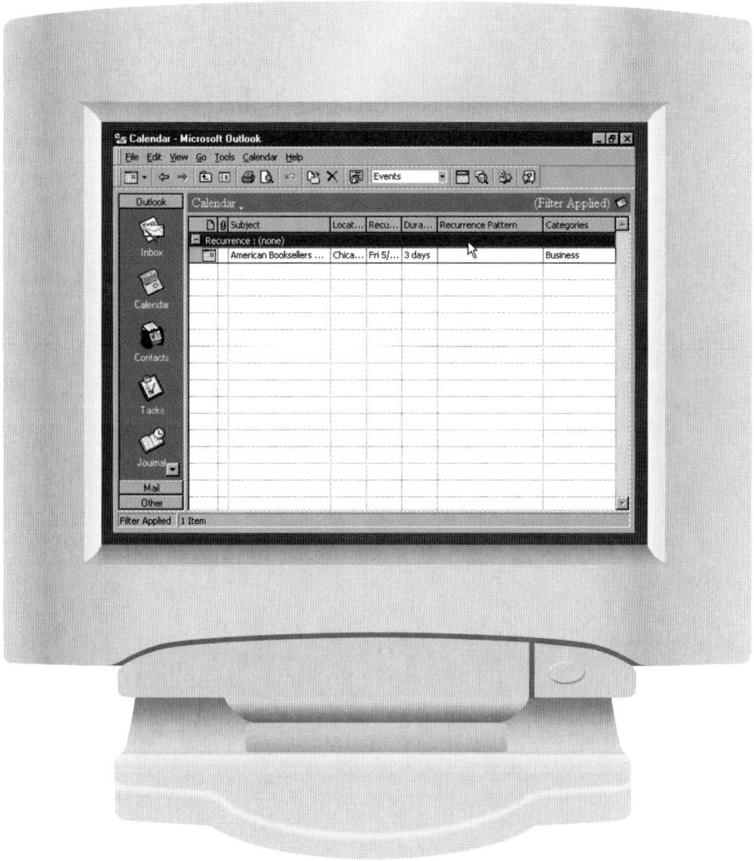

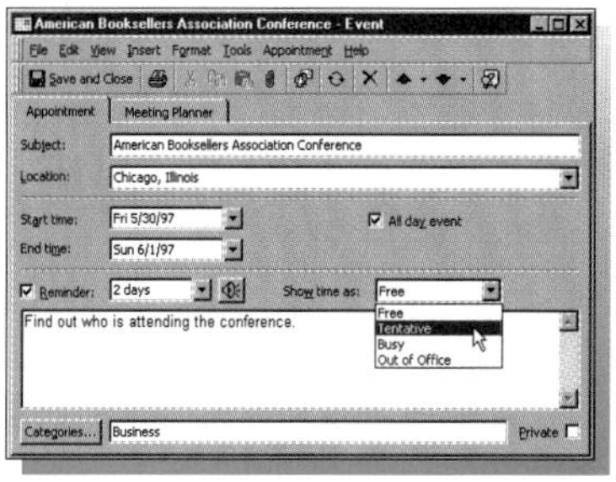

4 Type any notes about the event in the available space. You can also select a category for the event and specify whether the event you created should be private or not. Depending on your availability during the time of the event, you should choose the appropriate Show Time As selection from the drop-down list box. When you are finished filling in all the event information, choose the Save and Close button.

5 In the Calendar Month view, you can see that the event subject shows up on the appropriate date.

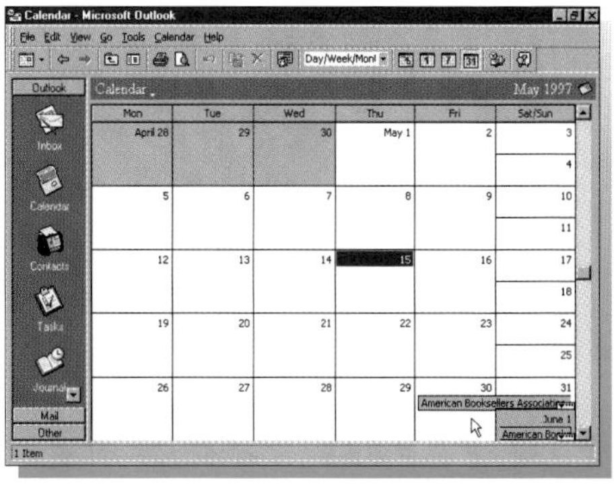

How to Use the Date Navigator

The small monthly calendar in the top right corner of the Calendar Window Information Viewer is the Date Navigator. It doesn't look like much, but it packs quite a bit of power. You can use it to change dates and to view your schedule information in a variety of ways.

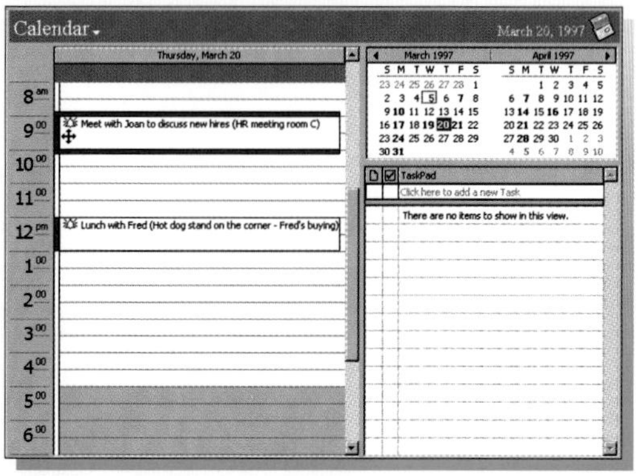

1 To change an appointment date using the Date Navigator, move your mouse pointer over to the left side of the appointment entry in the daily calendar. When the pointer turns into a pair of double-sided arrows (forming a cross), drag the appointment to the Date Navigator.

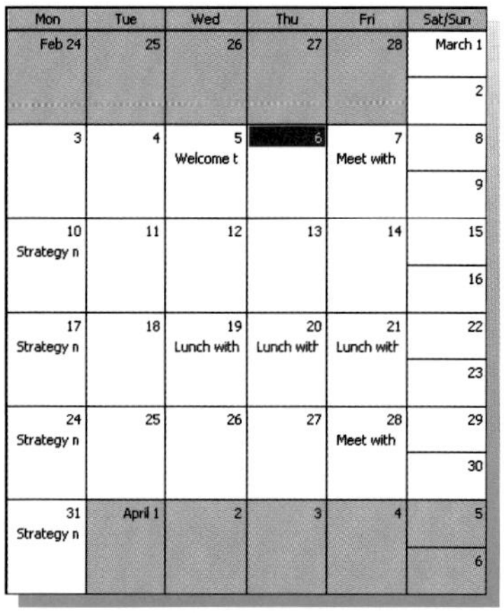

6 Click to replace the weekly view with a monthly view. Notice that the monthly view includes the last few days of the previous month and the next few days of the upcoming month.

FYI

- **To show two or more days in the daily calendar view, click on a date in the Date Navigator and drag your mouse to the adjacent date(s) you wish to include. If you include fewer than seven dates, they appear as separate columns in the daily calendar. If you choose more than seven dates, they appear as an expanded weekly calendar.**
- **By holding down the Shift key while selecting adjacent dates, you can show up to 14 dates as columns in the daily calendar.**
- **You can select as many as 14 non-adjacent days in the Date Navigator by holding down the Ctrl key as you select the dates using your mouse. They appear as columns in the daily calendar.**

2 Still holding down the left mouse button, position the mouse pointer over the desired date and drop the appointment listing on the new date. The date on the daily calendar changes to the new date and the appointment appears, scheduled for the same start and end times as the original appointment.

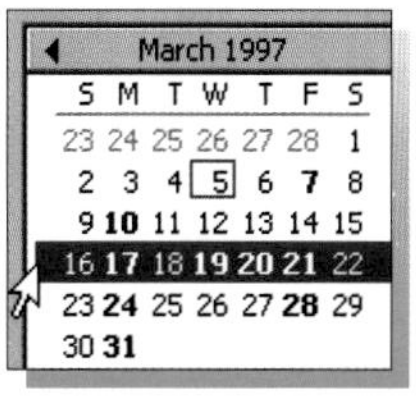

3 To view the weekly calendar, position your mouse pointer to the left of one of the rows in the Date Navigator. Be sure the mouse pointer changes from pointing to the top left to pointing to the top right, otherwise you will only succeed in highlighting the leftmost date in the row.

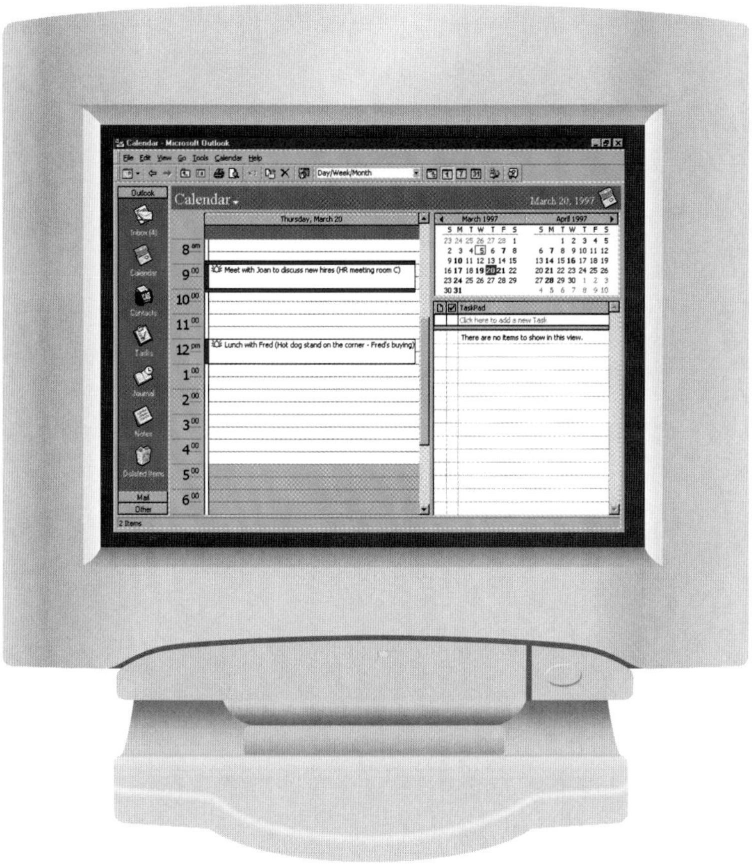

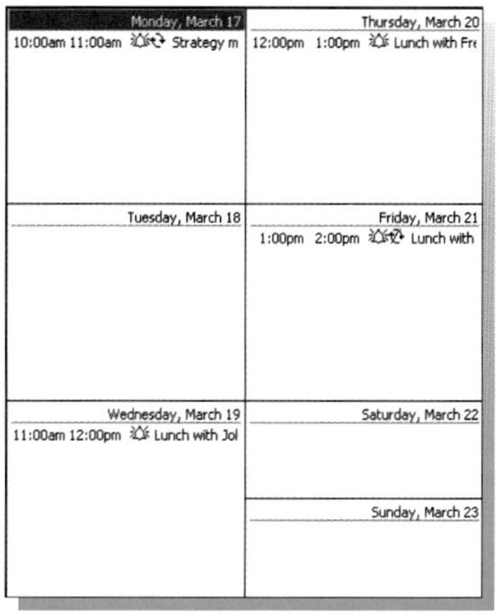

4 Click to highlight the row and automatically open the weekly calendar. The weekly calendar appears in place of the daily calendar, while the Date Navigator and the TaskPad remain the same.

5 You can also use the Date Navigator to change to a monthly calendar. Position your mouse pointer over one of the day headers (S M T W T F S) in the Date Navigator.

How to Use the Day/Week/Month View

Earlier you learned to use the Date Navigator to open the different views that the Day/Week/Month view affords. Now it's time to take it a step further and put those views to good practical use. An appointment calendar is not a static thing. Although the days and dates will probably remain consistent for the foreseeable future, your activities are bound to go through some changes. You can use the Day/Week/Month views to see that information and make any necessary changes. Since the daily calendar view was covered pretty thoroughly, we'll concentrate on the weekly and monthly views in this chapter.

FYI

- **To make a copy of an existing appointment on a date different from the original date, use the right mouse button to drag the appointment to the new date. From the pop-up menu that appears when you drop the appointment, choose Copy. The original appointment remains where it was and a copy is placed in the new date.**
- **You can edit a recurring appointment series by right-clicking on the appointment and choosing Edit Series from the pop-up menu.**

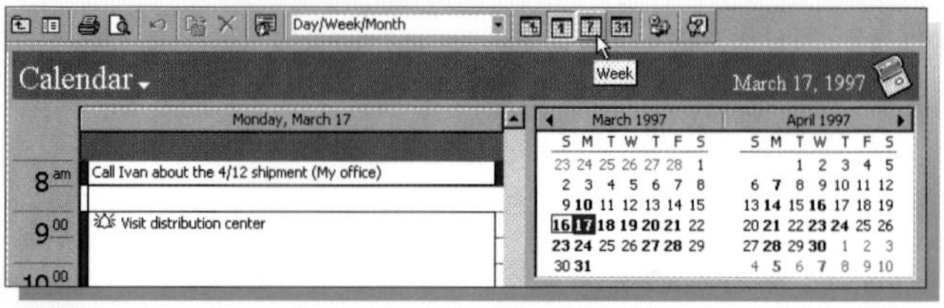

1 To open the weekly view, select a date that falls within the week you want to see, then click the Week icon in the Calendar toolbar. Note that the Day, Week, and Month icons are only available in the Day/Week/Month view.

6 To see the daily calendar for a particular date while in the monthly calendar, right-click in a blank area of a specific date box. From the pop-up menu choose Go to This Day to open the daily calendar for the selected date.

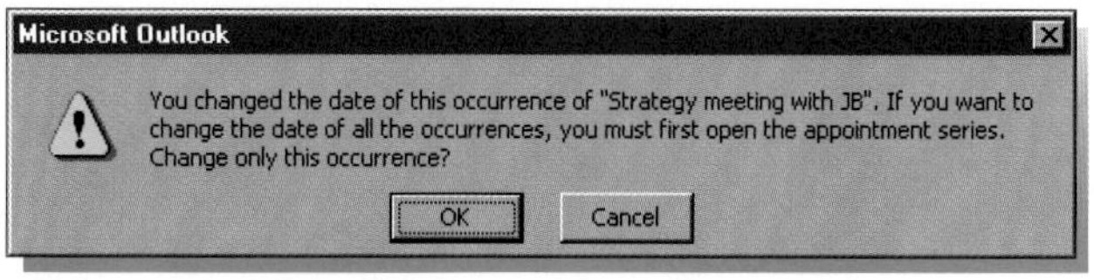

5 As in the weekly calendar, you can change the date of an appointment by dragging it from its original date to a new date on the calendar. However, when rescheduling a recurring appointment by dragging it, you can only change the occurrence you are dragging, not the entire series of occurrences. In both the monthly and weekly views you must open the recurring appointment to reschedule the series of occurrences.

2 Selecting the Week view brings up a weekly calendar with the current week displayed. Since most appointments occur on work days, which are generally Monday through Friday, those days are shown in full, while Saturday and Sunday share a time block.

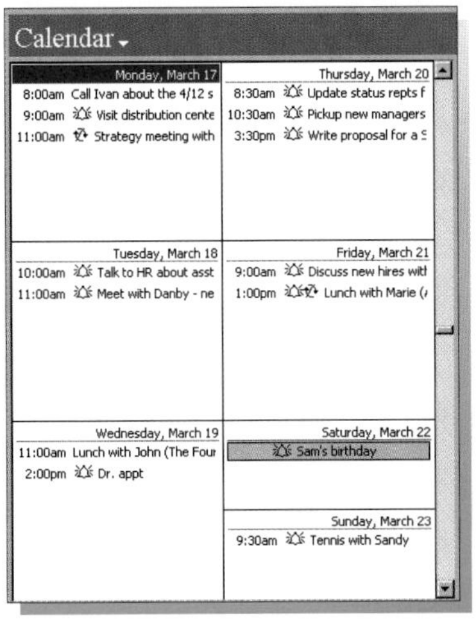

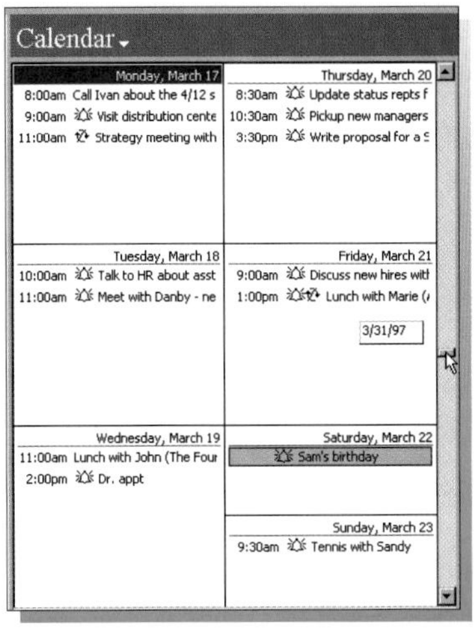

3 To change the week displayed in the weekly view, grab the scroll box in the scroll bar on the right side of the weekly calendar and drag it up or down to show previous or future weeks. As you drag the scroll box, a small window pops up indicating the week that will display if you release the mouse button at this point.

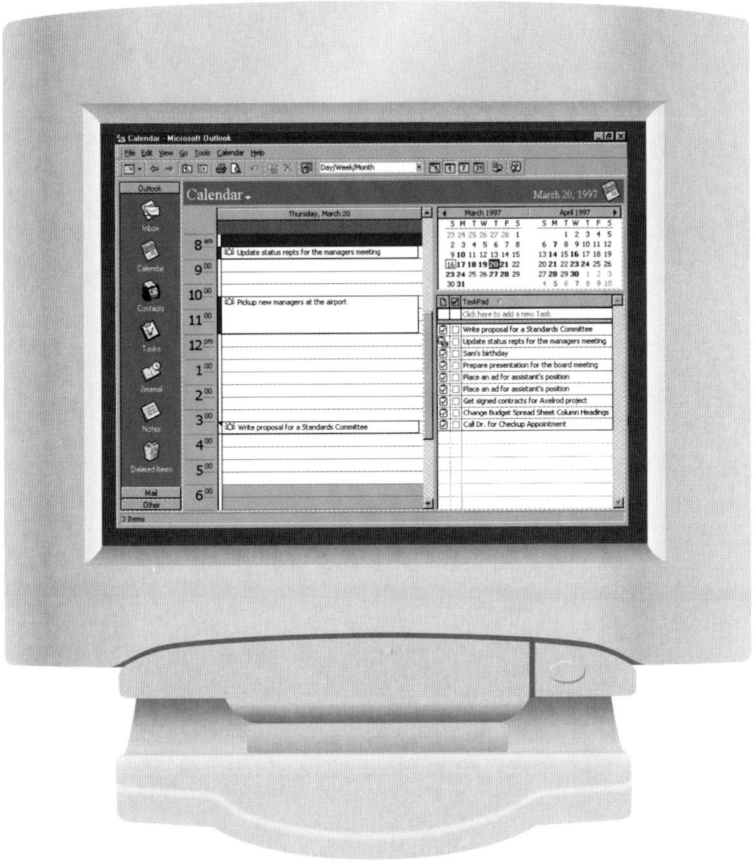

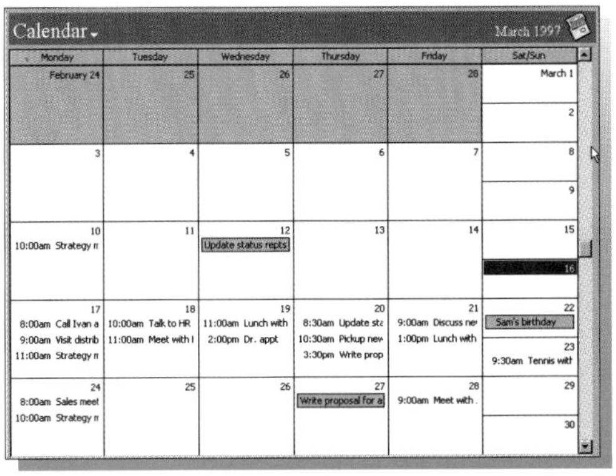

4 To open the monthly calendar, click the month icon on the Calendar toolbar. Unlike the daily and weekly views, the monthly view takes up the entire Information Viewer, causing the Date Navigator and TaskPad to disappear.

How to Use Calendar Table Views

The daily, weekly, and monthly views of the Calendar are very useful, but they are by no means the only views available for scrutinizing your schedule.

There are several table (list) views that you can use to help determine where you are spending your time, and that knowledge may improve your efficiency. Table views are set up in rows and columns. The rows represent single records and the columns represent the fields within each record.

1. To take a look at all of the upcoming appointments that are currently on your schedule, select Active Appointments from the Current View drop-down list on the Calendar toolbar.

FYI

- **To create a subgroup in a table view quickly, right-click the column header of the field by which you want to subgroup the appointments, and choose Group By This Field.**

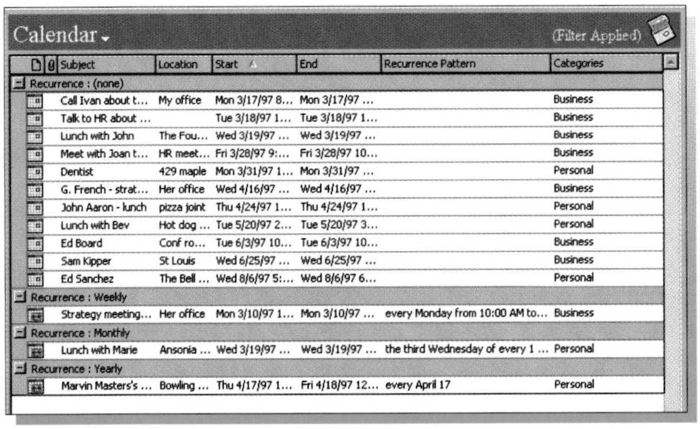

2 The Active Appointments view provides you with a listing of all appointments that are due from today forward. On the right side of the Calendar banner you see the words **(Filter Applied)**, indicating that a filter has been automatically applied to this view. All appointments with due dates earlier than today's date are filtered out.

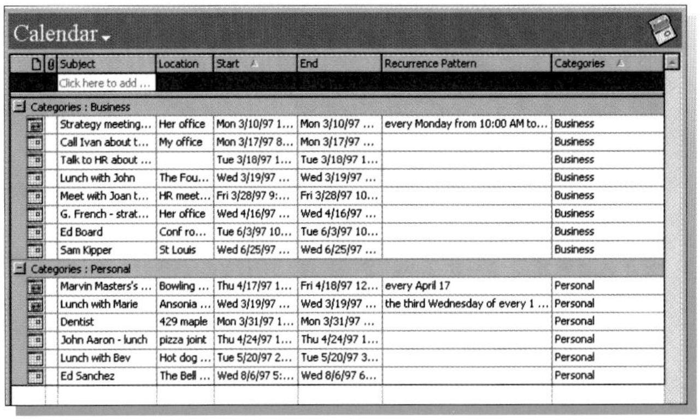

3 Another handy table view is the By Category view. It lists all appointments, past and present, and separates them into groups based on the categories to which they have been assigned (if you're using categories). It's an easy way to maintain both personal and business appointments on the same calendar.

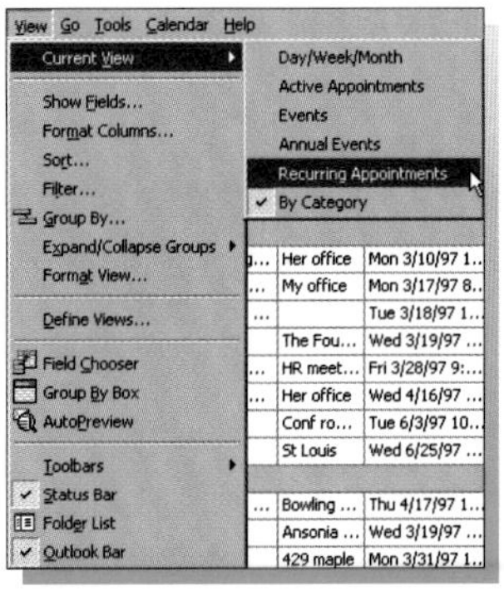

4 You can also switch views by using the menu bar. To see all your recurring appointments only, switch to the Recurring Appointments view by choosing View, Current View, Recurring Appointments from the Calendar menu bar.

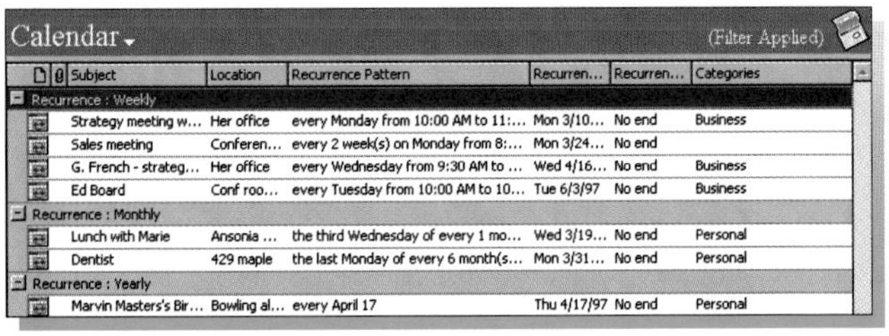

5 The Recurring Appointments view automatically filters out all appointments except recurring appointments, which it then groups by recurrence. The Recurring Appointments view provides an easy way to avoid scheduling conflicting appointments and to see the long-term effects of your scheduling decisions.

How to Modify Your Work Week

The Calendar work week settings determine the days and hours that are available for appointments and meetings on the daily calendar. Days and hours which are not considered work times appear grayed out on the daily calendar. Appointments can still be scheduled for these dates and times, it's just that the gray is a reminder that these are considered non-working hours.

The Calendar work week settings also determine the first day of your week as well as the first week of your year.

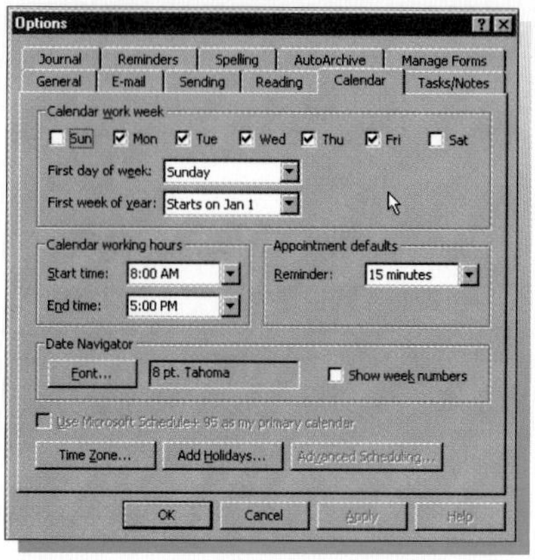

1 To change the Calendar work week, choose Tools, Options to open the Options dialog box. Click the Calendar tab to access options specific to the Calendar window.

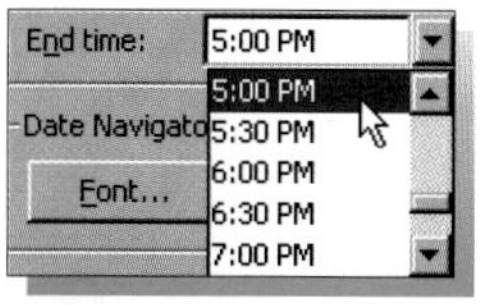

6 The next setting is the hour at which your workday ends. From the drop-down list in the End Time field select the hour that brings a close to your workday. The Start Time and End Time fields determine how the hours appear on the daily calendar. Click OK to save your changes and close the dialog box.

FYI

- **Changing the First Day of Week option automatically changes the days selected for the Calendar work week. If you wish to keep the workdays as they are and only change the first day of the week, remember to reset the days after selecting a new first day of the week.**

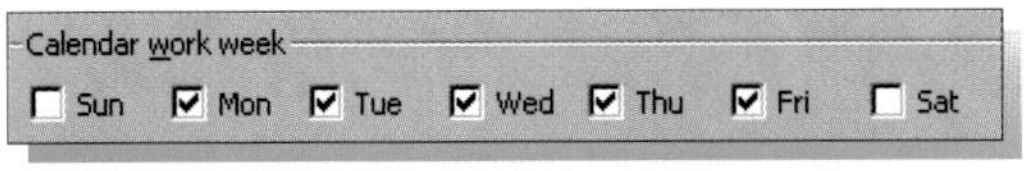

2 Click the box to the left of the days that make up your work week to place checkmarks in them, and remove the checkmarks from the boxes of those days that are not part of your work week.

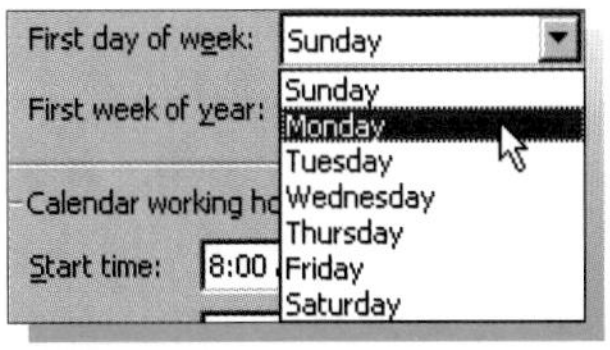

3 The next option is the First Day of Week option. This determines the start day of your work week. Click the down arrow at the end of the field and choose the day you want from the drop-down list. Whichever day you select appears in the leftmost day column of the Date Navigator.

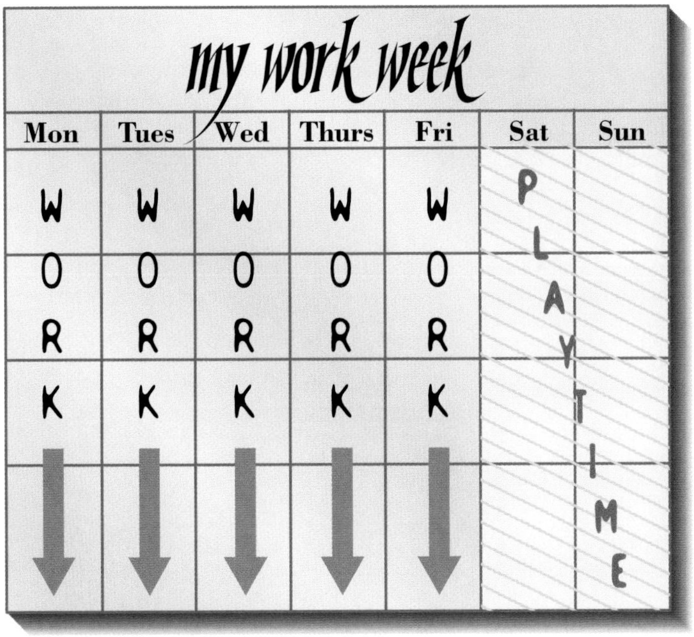

4 Move to the First Week of Year field to determine how your year starts. Click the down arrow at the end of the field and select the appropriate option. Your choices include Starts on January 1, the First 4-day Week of the Year, or the First Full Week of the Year. In other words your work year starts with the first day of the year, or with the first week that has only four workdays, or with the first week that has five workdays (no holidays).

5 Now it's on to the Calendar working hours. Set the hour at which your workday begins by clicking the down arrow at the end of the Start Time field, and making a selection from the drop-down list. You can also enter the time by typing it in, but be sure to get the A.M. or P.M. setting right.

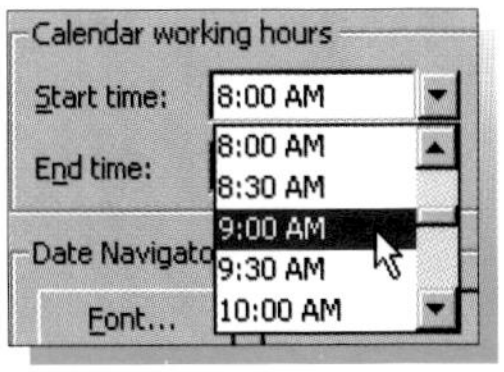

How to Set Reminder Options

Reminders help you stay on schedule by tapping you on the shoulder when an appointment or task is due. To get the most mileage from them you may have to change some of the reminder options. You can modify the amount of time prior to an appointment that a reminder displays. You can elect to have reminders display without playing a sound. You can even turn all reminders off temporarily if you need absolute peace and quiet to concentrate.

Both global reminder options (options that affect reminders anywhere in Outlook) and Calendar-specific reminder options can be modified from any Outlook window.

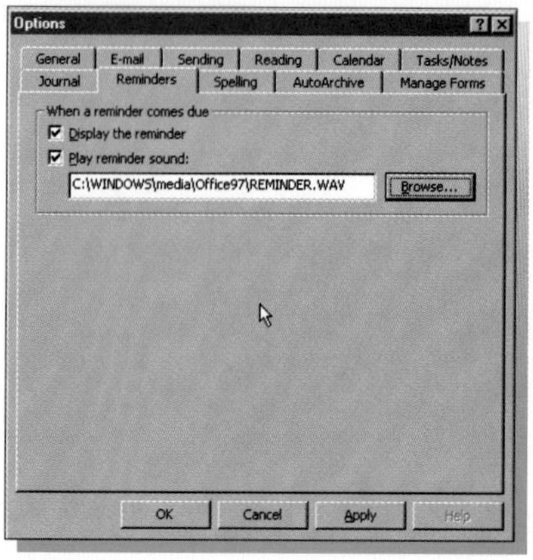

1 Choose Tools, Options from the menu bar to open the Options dialog box. Click the Reminders tab to access the reminders options. The Display the Reminder and Play Reminder sound options are enabled (checkmarked) by default. The REMINDER.WAV file, which plays a chiming sound when a reminder appears, is the default sound file.

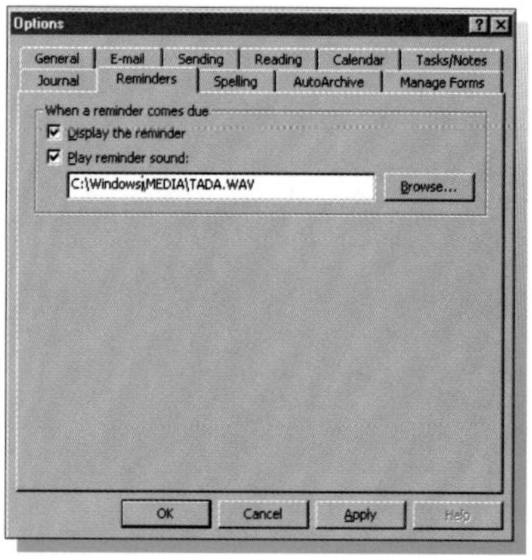

6 The new sound file and its location are inserted in the text box to the left of the Browse button. This sound will play with all reminders in Outlook. Click OK to make the changes permanent.

FYI

- **It's a good idea to set reminders well in advance of an appointment to give yourself time to prepare. When the reminder displays, you can opt to tell it to reappear at a time nearer the actual appointment.**
- **You can change the sound file played in conjunction with a specific appointment reminder by clicking the speaker icon next to the Reminder Time field in the Appointment form. Use the Browse button in the Reminder Sound dialog box to locate and select the sound file to use for this particular appointment.**

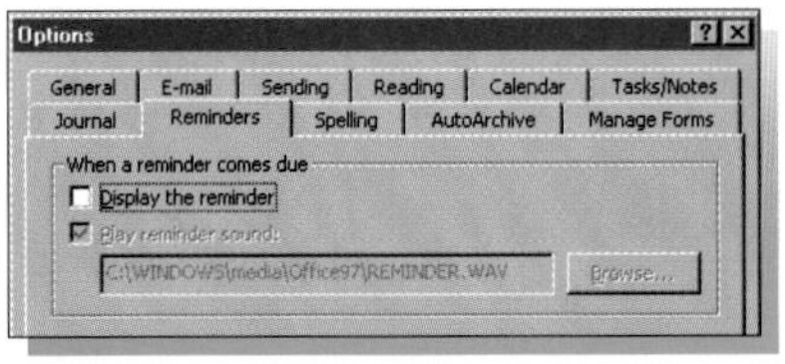

2 To disable all reminders throughout Outlook, click the Display the Reminder option to remove the checkmark. Until you click the checkbox again (which puts a checkmark back in this box), reminders are turned off. Note that the Play Reminder Sound and the Browse feature are now both grayed out (unavailable). You cannot set a sound to play without displaying a visual reminder as well.

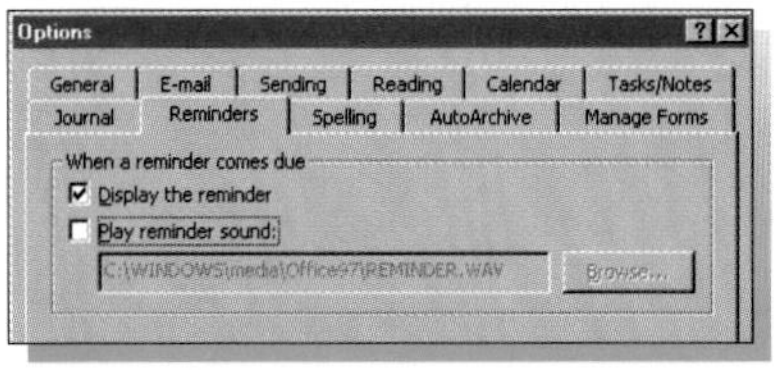

3 You can, however, display a visual reminder without playing a sound file. To eliminate the playing of a sound when reminders appear anywhere in Outlook, click the Play Reminder Sound option to remove the checkmark. From this point forward all reminders will be silent.

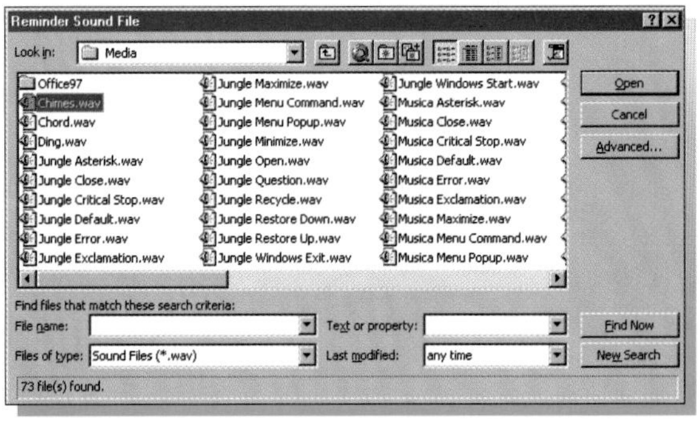

4 If you do want sounds with reminders, you can change the default sound. Find your sound files by clicking the Browse button, then moving to the folder where sound files are kept. You can usually find sound files in a folder named Media, under the folder for your operating system, for example C:\Windows\Media. Your operating system may be in a folder named Windows95 or Winnt.

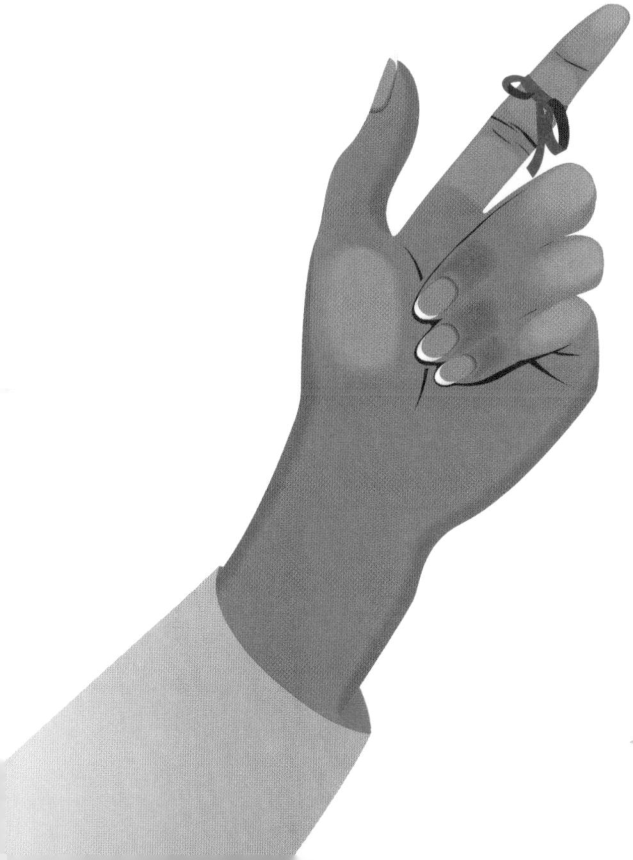

5 When you get to a folder with sound files (they have an extension of .wav), you can check out the sounds before you select one. Right-click the icon for a sound file and choose Play. The Windows Sound Recorder opens and you can hear the sound. When you find one you like, close the Sound Recorder and double-click the file.

How to Create an Additional Time Zone

If any of your business dealings involve contacts in another part of the country or another part of the world, or if you have relatives that live far away, you'll appreciate the ability to create a second time zone in the Outlook Calendar. The default time bar in the daily calendar is established using your Windows 95 or Windows NT time zone settings. You can use the Calendar Time Zone option to create a second time bar, adjacent to the default time bar.

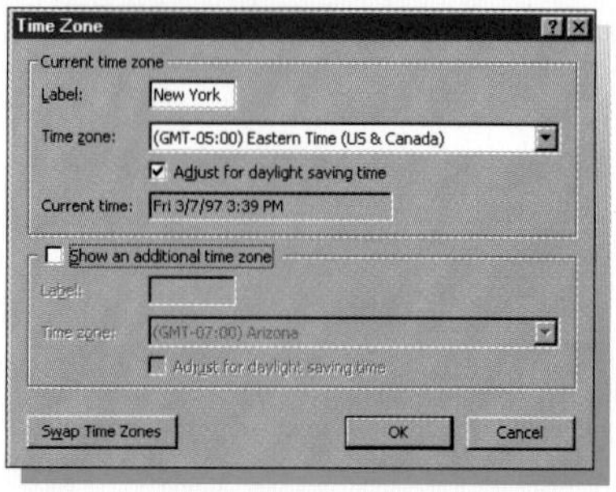

1 Select Tools, Options from the menu bar to open the Options dialog box. From the Calendar tab of the Options dialog box click the Time Zone button to open the Time Zone dialog box.

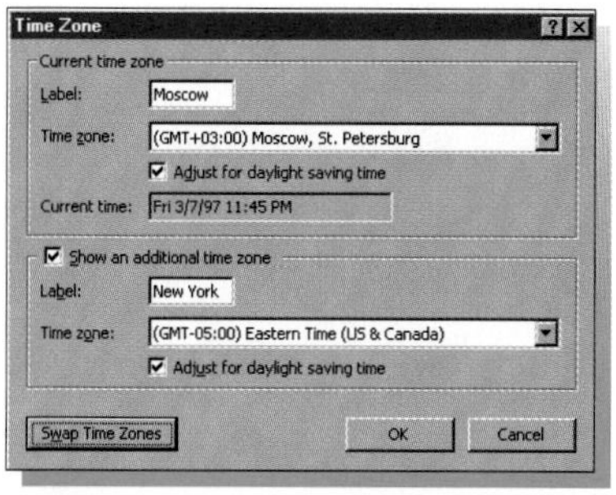

6 After you click the Swap Time Zones button, the current time zone and the additional time zone reverse locations on the Time Zone dialog box. The secondary zone becomes the current time zone and vice versa. When you're finished adding, swapping, or editing time zones, click OK on the Time Zone dialog box to return to the Options dialog box, then click OK again to close the dialog box.

FYI

- **Changing the current time zone in the Outlook Calendar options also resets the Windows 95 time zone setting for your computer. This affects all Windows programs that derive time and date settings from your computer's clock. Therefore, you should not reset your Outlook Current time zone to anything other than your own, unless you are prepared to have all time and date information adjusted accordingly.**
- **You can quickly add or change time zones by right-clicking on the time bar in the daily calendar and choosing Change Time Zone from the shortcut menu that pops up. When the Time Zone dialog box appears, make the necessary changes and click OK to return to the daily calendar.**

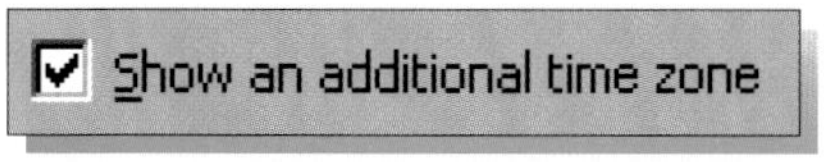

2 Click Show an Additional Time Zone to place a checkmark in the box and enable a second time zone.

3 In the Label field type a short title for the new time bar. Use something obvious like the city, state, or country name. Press the Tab key to move to the Time Zone field.

4 Click the down arrow at the end of the Time Zone field to open the drop-down list of available time zones. Select the appropriate time zone for the new time bar. If the new time zone supports daylight saving time, you can enable it by placing a checkmark in the Adjust for Daylight Saving Time checkbox.

5 If you occasionally travel between your home time zone and your second time zone, you can easily switch between the two by clicking the Swap Time Zones button.

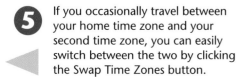

How to Add Holidays to the Calendar

Outlook comes with a large selection of national and international holidays that can be attached to your calendar. Since the selection is substantial, none of the holidays are automatically included in the calendar at installation. To put holidays in the Outlook Calendar you must select the holiday set you desire and import it. You can import as many sets of holidays as you wish.

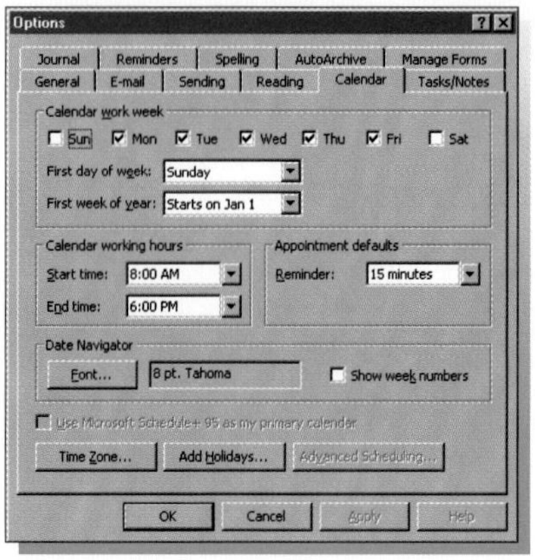

1 From the menu bar choose Tools, Options to open the Options dialog box. Click the Calendar tab to access the Calendar options. Click the Add Holidays button to open the Add Holidays to Calendar dialog box.

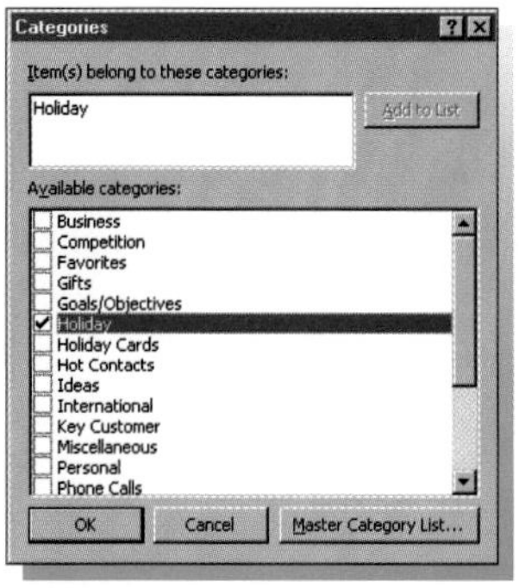

6 Click the Categories button to open the Categories dialog box. Select Holiday from the list, and click OK to return to the Recurring Event form. Click Save and Close to save the new holiday and return to Outlook.

FYI

- **You can type the name of holidays that occur on the same date every year into Outlook date fields rather than typing the date itself. For example, you could type Lincoln's Birthday in an appointment form start date if you didn't know it falls on February 12.**
- **If you are on an Exchange Server network, you can drag individual company holidays from the public folder that contains them onto your personal calendar.**

2 Scroll through the available holiday sets and place a checkmark next to each one you want to import. Select as many as you want, then click OK to begin the import process. After the import ends, click OK on the Options dialog box to close it.

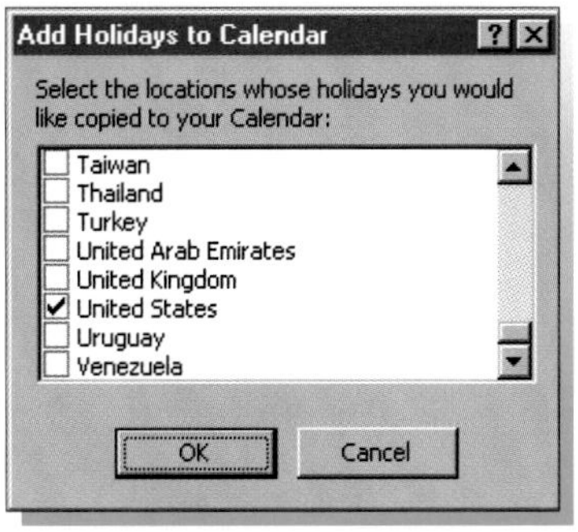

3 To ensure that the holidays have properly migrated to your calendar, change the date to that of a popular holiday such as July 4th. A brief description of the holiday appears in the daily calendar banner.

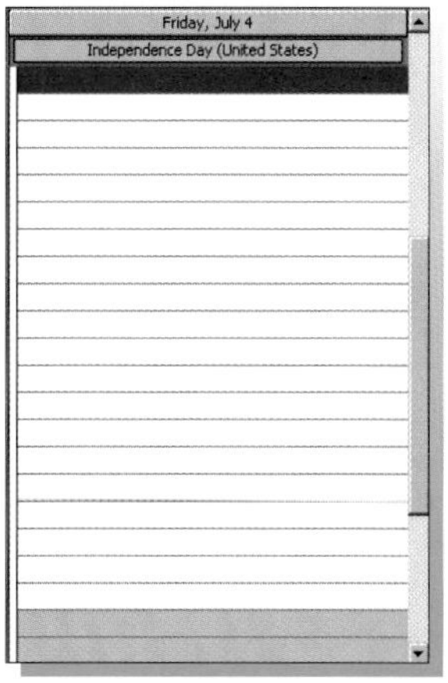

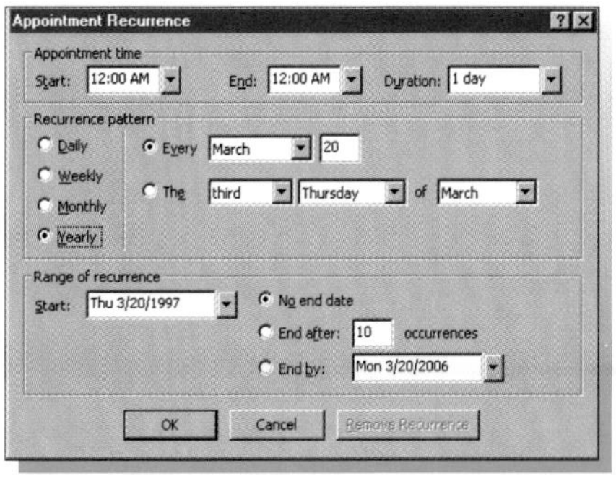

4 You can also create personal holidays for birthdays, anniversaries, or local celebrations. Choose Calendar, New Recurring Event from the menu bar to open the Appointment Recurrence dialog box. Fill in the appropriate information.

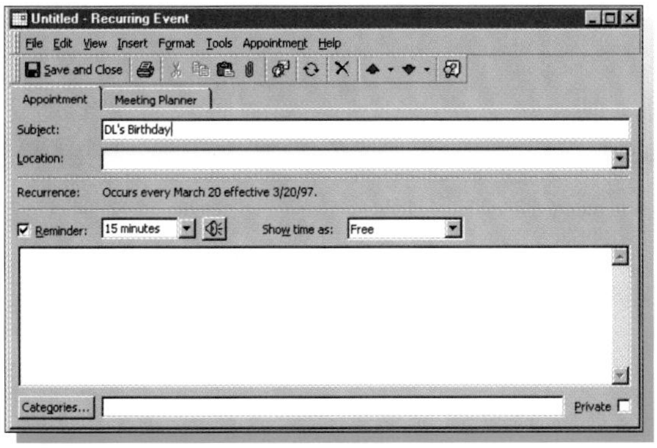

5 Click OK to save your changes and return to the Recurring Event form. Fill out the Recurring Event form. You can supply as little or as much information as you wish.

How to Print Your Appointment Schedule

Printing your appointment schedule can be a convenient way of keeping track of your appointments. For example, if you are going on a business trip, it is handy to have a copy of your meetings and appointments that you can refer to or even write notes on. You can print them by day, week, or however long you want. You can also change the specific days you want to print and how your appointments appear.

On this page, you'll learn how to select various options for printing your scheduled appointments.

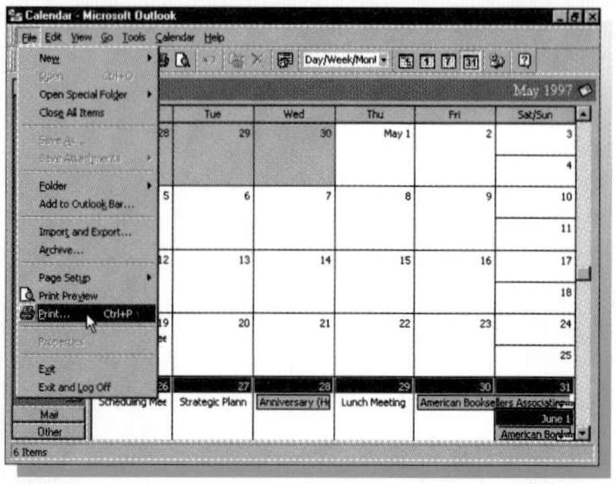

1 Click on the date or group of dates that contain the appointments you would like to print. You can choose to print a day, week, month, or even a year. For example, select seven consecutive days. Choose Print from the File menu.

FYI

- **A quick way to print anything in Outlook is to use the Print button on the toolbar. The button looks like a printer.**
- **If you print your appointment schedule and you do not see any appointments on the schedule, you probably need to make sure you have the correct start and end dates selected in the Print range.**
- **An alternative to printing your appointments by date is to print *all* your scheduled appointments in the Active Appointments view. Choose the Active Appointments option from the Current View drop-down list box on the toolbar. From this view, you might need to increase the width for some of the columns like Subject, Start, and End to make the information visible. Then click the Print button on the toolbar.**

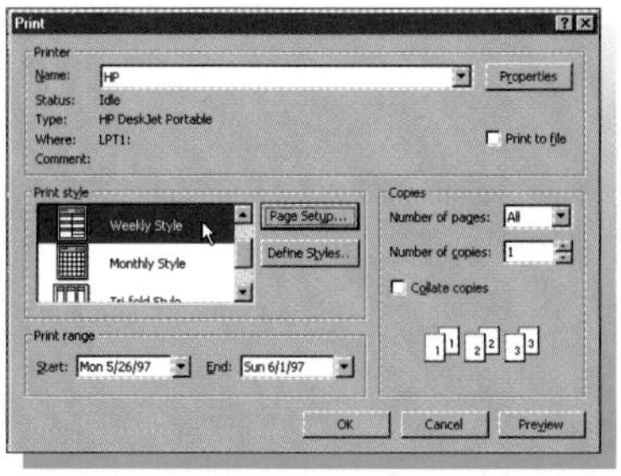

2 The Print dialog box will appear with numerous options to choose from. Choose the print style that you wish your appointments to be printed in. Because seven consecutive days were selected, click the Weekly Style option.

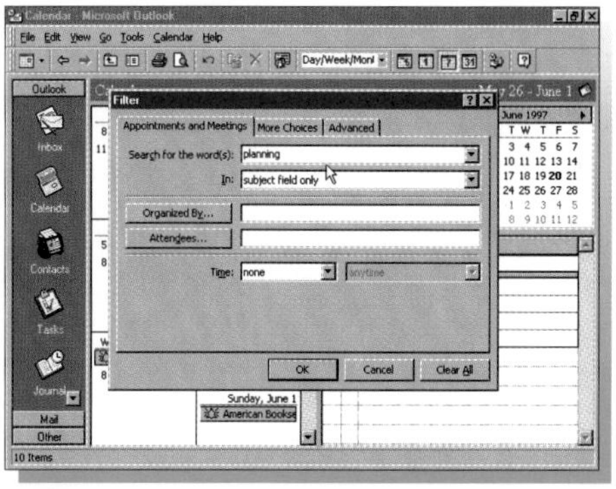

3 The dates you chose on the calendar should appear as start and end days for the Print range. If not, select the correct dates from the drop-down list boxes. Click on the Page Setup button to alter the look of your printout.

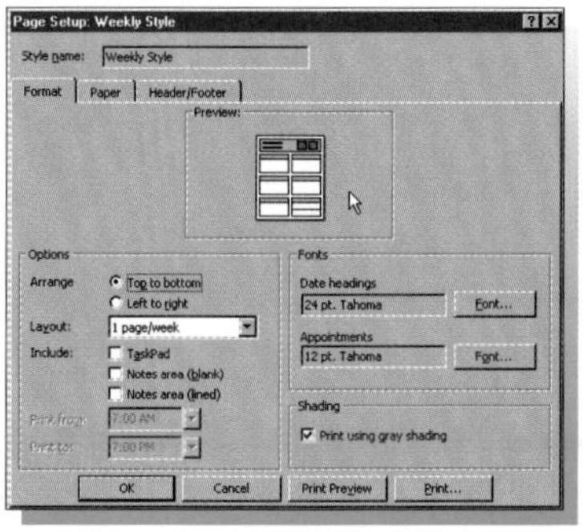

4 The Page Setup button allows you to alter the arrangement of your days: top to bottom or left to right. Click on the Left to Right button and you can see a preview of what the printout will look like. Click the OK button to return to the Print dialog box.

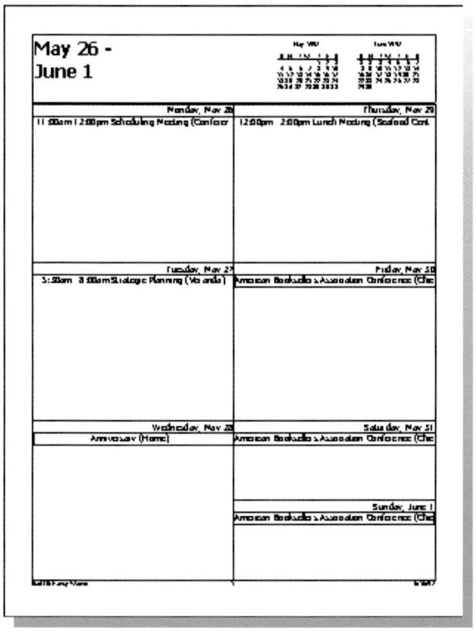

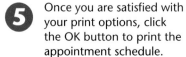

5 Once you are satisfied with your print options, click the OK button to print the appointment schedule.

How to Filter the Calendar View

Now that you have entered numerous different types of appointments, events, and holidays, your calendar might be looking a little cluttered. To alleviate this, you can view your calendar so that it only shows the specific events you wish to view. For example, if you must attend a week of planning meetings, you might have to miss other meetings you have scheduled. By simply filtering your calendar for only the planning meetings, you can organize your day accordingly. To do this, you will view only items that meet conditions you specify.

On this page, you'll learn how to filter calendar entries, which will help you organize your schedule.

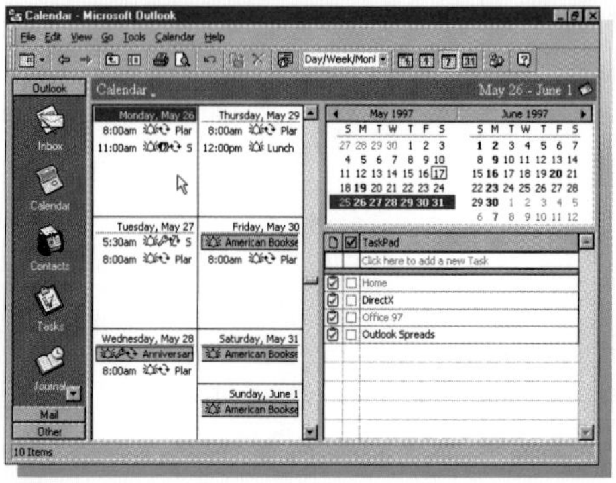

1 Open the Outlook group on the Outlook Bar. Click on the Calendar icon and the Week button on the toolbar. All the scheduled meetings, appointments, and events that you have made will be displayed in a calendar week.

6 The Calendar view will appear with the filter applied. Notice that there are only certain meetings that meet the specific filter criteria. Your other meetings are still on your calendar; they are simply not visible with this filter.

FYI

- **If you have numerous appointments with similar subject names, you might need to use a more sophisticated filter on your schedule. You can make your filter more selective by using the More Choices and the Advanced tabs in the Filter dialog box.**
- **To remove a filter on your Calendar view, choose Filter from the View menu. The Filter dialog box will appear with the criteria for your current filter. Click the Clear All button to remove the filter and clear the criteria. Then click the OK button to once again see all the entries in the Calendar view.**

2 Choose Filter from the View menu.

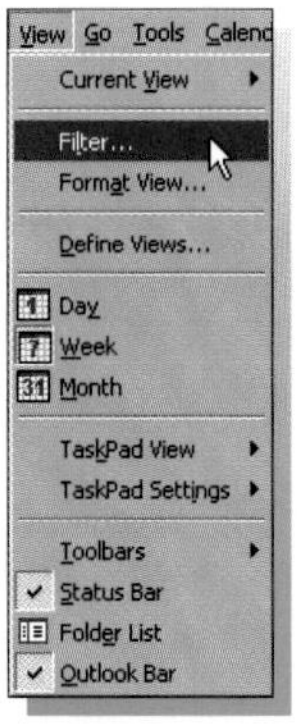

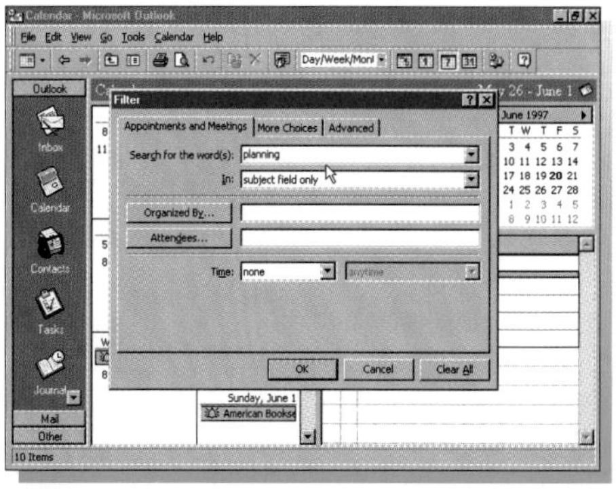

3 The Filter dialog box will appear, which will allow you to filter items in your calendar view by different criteria. From the Appointments and Meetings tab of the Filter dialog box, type a key word in the Search for the Word(s) list box. Select Subject Field Only from the In drop-down list box. When finished making your selections, click the OK button.

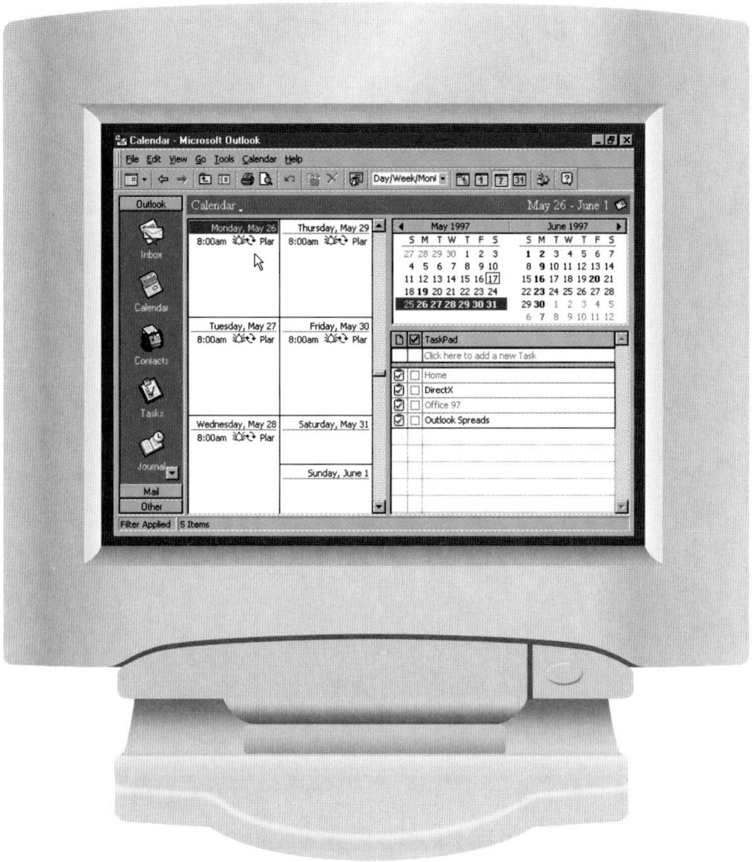

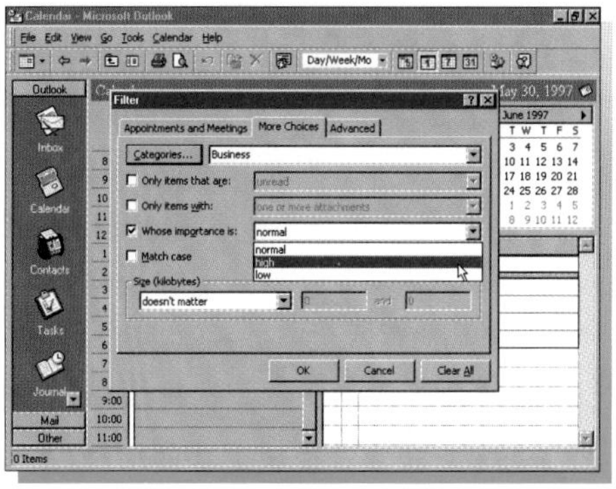

4 The Filter dialog box also has a More Choices tab that allows you to filter calendar items by category, item details, importance, case, or size. When you are finished making your selections, click the OK button.

5 The Filter dialog box also has an Advanced tab that allows you to define filter criteria. When you are finished making your selections, click the OK button.

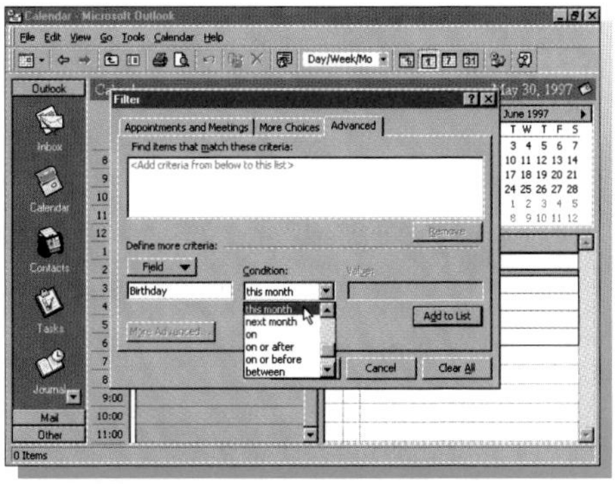

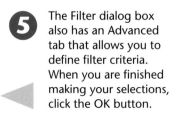

Ctrl + Shift + U=
New Task
Request
Ctrl + N=
New Task

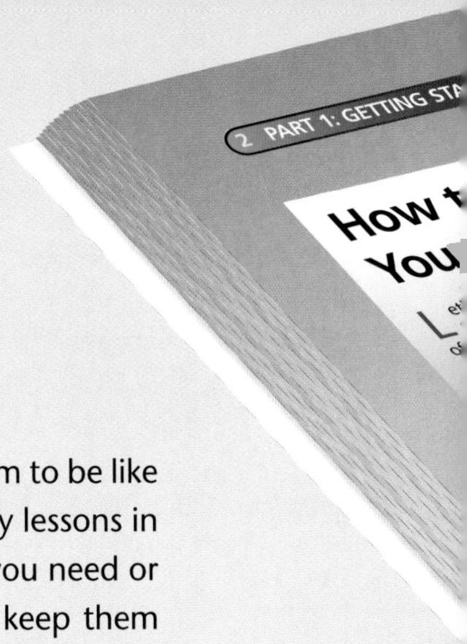

P A R T 4

Using Tasks

"USING TASKS" may not be the appropriate title for this part. Since tasks seem to be like amoebae because they reproduce spontaneously, you probably don't need any lessons in how to create them. You undoubtedly have more (tasks, not amoebae) than you need or want right now. As a matter of fact, what most of us could use is a way to keep them under control and prevent them from overwhelming us. And that is precisely what this part is all about.

The title of this part should be *Creating Tasks in Outlook so That You Can Become the Master of Your Tasks Instead of the Other Way Around.* For some strange reason the publisher of this book insists that such a part title is too long and convoluted for the Table of Contents. So we're stuck with Using Tasks, but at least you and I know what the part is really about.

To begin working with tasks, switch to the Tasks folder by clicking the Tasks icon in the Outlook Bar.

IN THIS SECTION YOU'LL LEARN

How to Create Tasks Quickly

Depending on the type of To Do list you require, you can make an Outlook task as simple or complex as you like. Outlook provides several ways to create a task. Since we're looking for the quickest way to create a task, let's start with the electronic equivalent of scribbling a quick entry on a lined notepad.

With that in mind, switch to the Tasks folder by clicking the Tasks icon in the Outlook Bar.

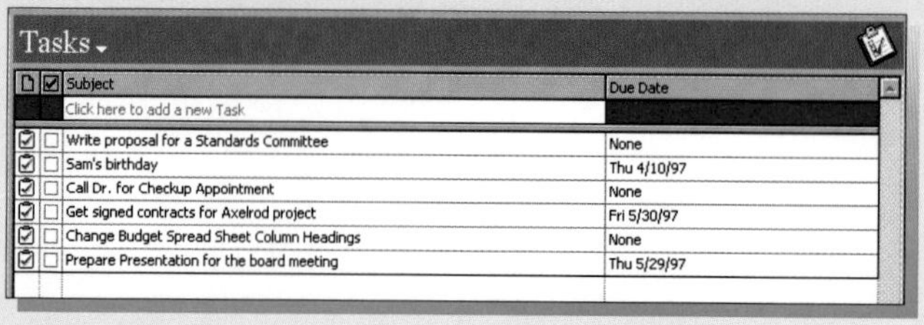

1 The default view in the Tasks information viewer is the Simple List. It doesn't get much simpler than a subject and a due date. The top line of the listing says "Click here to add a new task." Click there. The text disappears and you can enter the name of a task. Make the name a brief description of the task.

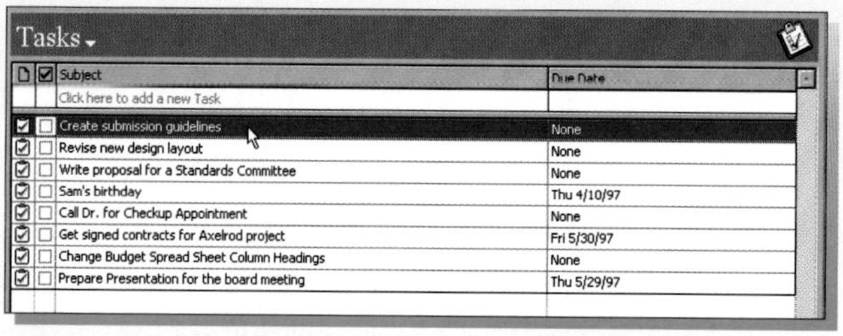

5 When you get back to the Tasks information viewer, you'll see that the new task you created in the TaskPad now appears on the Simple List. From here you can add a due date if you so choose.

FYI

- **It's not necessary to enter a due date when you create a task in the Tasks information viewer. However, as you learn more about using tasks and planning your time according to the tasks on your list, you'll find that being able to arrange tasks by due date is convenient. If you don't enter a due date when you create the task, be sure to go back and add it later.**

2 Click the Due Date text box to activate the down arrow at the end of the field. Click the down arrow and select a due date from the drop-down calendar that appears.

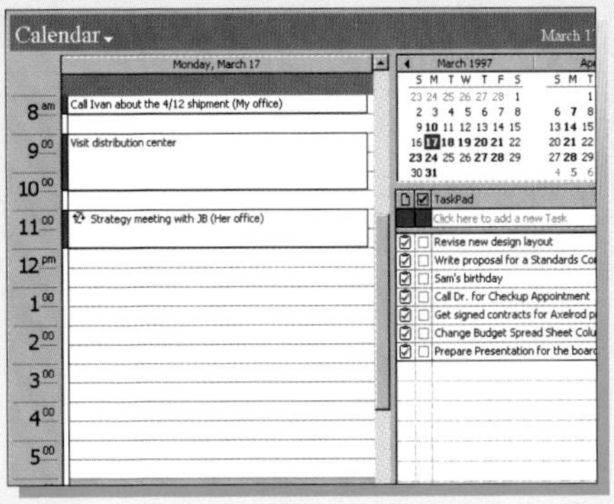

3 If you happen to be working in the Calendar and while you're creating an appointment (or checking up on one) you realize there's something you need to do to get ready for that appointment, you're in luck. Outlook conveniently provides a scaled-down version of the task list in the form of the TaskPad.

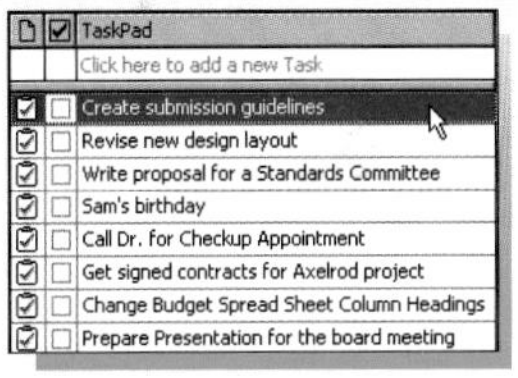

4 As in the Simple List of the Tasks folder, you can jot down a quick description of your new task in the blank line at the top of the TaskPad and press Enter to add it to the list.

How to Create Tasks with Details

When you're in a hurry and need to jot a task down before you forget it, you can't beat entering it in the Simple List or in the TaskPad. However, when the task calls for more information and closer tracking, you can use a Task card to provide the details that such a task requires.

If you're not in the Tasks folder click the Tasks icon in the Outlook Bar to switch to the Tasks information viewer.

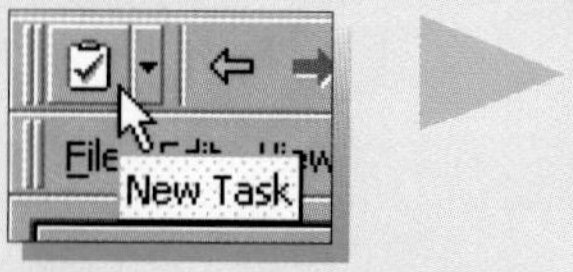

1 To open a new task card click the New Task icon in the toolbar.

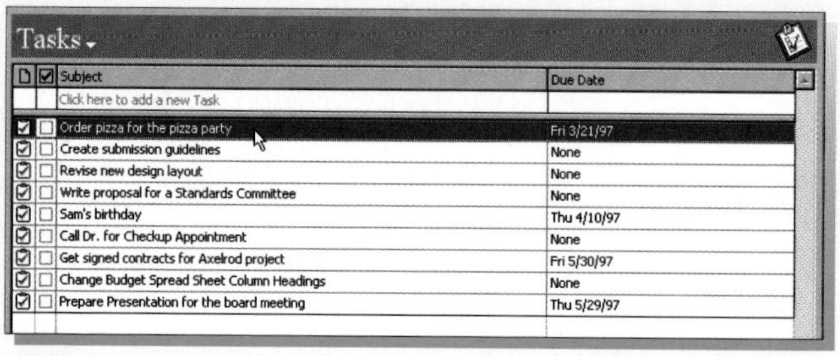

6 Move your cursor to the text box and type in any notes that you need to help complete the task. Click Save and Close to return to the Tasks information viewer, where you can see that the new task has been added to the Simple List.

FYI

- **You can reorganize the unsorted Simple List by dragging and dropping tasks from one place on the list to another. If the list has been sorted, the sort conditions override manual placement. To remove sort conditions choose View, Sort from the menu bar and click the Clear All button. Click OK twice to return to the now unsorted list.**

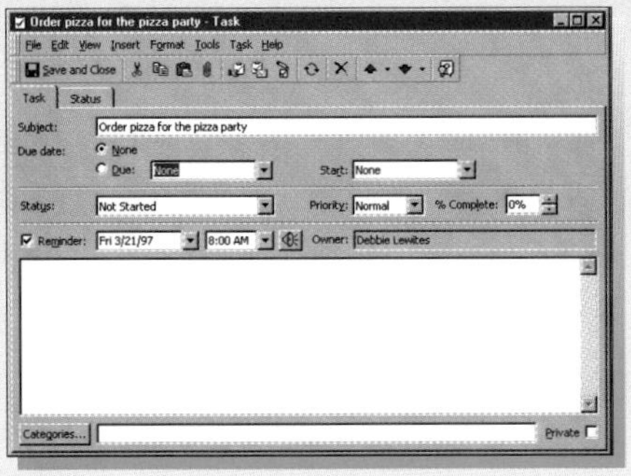

2 Enter a brief description of the task in the Subject field. Make it descriptive enough so you won't have difficulty deciphering it later on, when it's no longer fresh in your memory.

3 Click the down arrow in the Due field and select a due date from the drop-down calendar. You can also type in the date if you know it, or you can type in an English command such as **next Friday**, or **one week from Tuesday**.

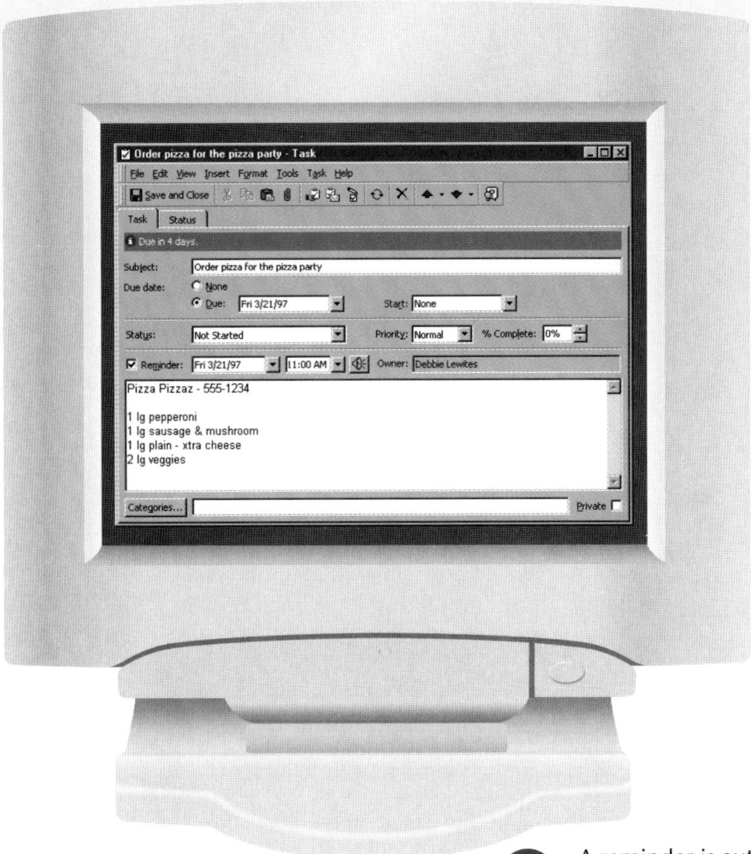

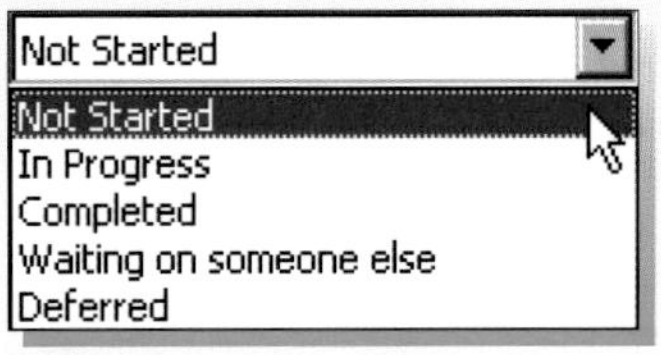

4 Move to the Status field and click the down arrow to the right to open the drop-down list of status options. The choices are self explanatory. Select one that best fits the situation.

5 A reminder is automatically set for 8:00 A.M. on the due date. You can change the date by using the drop-down calendar or typing in the date. To change the time at which the reminder appears, click the down arrow in the reminder time field and select the hour from the drop-down list.

How to Create and Manage Recurring Tasks

One of the most enjoyable things about a To Do list is crossing items off of it. Unfortunately, there is always a handful of tasks that just won't go away. Like the neighborhood dog who has a thing for your rosebushes, some tasks keeping returning on a regular basis, week after week or month after month.

There's only one thing to do with tasks like this—turn them into recurring tasks so that you don't have to keep adding them to your list every week or month.

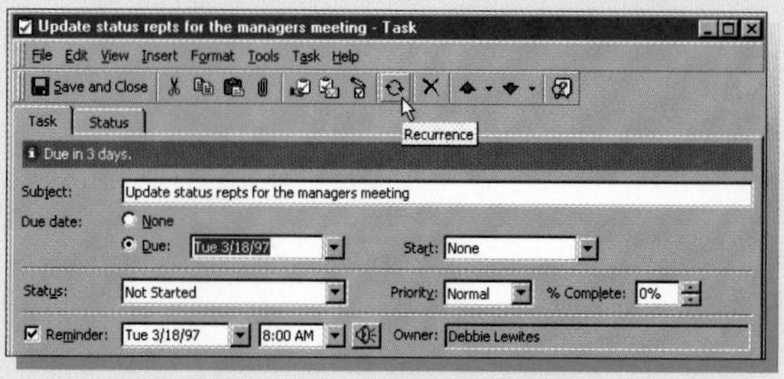

1 Click the Tasks icon in the Outlook Bar to return to the Tasks folder. Press Ctrl+N to open a new Task card. Fill out the Task card with the appropriate information. Then click the Recurrence icon in the Task Card toolbar to open the Task Recurrence dialog box.

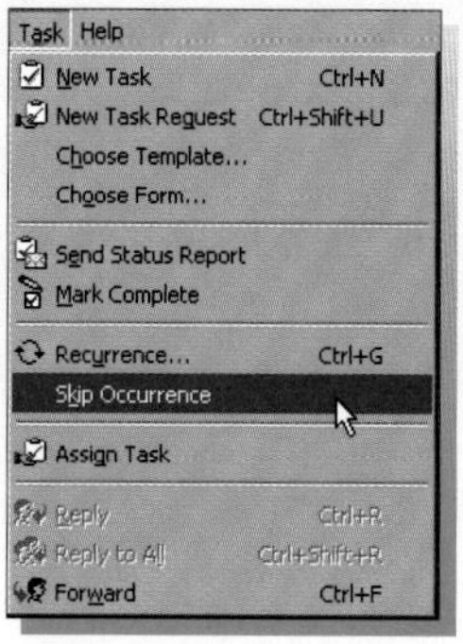

6 You can also skip an occurrence of a recurring task by double-clicking the task and opening the Task card. Choose Task, Skip Occurrence from the Task card menu bar. The upcoming occurrence is deleted and the following occurrence becomes the next one due.

FYI

- **When deleting a task you get no final warning. Once you select Delete All or Delete This One and click OK, the task is sent directly to the Deleted Items folder. If you've made a mistake you can switch to the Deleted Items folder and retrieve the task by dragging it onto the Tasks item in the Outlook Bar.**
- **Each time you finish an occurrence of a recurring task, you must mark it as completed before the next occurrence shows up on your To Do list. This is important to remember because the task's reminders will not work if the task on your list is an outdated one.**

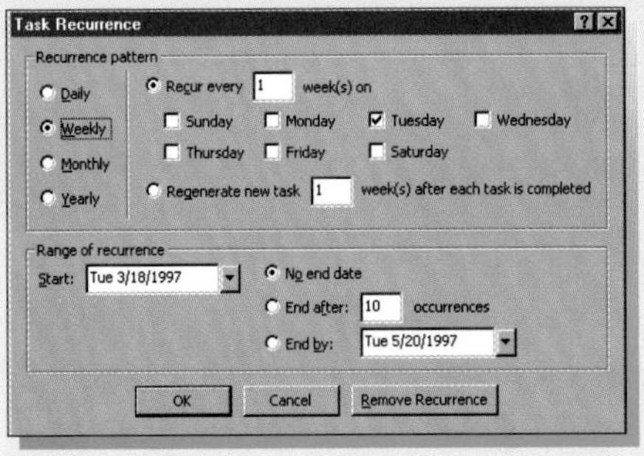

2 Select the recurrence pattern for the task. Based on the day and date you entered in the original Task card Due Date field, the default setting is for the Task to recur once a week on the day upon which the first task is due. You can choose a different pattern by clicking on your selection to place a checkmark in the box to the left. In the Range of Recurrence section indicate the start date, and the end date if there is one. Click OK to save your settings and return to the Task card.

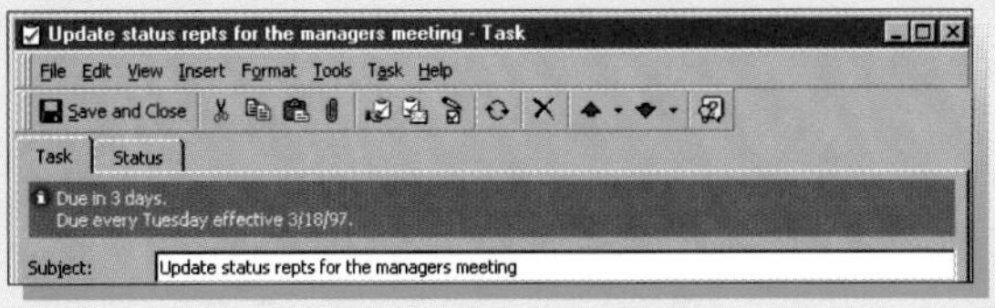

3 Notice that the Task card information banner now indicates the recurrence pattern of the new task. Click Save and Close to save the new task and return to the Tasks information viewer.

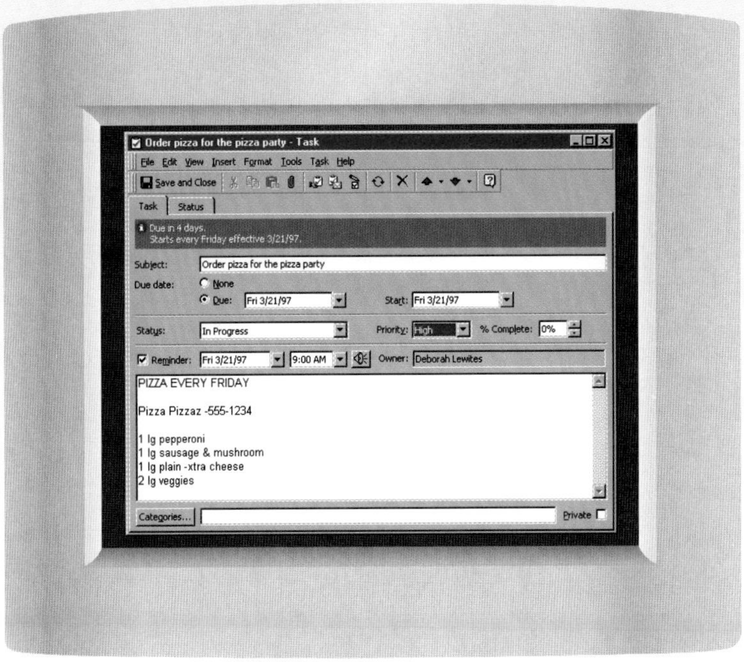

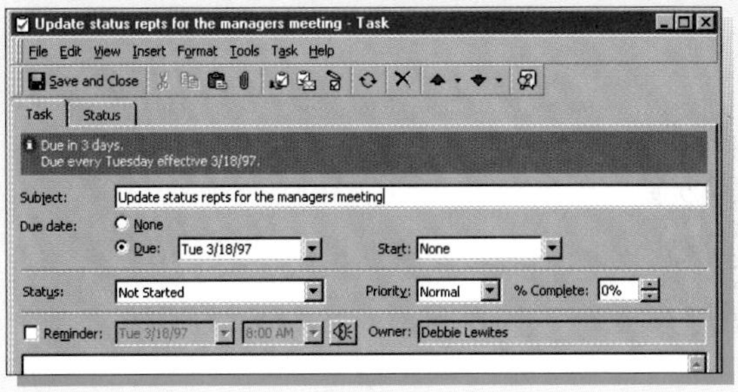

4 If you need to edit a recurring task for any reason, simply double-click on it to open the Task card. Make any necessary changes. If you need to change the recurrence pattern, click the Recurrence icon and make the appropriate edits to the Task Recurrence options. When you're through editing the task, click Save and Close to save the changes and return to the Tasks folder.

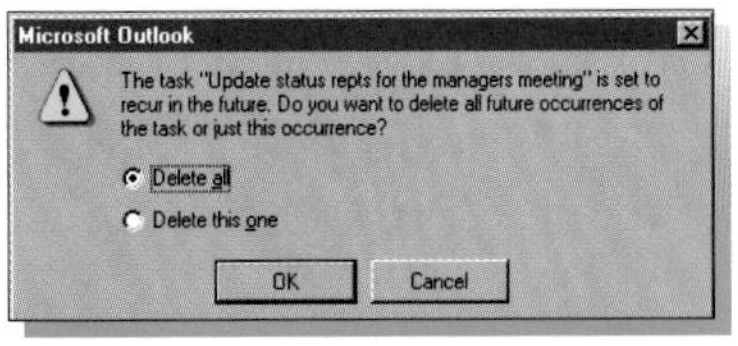

5 Occasionally fate grins broadly at you and a recurring task comes to an end. Other times fate only smiles at you and the task gets suspended temporarily. In either event you can delete a single occurrence of the task or the entire series of occurrences. Highlight the task and click the Delete icon in the toolbar. From the dialog box that appears select Delete All to eradicate the recurring task totally, or select Delete This One to eliminate this occurrence of the task only. After you make your selection, click OK to delete the task.

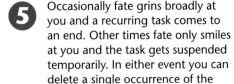

How to Use TaskPad Views in the Calendar Window

By now you have probably entered and completed numerous tasks in Outlook. If you want to look at a list of your tasks, there are different views that you can select. Some of the possibilities are All Tasks, Today's Tasks, Active Tasks for Several Days, Tasks for Next Seven Days, Overdue Tasks, and Tasks Completed on Selected Days. Taking a look at these different views will give you an idea of how successful you have been at organizing your tasks.

On this page, we are going to take a look at your tasks from all the different TaskPad views in Calendar.

FYI

- A fast way to select different TaskPad views is to right-click in a blank TaskPad area, click on TaskPad View, and select the specific view from the submenu.
- You can increase or decrease the visible TaskPad area within Calendar by dragging the separator bars up, down, left, and right.
- Tasks that are overdue appear in a different color (red). If you are in the Overdue TaskPad view and some of the tasks do not appear in black, this is because they do not have a set due date.

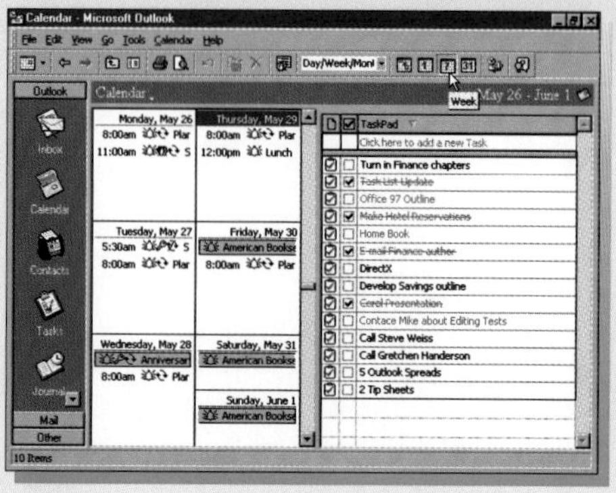

1. Click on the Calendar icon in the Outlook Bar and then click on the Week button in the toolbar. You can see all the tasks you have created from the default view (All Tasks).

7. Select the Tasks Completed on Selected Days command and the TaskPad will list only those tasks that you have completed on specific calendar days. This can give you an idea of what you have accomplished in any given set of days.

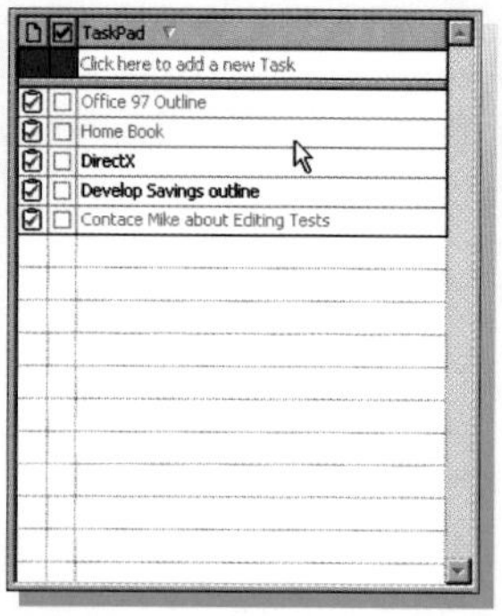

6. Select the Overdue Tasks command and the TaskPad will list only those tasks that you still need to complete. This can help you prioritize your tasks.

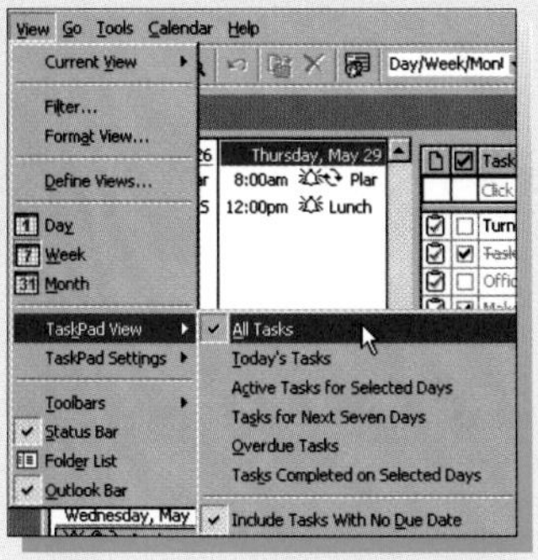

2 Select TaskPad View from the View menu to see the list of task views. The current task view has a checkmark to the left of the view. Notice that Include Tasks With No Due Date is also a default selection at the bottom of the menu.

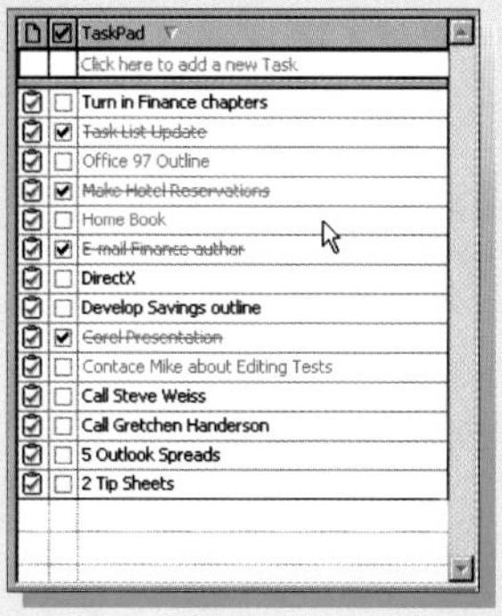

3 Select the Today's Tasks command from the View menu, TaskPad View, and the TaskPad will list only those tasks that you must complete today. This can help you organize your day. Notice that all tasks are listed; this is because technically you could do all those tasks today.

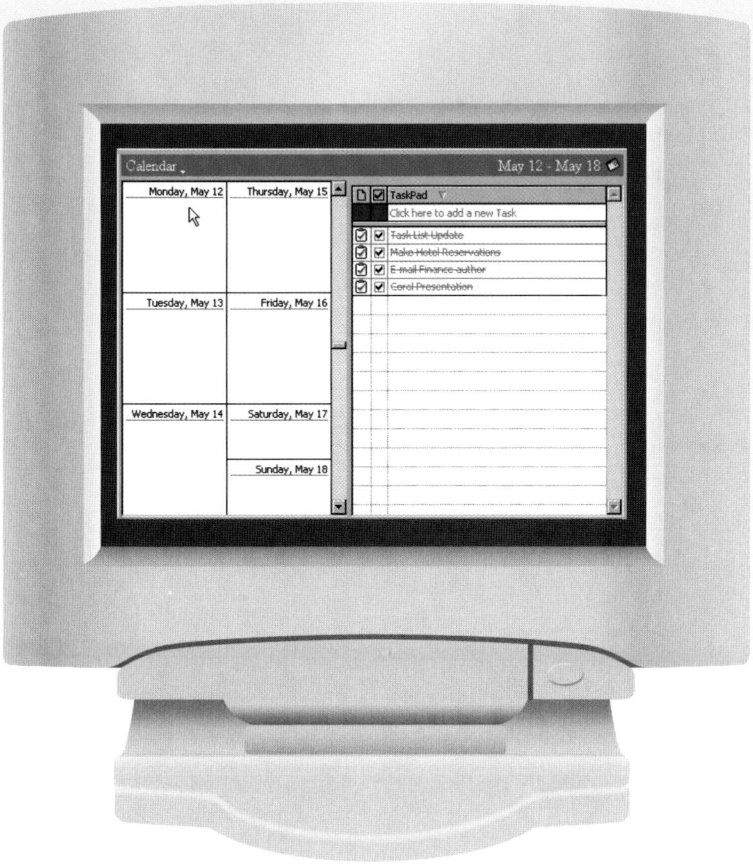

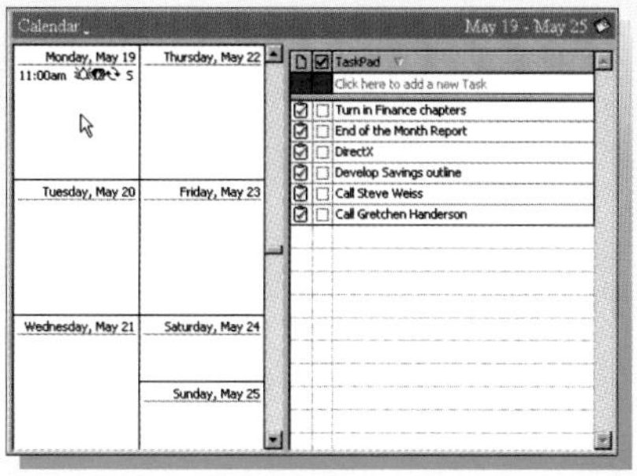

4 Select the Active Tasks for Selected Days command and the TaskPad will list only those tasks that you have to complete in the days that show on the calendar. This can give you an idea of what you need to accomplish in any given set of days.

5 Select the Tasks for Next Seven Days command and the TaskPad will list only those tasks that you have to complete in the next seven days. This can help you organize your week. Again, all tasks are listed because technically you could do all those tasks in the next seven days.

How to Update Tasks

There's no point in having a powerful information management system if you don't keep up with it. Taking the time to enter data is well worth the effort (and the few seconds of time it requires) because you'll never be stuck for an answer when you're asked to provide a detailed report on any of the work that's been assigned to you.

1 To keep yourself (and Outlook) on top of everything when you take a step toward the completion of a task, open the Tasks information viewer.

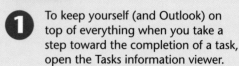

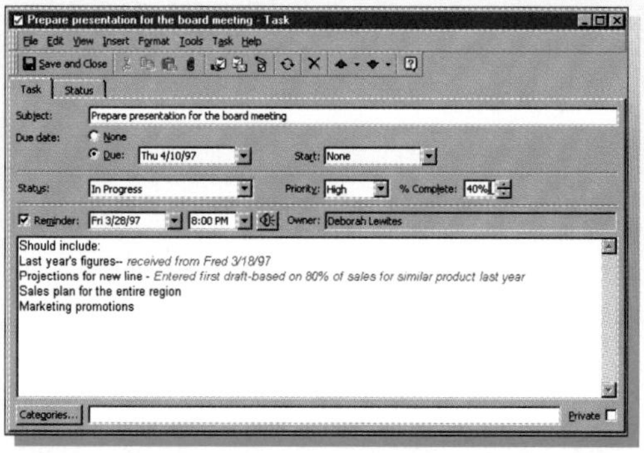

6 The Task form reflects your changes. If these tasks increased the percentage of this task that's been completed, update the %Complete field. Click Save and Close to complete your update and save the new information.

(Continues on next page)

FYI

- **You might also want to set a new reminder for yourself for the next step you need to complete in this task.**
- **The arrows on the %Complete field change the figure in 25% increments (only 25, 50, 75, and 100% are available). For any other percentage figure you must enter the number directly into the field (Outlook will add the percent sign (%) for you).**

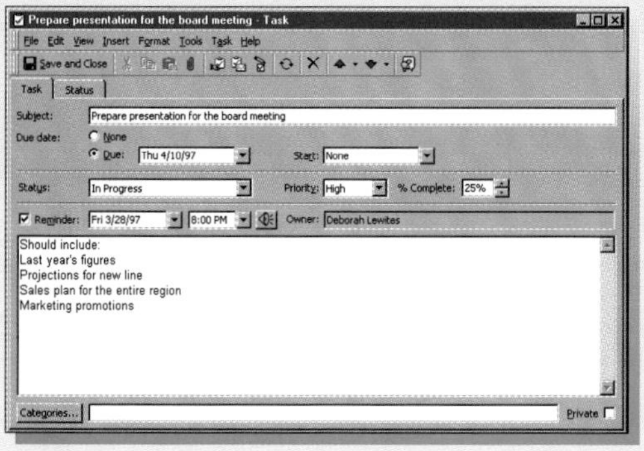

2 Select the task for which you just completed a step and double-click it to open it.

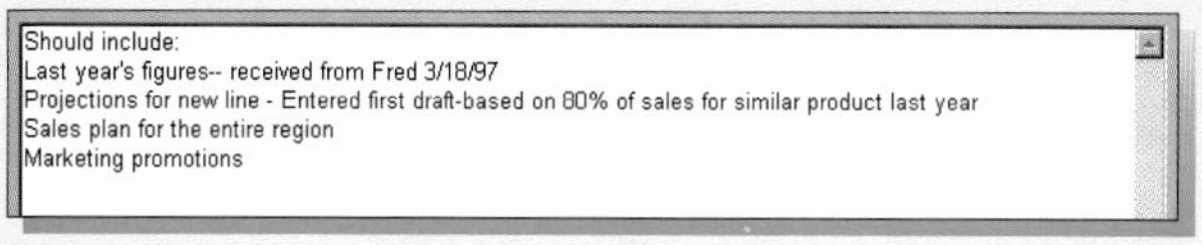

3 Move to the text box and enter a note describing the progress you've made.

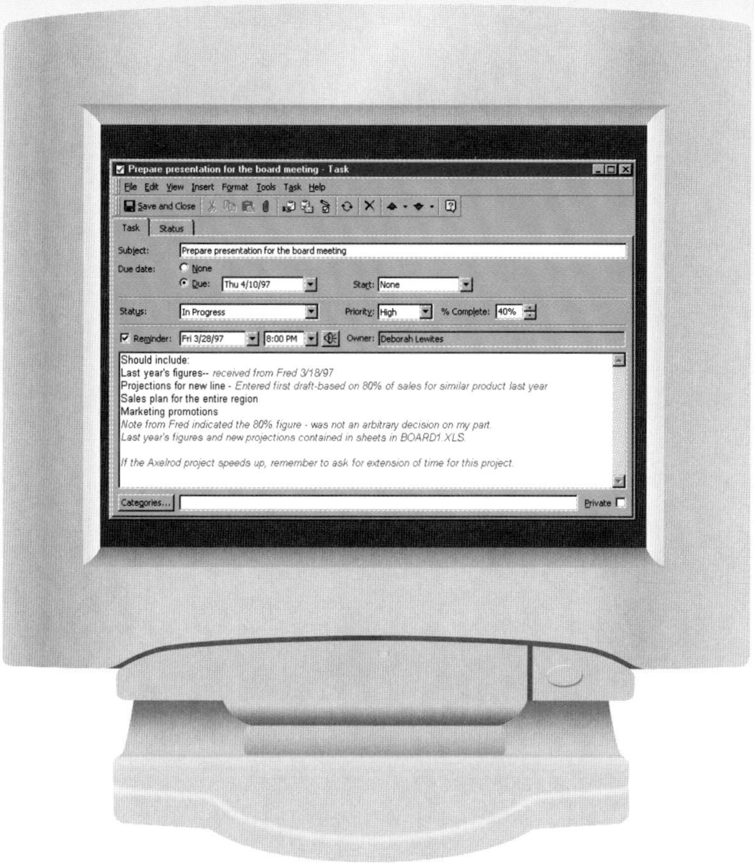

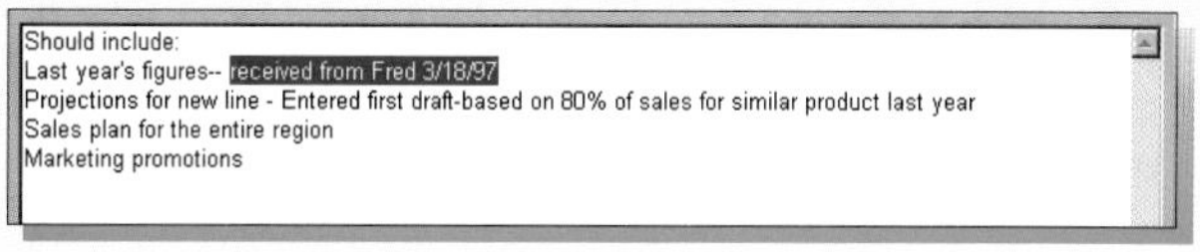

4 It might be easier to tell your original notes apart from your progress notes at a quick glance if you change the font for your progress notes. Highlight your new text and choose Format, Font from the menu bar.

5 When the Font dialog box opens, change the font, the font style, the size, or the color (or a combination of any of these). In this example, the font style is changed to italic and the color is changed to purple. (Changing the style is useful for reports because unless you have a color printer, the reader won't be able to tell the difference in color, but will be able to see your notes if they're italic or bold.) Click OK when you have made your changes.

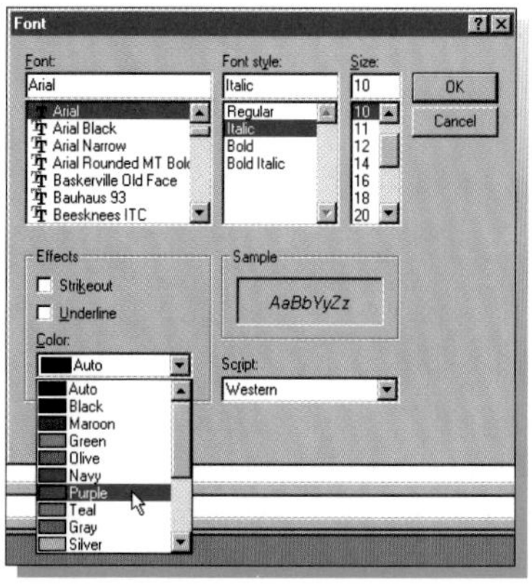

How to Update Tasks (Continued)

Besides entering your own notes about the tasks, there are some other things you can track as you work on this assignment. The Status tab of the Tasks form holds a number of choices for tracking information.

7 Click the Status tab to enter additional specific information about the task.

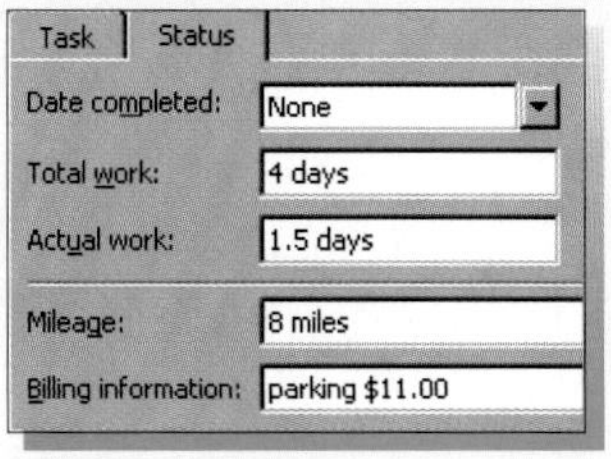

11 In the Status tab of the Task form, make sure you track mileage if you're reimbursed for it. Also track any expenses that are billable (either to a customer or as a reimbursable expense of your own). You can also track contacts and companies associated with this task. Click Save and Close when you have updated the task.

FYI

- **The Actual Work field has no ability to do math. You must enter your new total each time you update it; you cannot add a new figure to the old figure.**

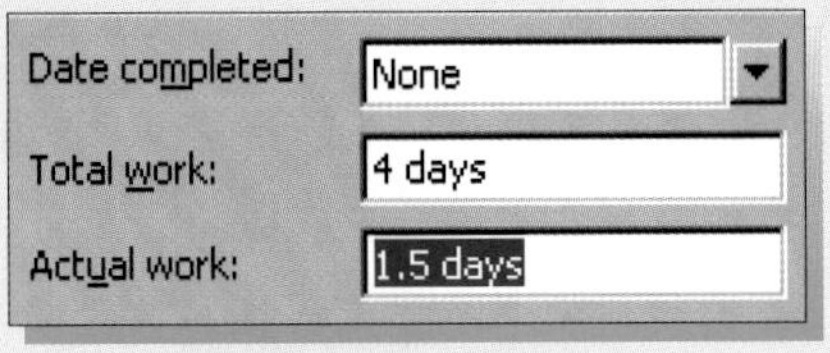

8 The Total Work section is the place to enter the amount of work you think is involved for the whole task, and also to track the actual work as you perform it. You can track hours or days. If you enter a number of days in the Total Work field, you can enter hours in the Actual Work field and Outlook will convert the hours to days.

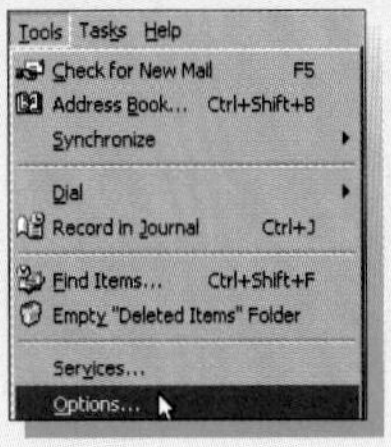

9 If accuracy in the number of hours in a day and in a work week is important (which it is if you are paid by the hour or if your time is billable to a customer), you can define those figures. By default, Outlook assumes you work an 8-hour day, 40 hours a week. To change that, choose Tools, Options from the Outlook menu bar and go to the Tasks/Notes tab.

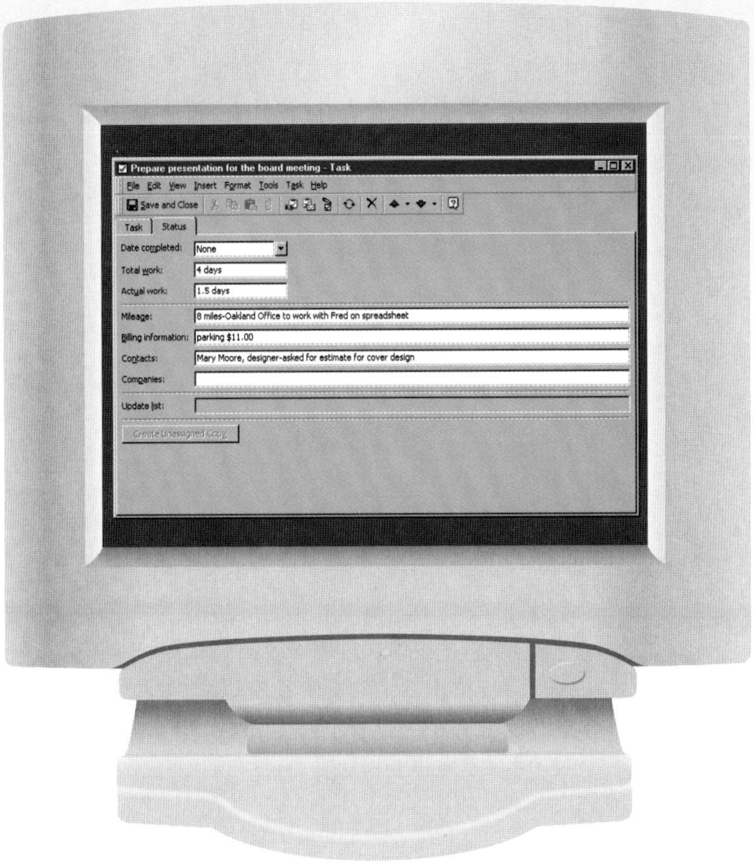

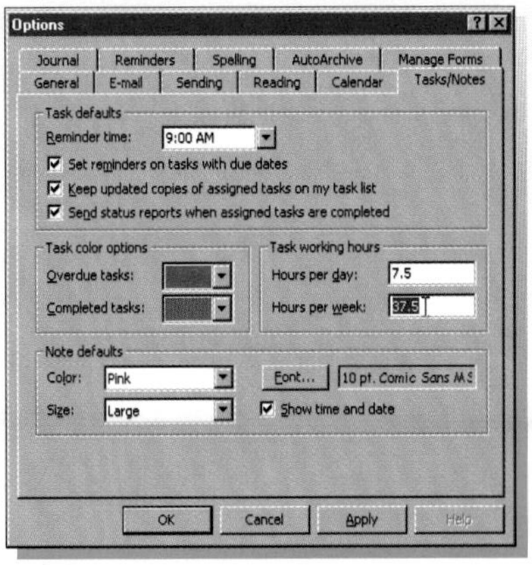

10 In the Task Working Hours section of the dialog box, specify your working hours per day and per week. Then click OK.

How to Record Tasks in the Journal

If you keep a journal and depend on it for tracking your time, or if you notify certain people about the progress of a task, you don't have to reenter the information you typed when you updated your task. You can record your work in tasks directly into other Outlook items.

1. Make sure the Tasks listing is the current Information Viewer, and put the Outlook icons on the Outlook Bar by clicking the Outlook title bar.

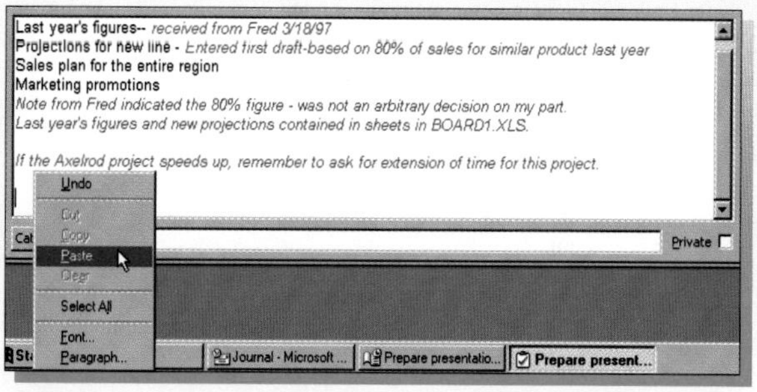

5. Double-click the Task icon in the Journal form (isn't it handy that it's right there?) and put your insertion point in the text area. Right-click and choose Paste. The note is placed in the task. Choose Save and Close on the Task form, then choose Save and Close on the Journal form.

FYI

- **If you enter a contact name in the Status tab of a task and then create a journal entry from the task, the journal entry has that contact name linked to it (even if the contact doesn't exist in your contact database).**

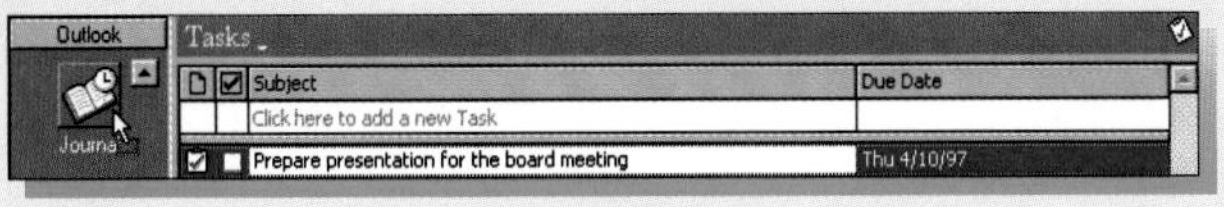

2 To create a journal entry for your work on a task, drag the task listing to the Journal icon on the Outlook Bar.

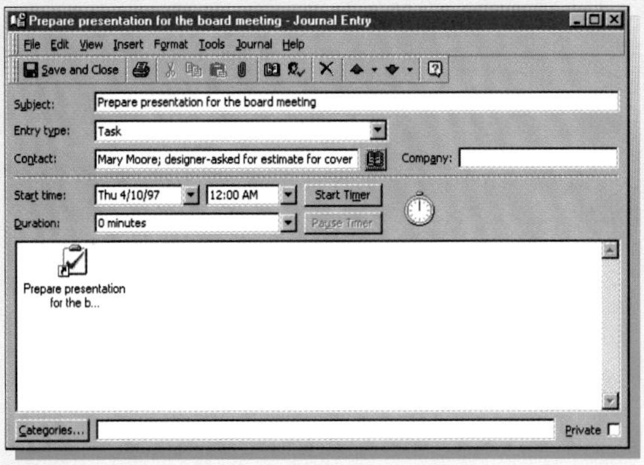

3 A new Journal Entry form appears and all the information is filled in, using the stuff you already typed into the Task form. The icon in the Journal Entry form is a direct link to the Task form, and double-clicking it opens the Task. Usually there's nothing more to add to this form (but you can add notes if you wish), so choose Save and Close.

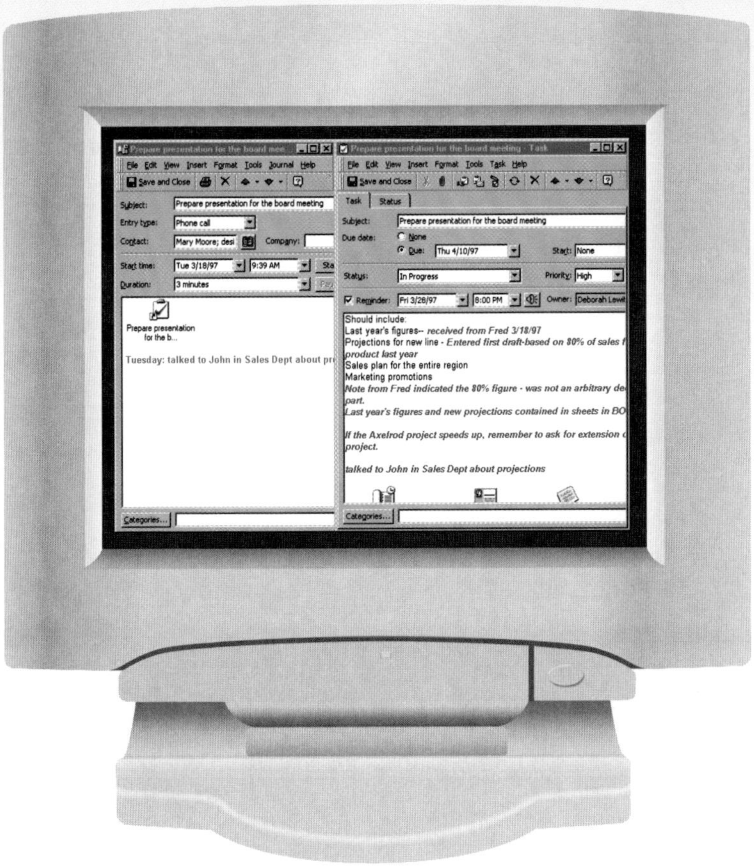

4 You can use the procedure in reverse order, too. Once you have a journal for the task, open it when you make a phone call or begin work on the task. When you finish the work, highlight your notes and right-click the highlighted text. Select Copy from the menu.

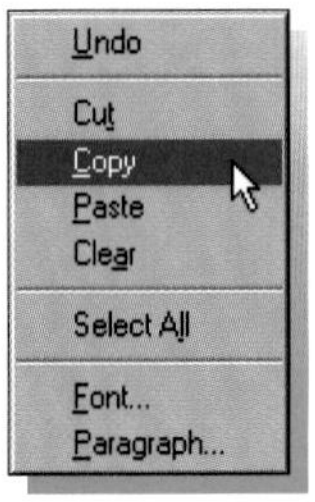

How to Create Status Reports on Tasks

Somebody is going to want to know what's going on with all those tasks you're working on. In fact, if you have lots of tasks to track, that somebody may be you. Instead of pulling together lots of files, little bits of paper, napkins with notes scrawled on them, and the notations on the backs of envelopes (I can never find blank paper or a notepad and always end up writing myself notes on the backs of envelopes), you can click your mouse a couple of times and give a full report.

There are several ways to report on the status of tasks and this section covers the methods you'll probably use most.

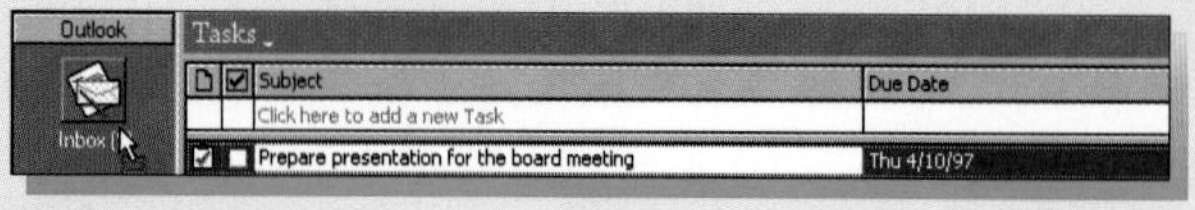

1 One quick way to let another person know about the status of a task is to send an e-mail message. You don't have to compose a long message in which you recite the details, you can let Outlook do the work. From the Tasks information viewer, drag the task you want to report on to the Inbox icon on the Outlook Bar.

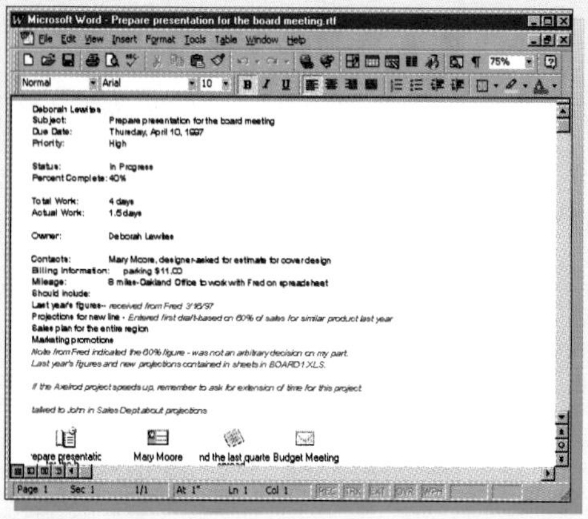

7 Double-click the listing to open the document. Your task report, complete with any formatting you used, is in the software window. Of course, you'll want to move things around, add text, and otherwise edit it to make a truly wonderful, professional-looking document.

(Continues on next page)

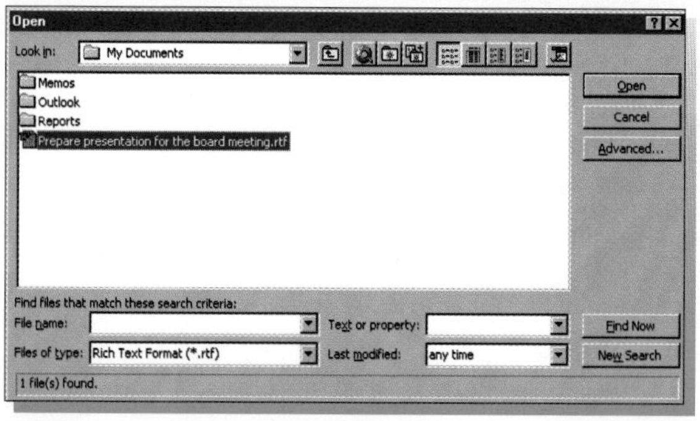

6 Your task report document is listed in the folder window.

FYI

- **If your task is open, you can click Send Status Report on the toolbar (or choose Task, Send Status Report from the menu bar) to open a new message form with all the task information.**
- **When you save the task as a document, any attachments you had in your Task form are also saved. If you don't need them for the final document, you should select them and press the Delete key to remove them.**

2 A new message form opens and everything anyone wanted to know about this task is included in the message. The task name is in the Subject field. All you have to do is enter a recipient in the To field (and recipients for the Cc field if you wish) and click Send.

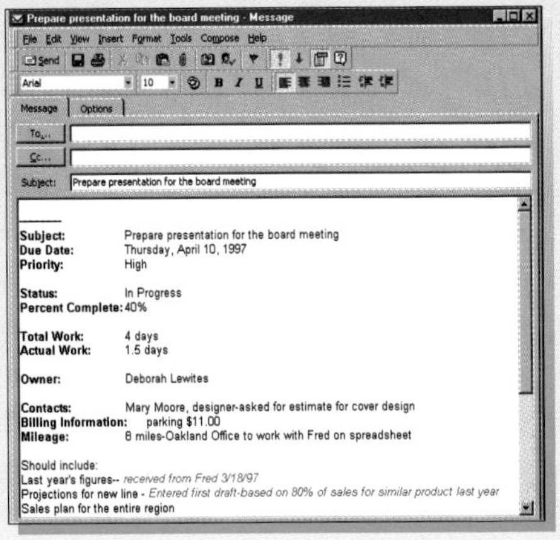

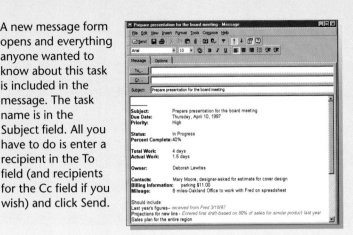

3 If you want to report on this task as part of a wonderful manuscript you're writing, you'll probably use your word processor for the final product. The quickest way to get the task report ready for such a project is to save it in a format your word processor can use. To do this, open the task and choose File, Save As from the menu bar.

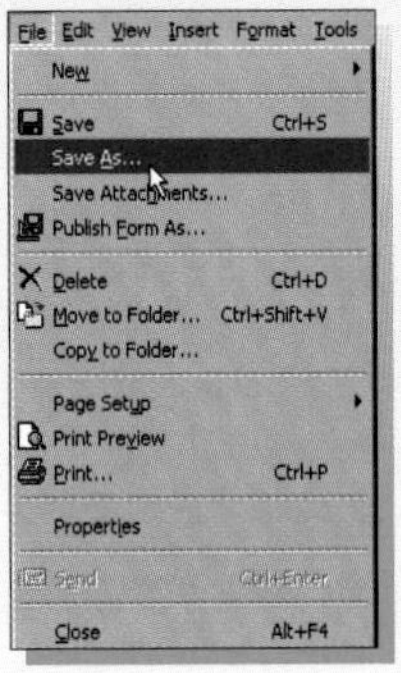

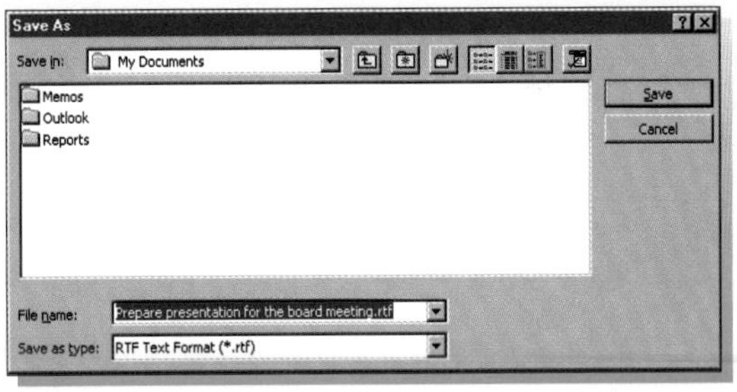

4 The Save As dialog box opens with the name of the task highlighted in the File Name field (you'll probably want to change that to something shorter and to the point). You have some choices about the file type for this file. By default, the file type is RTF (Rich Text Format), which most word processors can handle. You can also choose to save the file as a text file (with an extension of .txt), which any word processor or text editor can handle (but you'll lose any formatting in your task notes). Click Save when you have made the changes you want.

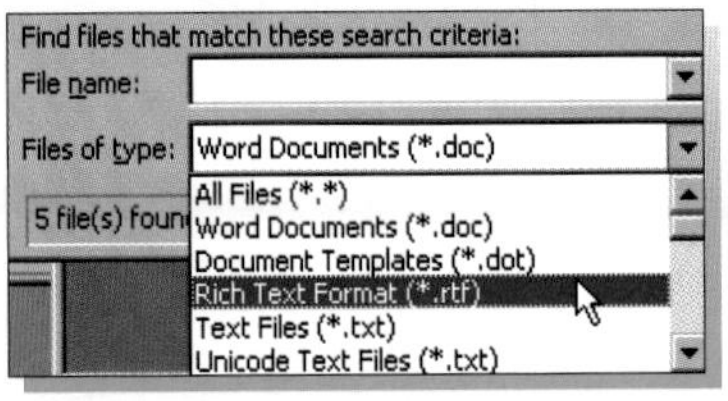

5 To work on the document, open your word processor, and then click the Open button on the toolbar. By default, your word processor displays files of the type associated with it (for instance, Microsoft Word displays files that have an extension of .doc). Click the arrow to the right of the box named Files of Type and choose the file type you used when you saved your task report.

How to Create Status Reports on Tasks (Continued)

You can, of course, print a status report on a task. And, as with everything else, Outlook provides several options for the printed report. We'll discuss those in this section.

8 To print a report on the status of a task, open the task and choose File, Print from the menu bar (or press Ctrl+P).

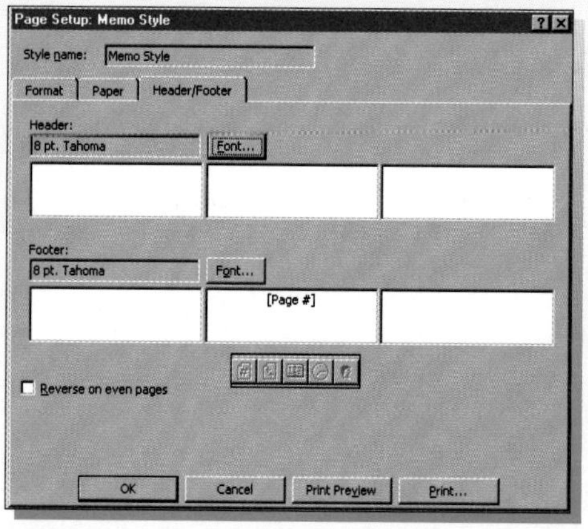

13 Move to the Header/Footer tab. By default there's a page number in the footer, and it's centered. You can enter header or footer text (or both). Notice that there are three boxes for both the header and footer, representing left, right and center justification. Click OK when you have made all your changes on all the tabs of the dialog box.

14 When you return to the Print Preview window, if everything looks right, click Print.

FYI

- By default, attachments do not print when you print a task status report. You can select the option to print attachments on the Print dialog box.

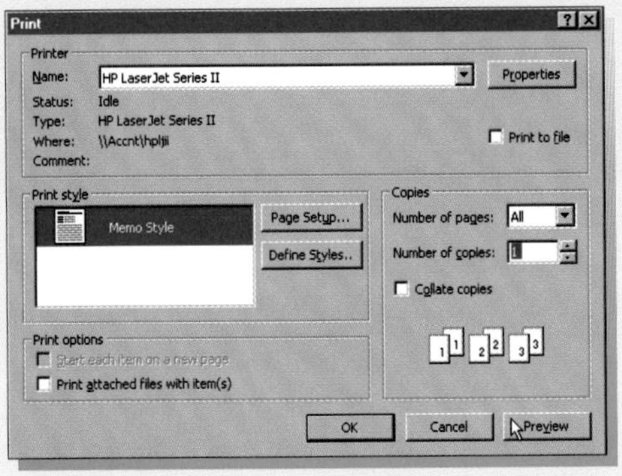

9 The Print dialog box opens. The default setup is for an Outlook Memo Style, which presents the report very much like a standard memo. For a quick glance before printing, click Preview.

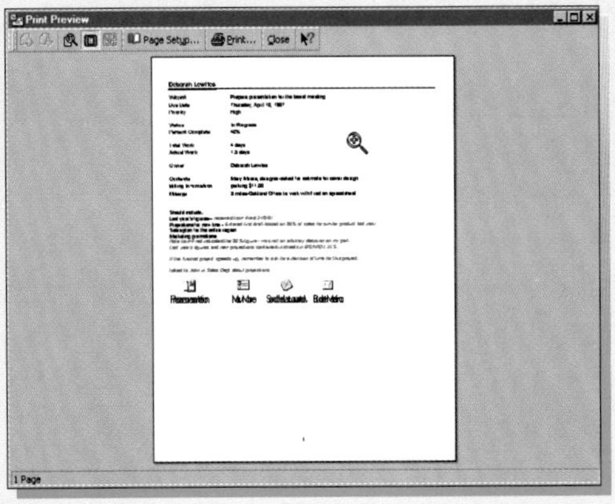

10 The Print Preview dialog box opens to display your report in a full-page view. It's rather difficult to read (which is okay because you already know what it says, you wrote it), but you can see the layout. If you want to get a closer look, your pointer is a magnifying glass, so just point and click and the page zooms closer. Click again to return to the full-page view.

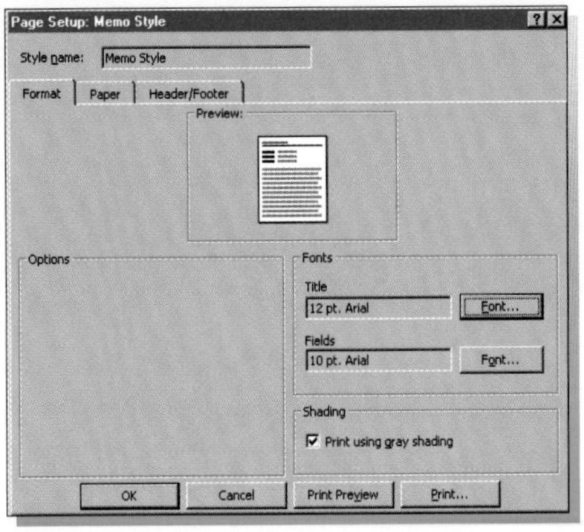

11 You can make some changes to the layout of the page by clicking the Page Setup button on the Print Preview toolbar. When the Page Setup dialog box opens, the Format tab is in the foreground and you can change the fonts for the Title of the report or the Fields (which really means the field names) by clicking the Font button. (We've gone over changing fonts so many times in this book that you probably don't need another lesson here.)

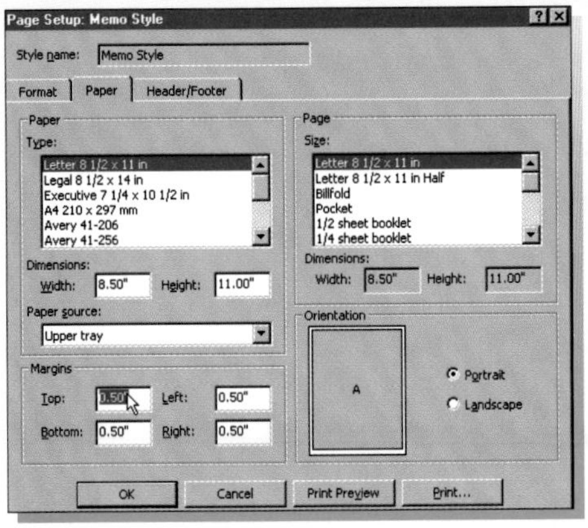

12 Click the Paper tab to move to the dialog box sheet that establishes the settings for the paper. Whether or not you can change the size of the paper is totally dependent on your printer's capabilities. However, you might want to change the margins. If your report is short, make the top margin larger to start the printing further down on the page. If your report is spilling over to a second page, but only using one or two lines on the second page, specify a smaller margin all around to try to fit everything on one page.

How to Manage Projects with Tasks

Renting a hotel ballroom for a party is a task. Putting together a major event like the 100th anniversary party for your company is a project. Renting the ballroom is just one task in a long list of things that have to be done.

In this section we'll plan such a party, and track each step with the Tasks feature in Outlook.

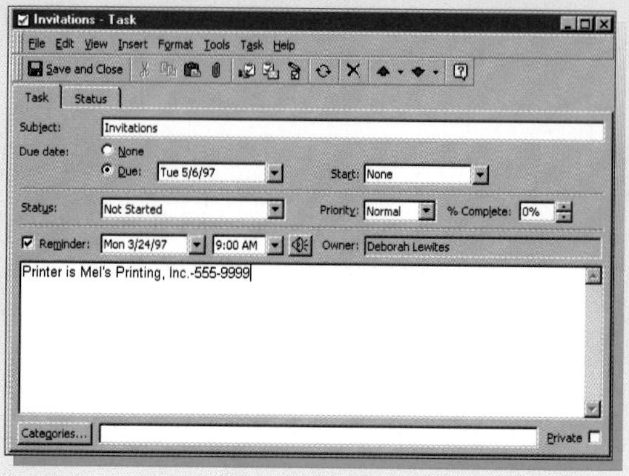

1 All trips start with the first step, and all projects start with the first task. In this case, the first task is to order the invitations. From the Tasks information viewer, click the New Task icon to open a blank form. Fill in as much information as you have.

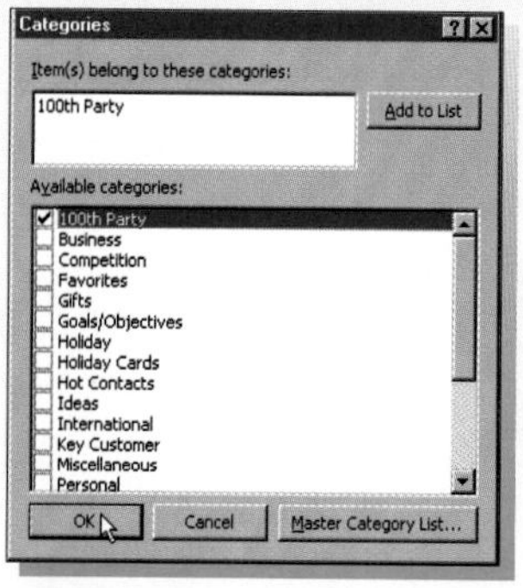

5 After you've filled in all the fields and written yourself whatever notes are necessary for the task, click the Categories button. When the Categories dialog box opens, find your project's category and click to select it. Then click OK. When you return to the task form, click Save and Close. Continue to do this for all the tasks involved with this project.

(Continues on next page)

FYI

- **At some point, you should make sure that due dates are entered in every task for the project. This gives you the ability to sort and view your tasks so you know what to do next; it's a step-by-step guide to completing the project.**

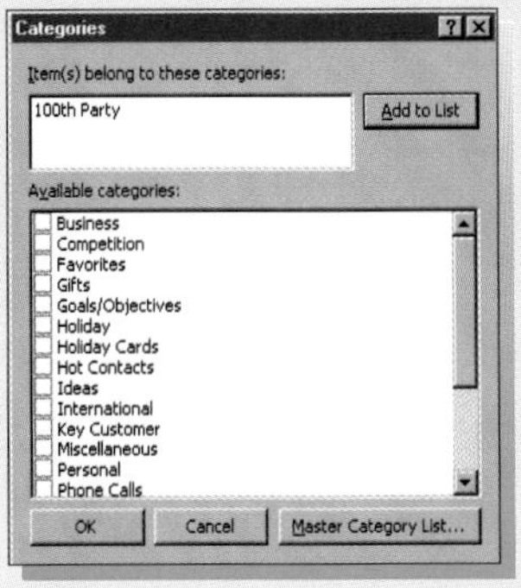

2 Now you must create the project this task is connected to. Once this project link is created, all the other tasks involved in completing this project will be linked to it. This is accomplished with the Categories feature in Outlook. Click the Categories button to begin. The Categories dialog box opens with the built-in available categories displayed. But in this instance you'll create a specific category for this project by typing its name in the top of the dialog box. After you've entered a new category name, click OK.

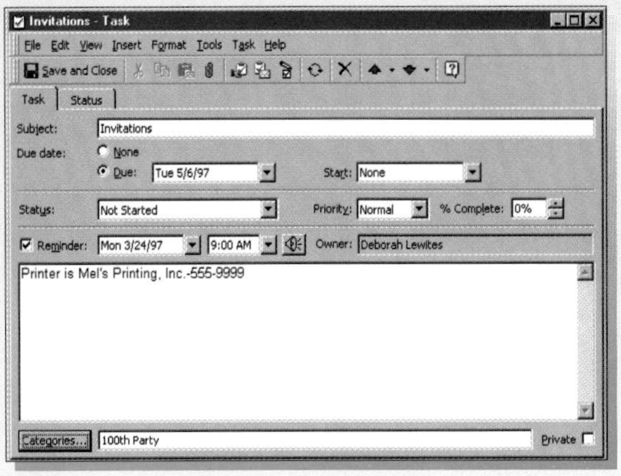

3 When you return to your task form, the category name is inserted in the Categories field. More important, your new category is in the Outlook system, available to all the features and functions. Click Save and Close.

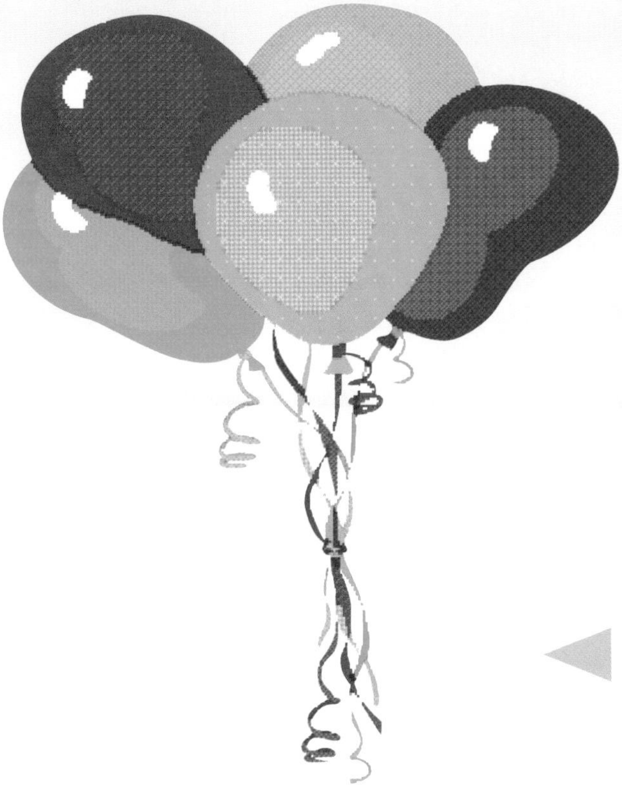

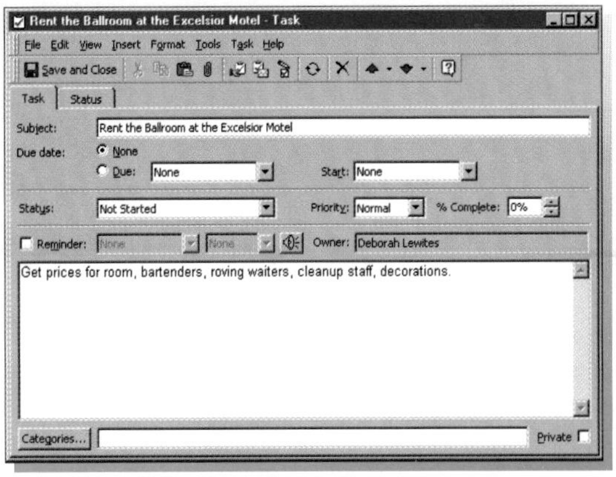

4 Open another blank task form by clicking the New Task icon on the toolbar and enter another task involved with this project.

How to Manage Projects with Tasks (Continued)

When you're tracking projects, you'll find that you're constantly entering new tasks; it's almost impossible to plan ahead for all the details you have to attend to. As the task list for the project grows larger, you'll be able to keep an eye on the project because of the link to the project (category).

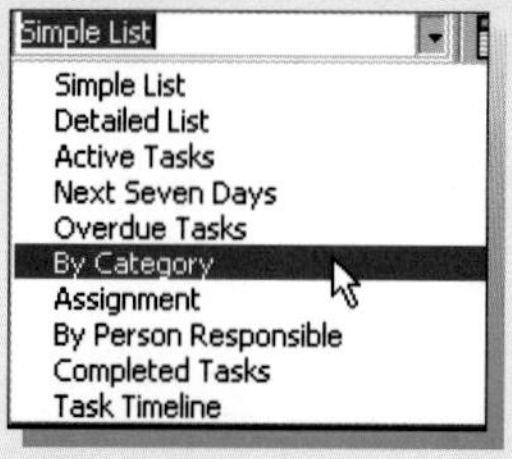

6 After you've entered a group of tasks for the project, the fact that you've linked them by category makes it easy to keep an eye on them. In the Tasks information viewer, click the arrow to the right of the Current View box on the toolbar. Choose By Category as a view.

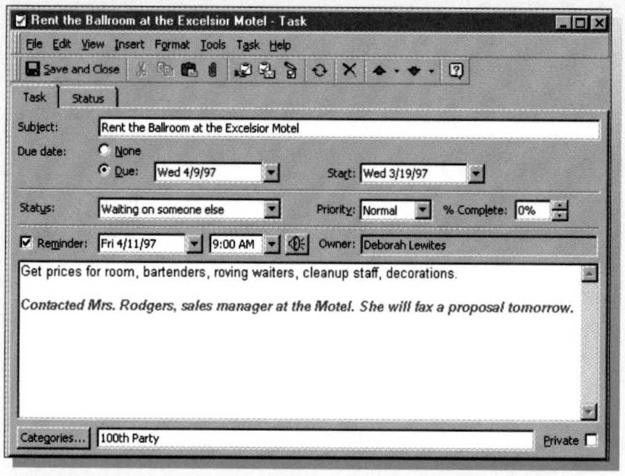

11 As you attend to the details for each task in the project, be sure to update the Task form. Don't forget that the moment you do anything, the tasks should receive a start date, a due date, and a status. Remember to set a reminder for the next step of the task. Click Save and Close to save your updates as you enter them.

(Continues on next page)

FYI

- **If the task itself doesn't yet have a firm due date, enter a due date based on the current step you're working on. Having due dates is important so you can set your priorities and arrange your time. (The closer you get to a project's end, the more crowded and confusing the task list becomes.)**
- **If running this project involves regular reporting to someone, or a regular call to someone for information, enter a recurring task and attach it to this project category.**

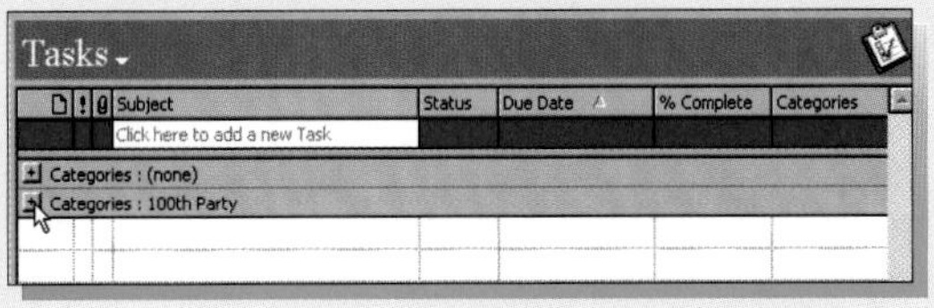

7 The categories are displayed instead of the tasks, and since most users find it's not necessary to put regular tasks into categories, there's usually a category of "none." Notice the plus sign (+) next to each category listing. Click the plus sign next to the category for your project.

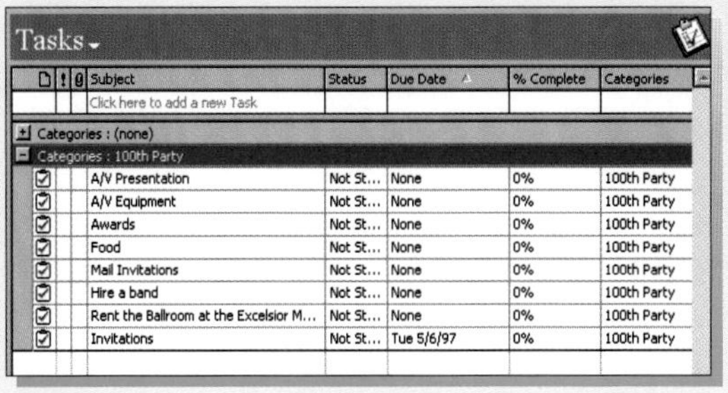

8 The category expands to display all the tasks connected to your project. Notice the arrow in the Due Date column heading. It indicates that within this category the tasks are arranged in order of due date. As you enter due dates in the tasks, this forms a "what to do next" list for you.

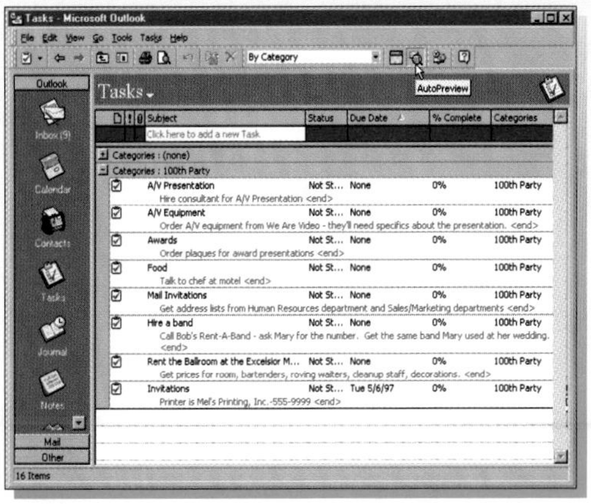

9 Click the AutoPreview icon on the toolbar to see any notes you've entered about the tasks. This is a fast way to get moving by seeing what you have to do without having to open a Task form.

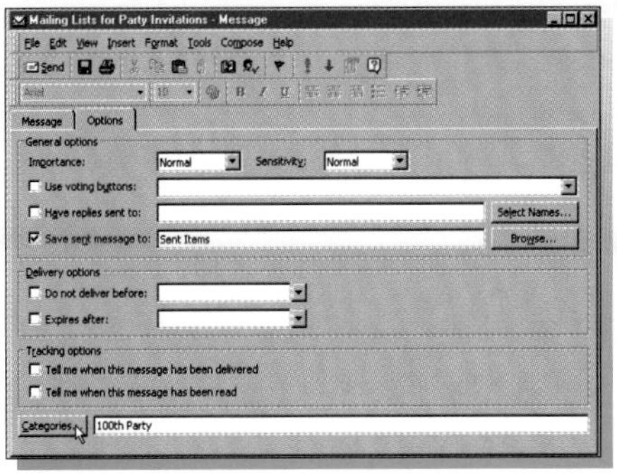

10 If you send e-mail related to this project, be sure to note the category on the Options tab of the e-mail message. Connecting everything you do with this project makes it much easier to track the project. In fact, the same is true for all Outlook items, such as contacts or appointments—be sure to choose this project for the Categories field.

How to Manage Projects with Tasks (Continued)

As you continue to enter and update tasks, create contacts, e-mail messages, and other Outlook items attached to the project's categories, you begin to see the project take shape. This section covers viewing and reporting on the project's progress.

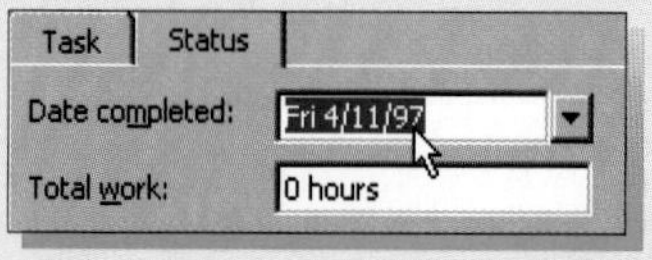

12 As you complete individual tasks, be sure to note the completion date in the Status tab of the task.

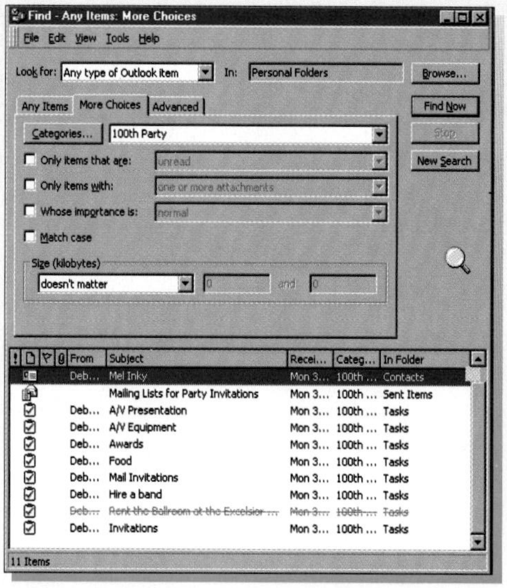

18 The results of the Find operation display in a box under the Find dialog box.

(Continues on next page)

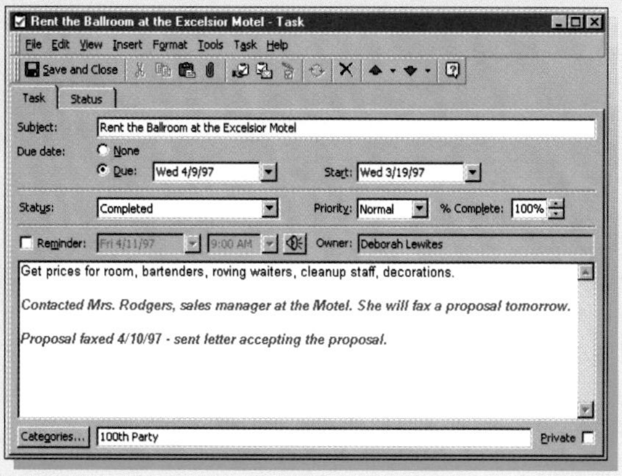

13 Once you enter a completion date in the Status tab of a task, the Task tab reflects that fact. The Status field on that tab is automatically changed to Completed.

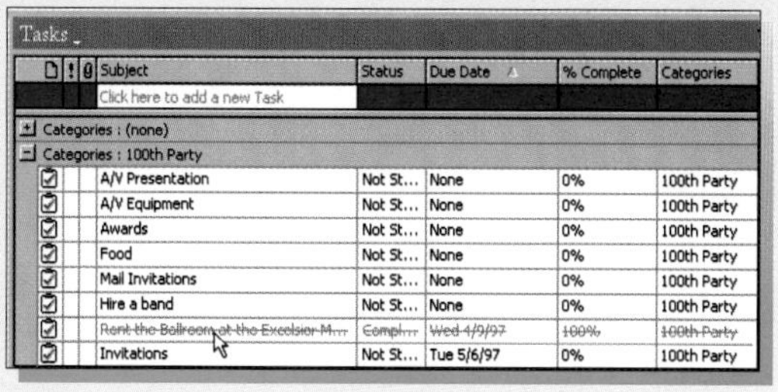

14 As tasks are completed, they're crossed off the list of things to do—isn't that a nice sight?

15 To gather all the Outlook items related to this project (tasks, contacts, and so on), use the Outlook Find feature. From any Outlook information viewer, click the Find Items icon on the toolbar

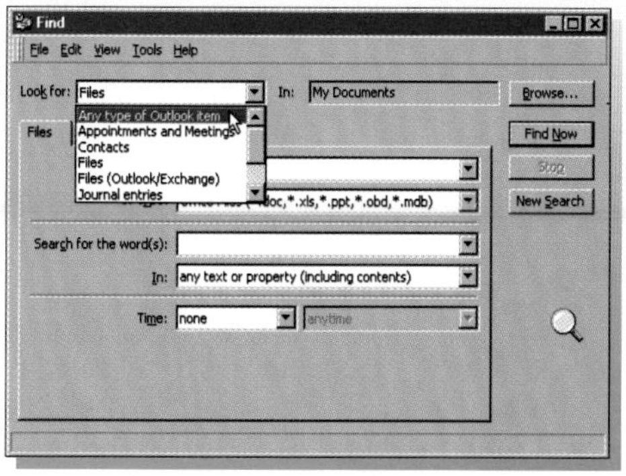

16 When the Find dialog box appears, click the arrow to the right of the Look For field and move to the top of the drop-down list to select Any Type of Outlook Item.

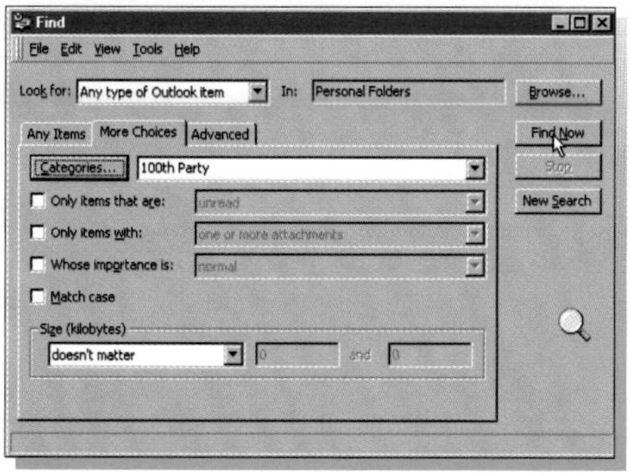

17 Move to the More Choices tab of the dialog box and enter the project name in the Categories field. Then click Find Now.

How to Manage Projects with Tasks (Continued)

Now that you have various Outlook items linked to your project and you can get a list of them using the Find feature, you can use the Find results to gain more information.

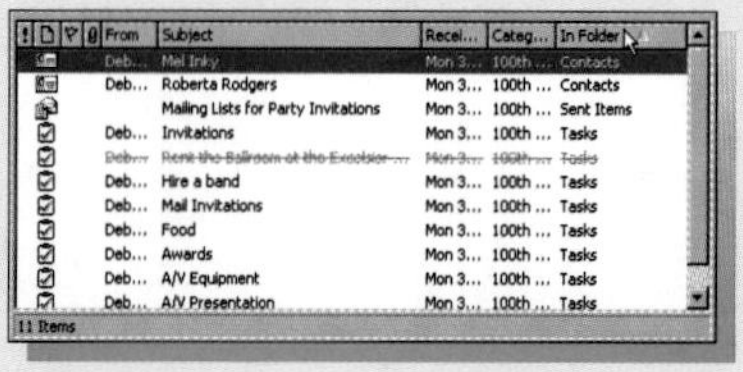

19 In the Find results display, you can arrange the found items by clicking one of the column headings. For example, clicking the In Folder heading not only arranges the items by folder, it gives you an idea of the type of items attached to this project (contacts, e-mail, or tasks, for example).

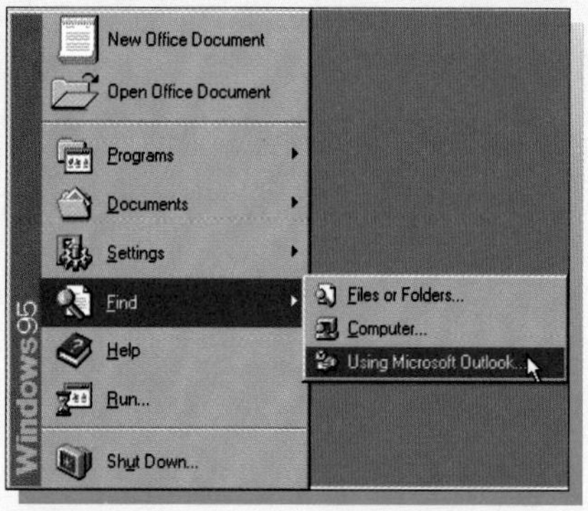

25 If you're not working in Outlook (perhaps you're working in your word processor and perhaps you're writing a report on the project), you can easily get the search results in order to examine the items. When Outlook was installed, Find Outlook Items was added to the options for your Windows 95 or Windows NT 4 operating system's Find feature. From your taskbar, click Start, then click Find, then click Using Microsoft Outlook. The same Find dialog box we've been using here appears so you can check on all the items connected to the project.

FYI

- **You only have to use Find when you want to look at all the different types of Outlook items at once. Otherwise, use the specific information viewer (check the status of tasks in the Tasks information viewer, check e-mail from the Sent Mail viewer, and so on).**

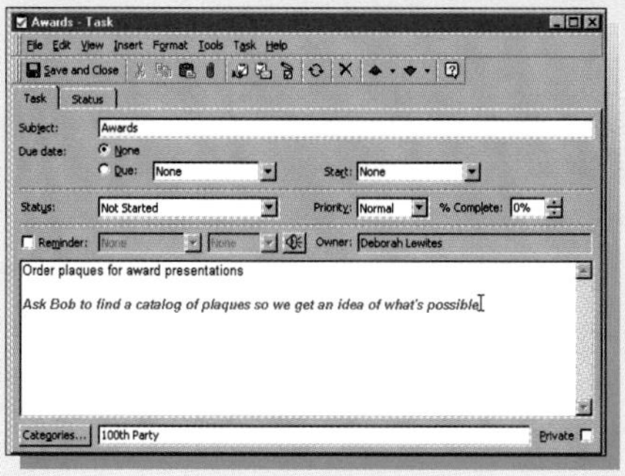

20 You can open any item by double-clicking it. Once it's opened, you can edit the contents if you wish. Be sure to click Save and Close if you make changes.

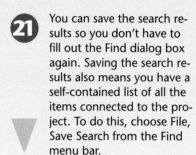

21 You can save the search results so you don't have to fill out the Find dialog box again. Saving the search results also means you have a self-contained list of all the items connected to the project. To do this, choose File, Save Search from the Find menu bar.

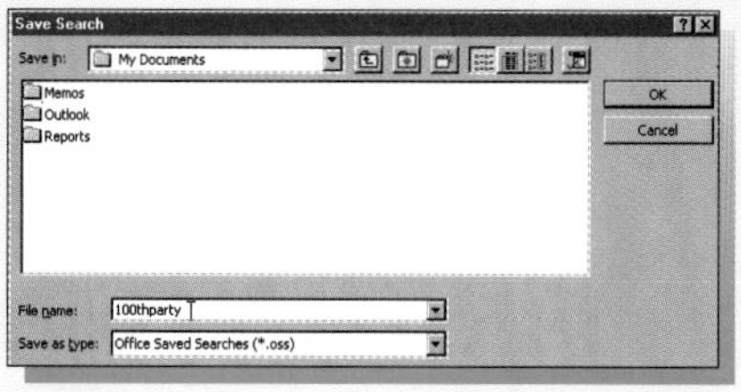

22 When the Save Search dialog box opens, name the file (choose something close to the name of the project) and click OK. Notice that the file is an Office Saved Searches file. You don't have to enter the .oss extension to the file name, Outlook will do that automatically when you click OK. Close the Find dialog box.

23 Later, when you want to see a status report on all items in Outlook relating to the project, you can recall the search results and see what's changed. Click the Find Items icon on the toolbar and when the dialog box opens choose File, Open Search.

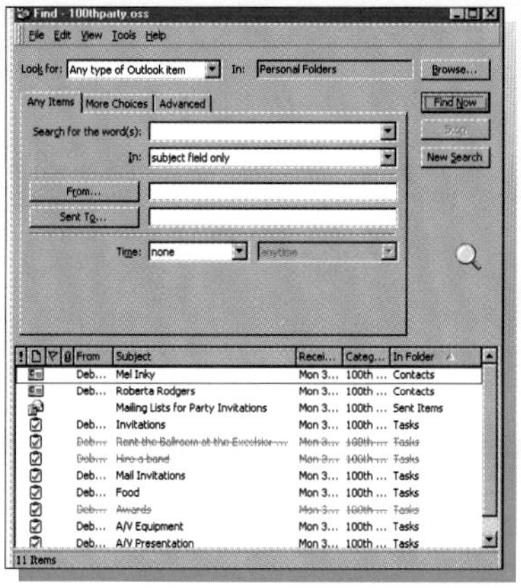

24 When the Open Saved Search dialog box appears, double-click the project's saved search file. The items display (in this case, more tasks have been completed, hooray!). You can open any item and examine it. Close the Find dialog box when you have finished looking at the items.

How to View Tasks

Changing the way you look at tasks in the Tasks information viewer helps you track information easily. You can change the view, sort the view, and filter the view. The choice you make helps you keep track of the tasks you're involved in.

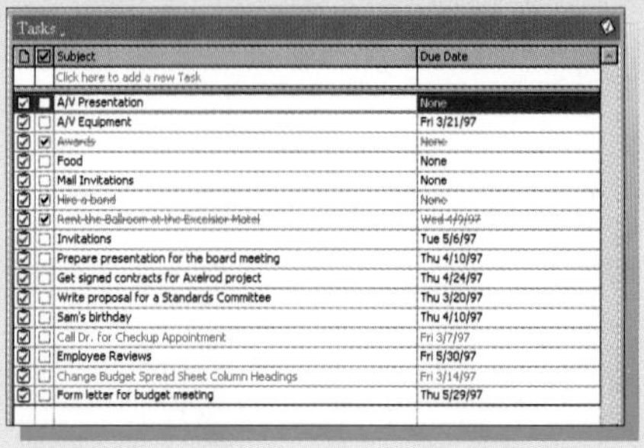

1 The default view for the Tasks information viewer is the Simple List view. It is, as the name implies, a simple list of all the tasks you've created and it is in the order in which you created the tasks (the first task is at the bottom of the list, the latest at the top). Additional information about some tasks is available, however. Completed tasks are displayed in gray type, the Completed icon is checked, and there is a line drawn through the listing and due date. Overdue tasks are displayed in red.

FYI

- **In any view except the Timeline, you can re-sort the listing by clicking the column heading you want to sort by.**
- **To Print the task list, select the view you want and choose File, Print from the menu bar (or press Ctrl+P).**
- **For more advanced ways to sort the view, read Part 2, "How to Change the View." All of the hints, tricks, tips, and instructions will work just as well on the Tasks information viewer.**
- **Tasks that are not given a due date don't appear in lists such as the Next Seven Days view. This can be deceptive because some of those tasks might be urgent. It's a good idea to give every task that's important a due date, even if it's being used as a To-do list entry.**

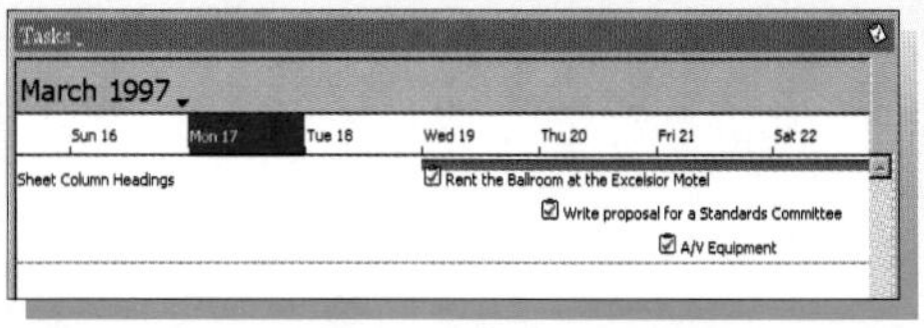

6 To get a look at your tasks arranged along the calendar, choose Task Timeline from the Current Views box. You can scroll through the months to see those days or weeks in which tasks are piled up. If there are periods in the calendar that seem extremely busy, that's a clue to start some of those tasks well ahead of their due dates so you don't get backed up.

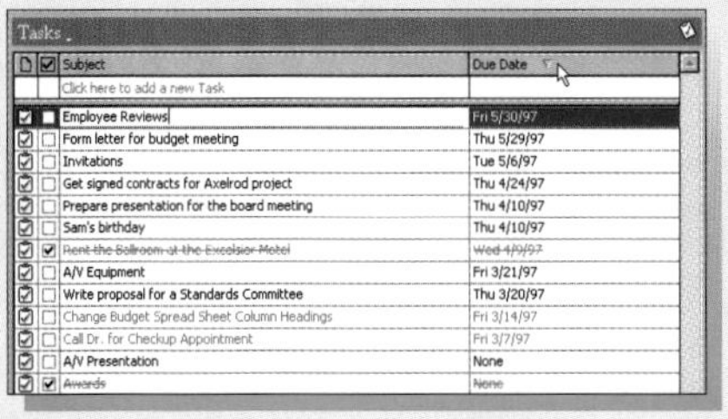

2 An easy way to plan your time is to put your tasks in the order in which they are due. Simply click the column heading for Due Date to rearrange the listing. Notice the arrow on the column heading, which indicates the direction of the sorting scheme (descending or ascending). To reverse the scheme, click the column heading again.

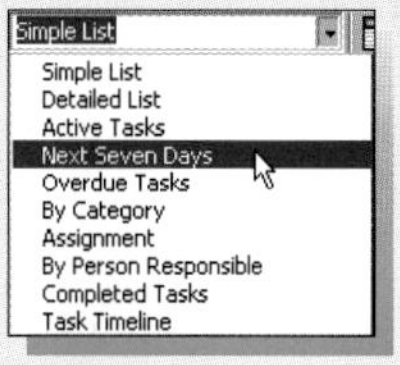

3 To see what you have to do right away, choose a view that shows the tasks needing attention now (I'm omitting the overdue tasks since they're screaming at you with their bright red listings—take care of them first, then move on to this step to plan your week). Click the arrow to the right of the Current View box on the toolbar and choose Next Seven Days.

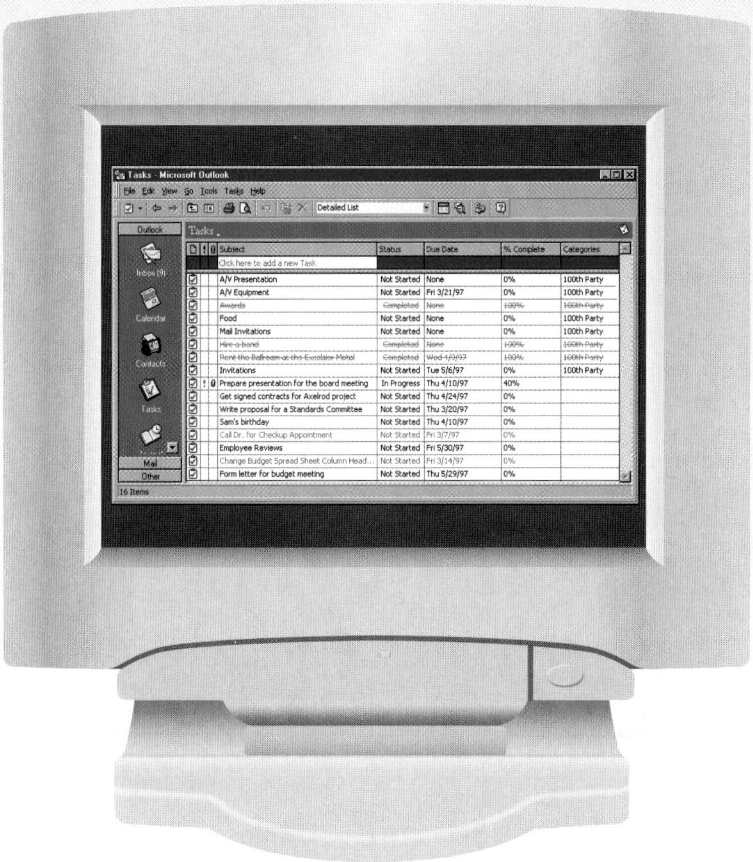

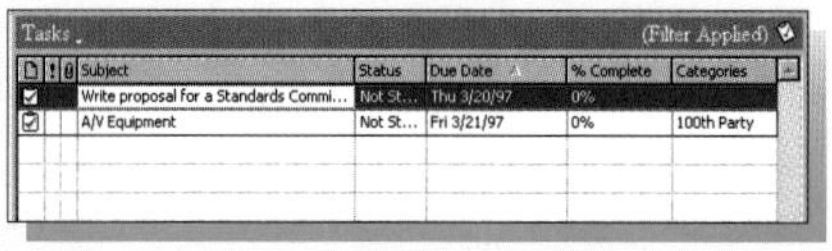

4 The task list is filtered to match the criterion of a due date within the current week (notice the indication of a filter on the bar above the column headings), and several additional columns are added to give you more information.

5 For a detailed view that has information about the status and % Complete, choose Detailed List from the Current View box.

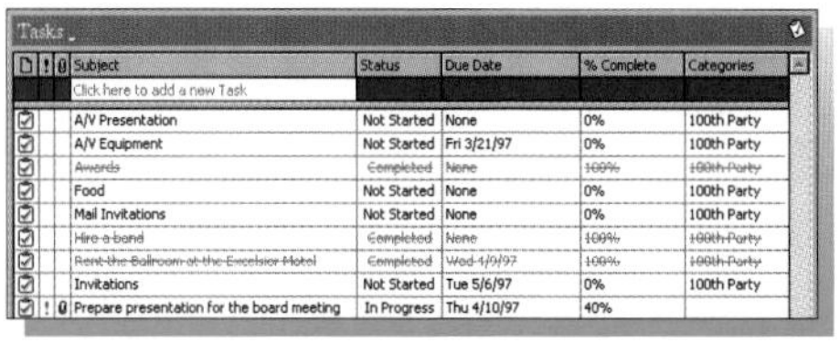

Ctrl + Shift + X=
Explore Web Page
Ctrl + N=
New Contact

P A R T 5

Using the Contacts Database

ONE of the information handling features that Outlook offers is a solid contact management tool. The Outlook Contacts window allows easy entry, importing, and outputting of contact information. If you've ever maintained an address book or rolodex file or scratched phone numbers on the inside of a phone booth, you've got the necessary skills to create a contact database.

In this part you'll learn how to create a single-contact form, multiple contacts from the same company, and contacts from e-mail messages, and how to import your address book into the Contacts database. To open the Outlook Contacts window, click the Contacts shortcut icon in the Outlook Bar.

IN THIS SECTION YOU'LL LEARN

How to Create a Contact Form

At its most basic level, contact management is the storage and retrieval of information you need in order to communicate effectively with another individual. The minimum requirements are a name to identify the contact, and either a postal address, phone number, e-mail address, or even a ham radio frequency in order to transmit information to the individual.

Of course, you can and should include all the information you want for each contact.

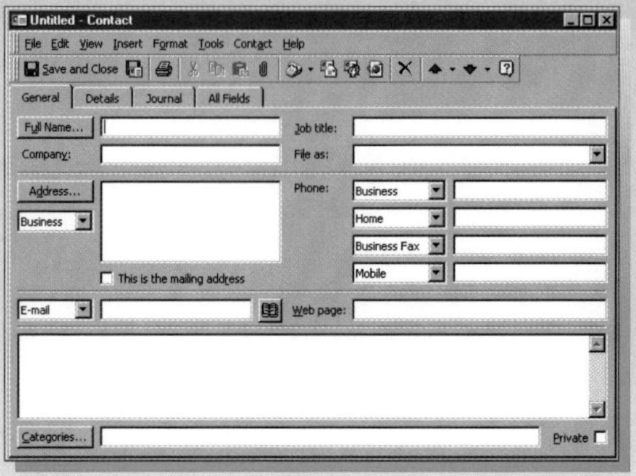

1 Click the New Contact icon on the Outlook toolbar to open a blank Contact form.

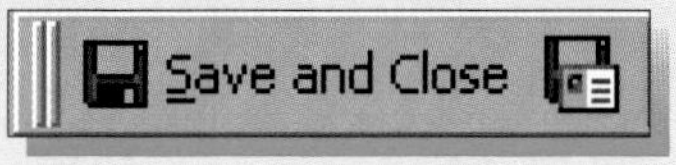

6 Click Save and Close to save the new contact form and return to the Contacts window.

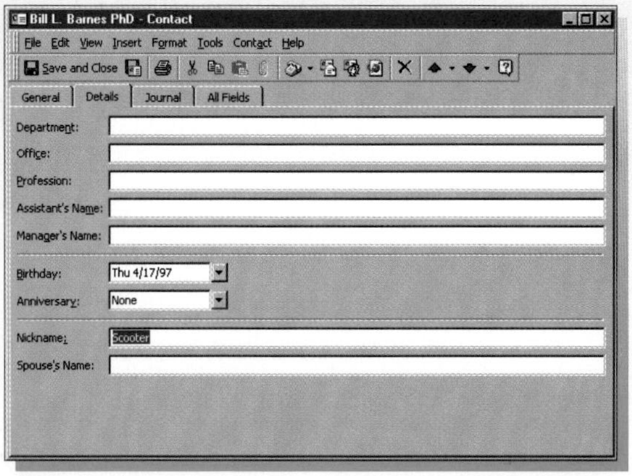

5 To include more detailed and personal information, click the Details tab on the Contact form to open the Details information sheet. Add any pertinent data and click the General tab to return to the Contact form.

FYI

- You can also open a blank Contact form by pressing Ctrl+N in the Contacts information viewer.
- To open more than one Contact form at a time, hold the Ctrl key down and highlight each contact you want to open by clicking it. After you've selected all the contacts you want to open, press Ctrl+O. Each of the Contact forms opens, one after the other.

2 Fill out the Contact form with as little or as much information as you wish. Remember, the purpose of the contact database is to provide you with the information you need, not necessarily every piece of information you possess. However, in some cases they may be the same thing.

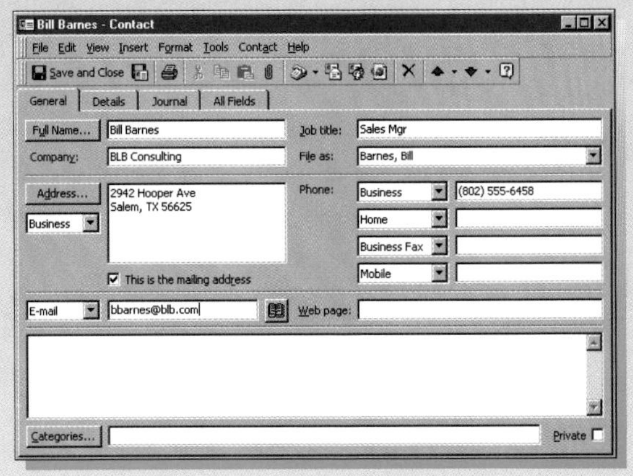

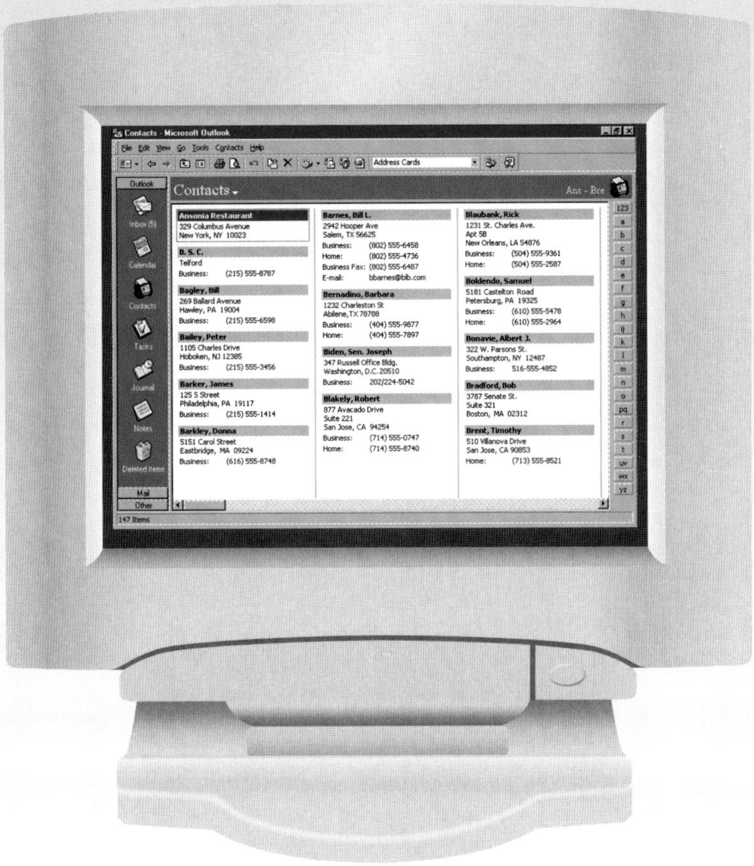

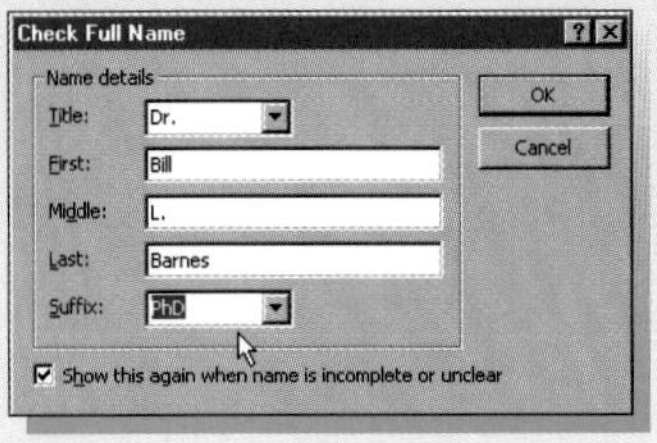

3 You can enter additional name information such as a title or suffix by clicking the Full Name button and opening the Check Full Name dialog box. Type the information and click OK to return to the Contact form.

4 The default address is a business address. To include a home or other address, click the down arrow on the right side of the Address Type field, select the type of address to enter, and enter the new address in the Address field text box. This does not replace the business address, but rather attaches a second address.

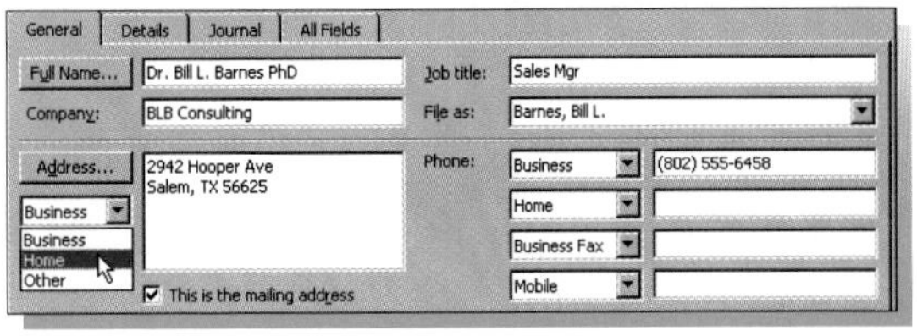

How to Break Down Contact Address Information into Fields

Outlook strives to let you view information in a way that is most useful to you. Here, you will learn how to view a contact's address information in its individual fields. You may find this an easy way to record and/or view this information.

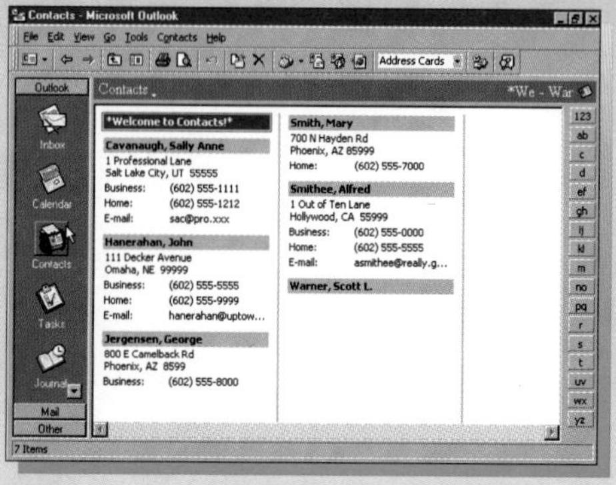

1 Click the Contacts icon on the Outlook Bar to open the Contacts folder. Right-click on one of the contacts listed to open the Quick menu.

FYI

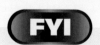

- **You can check the properties for any field from the All Fields section of the Contact form. In addition, you can add and remove custom fields.**
- **Information can be edited from within the All Fields section of the Contact form.**
- **You can tell Outlook not to open the Check Address dialog box when it is confused by an address that you have entered. Turn off that option by removing the checkmark for it at the bottom of the Check Address dialog box. This could save time if you are often prompted to clarify addresses that are correct.**

2 Choose Open from the Quick menu. You can also double-click on one of the contacts to open the Contact form.

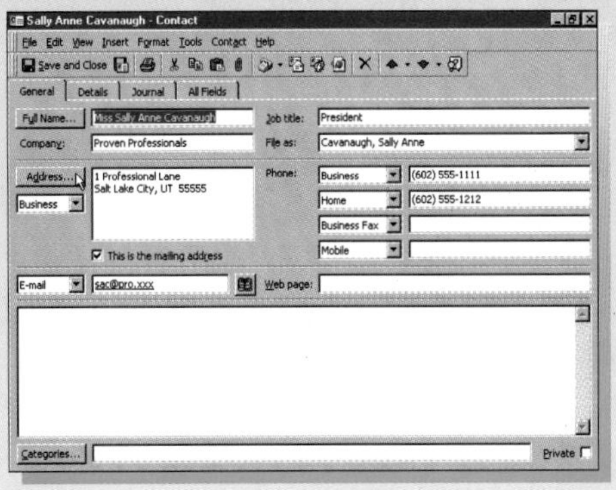

3 The information that was previously entered for this contact is displayed in the Contact form. Click the Address button.

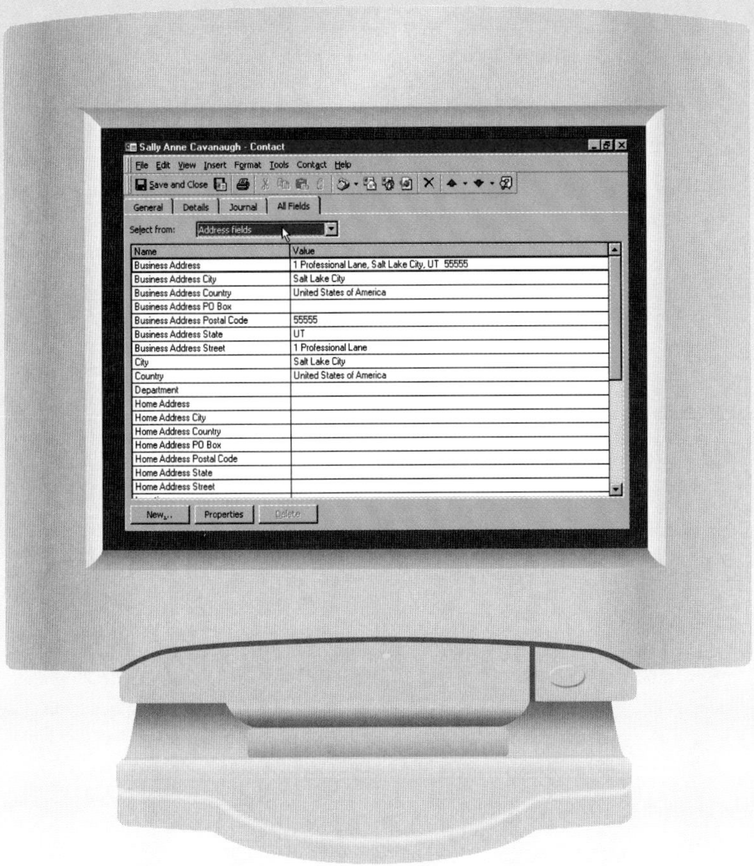

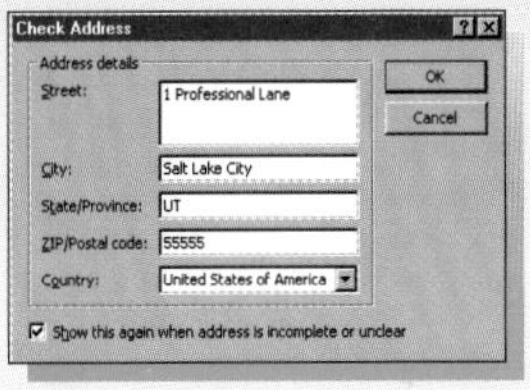

4 In the Check Address dialog box, notice that the information is automatically split into its individual fields—Street, City, State, Zip, and Country. Any time that Outlook is confused by an address, it displays this dialog box so that you can enter the information directly into the individual fields. Click OK to close this dialog box.

5 Click on the All Fields tab. As the name implies, all fields can be viewed individually from this section. Choose Address Fields in the Select From drop-down list box to view only those fields.

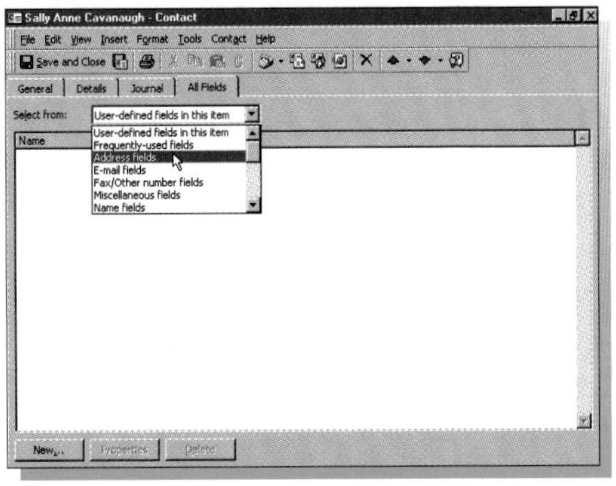

How to Add Multiple Contacts from the Same Company

Adding contacts is a necessary but time-consuming and tedious task at best. One Outlook feature that makes it a little less laborious is the New Contact from Same Company feature. Rather than input the same basic information each time you enter a contact from the same company, this Outlook feature carries over much of the information to a blank form.

FYI

- You can create a copy of a Contact form by highlighting the contact, pressing Ctrl+C to make the copy, and then pressing Ctrl+V to paste the copy in the view.
- You can edit contact information in the Address Cards view without opening the contact as long as the Allow In-Cell Editing option is enabled. Place your cursor in the field to edit and make the changes you want.

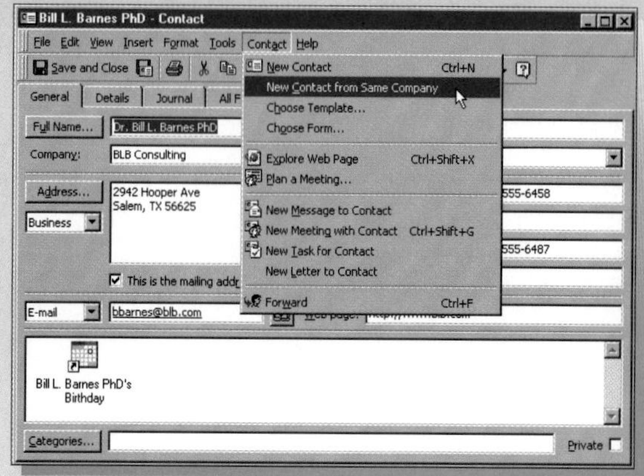

1 Open the Contact form of a person who works at the company from which you want to add more contacts. Choose Contact, New Contact from Same Company from the menu bar.

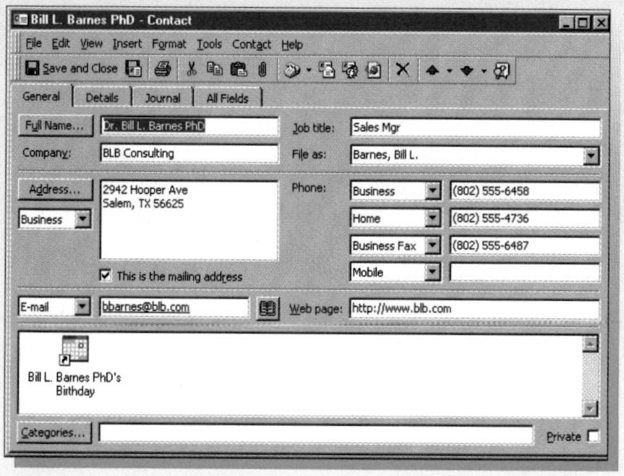

7 Open the copy, and replace all necessary information to create an entry for the new contact. Click Save and Close to save the new Contact form and return to the Calendar window.

6 An identical copy of the highlighted entry is placed after the original contact.

2 Note that the new Contact form that opens is not blank. The Company Name, Business Address, Business Phone, and Business Fax fields are all filled in with information from the previous Contact form.

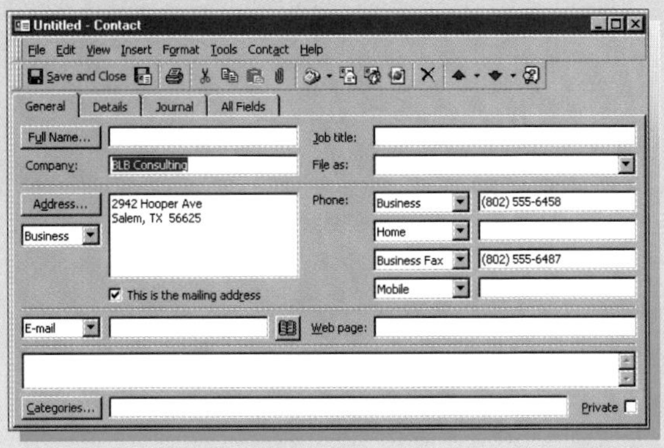

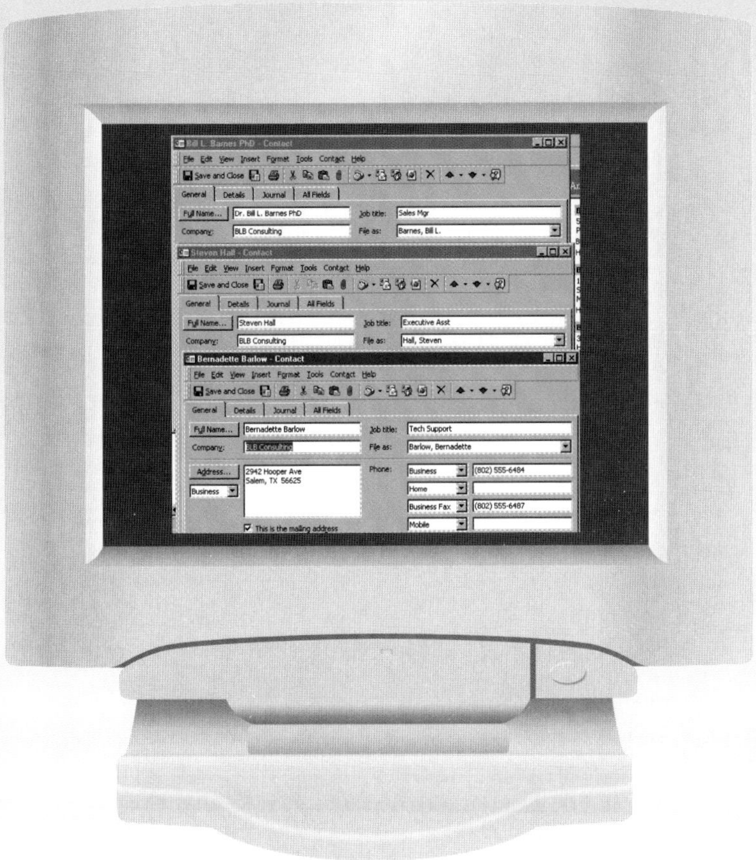

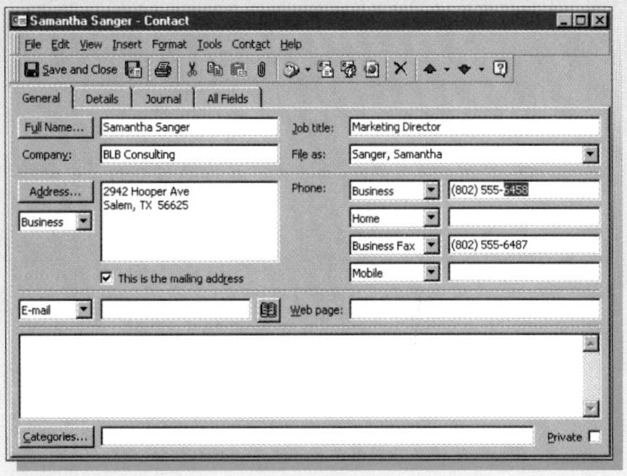

3 Complete the blank fields in the new form and, if need be, edit the phone numbers to reflect the correct extensions. When you're finished, click Save and Close to save the new Contact form and return to the Contacts window.

4 Another way to create a Contact form from the same company is to make a copy of an existing record and edit the information to suit the new contact. Highlight the Contact form to copy and select Edit, Copy to Folder from the menu bar.

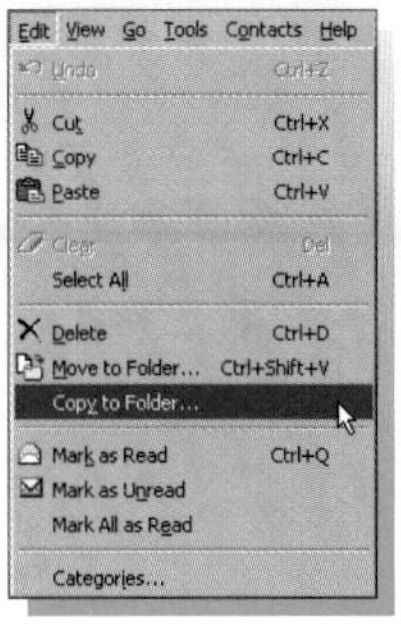

5 Choose Contacts from the Copy Items dialog box, then click OK to return to the Contacts window.

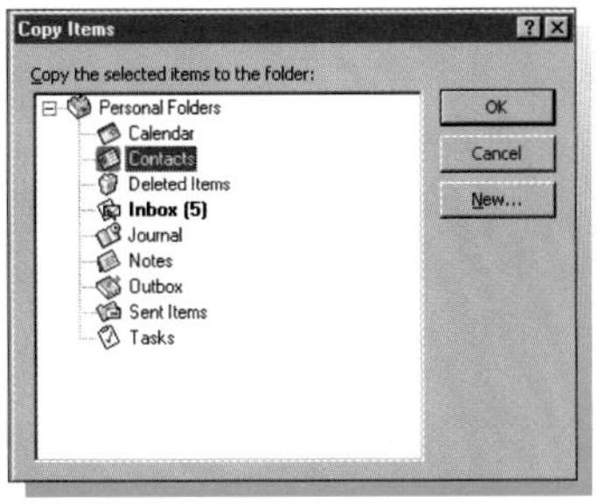

How to Import Contacts from Your Personal Address Book

Another time-saving feature that Outlook provides is the ability to transfer information from your Personal Address Book to your Contacts database without having to reenter all the information. You can import the contents of your Personal Address Book directly into the Contacts database by using the Import and Export feature.

FYI

● **Personal Distribution Lists from the Personal Address Book are not imported into the Contacts database. However, the individual members of Personal Distribution Lists are imported. Since members of a Personal Distribution List are also listed separately in the Personal Address Book, they will actually be imported twice. To eliminate the duplicate records, switch to the Phone List view in the Contacts window and click on the Full Name field header to sort the list by full name. Highlight duplicate records by holding down the Ctrl key and clicking each duplicate. With all duplicates highlighted, click the Delete icon in the toolbar.**

1 To open the Import and Export Wizard, choose File, Import and Export from the menu bar.

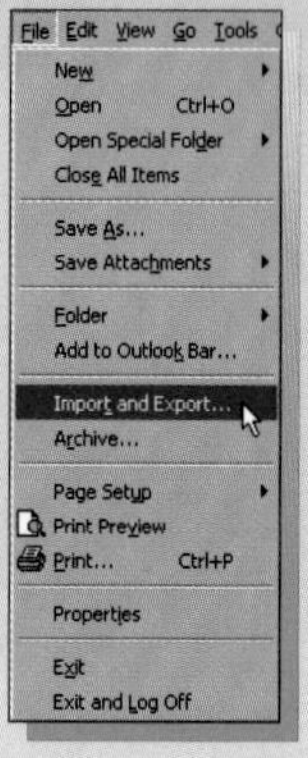

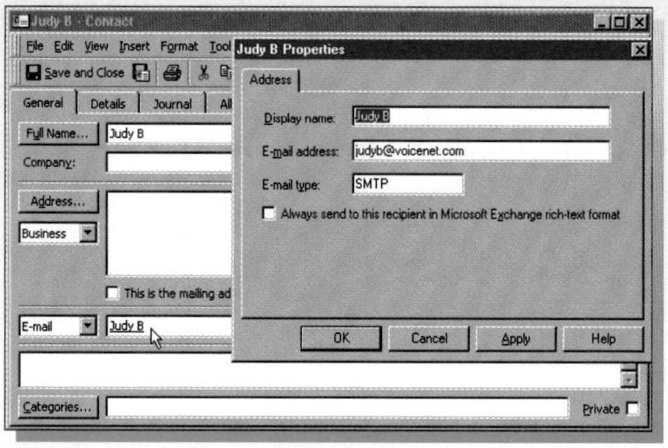

6 All the data in the Personal Address Book is imported into the Contacts database.

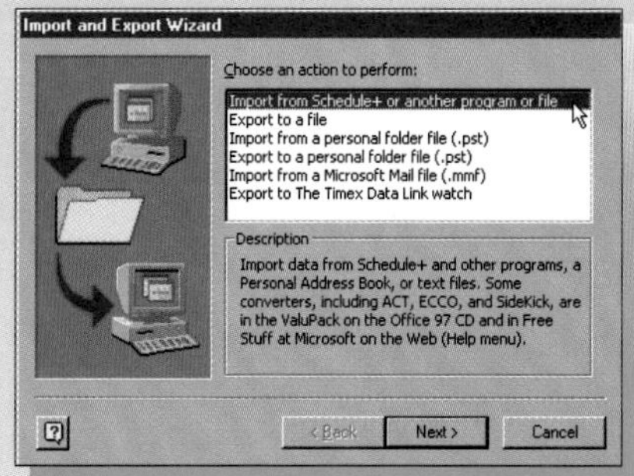

2 When the Import and Export Wizard opens, select Import from Schedule+ or Another Program or File. Then click Next to move on.

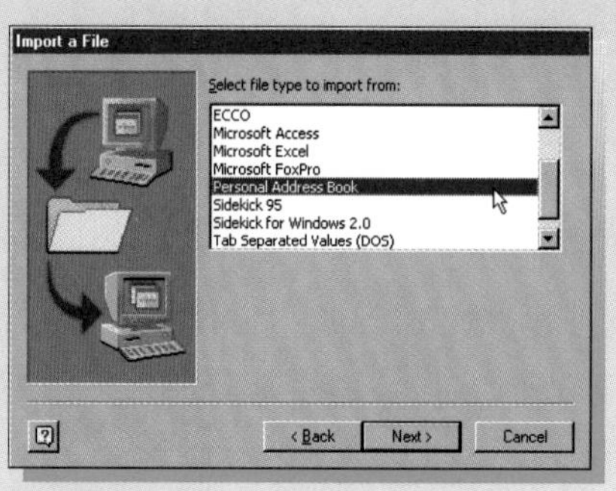

3 In the Import a File dialog box, scroll through the File Type list to find Personal Address Book, and select it. Note the variety of programs from which Outlook allows you to import files. Click Next to proceed.

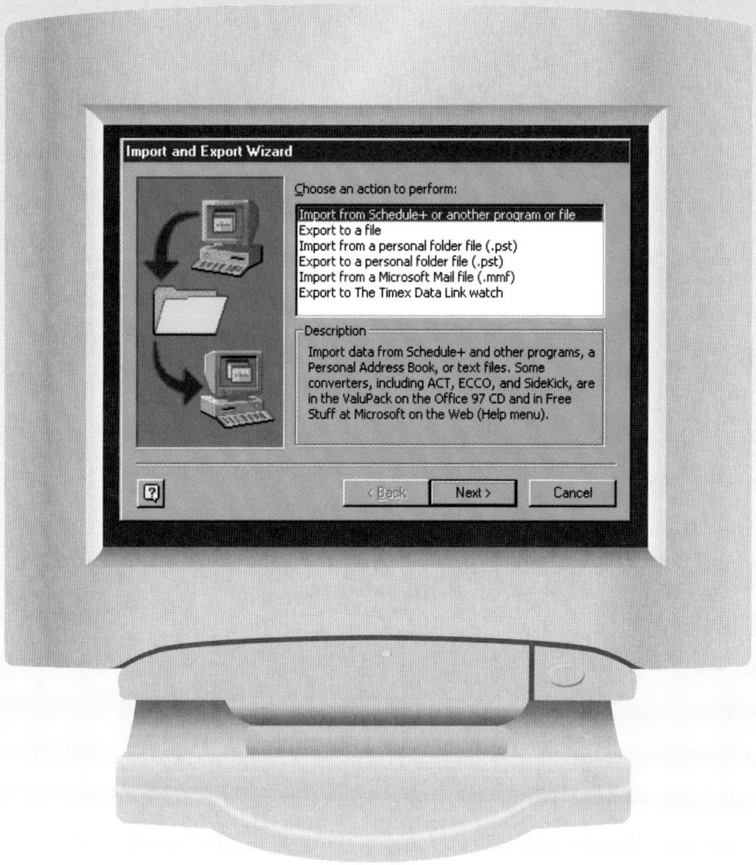

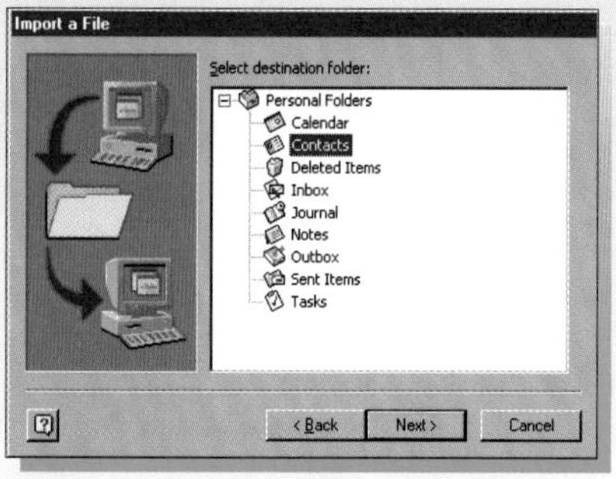

4 From the Select Destination Folder list choose Contacts and click Next to open the final Import a File dialog box.

5 Make sure the Import Personal Address Book option has a checkmark in the box to the left. At this point you are ready to import your Personal Address Book. Click the Finish button to begin the import.

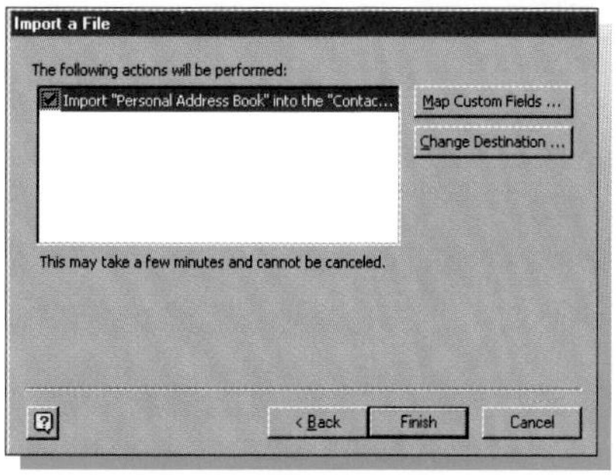

How to Add Outlook Contacts to the Address Book

After building an extensive database, it stands to reason that you want to be able to use the contact data when sending e-mail messages. Fortunately, Outlook provides a way for you to do just that. First you have to set up an Outlook Address Book as an Outlook information service, in addition to your Personal Address Book. Then you can use the Contacts folder as an E-Mail Address Book.

After you create an Outlook Address Book, you can also use it as a data source for performing mail merges with Microsoft Word.

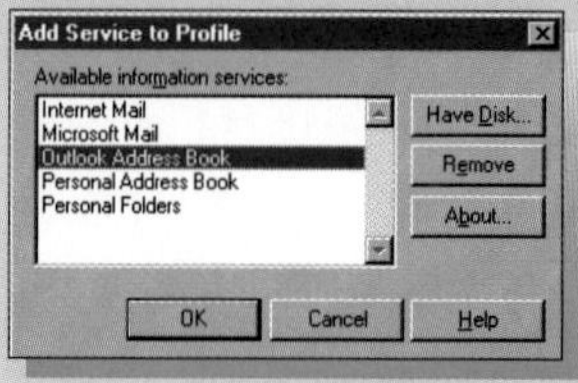

1 Choose Tools, Services to open the Services dialog box, and then click the Add button to open the Add Service to Profile dialog box. Select Outlook Address Book from the list of available information services and click OK.

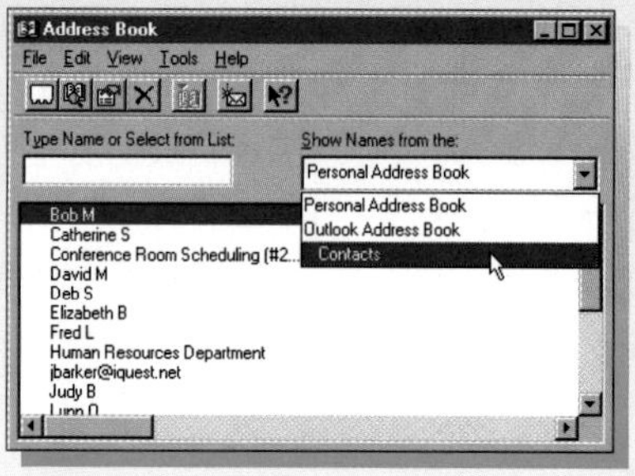

6 Press Shift+Ctrl+B to open the Address Book. From the Show Names From The: drop-down list, select Contacts to open the new Outlook Address Book called Contacts. Notice that Contacts is indented below Outlook Address Book, indicating it is a subset of Outlook Address Book. This means that you can have more than one Outlook Address Book.

FYI

- **You can have multiple Contacts databases and therefore multiple Outlook Address Books. If you want to separate business and personal contacts, simply choose File, New Folder to create a new folder. Name it Personal Contacts, make sure that it contains contact items, and make it a subfolder of Personal Folders or Contacts. Add personal contacts following the same steps used to create contacts. Then follow the steps in this exercise to add the Personal folder to the Address Book.**

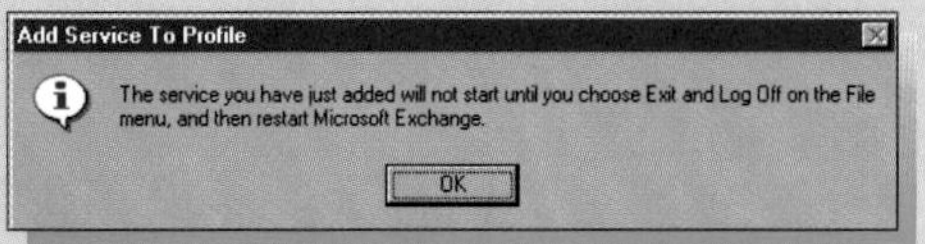

2 An informational dialog box appears, notifying you that you must exit and reenter Outlook before this service is added. Click OK to close the dialog box, and then click OK to close the Services dialog box.

3 Choose File, Exit and Log Off from the menu bar to close Outlook. Be sure to use Exit and Log Off rather than Exit.

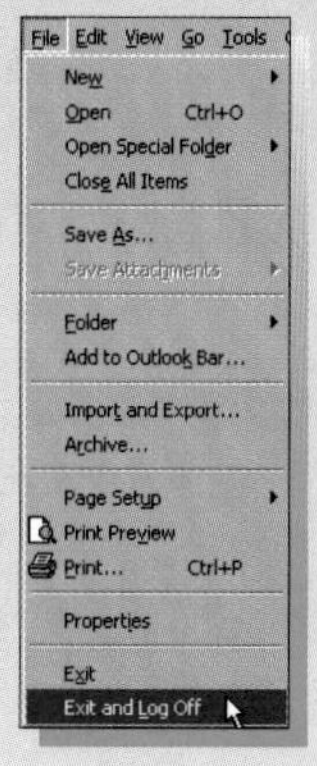

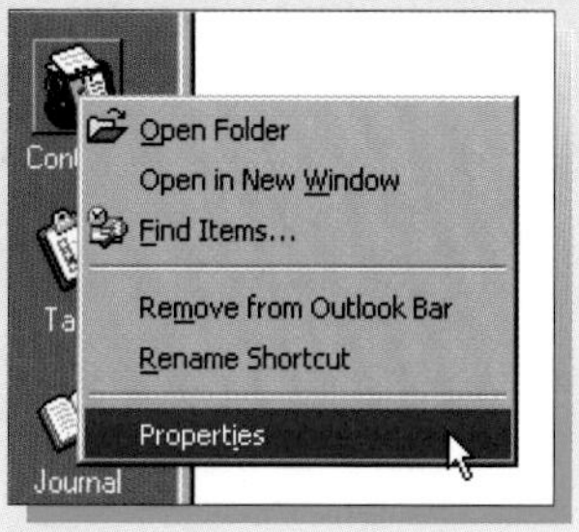

4 Reopen Outlook and right-click the Contacts icon on the Outlook Bar. Select Properties from the pop-up menu to open the Contacts Properties dialog box.

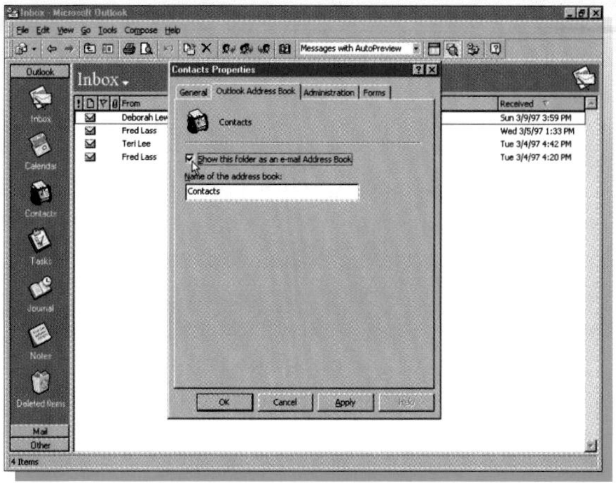

5 Click the Outlook Address Book tab and enable the option named Show This Folder as an E-Mail Address Book by placing a checkmark in the box to the left. Click OK to close the dialog box.

How to Create a Contact from an E-Mail Message

As you've seen from the other exercises in this chapter, adding contacts to the Contacts database is a chore that can to some extent be automated. One important source of contact information is your incoming e-mail. Recognizing this, Outlook provides a way for you to convert an e-mail message into a contact entry with a couple of mouse clicks.

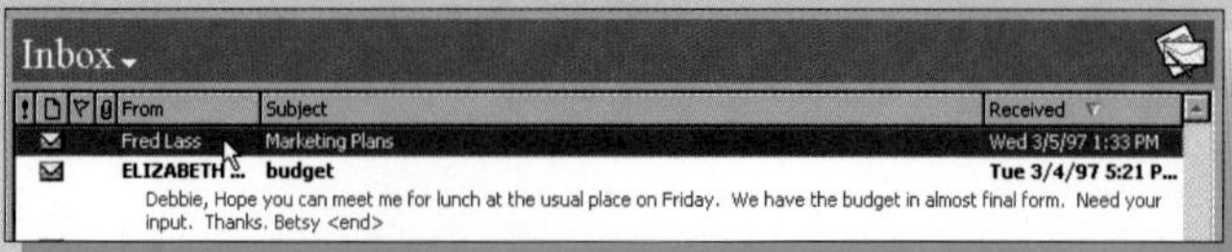

1 Click the Inbox Shortcut icon in the Outlook Bar to open the Inbox window. Select an e-mail that came from someone you want to add to the Contacts database.

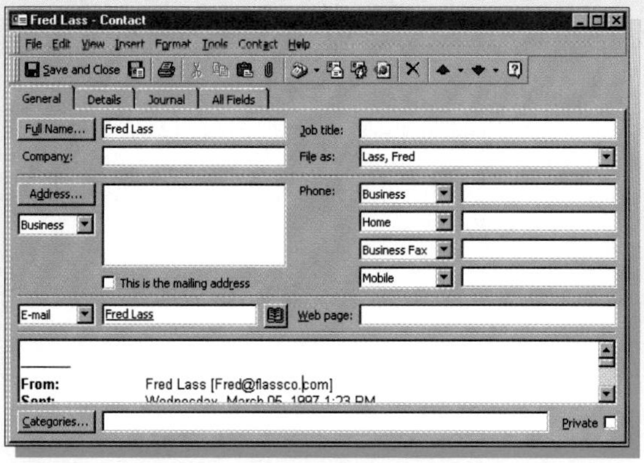

6 A new Contact form appears, filled out with basic information for this e-mail message sender. The bottom text box (used for your own notes) has the header and message of the e-mail. Fill in the additional information you need in the Contact card, then click Save and Close.

FYI

- **You can create a new contact from an e-mail message and attach the message to the Contact form at the same time. Highlight the contact in the Inbox and click the Move to Folder icon on the toolbar. A new Contact form for the sender of the message opens and the message itself is inserted in the Contact form text box. Fill in the missing information and click Save and Close.**

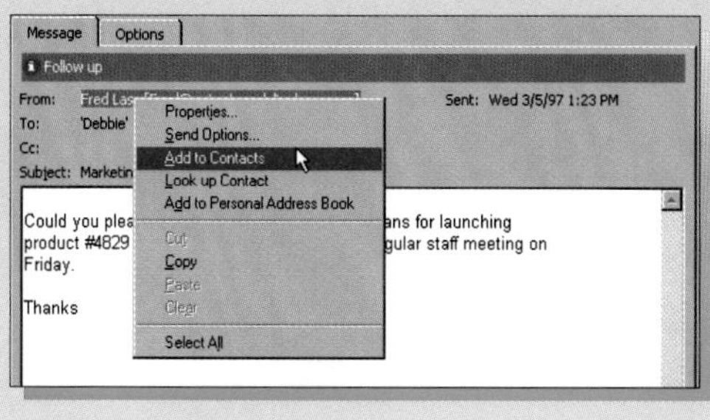

2 Double-click the e-mail message to open it. Position your mouse pointer over the From address in the message header, and right-click to access the pop-up menu. Choose Add to Contacts.

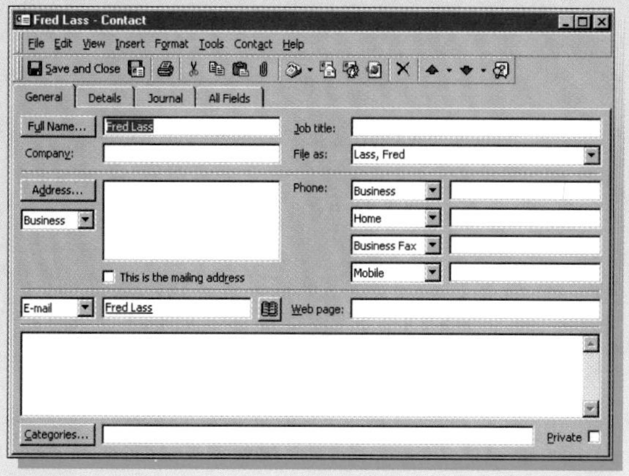

3 Notice that the new Contact form contains basic information from the e-mail address of the message. The Full Name, E-Mail Address, and File As fields are filled out.

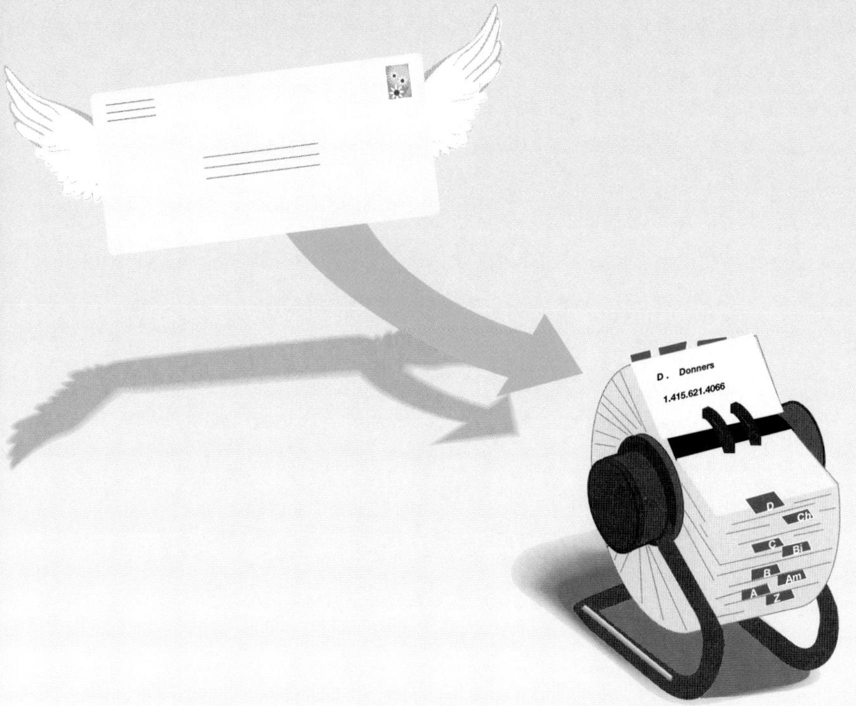

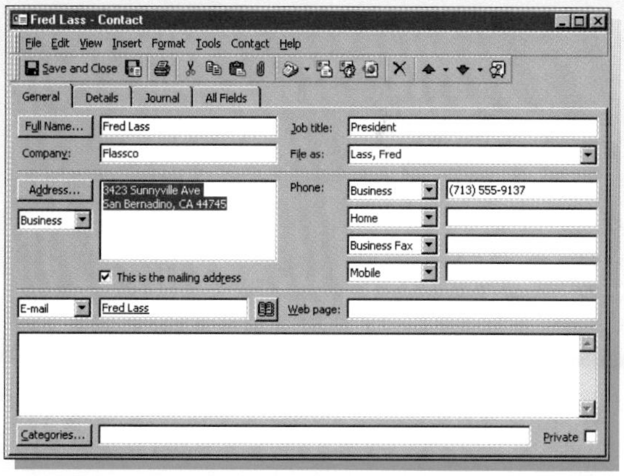

4 Add additional information to the Contact form as necessary and click the Save and Close button to save the new contact and return to the e-mail message. Press Alt+F4 to close the e-mail message and return to the Inbox window.

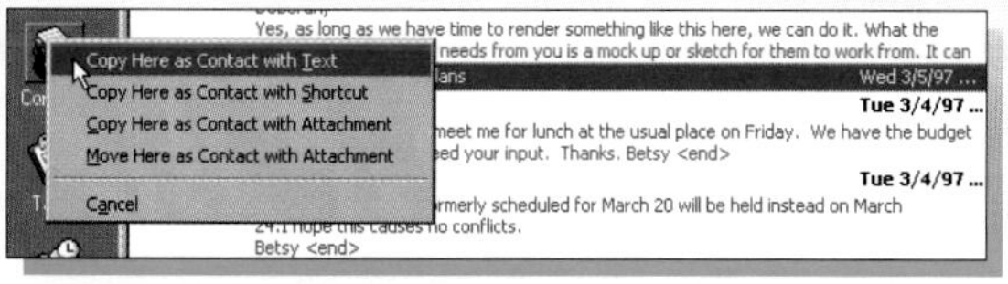

5 If you're comfortable with dragging objects using your mouse, there's a shortcut to creating a contact. From the message listing in the Inbox, right-drag (press and hold the right mouse button while you drag) the Message icon to the Contacts icon in the Outlook bar. When you release the mouse button, a menu appears. Choose Copy Here as Contact with Text.

How to Send E-Mail to a Contact

Sending e-mail to a contact is a simple matter of opening the Inbox and filling out the header, then composing a message. The job of an information manager is to simplify your life; therefore, the contact system in Outlook has an easier way.

You can perform a number of contact-related actions from within the Contacts information viewer, including sending e-mail quickly and easily.

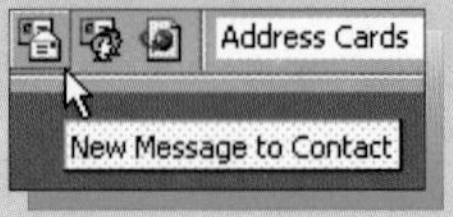

1 To send an e-mail message to someone listed in your Contacts database, just highlight the contact and click the New Message to Contact icon on the toolbar.

FYI

- **You can also use the drag-and-drop method to create an e-mail message to a contact. Simply drag the contact listing by holding down the left mouse button, and drop it on the Inbox icon on the Outlook Bar. A new Message form appears with the contact's e-mail address inserted in the To field.**
- **The drag-and-drop method can also be used to address a single e-mail message to more than one contact at a time. Highlight the multiple contacts you want to use by holding down the Ctrl key and clicking each contact. Then drag (using the left mouse button) any one of the highlighted contacts to the Outlook bar and drop it on the Inbox icon. A new Message form pops up with each of the selected contacts' e-mail addresses in the To field.**

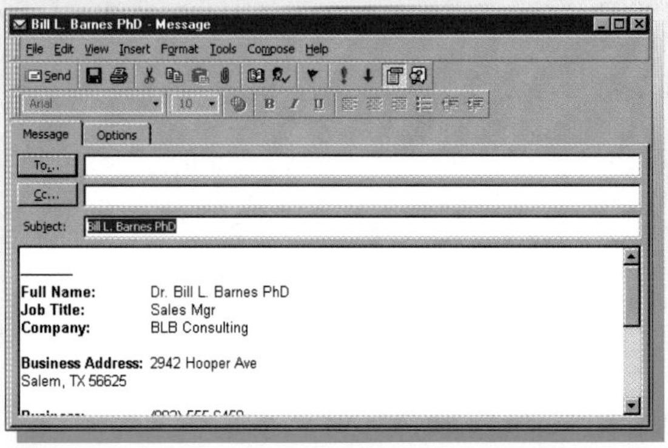

6 A new Message form opens and the contact name is inserted in the Subject field. The contact data is included in the message body. All you have to do is fill out the name of the recipient (the person you wanted to pass this contact information to). It's probably a good idea to add some additional text, such as "Here's the information you wanted," or at least "Hello." Then click Send.

2 A new Message form opens with the contact's e-mail address already inserted in the To field. Complete the header as necessary, compose your message, and click Send to dispatch your e-mail.

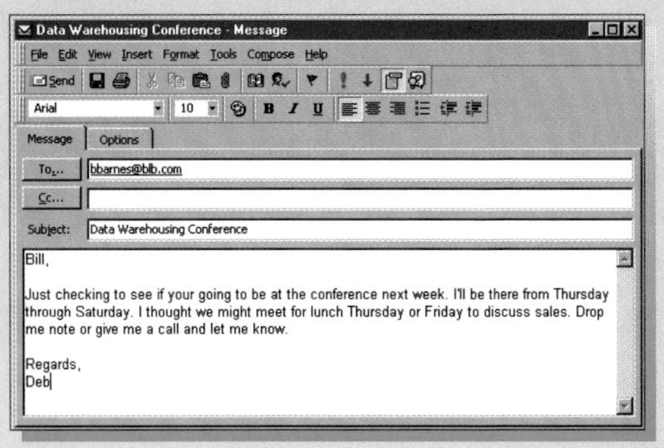

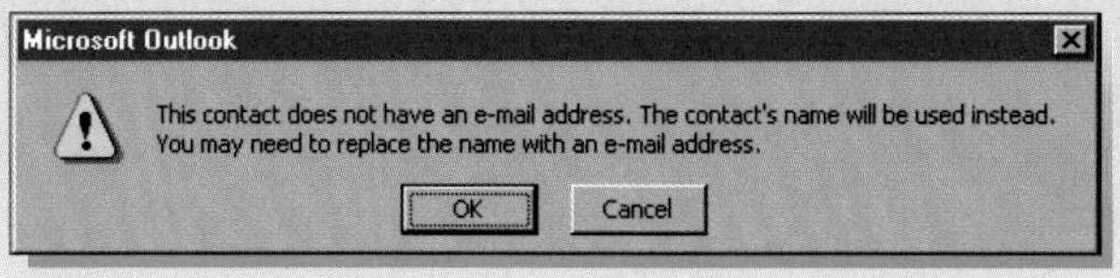

3 Occasionally you may find you entered a contact into your database without an e-mail address. If you attempt to send a message to that contact by following these steps, a dialog box appears informing you that the contact has no e-mail address and you must therefore enter it manually. Click OK to proceed.

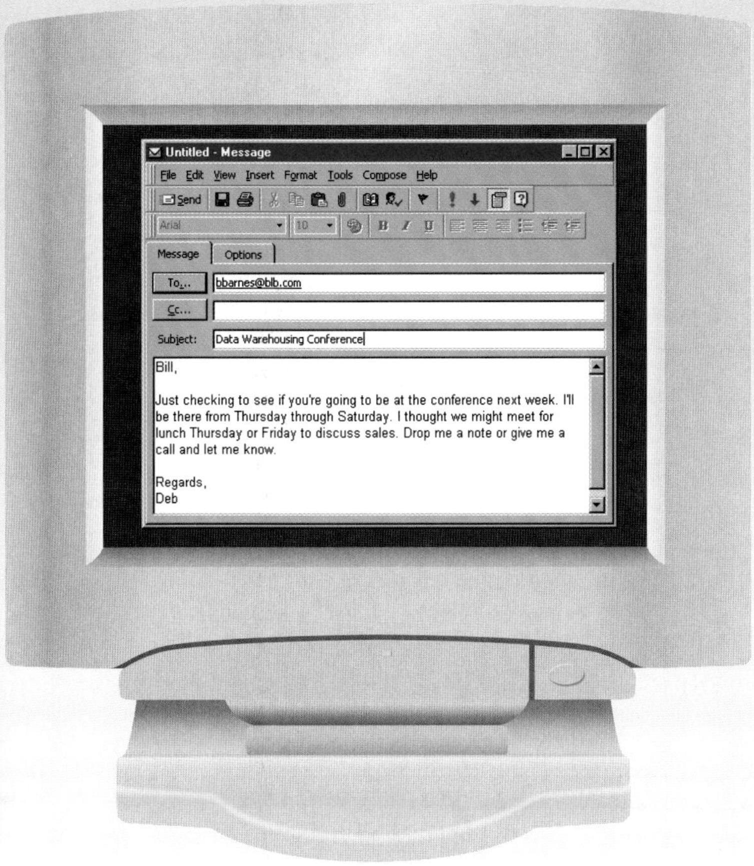

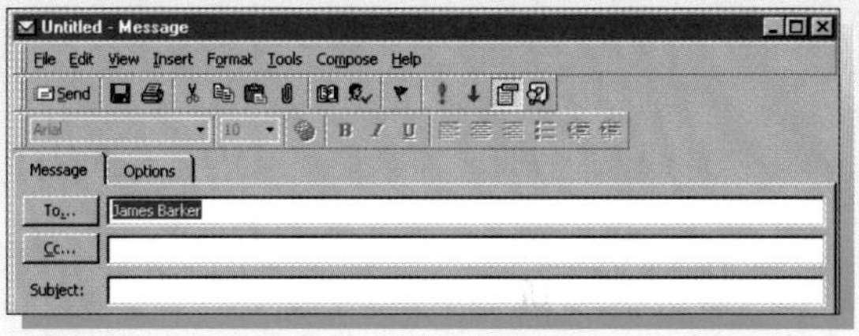

4 A new Message form opens with the contact's name inserted in the To field. Move to the To field and type the correct e-mail address for the contact to remove the name, replacing it with a valid e-mail address. Then complete the message and click Send to transmit the message.

5 Another handy e-mail feature available in the Contacts window is the ability to create an e-mail message with a contact as the subject of the message, and include data about the contact in the message text. This is useful when you're sending e-mail to someone who wants information about that contact. Use the right mouse button to drag and drop the contact listing onto the Inbox icon on the Outlook Bar. When you release the mouse button, a pop-up menu offers a number of choices. Choose Copy Here as Message with Text.

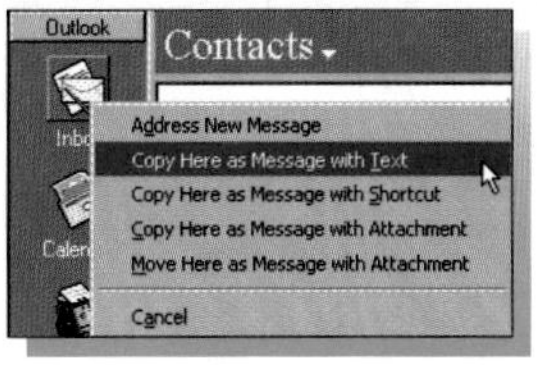

How to AutoDial Contacts

If you have a modem connected to your PC, you can use the Outlook AutoDial feature to call contacts.

Besides the modem, you have to have a real telephone. The modem is attached to the wall jack with a telephone cord, and the cord from the telephone (the real one) plugs into the other modem jack. All modems except PCMCIA cards have two jacks, one that connects to the wall and another for a telephone instrument. If you're working with a portable computer that has a PCMCIA modem, you can't use this feature.

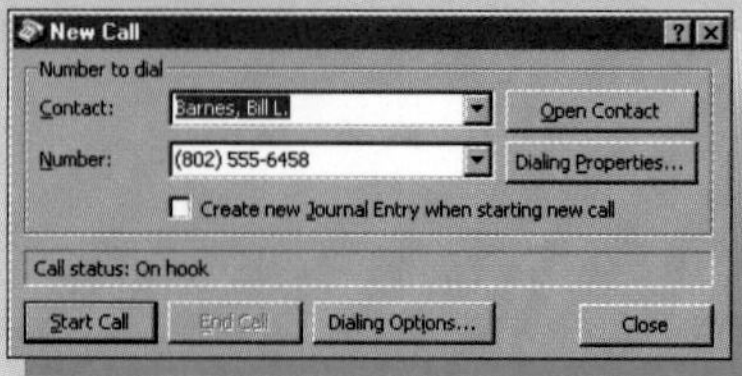

1 In the Contacts information viewer, highlight the contact you wish to call, then click the AutoDialer icon in the Contacts window toolbar to open a New Call dialog box. The name and business phone number of the contact are filled in.

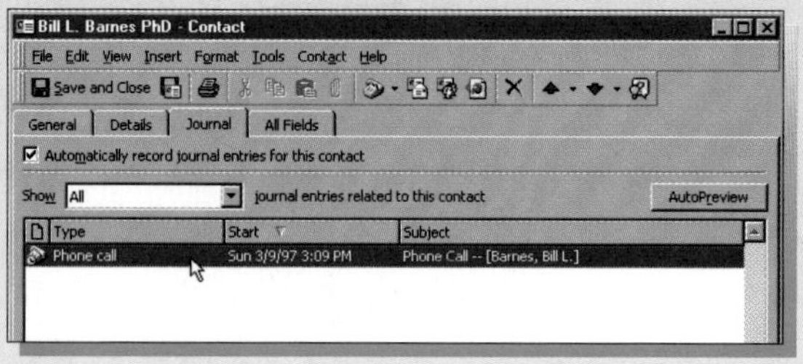

6 Whenever you want to view the journal entry for this phone call, double-click the contact card, and when it opens, click the Journal tab. You see the journal entry (it's a listing), and you can double-click it to open it so you can view or edit it.

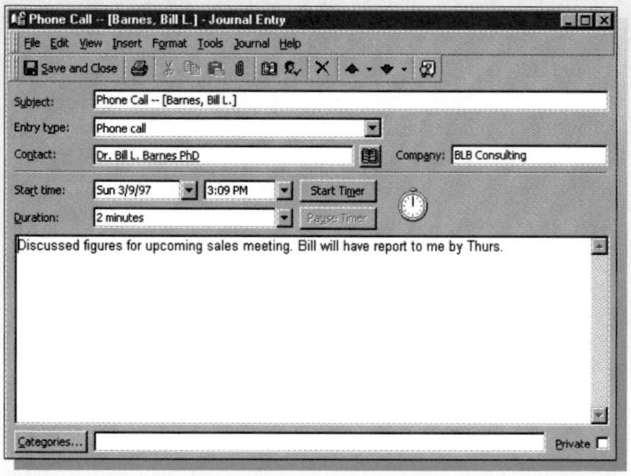

5 When you click Talk, the timer in the Phone Call Journal Entry form begins tracking the time. Note that the contact name, as well as the date and time of the call, are already recorded for you. You can take notes on the conversation in the text window. When you finish the conversation, click Save and Close to save the Journal entry and close its window. When you return to the New Call dialog box, click End Call to hang up. Then click Close to return to the Contacts information viewer.

FYI

- **You can also activate the AutoDialer by right-clicking the contact and selecting AutoDialer from the pop-up menu.**
- **Press Ctrl+Shift+D to start a new call and then manually enter the name and phone number.**

2 Click the Dialing Properties button to open the Dialing Properties dialog box. Make sure that the area code field reflects your correct area code. In the How I Dial from This Location section, add any prefix numbers that you need to dial in order to get an outside line (usually a 9). Do not include the number 1 in the long-distance field—Outlook automatically dials a 1 before making a long-distance call. Click OK to return to the New Call dialog box.

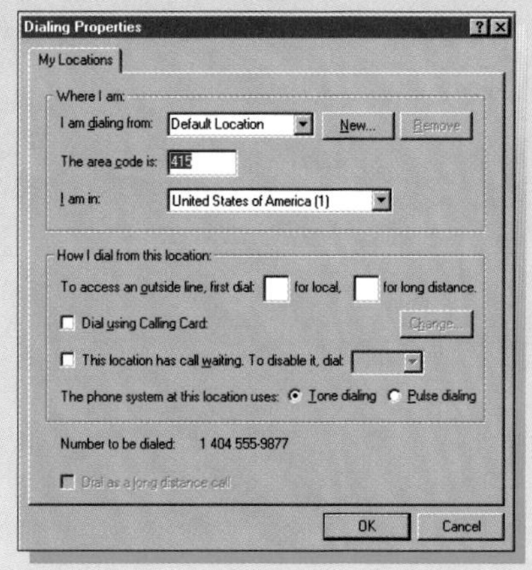

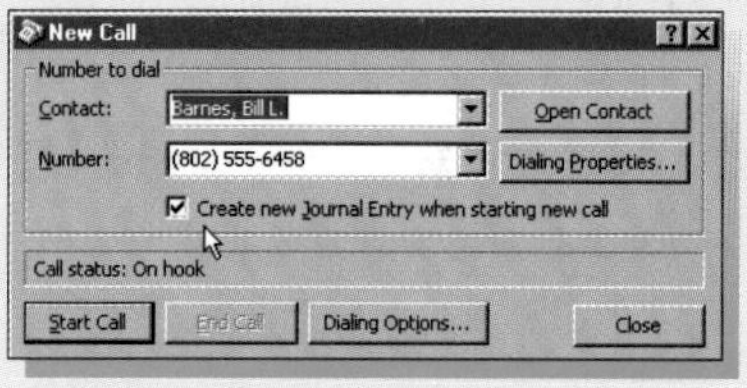

3 If you want to take notes and log the call (it's called a Journal entry and there's more information about Journal entries later), click the option named Create new Journal Entry When Starting New Call. Now, click Start Call to dial the number.

4 Several things happen simultaneously. The modem dials the phone number, a Journal Entry form opens, and a dialog box pops up informing you that you should lift the receiver and click Talk to talk, or click Hang Up to disconnect.

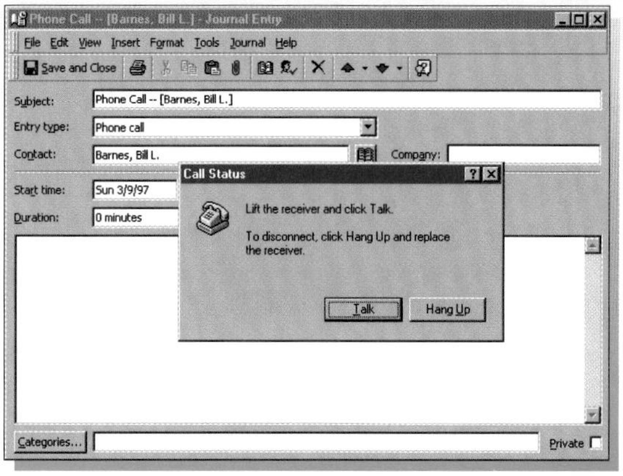

How to Create a Speed Dial List

Outlook can store information about people that you contact on a regular basis. It will maintain their names, addresses, phone numbers, e-mail addresses, and even their Web addresses, if they have one.

A nice feature of Outlook is its ability to dial phone numbers for you. No fumbling through a card file or organizer; you simply find the person in your contact list and instruct Outlook to dial the number. However, you may call some people so often that repetitively locating them in your contact list becomes burdensome. Outlook uses a phone trick to take care of this problem. It allows you to create a Speed Dial list to quickly make phone calls.

This page will show you how to add numbers to your speed dial list and how to dial using the Speed Dial list.

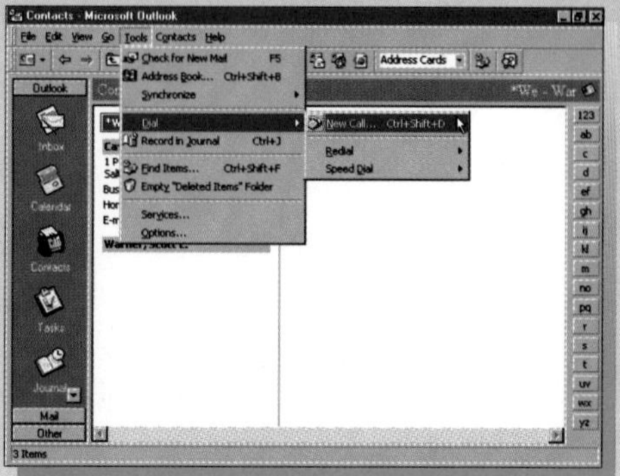

1. Under the Tools menu, choose Dial, New Call.

FYI

- **When adding someone's name to your Speed Dial list who also appears in your Contacts database, Outlook will automatically fill in the phone number. If the person has more than one phone number, Outlook will place all the numbers in a drop-down list box and let you choose which to place on the Speed Dial list.**
- **Add people to the Contacts database before adding them to the Speed Dial list. If you cannot reach them by phone, you will have all of their contact information readily available.**

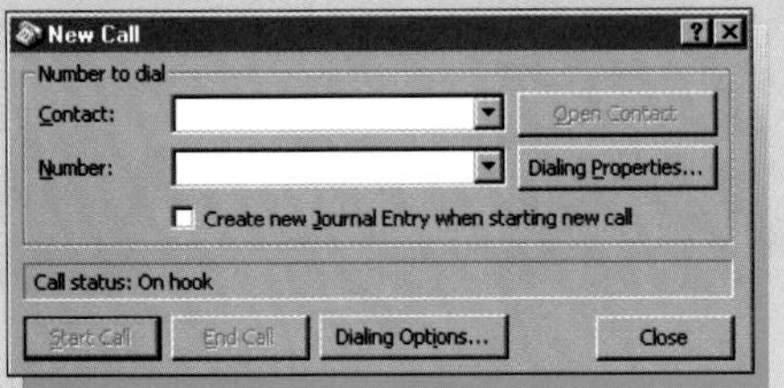

2 The New Call dialog box appears. This is where you enter a name from the Contacts database or a phone number to start a phone call. Click the Dialing Options button.

3 The Dialing Options dialog box opens. Type a name into the edit box labeled Name, and a phone number into the edit box labeled Phone Number. Click the Add button to add the person's name to the Speed Dial list. Phone numbers can be removed from the list by highlighting them on the list and clicking the Delete button. Next, click the OK button and then click the Close button of the New Call dialog box.

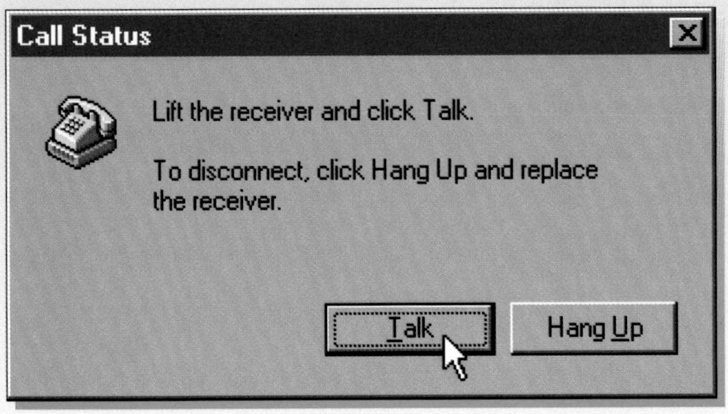

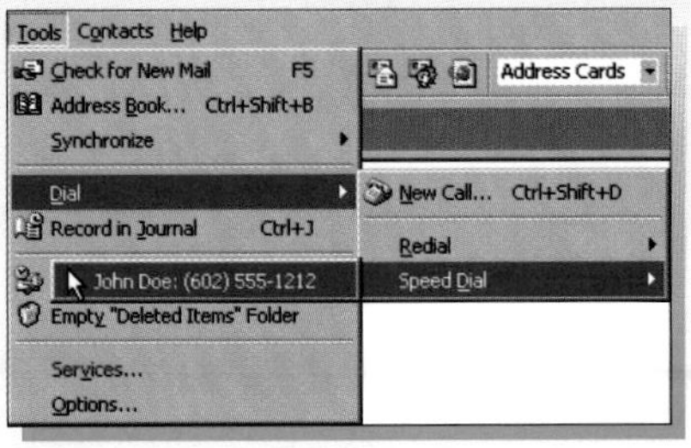

4 Choose the entry that you just made in the Speed Dial list by selecting it from Tools, Dial, Speed Dial. Outlook will automatically call the contact.

How to Create a Journal Entry in a Contact Card

Many tasks that you complete using Outlook are automatically added to your Journal. You can review the Journal to see when you last edited a document and how long you spent editing it. Or you could see all of the messages that you have sent or received for any given period of time.

You can take advantage of the abilities of the Journal to keep track of tasks performed for people listed in your Contacts database. This gives you a record of the tasks you have performed and whom you have performed them for.

This page will show you how to record a Journal entry, associated with someone in your Contacts database, directly from their Contact card.

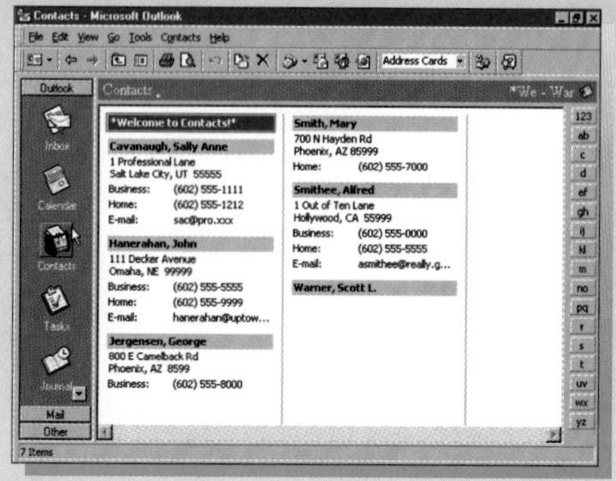

1 Click the Contacts icon on the Outlook Bar to open the Contacts folder. Double-click on one of the contacts listed to open the Contact form for that person.

FYI

- **If you have trouble tracking the amount of time you spend dealing with people, create a Journal entry each time you perform a task for that person and use the timer to track the time for you. Click the Start Timer to begin and click the Pause Timer button anytime you stop.**
- **You can associate more than one person with a Journal entry. Click the Address Book button and add the other contacts that the Journal entry affects.**
- **Limit the types of Journal entries that you view in the Journal section of the Contact form by selecting a type of entry to view from the Show drop-down list box.**

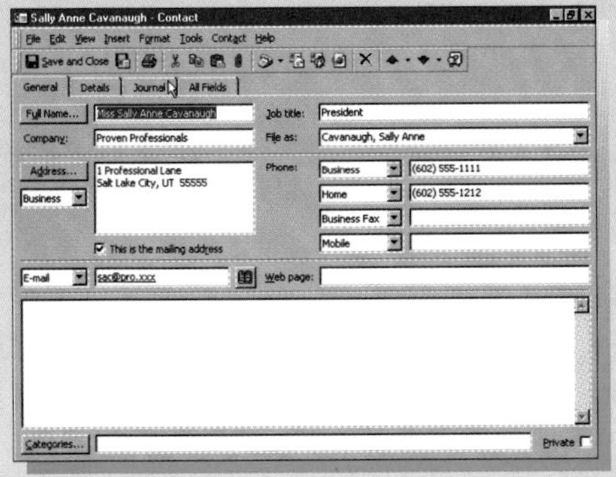

2 Notice all the information about a contact on the General tab. If you need to change any address or personal information, you can do so now. Click the Journal tab. Notice the checkbox that will allow you to automatically record Journal entries for a contact.

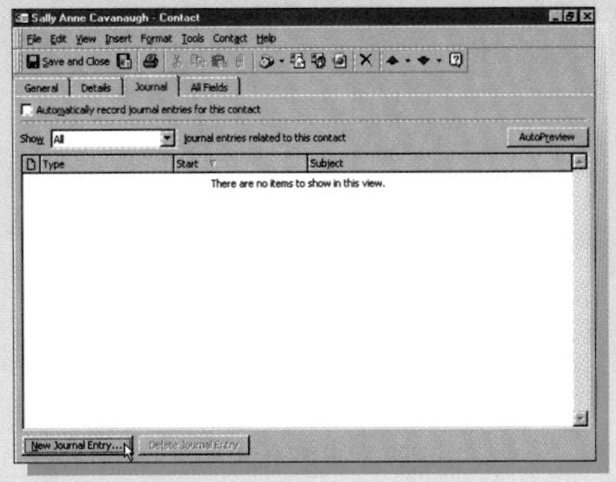

3 Click the New Journal Entry button at the bottom of the screen to create a new Journal entry. If you had any Journal entries already recorded, then you could have chosen the Delete Journal Entry button.

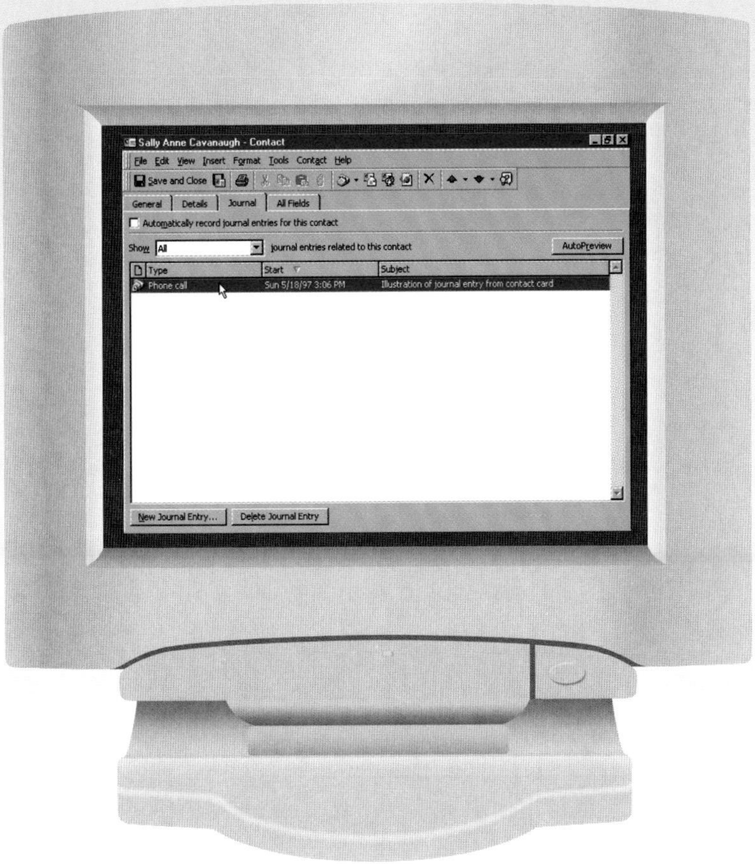

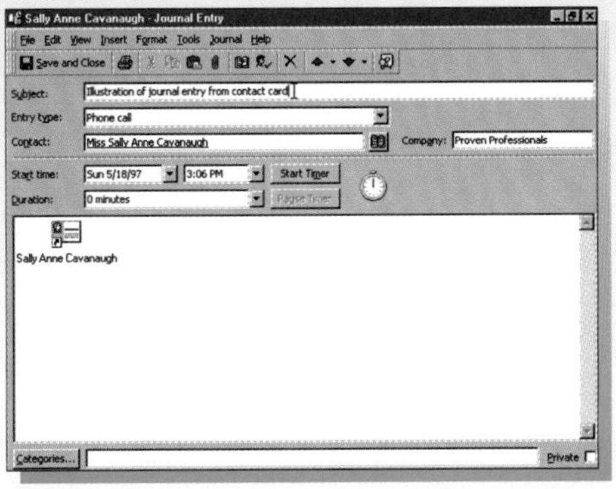

4 Fill out the information for the Journal entry. Notice that you can click the Start Timer button to start timing the Journal entry. Click the Save and Close button when finished and the new entry will appear.

How to Print Your Contact List

Printing your contact list can be a convenient way of having contact information with you when you are not at your computer. For example, if you are going on a business trip, it is handy to have a copy of your contact list so you can reach someone if you need to. You can select specific contacts that you want to print and you can print them in many different styles.

On this page, you'll learn how to select various options for printing your contact list.

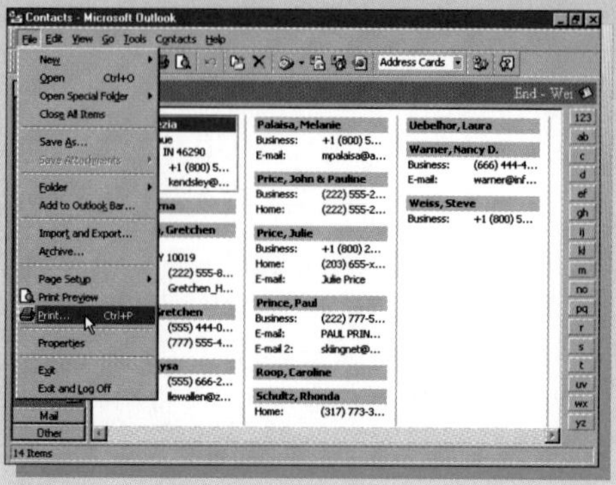

1 Select Address Book from the Current View drop-down list box on the toolbar. (Note: you can print from any current view.) Choose Print from the File menu.

FYI

- **A quick way to print anything in Outlook is to use the Print button on the toolbar. The button looks like a printer.**
- **To select multiple contacts to print: hold down the Shift key while selecting consecutive contacts with the mouse pointer or hold the Control key down while selecting nonconsecutive contacts with the mouse pointer. Make sure you choose the print range as Only Selected Items from within the Print dialog box.**
- **Right-click on the name of the contact that you want to print and choose Print from the Quick menu. Outlook will automatically print that contact's information in the Memo style. You can also do this for multiple contacts.**

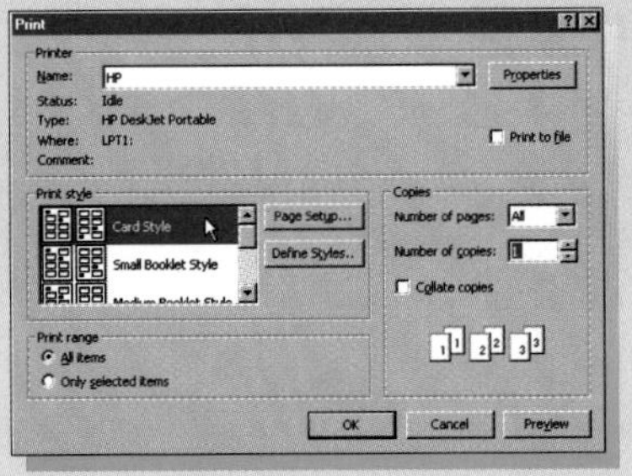

2 The Print dialog box will appear with numerous options to choose from. choose the print style that you wish your contacts to be printed in. Because you are printing *all* your contacts, the default print range is All Items. Click on the Page Setup button to alter the look of your printout.

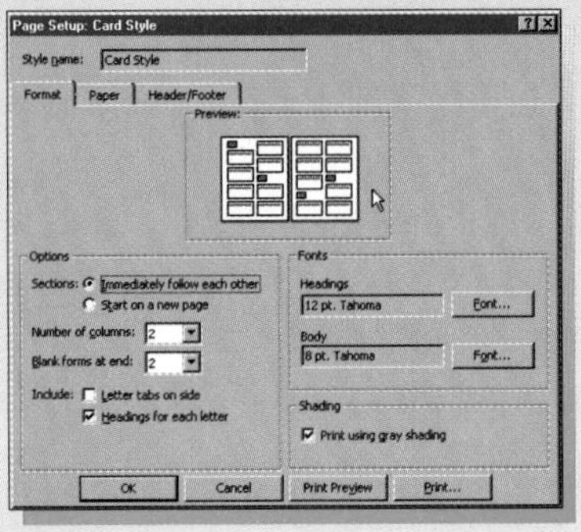

3 On the Page Setup dialog box, you can change more options. Some of the options are the number of columns and whether the sections start at a new page or immediately follow each other. When you have finished making your changes, click the OK button to go back to the Print dialog box.

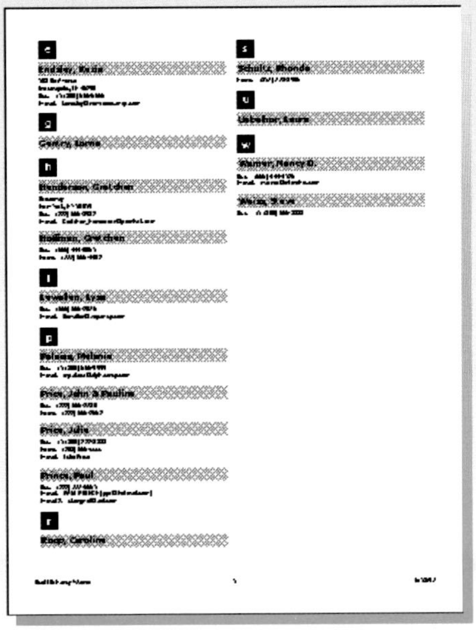

4 When you are satisfied with your print options, click the OK button to print the contact list.

How to Use Microsoft Word Mail Merge with the Contacts Database

You may find that you need to send the same letter to several people in your Contacts database. It would be very time-consuming to type each name and address into a separate letter. Microsoft Word has a tool called Mail Merge that allows names and other information contained in a data file to be merged with a special document. This, in turn, creates a new document for each name in the data file.

On this page you will learn how to create a Mail Merge document using an Outlook Contacts database as the data source.

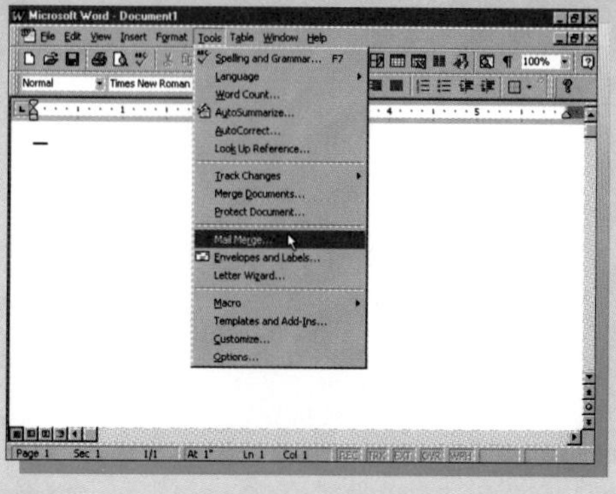

1 Open Microsoft Word and choose Mail Merge from the Tools menu. You must be in a document to see the menu option.

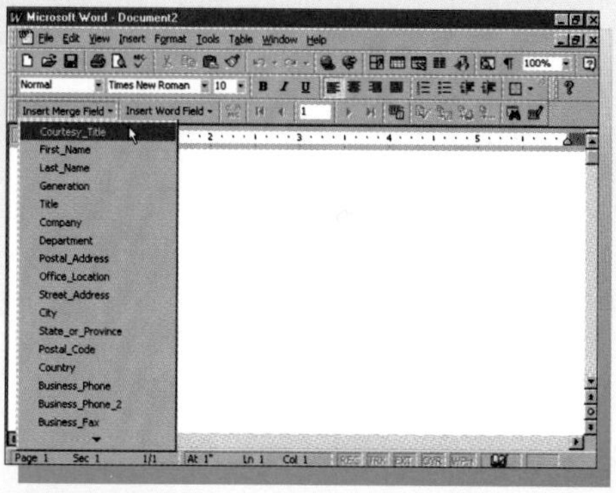

7 The Mail Merge Helper dialog box closes. Notice that there is an extra Word toolbar on your screen now. This is the Mail Merge toolbar. Create your letter and insert a Mail Merge field anywhere you want information from your Contacts database to be placed. Insert Mail Merge fields by clicking on the Insert Merge Field button and choosing a field name.

8 Edit the document and then click the Mail Merge Helper button on the Mail Merge toolbar to return to the helper's dialog box.

(Continues on next page)

FYI

- **You can export the Contacts folder to let someone else use the information contained in your Outlook Contacts database. This must be done if the mail merge is not being performed in Word 97 or higher.**
- **Non-Outlook data sources can also be used to create Mail Merge documents. There are more steps involved, but it is easier than entering a large amount of data into Outlook to perform a single mail merge.**
- **You can always save your documents to be used again later. The query options can be changed or the text can be altered to update the document.**

2 Click the Create button and choose Form Letters from the pop-up menu. You could also create mailing labels or envelopes by choosing the appropriate option.

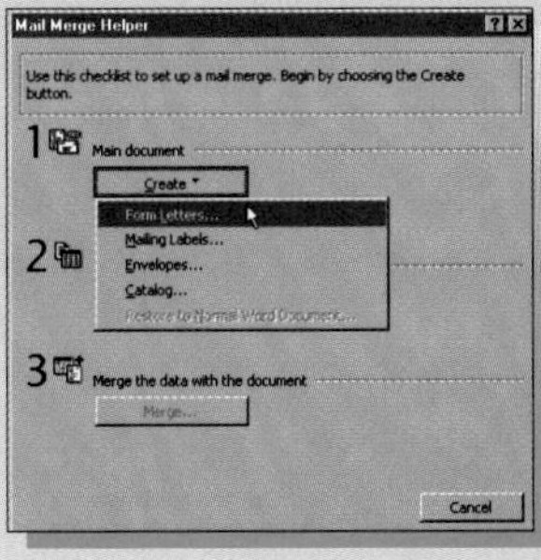

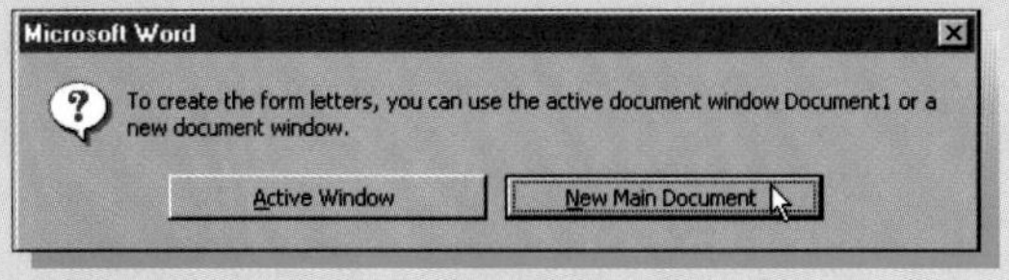

3 A dialog box appears asking if you would like your Mail Merge document to be created in the active window or in a new main document. Click the New Main Document button. The active window would be a form letter you have already created.

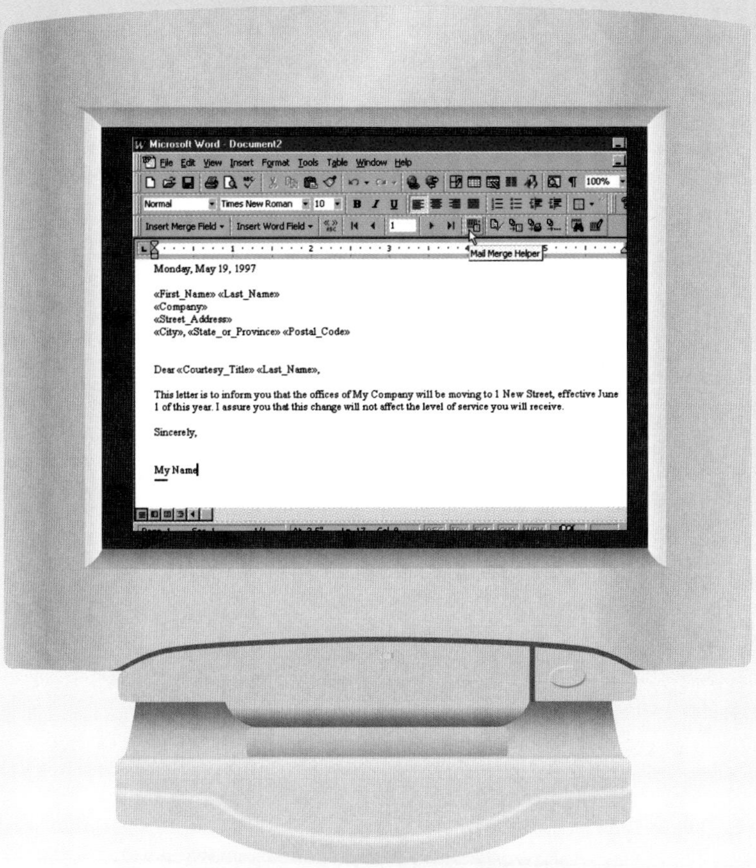

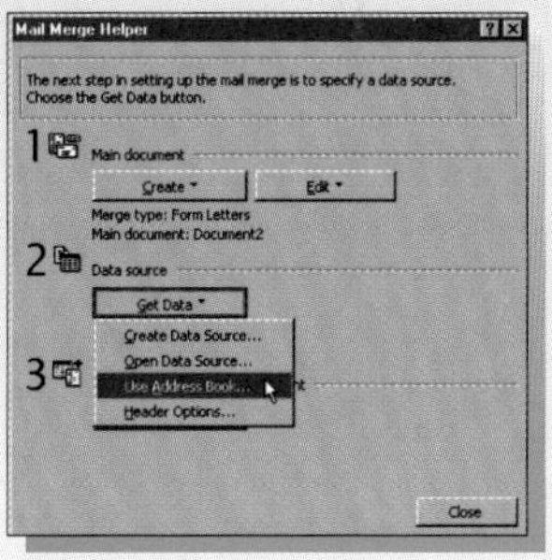

4 An Edit button appears next to the Create button. Click the Get Data button and choose Use Address Book from the pop-up menu.

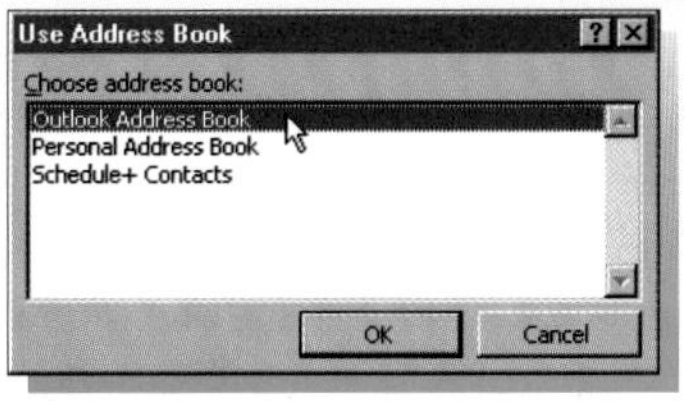

5 The Use Address Book dialog box appears. Select Outlook Address Book from the list and click the OK button.

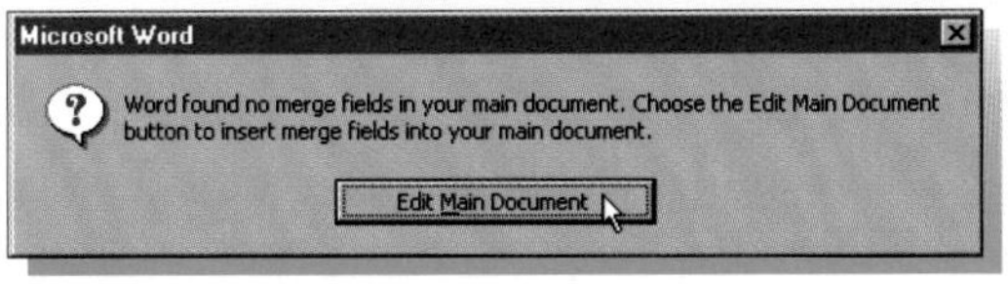

6 A dialog box appears. It informs you that you have no Mail Merge fields and asks if you would like to edit the document to insert some. Click the Edit Main Document button.

How to Use Microsoft Word Mail Merge with the Contacts Database

(Continued)

Using the Contacts database to create many documents saves time. However, there may be situations where you want to use only a few of the contacts in your database. This can be accomplished by using the query options in your Mail Merge. Query options let you limit the entries used from the Contacts database.

On this page, you will learn how to set Mail Merge options, including the query options, and how to perform the mail merge.

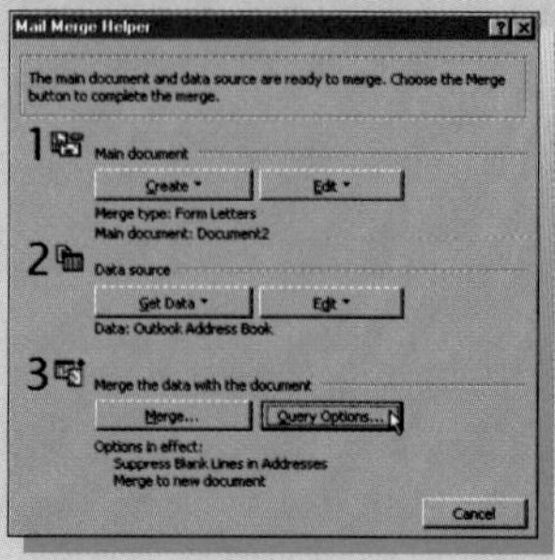

9 An Edit button appears next to the Get Data button, and a Query Options button appears next to the Merge button. The Edit button is used to edit a data source. However, when using the Outlook Address Book as the data source, it is best to edit the data from within Outlook. Click the Query Options button.

15 Click the Merge button when you are returned to the Merge dialog box. The mail merge will be completed according to the options that you chose.

FYI

- The mail merge does not have to apply only to a letter that is printed. You can also have a mail merge produce e-mail messages. Choose Electronic Mail in the Merge To drop-down list box. Then, click the Setup button and select the field that contains the e-mail address.
- You can use the Mail Merge toolbar after you become used to the mail merge process. The Mail Merge Helper is easy to use but might slow down an experienced user.

14 The Checking and Reporting Errors dialog box appears. As its title suggests, it lets you determine how errors should be identified and how they should be reported. Make your choice and click the OK button.

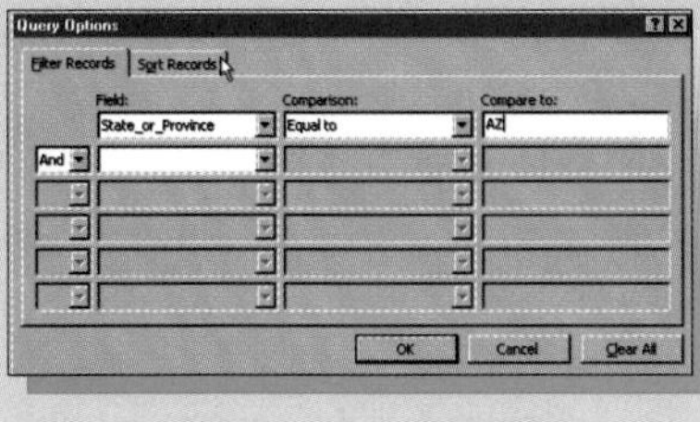

10 Select State_or_Province from the Field drop-down list box, Equal To from the Comparison drop-down list box, and type **AZ** in the Compare To edit box. Choosing these options will cause only the contacts from Arizona to be used in the mail merge. Click the Sort Records tab.

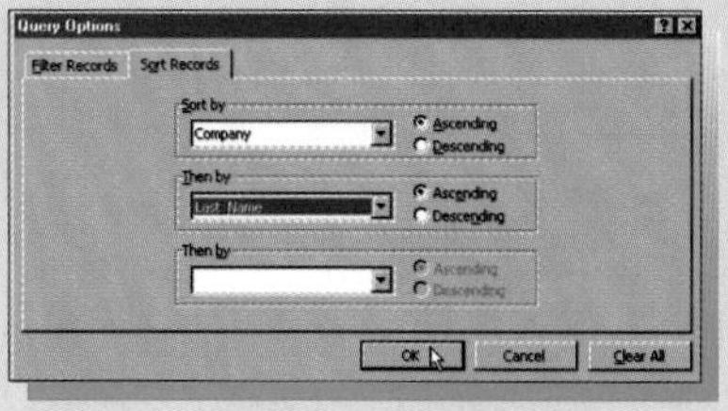

11 Choose to sort by company in ascending order and then by last name in ascending order. You could choose one more field to sort by if you wish. Click the OK button to apply the options you have selected and close the Query Options dialog box.

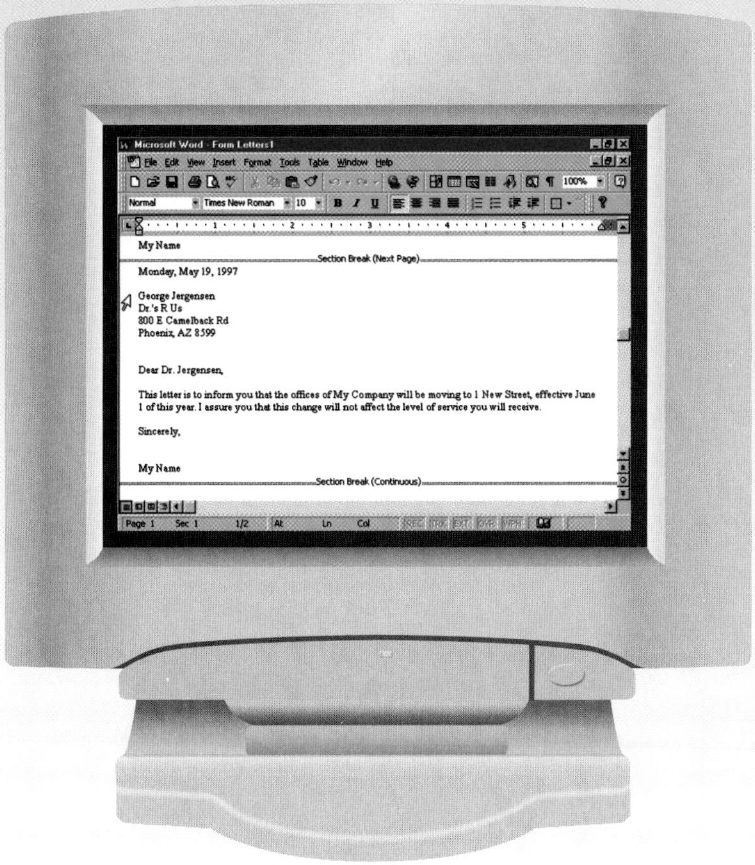

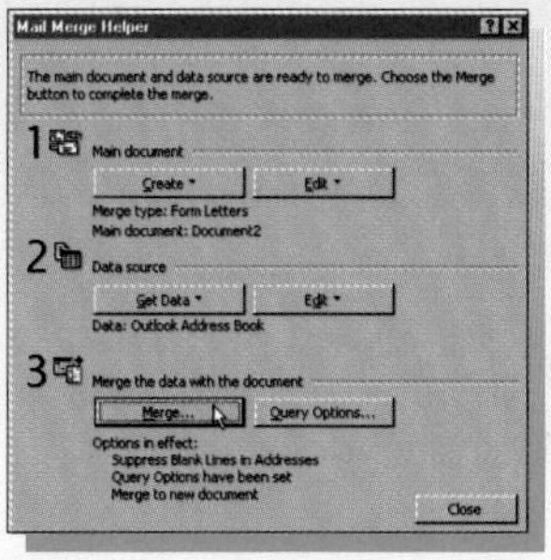

12 The Mail Merge Helper dialog box lists the options in effect. You will notice that the query options are listed. Click the Merge button.

13 The Merge dialog box appears. There is a Query Options button if you need to change the filter or sort criteria. Click the Check Errors button.

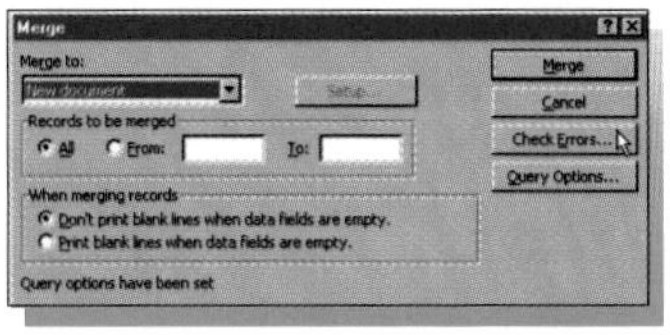

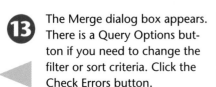

How to Sort and Filter the Contact View

Now that you have added numerous contacts to your Contacts database, you can begin to sort and filter them for your reference. You might be interested in sorting your contacts by name, company name, or other sort options. Outlook lets you sort your contact entries in any manner you wish.

When you want to view only contacts that meet conditions you specify, you can use a filter. For example, you can filter all contacts that are of a personal nature to see just their information alone.

On this page, you'll learn how to sort and filter contact entries, and this will help you keep track of and locate your contacts.

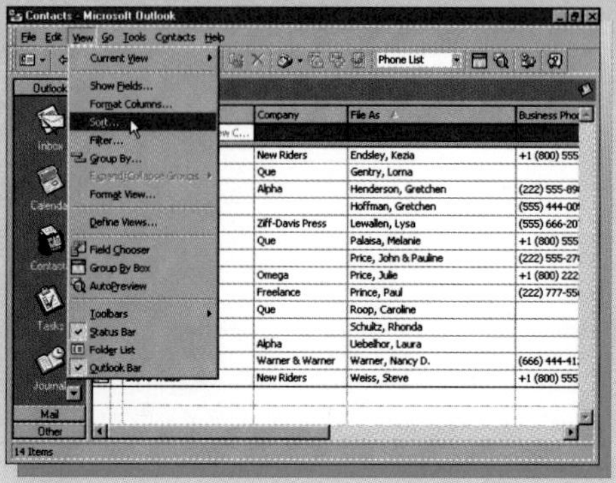

1 Open the Outlook group on the Outlook Bar. Click on the Contacts icon. It looks like a rolodex. All the entries that you have made in your Contacts database will be displayed. Choose Sort from the View menu.

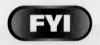

6 The Contact view will appear with the filter applied. Notice that there are only a few entries that meet the specific filter criteria.

FYI

- **You can click the heading at the top of any column to sort the list by the information in that column. For example, if you want to sort your entries by company name, click the header that says Company. The list will be sorted alphabetically by company.**
- **The upper-right corner of the Folder banner shows the words "Filter Applied" when a filter is applied to a selected folder. This will let you know that certain items have been *filtered out*. When you remove a filter, "Filter Applied" will disappear.**
- **To remove a filter on your Contact view, choose Filter from the View menu. The Filter dialog box will appear with the criteria for your current filter. Click the Clear All button to remove the filter and clear the criteria. Then click the OK button to once again see all the entries in the Contacts view.**

2 The Sort dialog box will appear, which will allow you to sort items in your Contacts view by different criteria. Click on the drop-down list box in the Sort Items By field. You can scroll through the various sort options. Notice that these options correspond with the Contact View column headers. Choose to sort items by company in ascending order. Then, click the OK button.

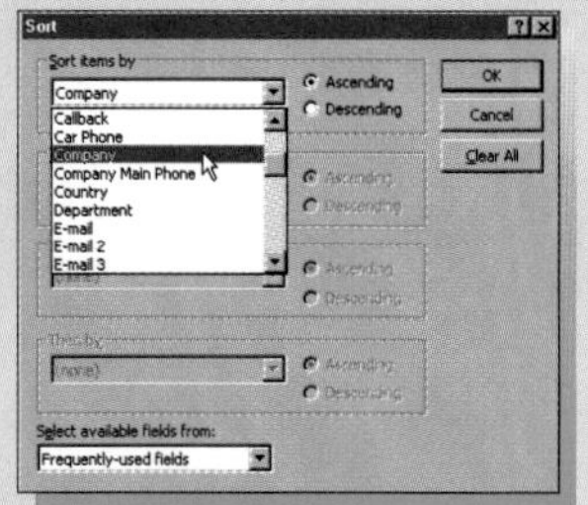

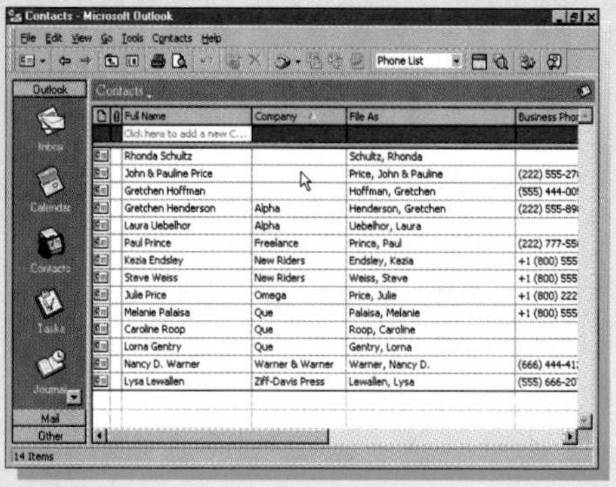

3 The Contacts entries will automatically sort by the company name in alphabetical order. You can even sort your entries by multiple items. For example, you can sort first by company, then select the Then By drop-down list box and choose to sort second by full name within a subject. This is handy if you have multiple entries for your companies. Outlook allows you to sort by up to four different items at a time.

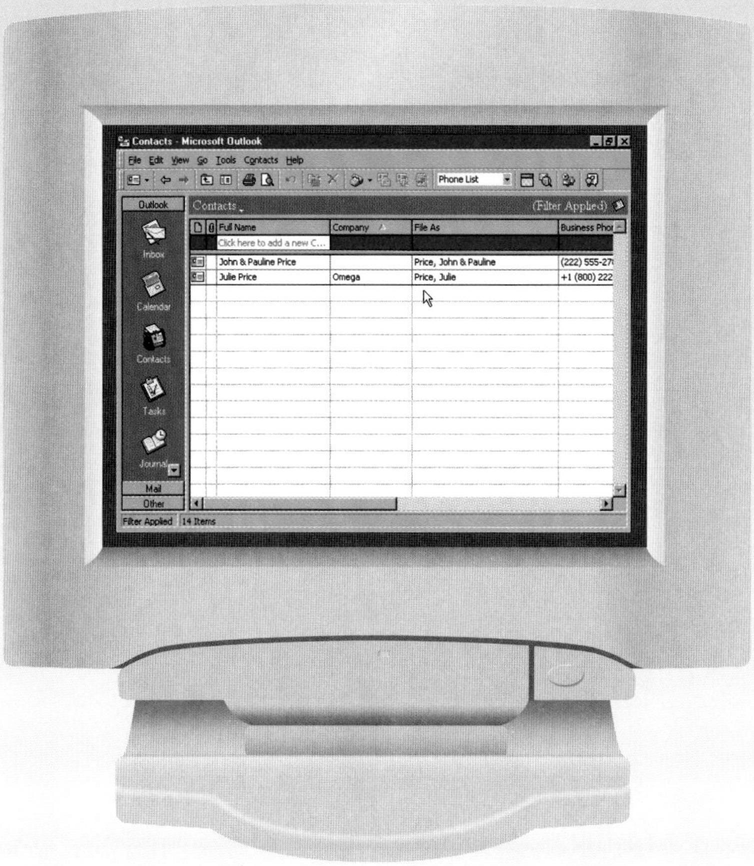

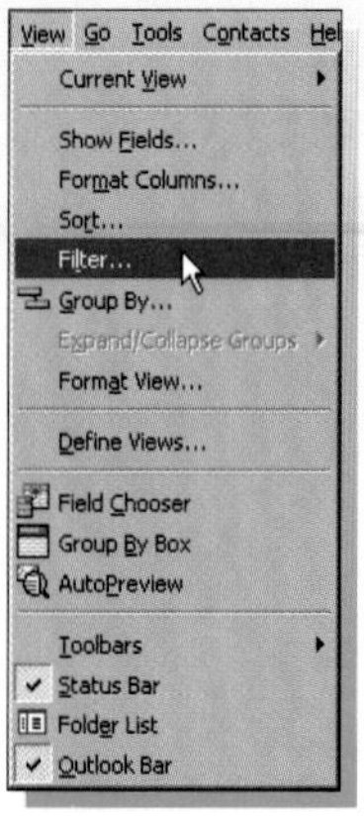

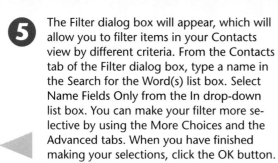

4 Choose Filter from the View menu.

5 The Filter dialog box will appear, which will allow you to filter items in your Contacts view by different criteria. From the Contacts tab of the Filter dialog box, type a name in the Search for the Word(s) list box. Select Name Fields Only from the In drop-down list box. You can make your filter more selective by using the More Choices and the Advanced tabs. When you have finished making your selections, click the OK button.

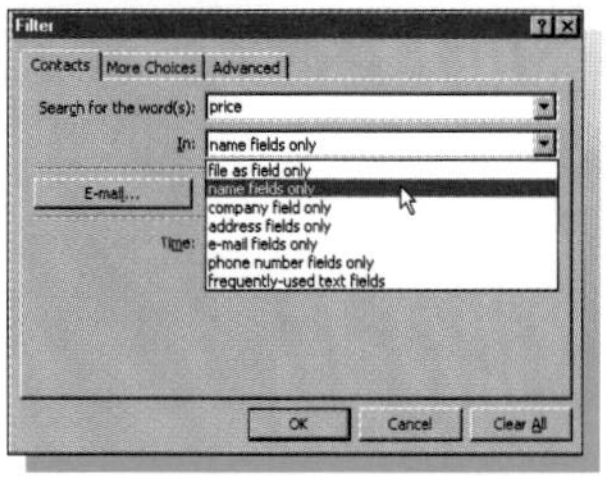

Ctrl + N=
New Journal
Entry
Ctrl + A=
Select All

P A R T 6

Using the Journal

REMEMBER that Outlook is an information manager. If you're only using it as an appointment calendar or address book, you're missing out on a great deal of the power that it packs. Creating a contact database, and using it to write e-mail messages and autodial your contacts is fine, but it just scratches the surface of what you can really accomplish with your contact information.

The Outlook Journal offers you the ability and flexibility to organize phone calls, e-mail messages, letters, chats in the hall, and just about any other exchange of information you have with a contact. This chapter walks you through setting up and using the Outlook Journal.

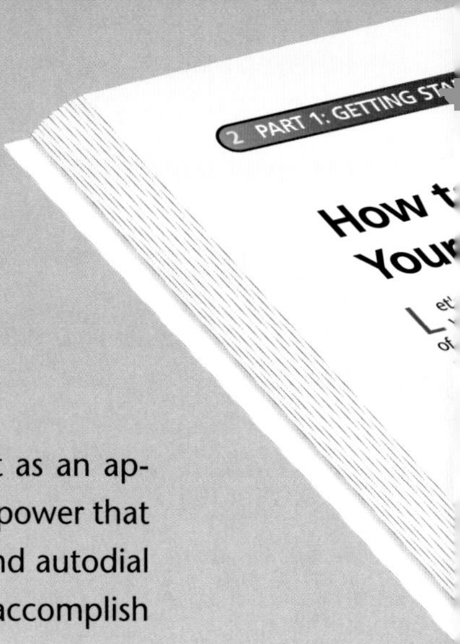

IN THIS SECTION YOU'LL LEARN

How to Set the AutoJournal Options

The Outlook AutoJournal feature automatically records the e-mail messages that you send to selected contacts. If you are on an Exchange Server network, it also records meeting and task requests sent to contacts on the same network.

The first thing you must do to ensure that the automatic Journal entries are properly recorded is set the global Journal options.

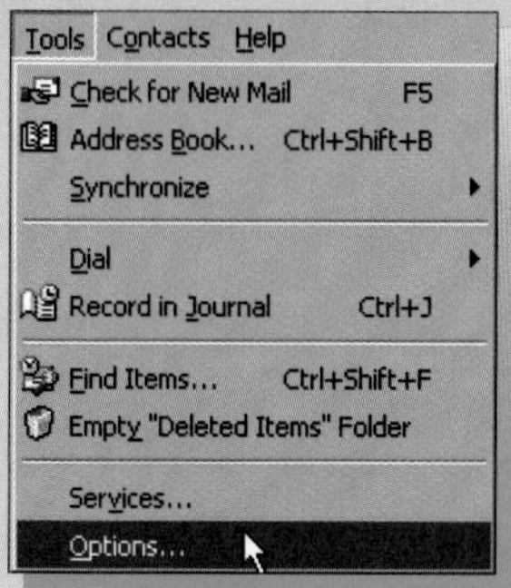

1 Since global options apply to the entire Outlook program, you can access them from any Outlook window. Choose Tools, Options from the menu bar to open the Options dialog box.

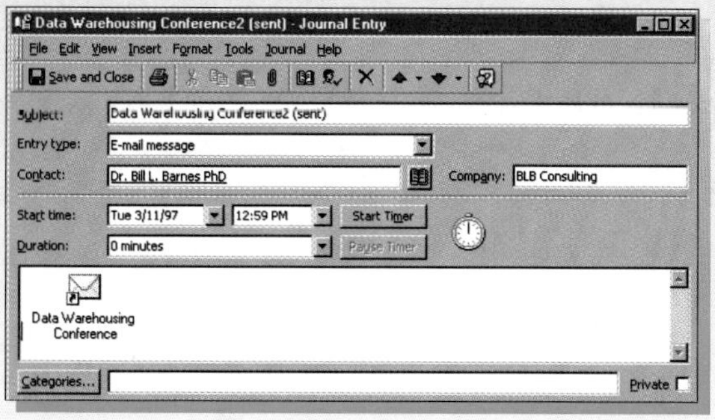

6 Depending on your choice in the Double-Clicking a Journal Entry option, either the Journal entry itself or the item (e-mail message, letter, or so on) to which it refers will open when you double-click a Journal entry. Journal entries that contain only your own notes (and have no files, e-mail messages, or documents) have no associated items to open. Consequently, the Journal entry itself opens regardless of the settings of this option.

FYI

- **If you change the global options for recording Microsoft Office documents in the Journal, you must reboot your computer before the new option setting takes effect. Merely exiting and logging off from Outlook does not reset the option. This is a rather annoying way to enable options, made worse by the fact that the program doesn't even advise you that you must reboot.**
- **The Automatic Journal Recording option can be turned on and off for any specific contact by accessing the Journal tab in the Contact form and clicking Automatically Record Journal Entries for this contact. A checkmark enables automatic recording, no checkmark disables the option. Note that changing this option resets the global Journal option for this contact.**

2 Click the Journal tab to access the Journal options. You can see that it contains four sections of options—items to automatically record, contacts for whom you want the items automatically recorded, Microsoft Office programs from which you want all files automatically recorded, and double-clicking options for Journal entries.

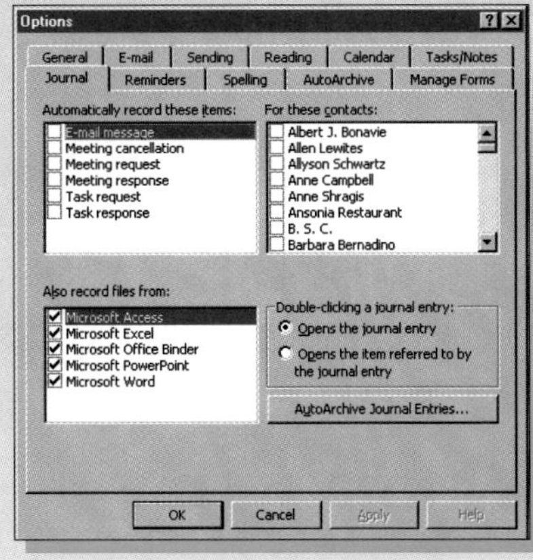

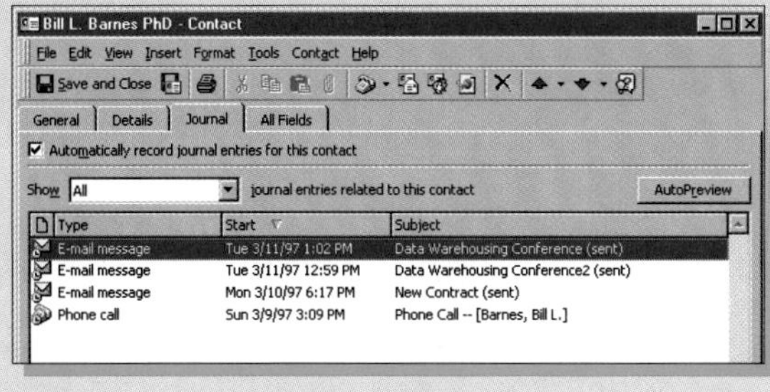

3 In the Automatically Record These Items display box, click each of the items you want automatically recorded. Remember that unless both you and the contact are on the same Exchange Server network, only the e-mail feature works. Automatically recorded items appear in the Journal information viewer, and, as seen here, they also appear in the Journal tab of the Contact card for the associated contact.

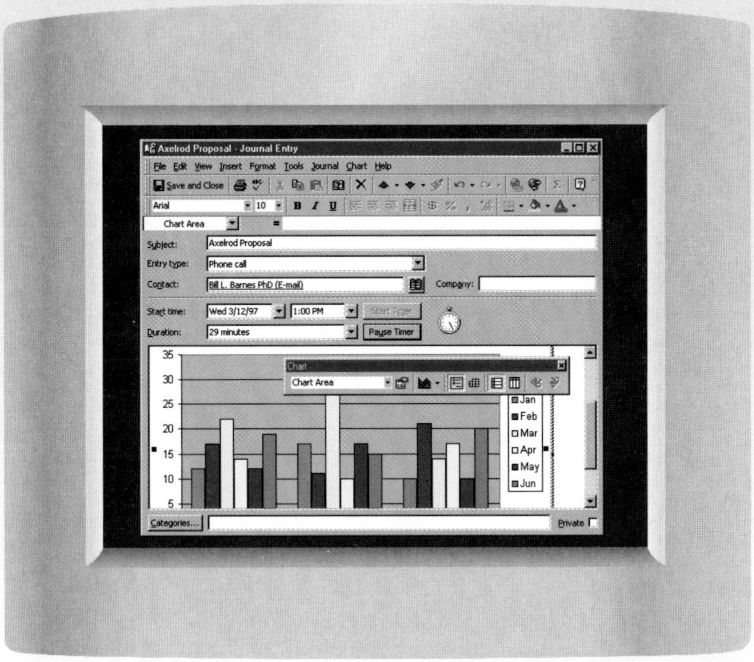

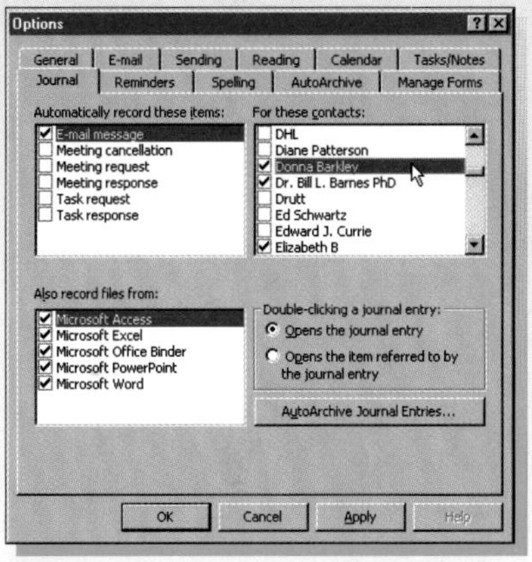

4 The next step is to decide which contacts to apply the AutoJournal feature to. From the For These Contacts list select the contacts you wish to include. If you have casual contacts with whom you rarely exchange important data, there's probably no reason to add them to the list. Place a checkmark next to the contacts you want to include by clicking the appropriate names.

5 A Journal feature that you'll either love or hate is the automatic logging of all Microsoft Office documents you create. This can be rather overwhelming if you do a lot of work in Office. If you decide you can't take it anymore, just turn it off. To eliminate the automatic recording of Office documents, deselect (remove the checkmarks of) the desired Office programs from the Also Record Files From box by clicking the checkbox.

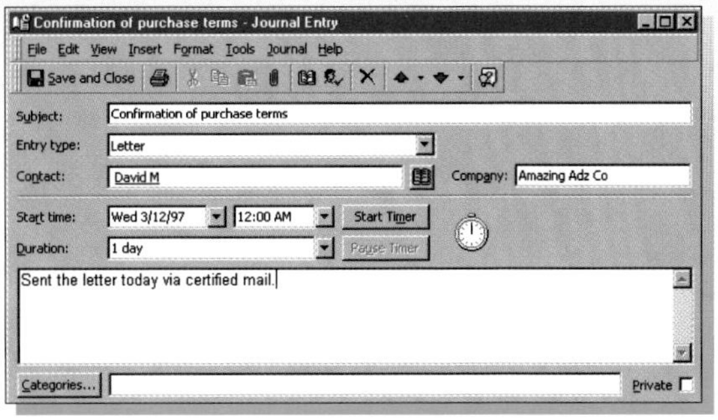

How to Record Manual Journal Entries

AutoJournal works fine for e-mail (and meetings and tasks if you're on Exchange Server), but that leaves quite a few other types of information unrecorded. No problem; you can record just about anything in Outlook as a Journal Entry. You just have to do a little more of the work yourself.

While you can create a journal entry anywhere in Outlook by pressing Ctrl+Shift+J, this exercise begins in the Journal window. So before proceeding, click the Journal icon in the Outlook Bar to open the Journal information viewer.

1 To open a blank Journal Entry form, click the New Journal icon on the toolbar (or press Ctrl+N).

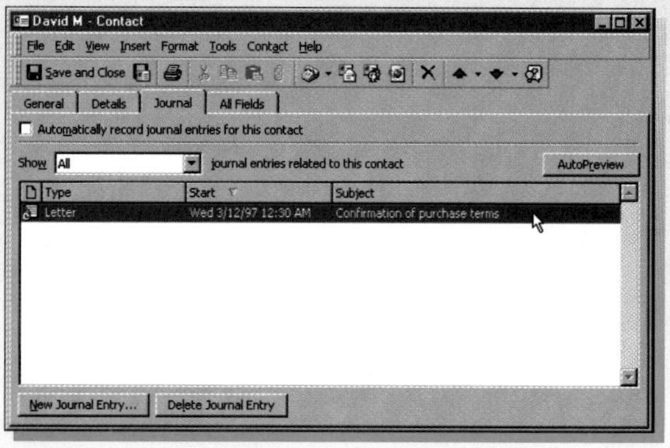

6 Associating the manual Journal entry with a specific contact results in the entry being logged into the Journal sheet of the individual's Contact form. Open the Contacts information viewer by clicking the Contacts icon in the Outlook Bar. Double-click the contact you associated with the new Journal entry to open the Contact card, and click the Journal tab to see the new entry.

FYI

- **You can quickly create a manual Journal entry by dragging a contact onto the Journal icon in the Outlook Bar. As soon as you drop the contact on the Journal icon, a new Journal Entry form opens for the selected contact. Fill in the necessary information and save the Journal entry.**
- **Manual Journal entries are perfect for recording phone conversations with contacts. Open the contact in the Contacts window and use the autodial feature (if you have a modem and telephone connected) to place the call, then move to the Journal tab and click New Journal Entry to enter a manual Journal entry for the call.**

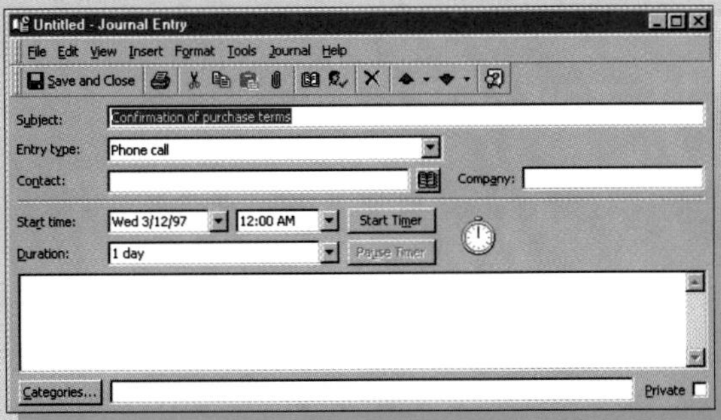

2 The Journal Entry form allows you to enter a subject, the type of Journal entry, the contact with whom it is associated, and additional information to create an electronic paper trail for tracking a contact or project. Begin by filling in the Subject field with a brief description of the Journal entry.

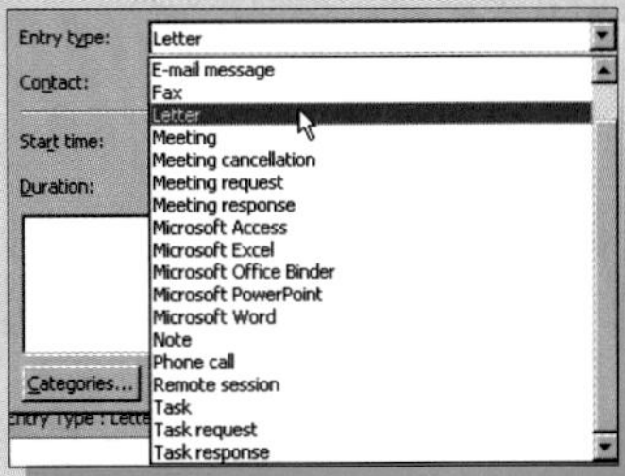

3 The default entry type is Phone Call. Since it is already inserted, it's easy to pass right by and leave it as a phone call even when it is something else. For it to be truly useful, it's important to identify the entry type properly. Click the down arrow at the end of the Entry Type field and select the correct entry type from the drop-down list.

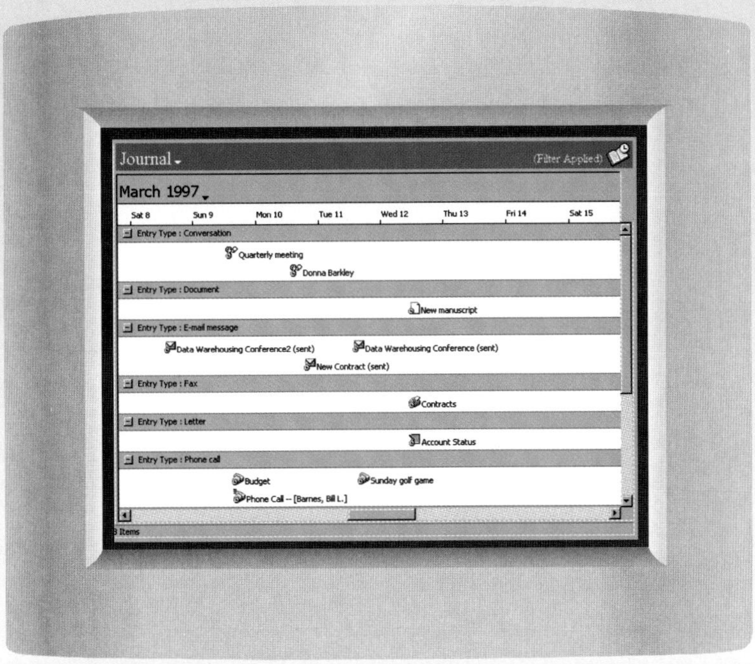

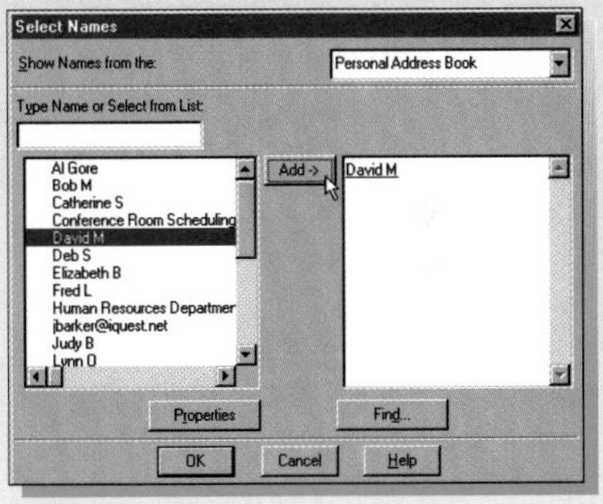

4 Associating a Journal entry with a contact saves a lot of time and aggravation by allowing you to refer directly to a specific phone call or e-mail message to resolve a question or find a piece of important information. To associate the Journal entry with one or more contacts, click the Address Book icon at the end of the Contact field and select the contact(s) from the Select Names dialog box that appears. Click the Add button to include them, then click OK to return to the Journal Entry form.

5 Complete the remainder of the form with appropriate information. The timer is great for phone calls or meetings that take place in real time. Adding notes may not seem necessary at the moment, but you'll be glad you did later on when the event is no longer fresh in your mind. When you're through, click Save and Close to save the new entry and return to the Journal window.

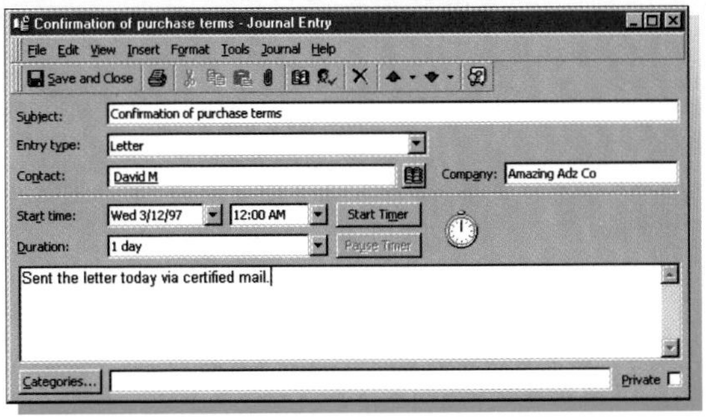

How to Attach Items to Journal Entries

You create Journal entries to keep track of information, which sometimes requires more than just notes. Often a Journal entry refers to files, Outlook items, or other objects that would be handy to have available when you open the entry to find information or refresh your memory.

Looking back at your Journal entry, logging a phone call about a previously submitted proposal would be a lot easier to understand if a copy of the proposal and other associated documentation were included. Fortunately, Outlook provides a quick and easy way to attach objects to any Journal entry.

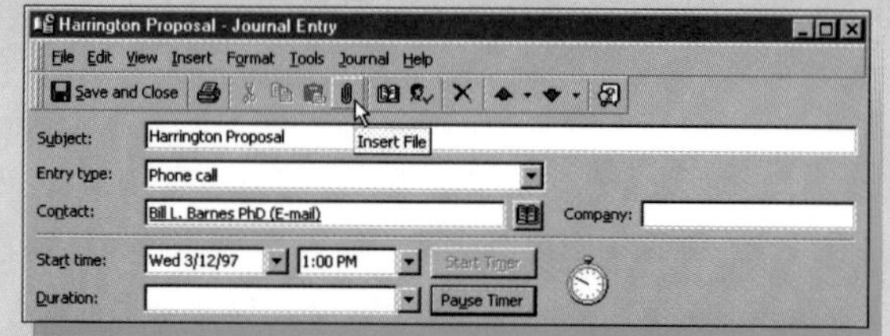

1 Press Ctrl+Shift+J to open a blank Journal Entry form. Fill in the appropriate information regarding subject, entry type, contact, and so forth. Then click the Insert File icon on the entry form toolbar to open the Insert File dialog box.

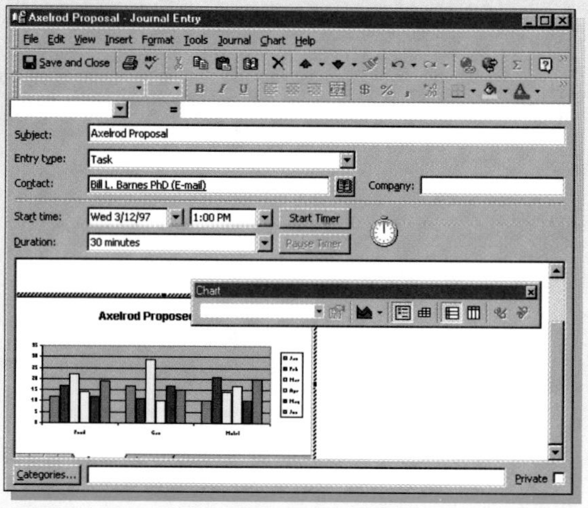

6 When you create the object from scratch, an object (worksheet, graph, chart, or so forth) from the selected application appears in the text box of your entry form. The menu bar and toolbars of the application become available in the Journal Entry form as well. When you're finished creating the object, click any area around the object in the text box to close the application. Click Save and Close to save the Journal entry.

FYI

- **You can insert a portion of a file into a Journal entry by opening the file in its parent application and copying the part you want to include (select the part you need, then choose Edit, Copy from the application's menu bar). Then open the Journal entry, click the text box where you want to insert the object, and choose Edit, Paste Special from the menu bar. If the parent application supports object linking, you can select Paste Link to ensure that any changes in the part of the original object you copied will be reflected in the object inserted in the Journal entry.**

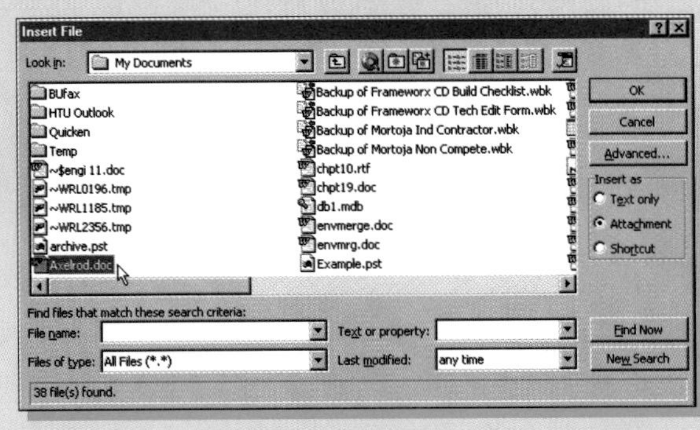

2 The Insert File dialog box opens, and if the file you wish to insert is located in the folder that displays, double-click it to insert it in the Journal entry. If it is located elsewhere, move to the correct folder, locate the file, and double-click it.

3 In addition to attaching files to Journal entries, you can also include Outlook items, such as e-mail messages, tasks, notes, other contacts, and so on. Choose Insert, Item from the menu bar to open the Insert Item dialog box.

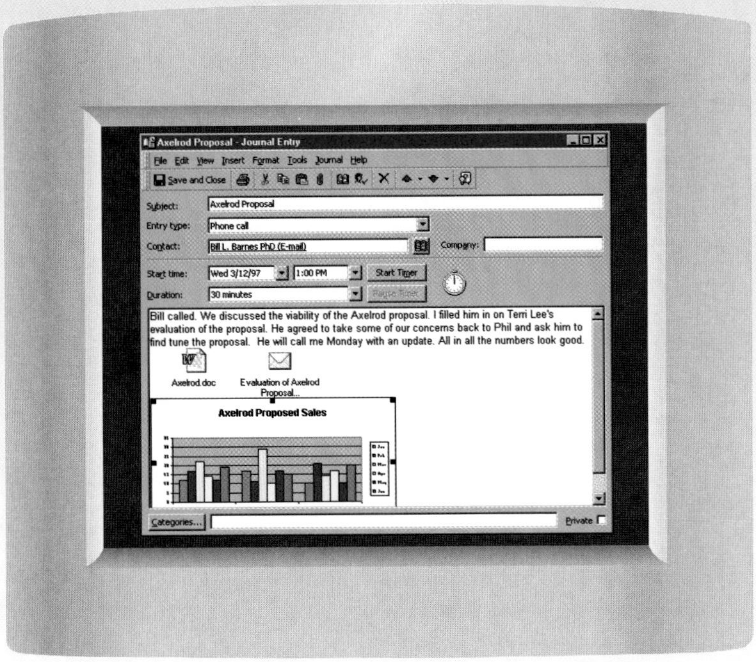

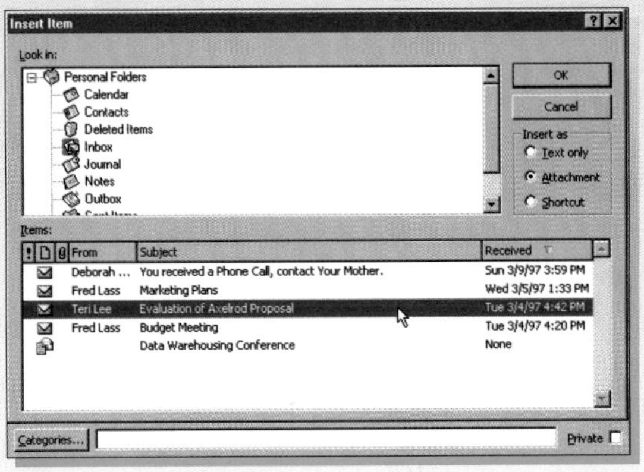

4 To insert an item, you must first indicate the Outlook folder in which the item resides, and then select the item itself. In the Look In display box, click the Outlook folder that contains the item. Then move to the Items display window and double-click the item you want to insert.

5 A third category of attachable items is objects. This includes bitmap images, sound files, video clips, charts, graphs, and more. Choose Insert, Object to open the Insert Object dialog box. Decide whether to create an object from scratch or use an existing file, and select the appropriate option. To create a new object, scroll through the Object Type list and double-click the one you need.

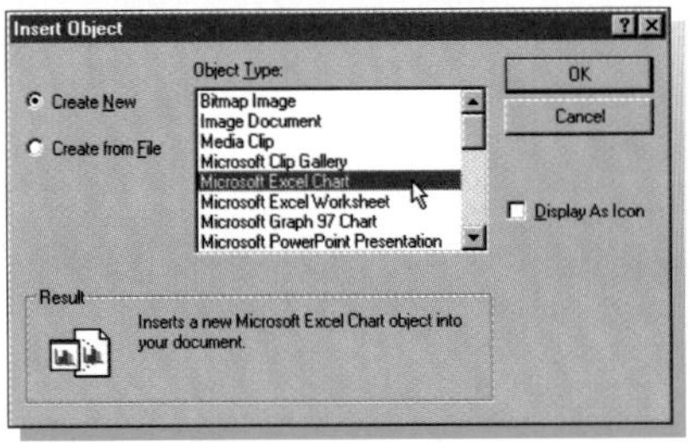

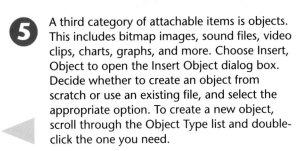

How to Sort and Filter the Journal View

Now that you know how to add numerous different types of Journal entries to your database, you can begin to sort and filter them for your reference. You might be interested in sorting your types of entries, the subjects that you enter, the order that you started them, or other sort options. Outlook lets you sort your Journal entries in any manner you wish.

When you want to view only items or files that meet conditions you specify, you can use a filter. For example, you can filter all items with a specific name in the From field to see only items from that person.

On this page, you'll learn how to sort and filter Journal entries, which will help you organize your Journal.

FYI

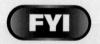

- **You can click the heading at the top of any column to sort the list by the information in that column. For example, if you want to sort your entries according to a type of entry, click the header that says Entry Type. The list will be sorted alphabetically by type of entry.**
- **The upper-right corner of the Folder Banner shows the words "Filter Applied" when a filter is applied to a selected folder. This will let you know that certain items have been *filtered out*. When you remove a filter, "Filter Applied" will disappear.**
- **To remove a filter on your Journal view, choose Filter from the View menu. The Filter dialog box will appear with the criteria for your current filter. Click the Clear All button to remove the filter and clear the criteria. Then click the OK button to once again see all the entries in the Journal view.**

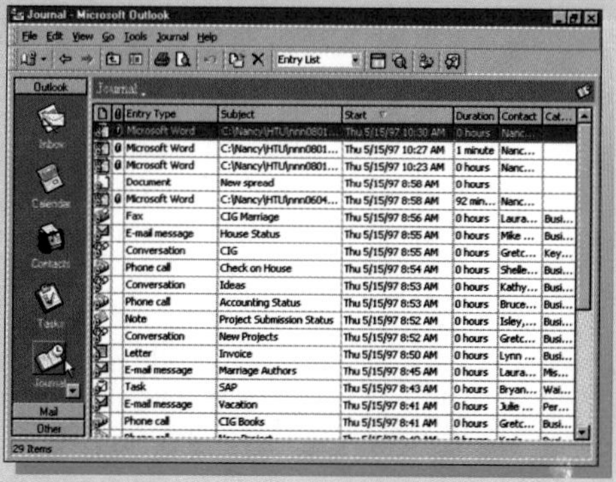

1 Open the Outlook group on the Outlook Bar. Click on the Journal icon. It looks like an open book with a clock in the upper right-hand corner. All the entries that you have made in your Journal will be displayed.

7 The Journal view will appear with the filter applied. Notice that there are only a few entries that meet the specific filter criteria.

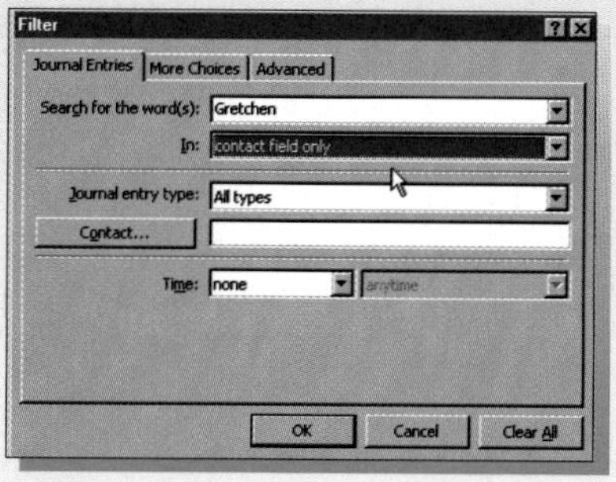

6 The Filter dialog box will appear, which will allow you to filter items in your Journal view by different criteria. From the Journal Entries tab of the Filter dialog box, type a name in the Search for the Word(s) list box. Select Contact Field Only from the In drop-down list box. In the Journal Entry Type field you can keep All Types selected or you can choose Contact. By choosing All Types, you make sure you have all entries that have to do with the name you entered, even if the Contact field is blank. You can also select a Journal entry by a specific contact name or time. You can make your filter more selective by using the More Choices and the Advanced tabs. When finished making your selections, click the OK button.

2 Choose Sort from the View menu.

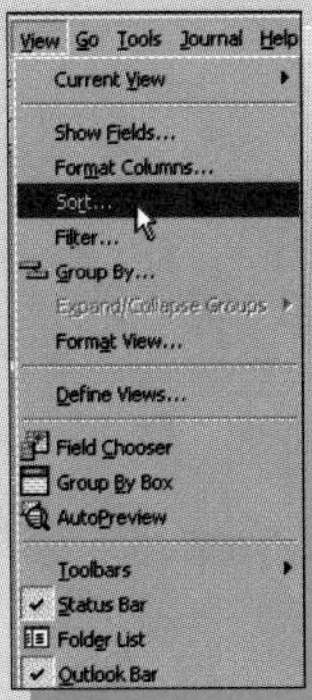

3 The Sort dialog box will appear, which will allow you to sort items in your Journal view by different criteria. Click on the drop-down list box in the Sort Items By field. You can scroll through the various sort options. Notice that these options correspond with the Journal View column headers. Choose to sort items by entry type in ascending order. Then, click the OK button.

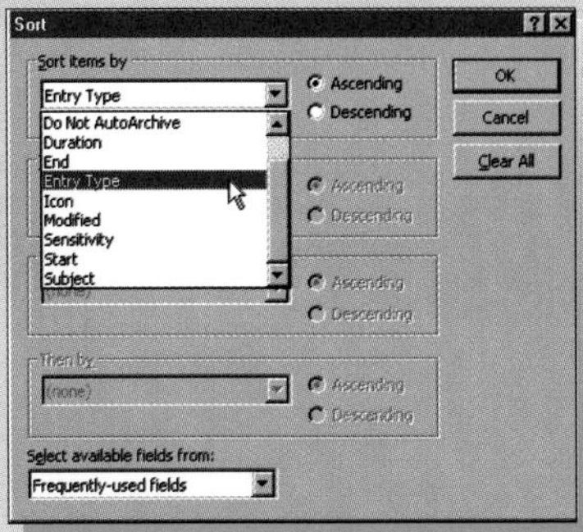

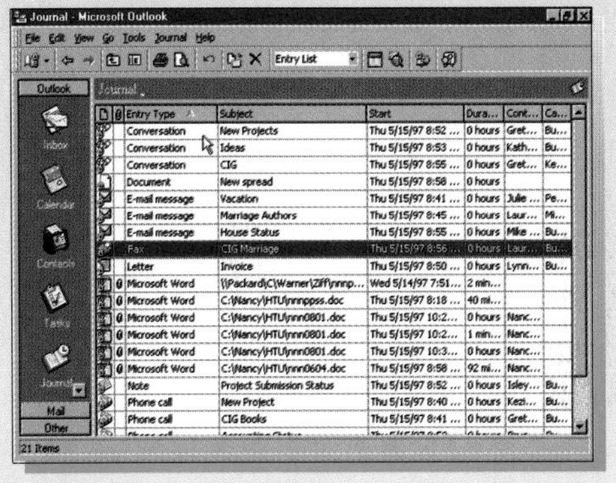

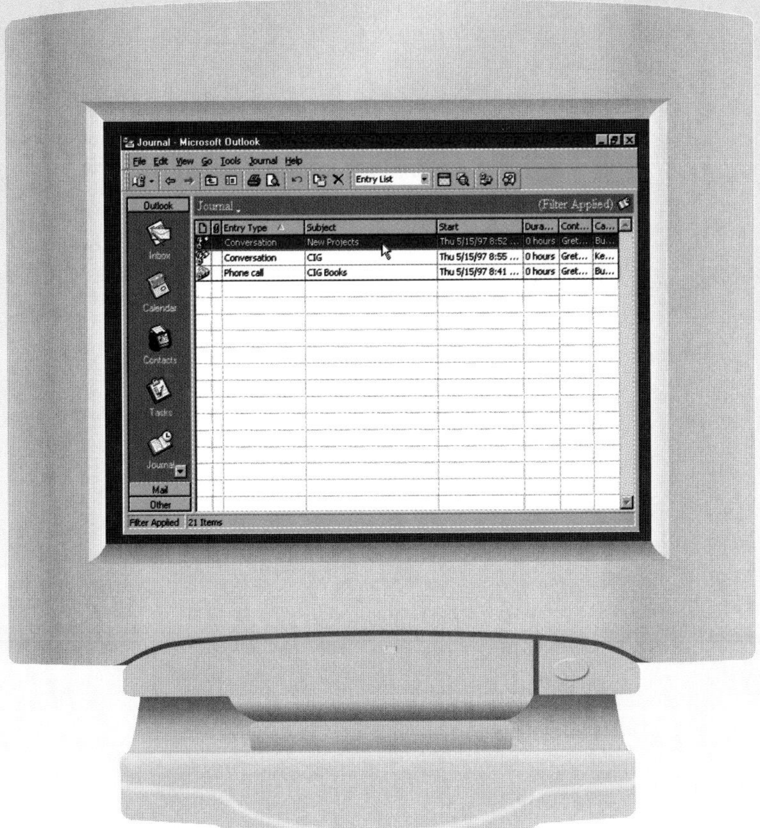

4 The Journal entries will automatically sort by the type of entry in alphabetical order. You can even sort your entries by multiple items. For example, you can sort first by subject, then select the Then By drop-down list box and choose to sort second by start time within a subject. This is handy if you have multiple entries for your subjects. Outlook allows you to sort by up to four different items at a time.

5 Choose Filter from the View menu.

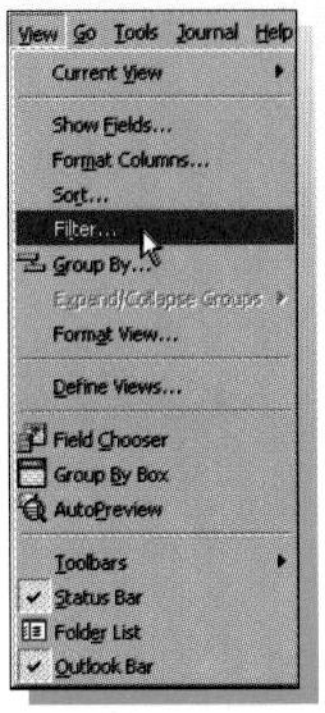

Ctrl + N=
New Note
Ctrl + D=
Delete

PART 7

Using Notes

OUTLOOK notes are like post-it notes and they're just as easy to use and as helpful as their physical counterparts. You can leave them on your screen or in a folder. You can use them as reminders or stick them onto Outlook items. The number of uses is limited only by your own imagination.

This chapter covers creating and using notes, as well as setting up the options for notes so you get the most out of this nifty feature.

IN THIS SECTION YOU'LL LEARN

How to Create a Note

The only way to have all those handy reminders in front of your face is to write them. Most of the time nobody else will see them so you don't even have to worry about spelling, grammar, or punctuation. That's even better than writing the notes you put on your refrigerator because other people probably use your refrigerator. It's unlikely that anyone else uses your computer, especially your Outlook files.

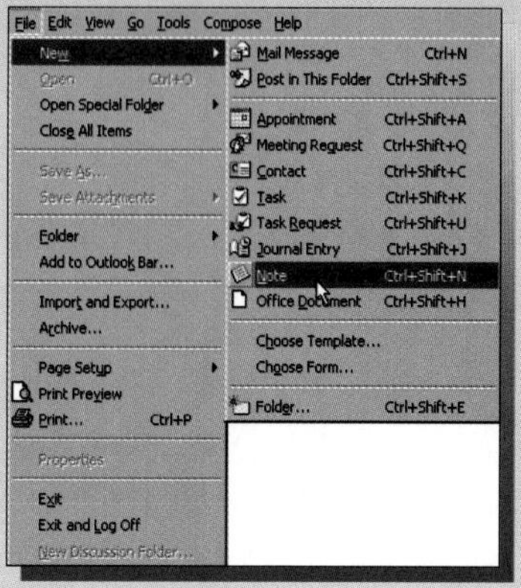

1. To create a Note, choose File, New, Note from the menu bar (or press Ctrl+Shift+N).

6. Close the note (use the Close button on the note if you work in Windows 95 or Windows NT 4, use Close from the menu if you work in Windows NT 3.51). The note is automatically saved in the Outlook Notes folder.

FYI

- **If you want to make the note smaller so it fits on your desktop, place your pointer on the hash marks in the lower right corner of the note. When the pointer turns into a diagonal double arrow, drag the corner up, sideways, or at an angle.**

2 A Note form appears on your screen. It has a title bar at the top, a Note icon to the left of the title bar, and the date and time is displayed at the bottom. Your insertion point is at the top of the note, just below the Note icon.

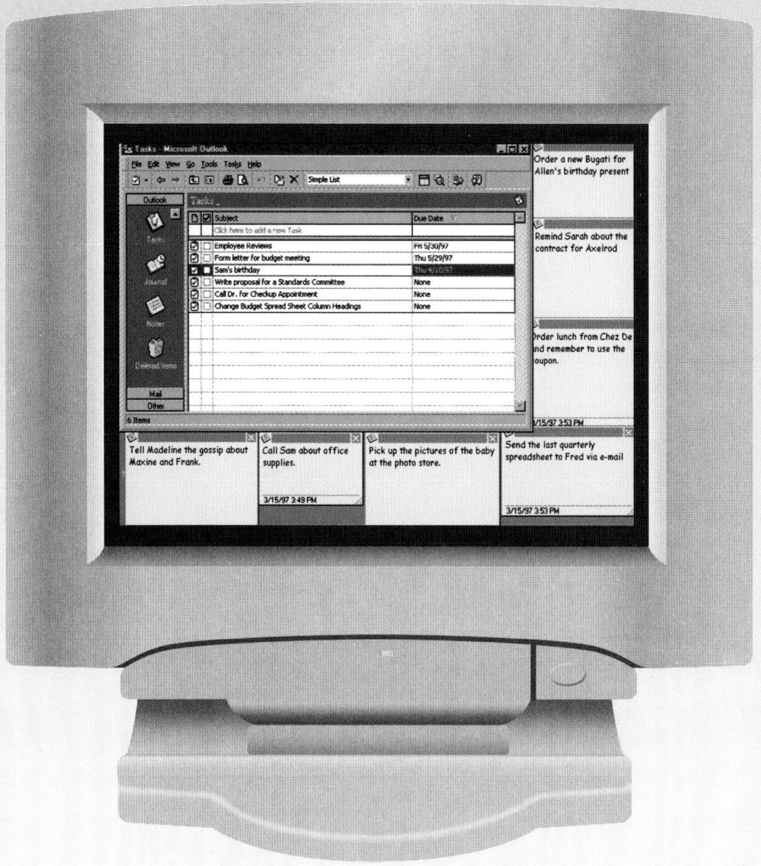

3 Click the Note icon so you can learn what's on the Note menu. Then click anywhere on the yellow note to remove the menu.

4 Enter a note, perhaps a reminder to do something or a funny line you heard that you want to remember.

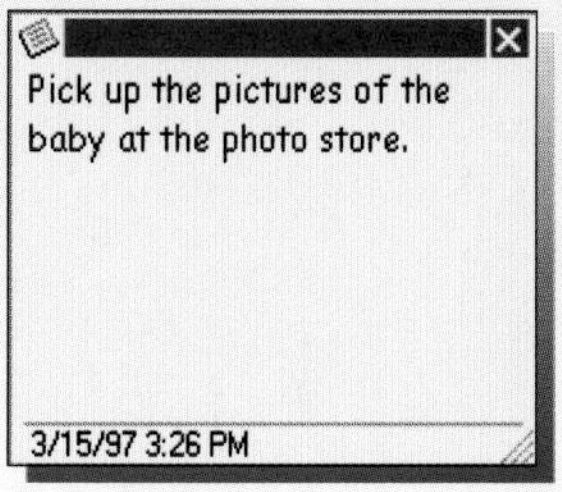

5 If you want to keep the note in front of you, drag it out of the Outlook window and onto your desktop. Then continue to work in Outlook, while the note continues to stare you in the face (handy arrangement if the note is a reminder). If you like to work in Outlook with your window maximized, this isn't an option.

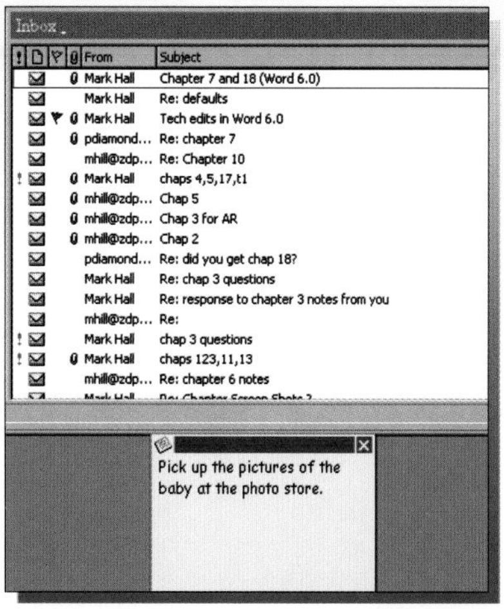

How to Customize Notes

If you find you're constantly changing the size of your notes, either making most of them much smaller (so they fit on your desktop) or larger (because you tend to write long notes), you can change the default size of the notes. There are several changes you can make in the appearance of notes, and this section discusses them.

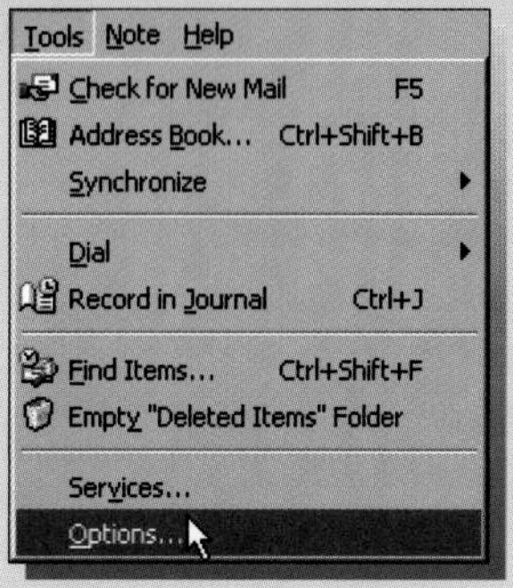

1 To set the options for Outlook notes, choose Tools, Options from the menu bar.

6 When you are finished changing options, click OK. The new options take effect with the next note you create; existing notes are not changed.

FYI

- **Remember that no matter what settings you establish for the default color or size, you can change any individual note to suit your own needs or taste.**
- **If the way you use notes doesn't require a date and time on every note, click the box named Show Time and Date to remove the checkmark.**

2 Click the Tasks/Notes tab on the Options dialog box. The Notes options are at the bottom of this dialog box sheet.

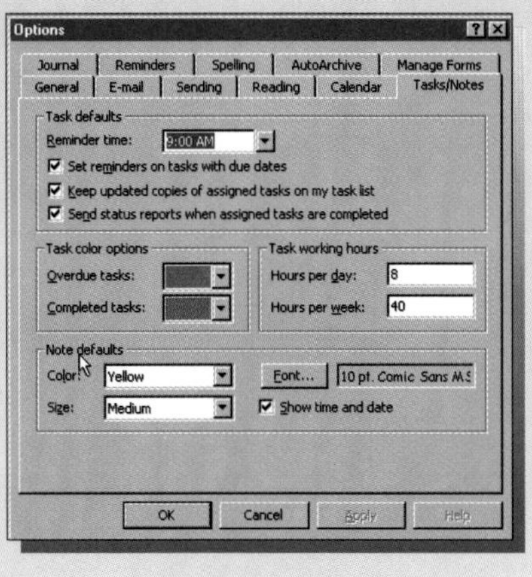

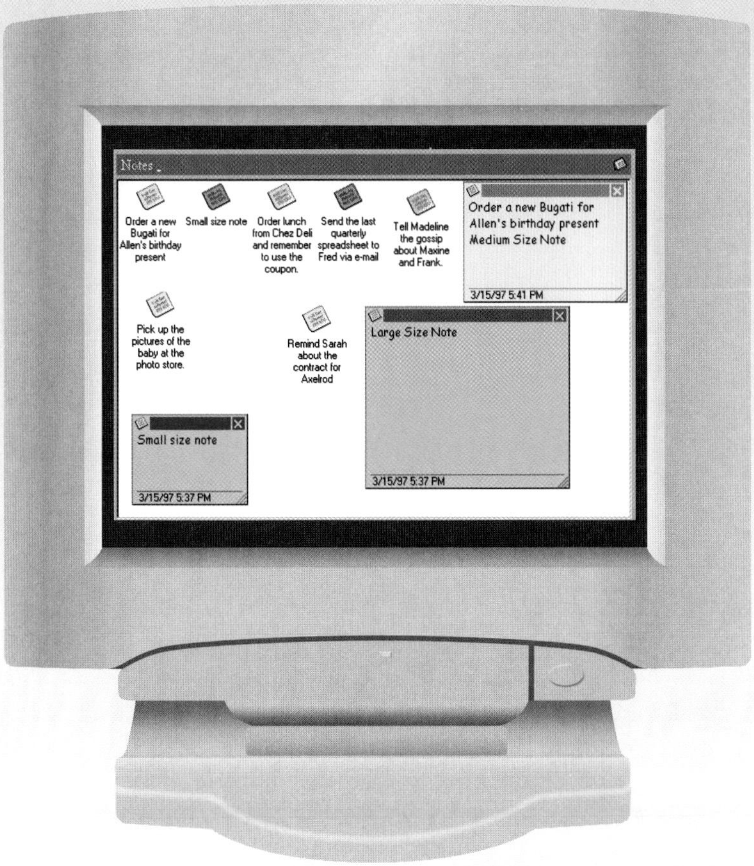

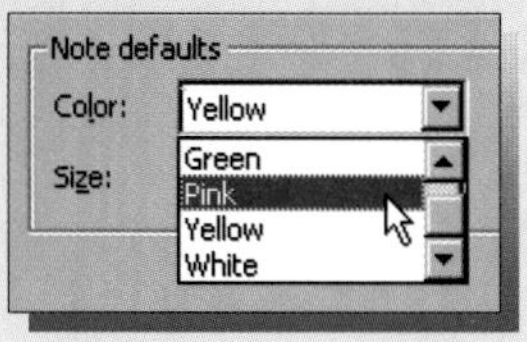

3 To change the default color from yellow to another color, click the arrow to the right of the Color field and choose the new hue.

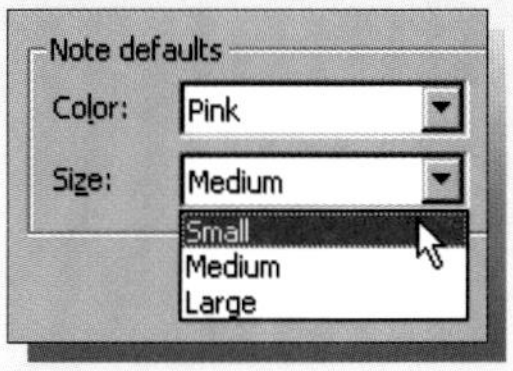

4 To change the default size from medium, click the arrow to the right of the Size field and pick either small or large.

5 If you want to change the font for notes, click the Font button and pick a font, style and size. You can also change the color of the font. Click OK to leave the Font dialog box and return to the Options dialog box.

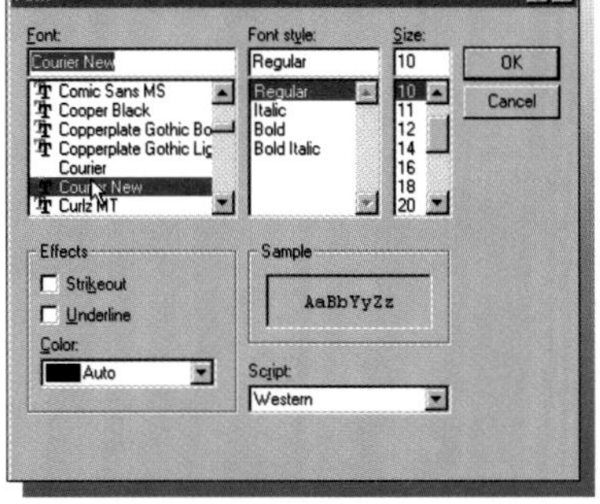

How to View and Use Notes

There is, of course, more to the Outlook Note feature than the ability to have little yellow sticky notes on your screen. You can use the notes in other Outlook items.

This section covers viewing your notes and using them throughout Outlook.

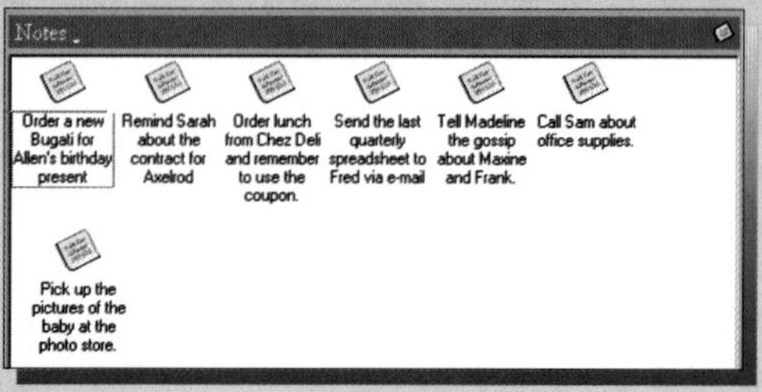

1 To see your notes, click the Notes icon on the Outlook Bar. By default, all your notes are displayed as icons with the text below the icon.

7 To delete a note, select it and hit the Delete key (or right-click it and choose Delete from the menu).

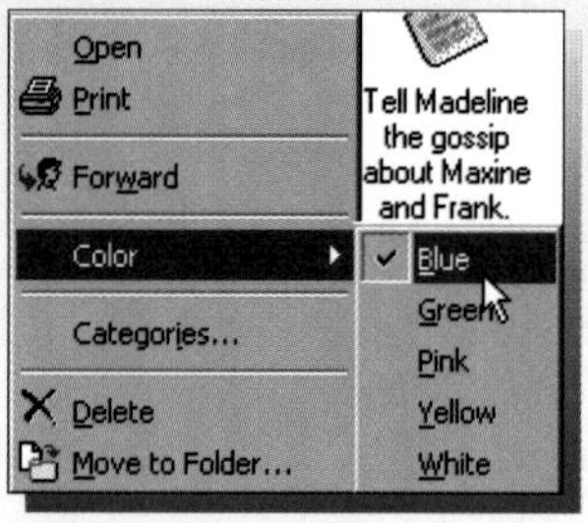

6 You can change the color of the note's icon by right-clicking on the note and choosing Color, then selecting a color. This is a useful way to keep notes by category, and each category is instantly recognizable. The new color only displays in the Notes folder—if you move the note to another item or to the desktop, it's yellow again (or whatever the default color is).

FYI

- **To print a note, right-click it and choose Print. Your name appears on the printout, followed by the date and time of the last modification of the note. Beneath that is the text of the note.**
- **When you drag a note from the Notes folder to your desktop or to any other item, it becomes a copy of the note and the original note stays in the folder. If you delete a note from the desktop or from inside an item, only that copy is deleted. The original remains in the Notes folder.**

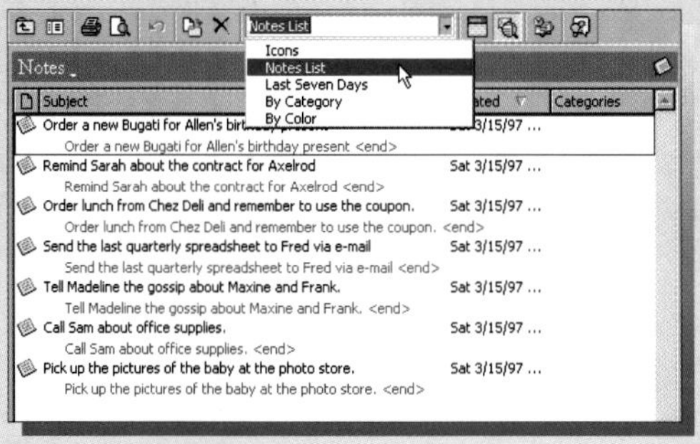

2 You can use the choices in the Current View box on the toolbar to change the way the notes are displayed. If you want to see the notes in a listing, you can turn the display of the text off and on with the AutoPreview button on the toolbar.

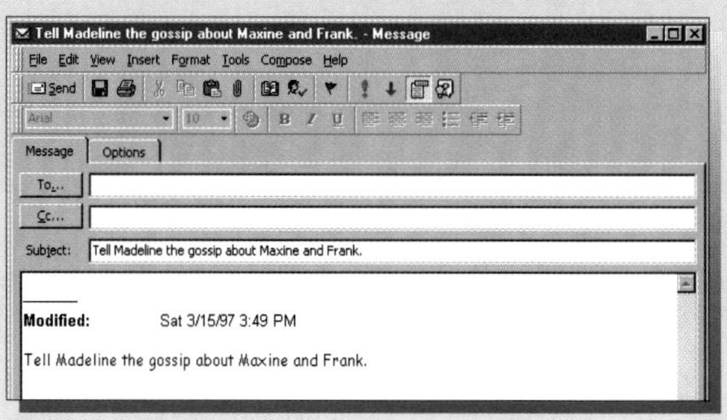

3 To put a note into an Outlook item, drag the note from the Notes folder onto the appropriate icon. For instance, if you want to put a note into an e-mail message, drag the note to the Inbox icon. A new message form opens, and the note is the Subject line. It also appears in the Message box. You can change either the subject or the message so your note doesn't seem overly repetitive. Enter any additional message text you wish to, then enter a recipient and send the note.

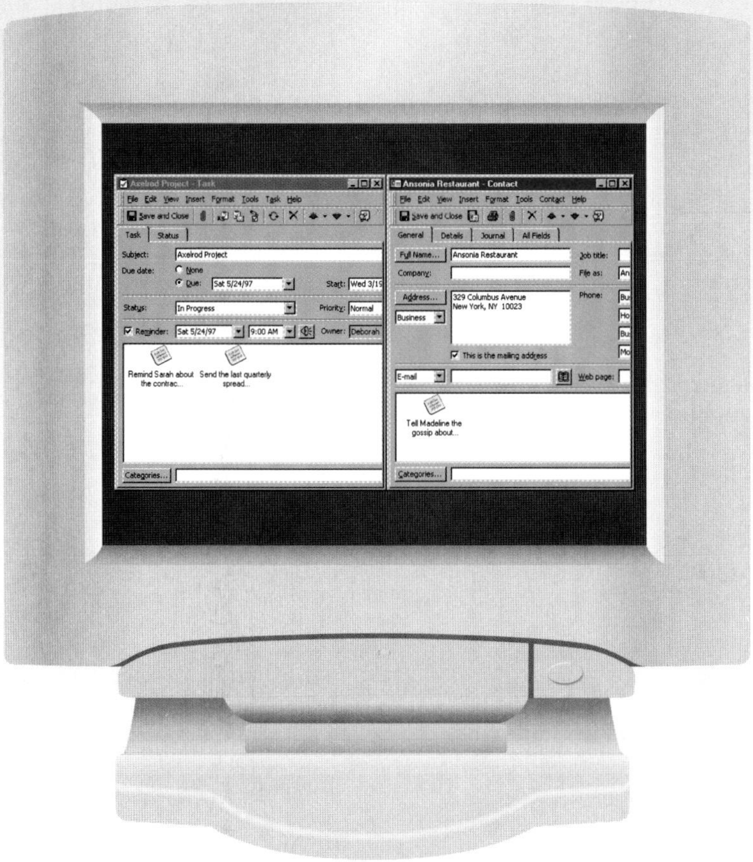

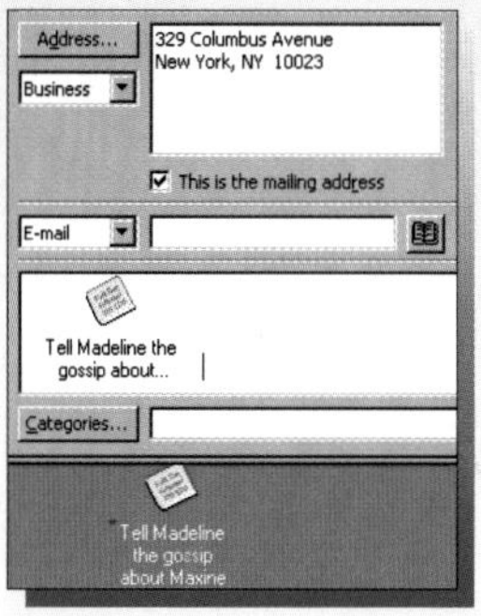

4 A quick way to put a note into an existing item (such as a task or a Contact card) is to drag the note to the desktop and park it there. Open the item, and then drag the note into the text box of the item.

5 To edit a note, open it by double-clicking on it. Add, delete, and change text as you wish. Don't be fooled by the size of the note, you can keep typing and your characters will scroll below the bottom of the note. You can use the arrow keys to move through the note when you want to read it, or you can enlarge the note to see all the text. Close the note when you have finished making changes.

Ctrl + Shift + F=
Find Items
Ctrl + Y=
Go to Folder . . .

P A R T 8

Managing the Outlook Folders

LIKE death and taxes, deleting is inevitable. No matter where you're working in Outlook, you're bound to encounter information that's useless, obsolete, dead wrong, annoying, or just plain boring. When it happens, you'll probably reach for the Delete key and zap the item. So far so good. But what actually happens when you delete something? What if you were just kidding and didn't really mean to delete it? Okay, what if you meant it at the time, but are now having second thoughts?

The Deleted Items folder provides a holding pen for Outlook items that you retire. There are several options for handling, using, and retrieving deleted items. This chapter takes you on an excursion through the desolate domain of Deleted Items.

IN THIS SECTION YOU'LL LEARN

How to Use the Folder List

The Folder list shows or hides the list of all your Outlook folders. When you're using the Outlook group, the Folder list does many of the same things that the Outlook Bar does. But when you change to a different Outlook group, like Other, you can manage your files and folders directly in the Folder list. This is useful when you want to view, copy, and move files without having to leave Outlook.

On this page, you'll learn how to use the Folder list to view items on your hard drive from within Outlook.

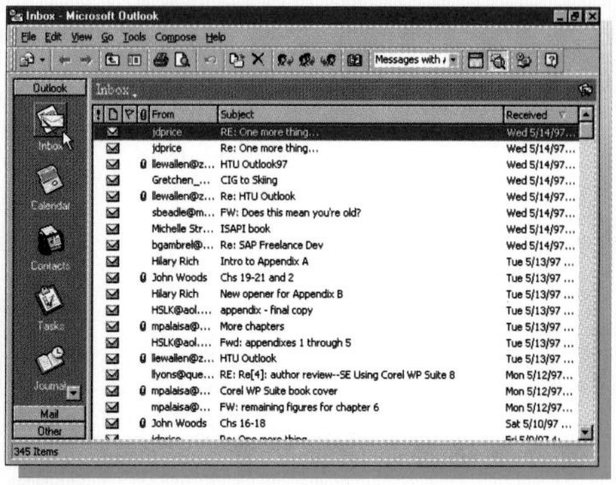

1 In Microsoft Outlook, click the Inbox icon from the Outlook group.

FYI

- Another way to select the Folder list is to use the Folder List button on the toolbar. The Folder List icon looks like a two-column spreadsheet.
- To quickly see the Folder list and automatically hide it when you select a folder, click the down arrow to the right of the title of the open folder, such as Inbox, in the Folder banner. When the Folder list is displayed using this method, it will automatically close after another folder is selected.
- You can increase the width of the Folder list to view folder names. Click on and drag the separator bar to the right until you can clearly see your folder names.

2 Choose Folder List from the View menu.

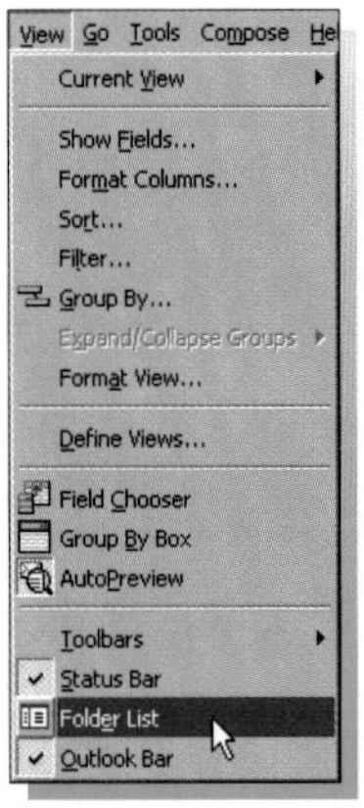

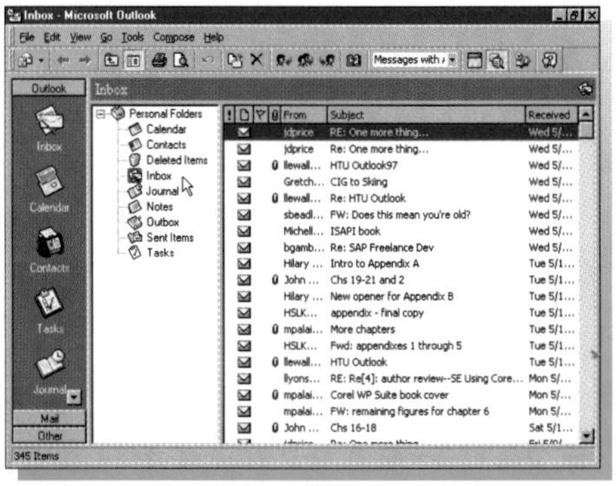

3 The Inbox now has another column that contains all the items in your Personal folders. You can click on any of the items and the information viewer will display the contents.

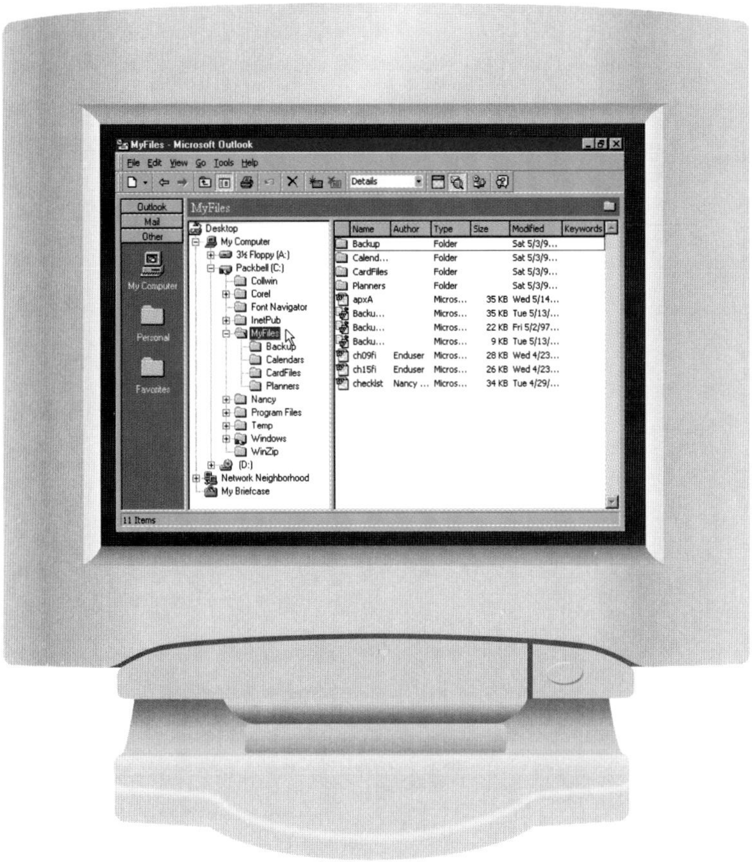

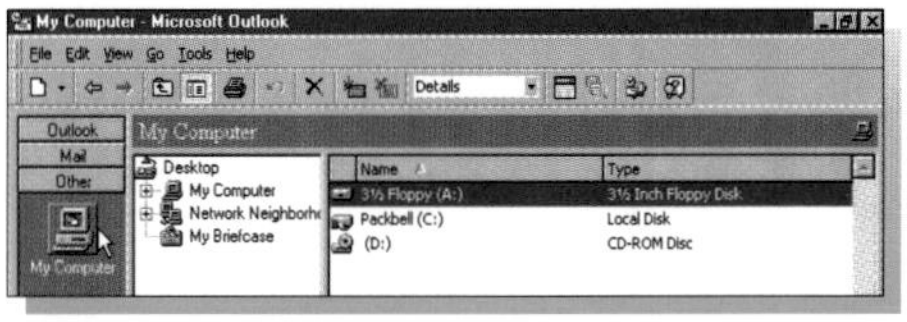

4 Click the Other group in the Outlook Bar and then click the My Computer icon. Your files are displayed in a similar fashion to an Explorer window.

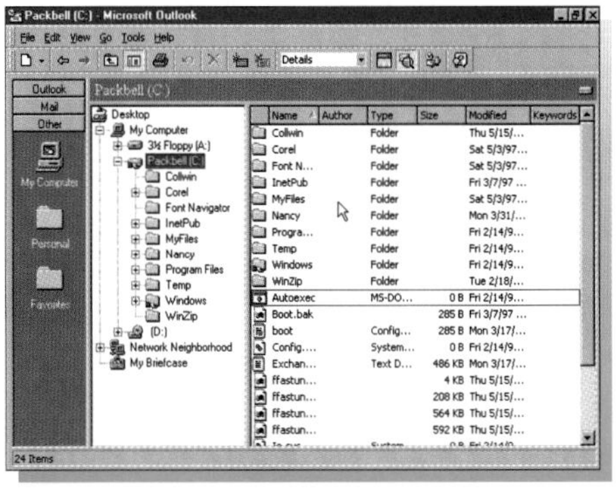

5 Click the plus sign next to the My Computer icon in the Folder list. Next, click the plus sign next to your hard drive (most likely labeled C:), and then open another folder. You see the names of all your files in the information viewer.

How to Set Deleted Items Options

On the surface, deleting is pretty simple and straightforward. If you don't like an item, you highlight it, hit the delete key, and the item moves to the Deleted Items folder. There are, however, several settings that affect deleted items, and you should familiarize yourself with them.

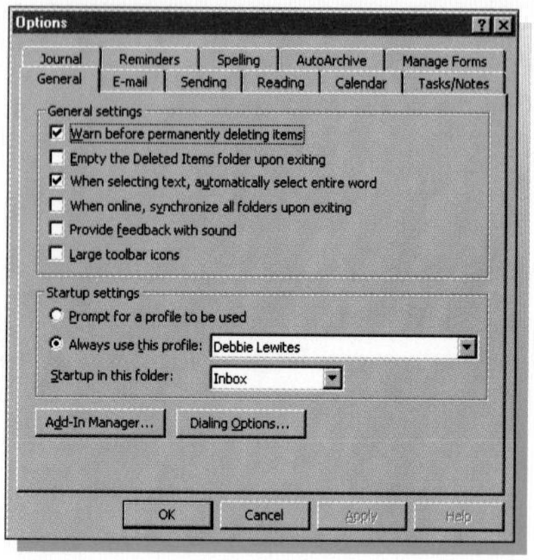

1 The deleted items options are found in the General Settings section of the Options dialog box. Choose Tools, Options to open the Options dialog box. Then click the General tab to access the General settings.

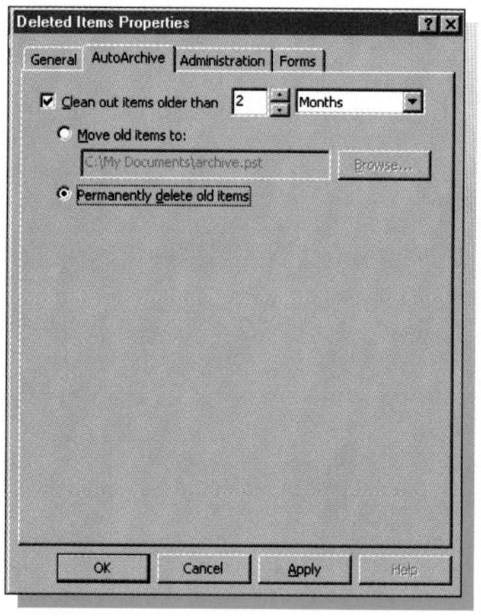

5 Click the AutoArchive tab to open the AutoArchive properties sheet. These settings determine the actions taken during an automatic archive. The default settings will delete old items in the Deleted Items folder, rather than move them to the Archive file. That means they are permanently deleted, gone forever, unrecoverable. If you wish to save deleted items in the Archive file, click the option named Move Old Items To and then select the Archive file in which to save deleted items. Click OK to return to Outlook.

FYI

- **Do not make the mistake of confusing the Deleted Items folder with the Windows 95 or Windows NT 4 Recycle Bin. They do not work in conjunction with one another. Items that are permanently deleted in Outlook are absolutely and unequivocally deleted and do *not* end up in the Windows 95 Recycle Bin.**

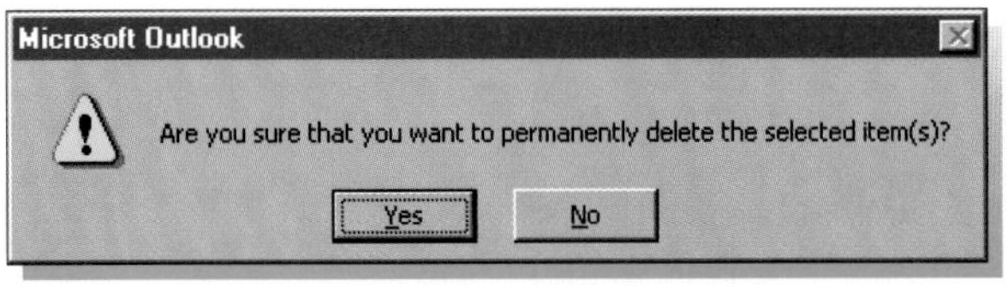

2 The first option that deals with deleted items is the Warn Before Permanently Deleting Items option, which simply means that every time you delete an item from the Deleted Items folder, Outlook will pop up a message warning you that you're crossing the point of no return. The Deleted Items folder is the last refuge for items you no longer want. Since the fate of an item which you erase from the Deleted Items folder is everlasting oblivion, turning on this option warns you, before you delete a deleted item, that you cannot undo this action. By default the option is turned on. To turn it off, click the box to the left to remove the checkmark. Your best bet is to leave it turned on though, because that warning can be useful.

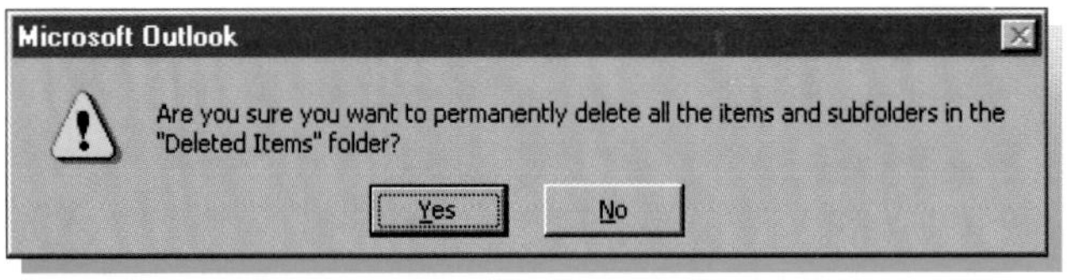

3 The second deleted items option is Empty the Deleted Items Folder Upon Exiting. This option is turned off by default due to the serious and unalterable consequences of turning it on. Unless you have a specific reason for turning it on, it is best left off. With it turned on, the entire contents of the Deleted Items folder is erased when you exit Outlook. However, before you exit, a dialog box appears, warning you that all items and subfolders will be deleted, giving you a final chance to change your mind. Click No to return to Outlook or Yes to exit and delete the contents of the Deleted Items folder.

4 A third option regarding the removal of the contents of the Deleted Items folder can be found in its AutoArchive properties sheet. Right-click the Deleted Items icon in the Outlook Bar, and select Properties from the pop-up menu.

Deleting and Restoring Deleted Items

Since the Deleted Items folder is a halfway house for abandoned items, there are only two alternatives for dealing with them. You can either permanently remove them from the Deleted Items folder, or you can restore them to a productive and meaningful existence. The choice is yours.

The reason that deleted items end up in the Deleted Items folder is, more often than not, because they belong there. When that fact becomes overwhelmingly clear, the obvious choice is to delete the item(s) from the Deleted Items folder.

In those rare instances when you make a mistake, or if circumstances change, or when you're just feeling kindhearted and carefree, you may decide to restore a deleted item to its original folder. Whatever you decide to do, move to the Deleted Items folder by clicking the Deleted Items icon in the Outlook Bar.

FYI

- **To delete multiple deleted items without emptying the entire Deleted Items folder, highlight the desired items by holding down the Ctrl key and clicking each item you want to delete. When all the items are highlighted, click the Delete icon on the toolbar or press the Delete key.**
- **When restoring multiple deleted items to their original folder, be sure that all the items selected are of the same type. For example, you may want to restore e-mail messages to the Inbox folder. If you have just one item of a different type among the group of selected items, none of the items will be restored. Instead, a single new item will be created and all the deleted items you have gathered up will be added to that one item. What's worse is that the process is irreversible. Once you begin the creation of that new item you can't change your mind. If you do, all the deleted items you tried to restore are permanently removed.**

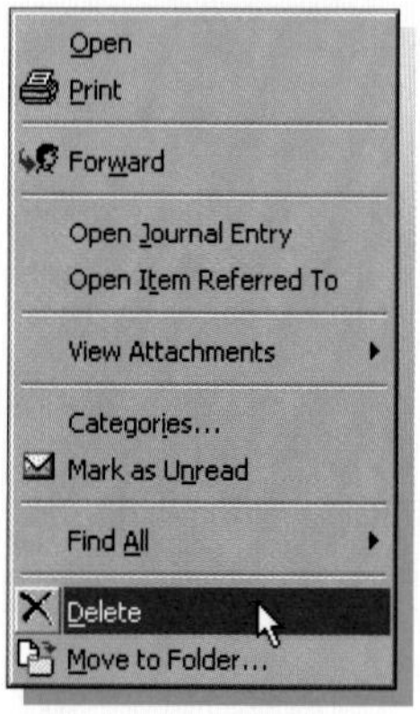

1 The quickest way to delete a single item in the Deleted Items folder is to right-click the item you want to delete and select Delete from the pop-up menu. If you're sure you want to get rid of the item, click Yes in the dialog box that appears warning that this action is permanent.

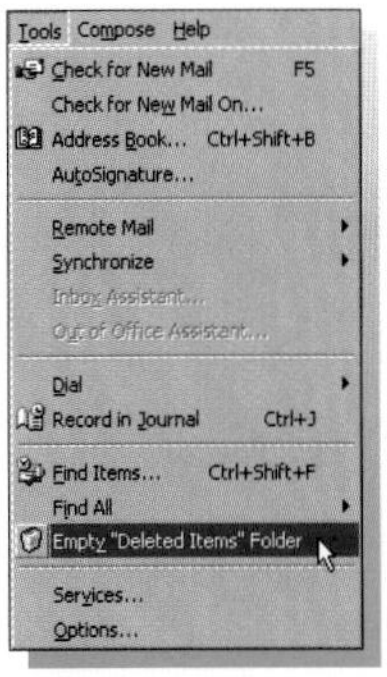

2 If you decide it's time to clean house and get rid of everything in the Deleted Items folder, you can accomplish this with a couple of mouse clicks. Choose Tools, Empty Deleted Items Folder from the menu bar. If you're secure in your decision, click Yes in the dialog box that pops up, otherwise click No and reconsider your action.

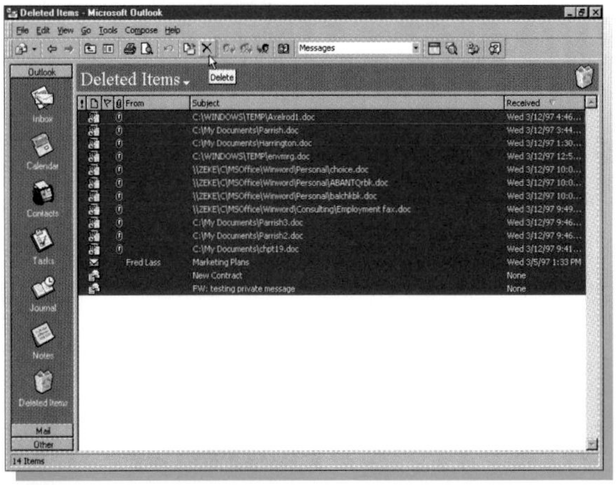

3 An alternative way to delete the entire contents of the Deleted Items folder is to open the folder and press Ctrl+A to highlight all the deleted items in the Deleted Items information viewer. Then click the Delete icon in the toolbar. The same informational dialog box pops up asking if you're sure you want to permanently delete the selected items. If you are, click Yes, otherwise click No.

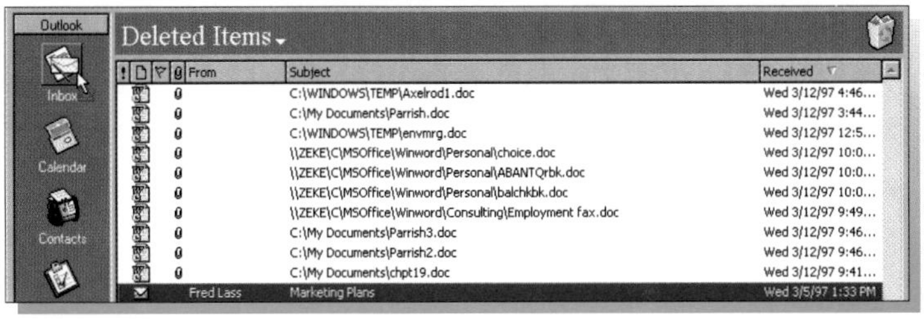

4 If you decide to give a deleted item a reprieve, you can restore it to its original folder by dragging the selected item to the Outlook Bar and dropping it onto the icon of the folder from which it originated. It immediately disappears from the Deleted Items folder and reappears in the original folder.

5 The rehabilitation of a deleted item can also be accomplished by making it a part of a new item of a different type (a deleted message item can be sent to the Tasks folder, for instance). Right-click the deleted item and select Move to Folder from the pop-up menu that appears. In the Move Items dialog box choose the target folder and click OK to proceed. A new item is created in that folder, and the information from the original item is included in a text box or comments box (depending on the new item type).

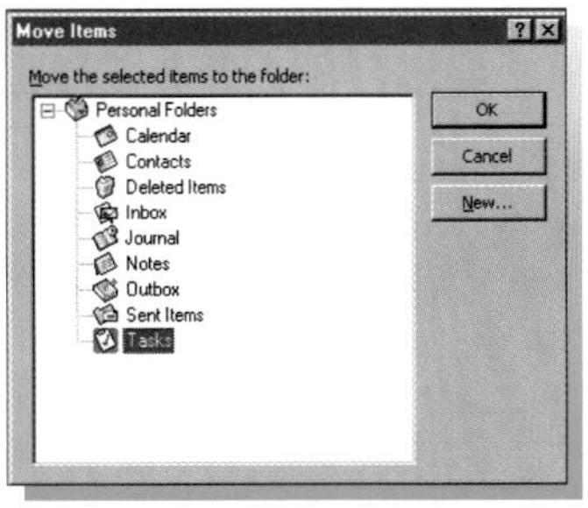

How to Set AutoArchive Options

The Outlook AutoArchive feature automatically creates an archive, and periodically copies the Outlook items you specify into the archive. Since Outlook cannot read your mind, you have to tell it when and how to perform these periodic archiving tasks. You accomplish this by setting the AutoArchive options.

Setting AutoArchive options requires two separate operations. The first is setting the global options, the second is setting the individual folder AutoArchive options. Note, however, that all folder-specific AutoArchive options take precedence over the global AutoArchive options. For example, if you specify archive.pst as the default archive file in the global options, but set it to inbox.pst in the Inbox properties, all Inbox archiving is done using inbox.pst.

All original Outlook folders, with the exception of Contacts, can be AutoArchived. AutoArchiving rules are based on the creation or edit dates of items. Since contacts are more or less permanent entries, they are not considered candidates for AutoArchiving.

1 You can set global AutoArchive options from any folder. Choose Tools, Options from the menu bar to open the Options dialog box.

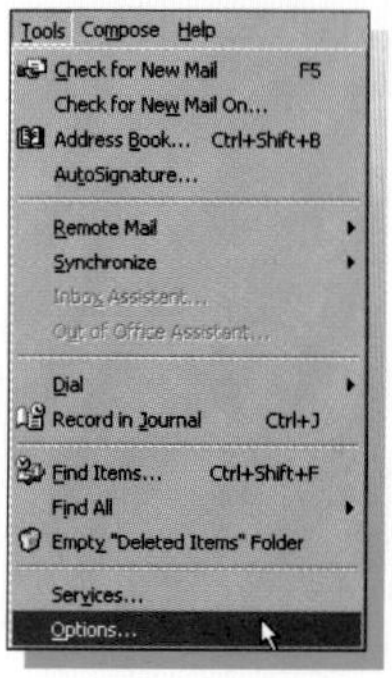

6 If the AutoArchive option is turned off, click the option named Clean Out Items Older Than. This places a checkmark in the box to the left and enables AutoArchiving for the folder. Then set the age condition. Be careful when making your selection of the final option. Choosing Permanently Delete Old Items results in the irretrievable loss of any items meeting the criteria you specified when an AutoArchive is performed.

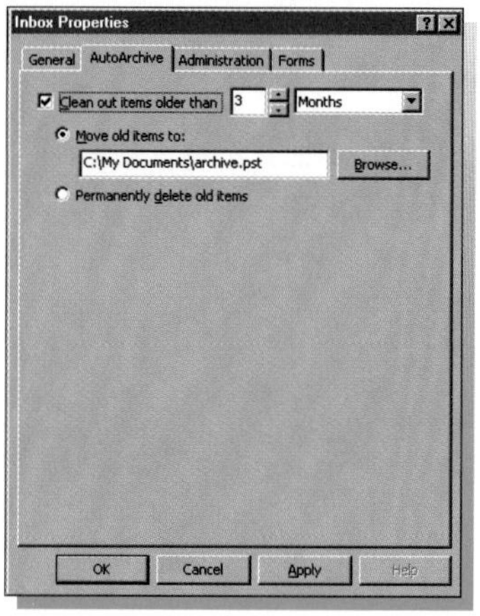

5 Click the AutoArchive tab to open the AutoArchive properties sheet. The global options turn on AutoArchiving and determine the frequency, but without enabling the individual folder AutoArchiving options, nothing will happen at the specified time intervals. It's like setting a timer for a coffee maker that's not turned on. The timer makes the electricity available to the coffee maker at the appropriate time, but you don't get your morning coffee because the coffee maker is switched off.

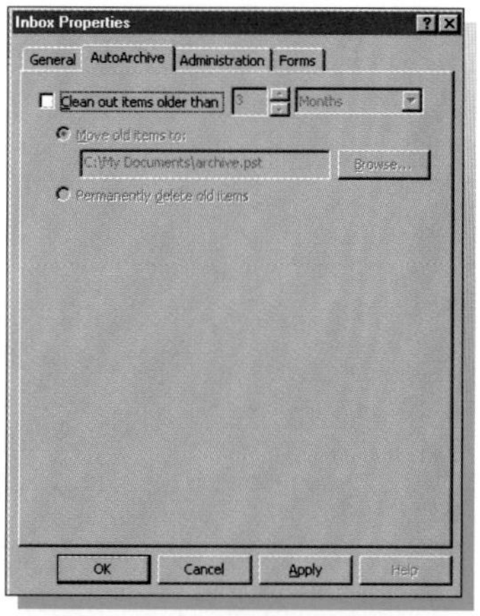

FYI

- **The default AutoArchive settings for the Deleted Items folder is Clean Out Items Older Than Two Months, with Permanently Delete Old Items selected. Since you deleted the items in the first place, there is probably no reason to change this setting, but you should be aware of it just in case.**

2 Click the AutoArchive tab to access the AutoArchive options. The first of five available options is to enable or disable AutoArchiving. If you disable AutoArchiving, no other options are available. If you enable it, the remaining options are the frequency of AutoArchiving, whether or not to display a prompt before AutoArchiving, an option to delete expired e-mail, and the default Archive file.

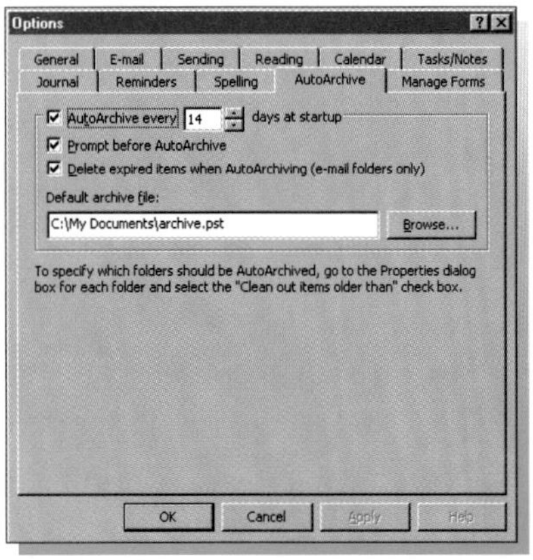

3 Enabling the prompt before AutoArchiving causes a dialog box to display each time Outlook is about to AutoArchive, informing you of its intentions, and asking for your confirmation. This provides you with an opportunity to stop the process in the event you need access to an item that is about to be removed to the Archive file.

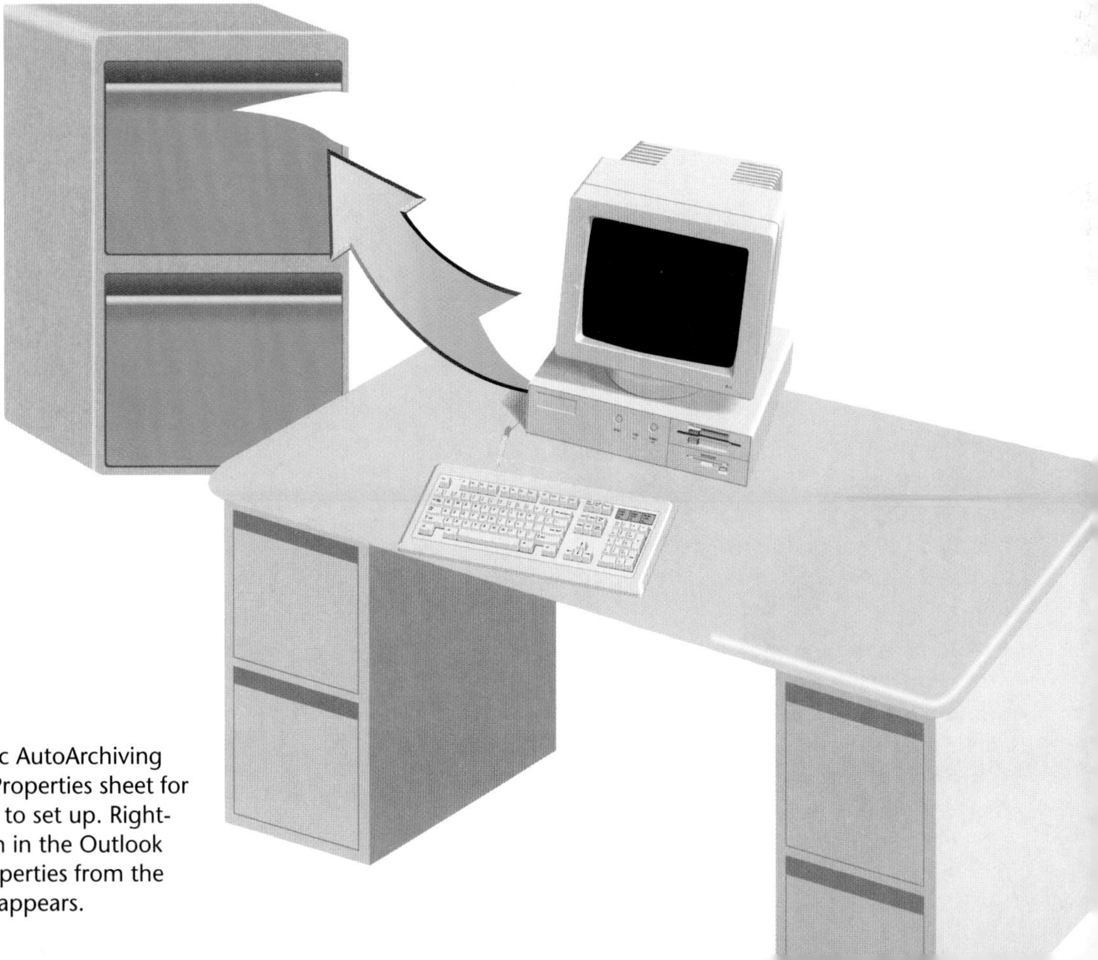

4 To set folder-specific AutoArchiving options, open the Properties sheet for the folder you wish to set up. Right-click the Folder icon in the Outlook Bar and choose Properties from the pop-up menu that appears.

How to Archive Manually

Regardless of what your AutoArchive settings are, there may come a time when you want to perform an archive without waiting for the next scheduled session. If you've recently finished a large project that resulted in volumes of e-mail, notes, and appointments, you might want to clean up Outlook by performing a manual archive that overrides the aging conditions set for a particular folder. Or you may decide to perform an archiving session using the individual folder AutoArchive settings, instead of waiting until the AutoArchive is scheduled.

FYI

- **The Outlook archiving feature uses the most recent of several dates to determine whether or not to archive an item. One of those dates is the last modified date. This means that if you have a journal entry that you created three months ago but made a change to only last week, it will be archived on the basis of the date you changed it, not the date you created it.**
- **Although the Contacts folder is not eligible for AutoArchiving, it can and will be archived if you perform a manual archive and select Personal Folders from the Archive This Folder and All Subfolders option in the Archive dialog box. The creation or last-modified date (whichever is later) will be used to determine eligibility based on the date you enter into Archive Items Older Than on the Archive dialog box.**

1 To begin a manual archive, choose File, Archive from the Outlook menu bar. You can perform a manual archive from any Outlook folder.

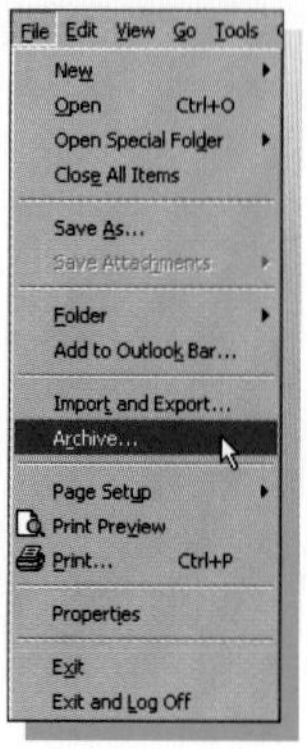

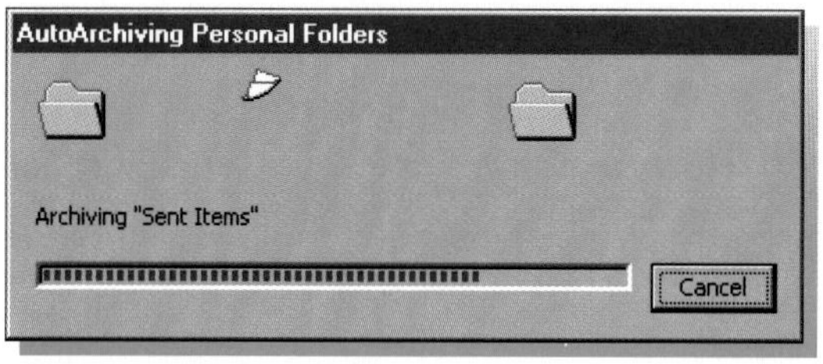

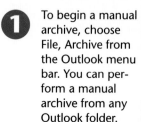

6 After you've made your selections, click OK to begin the archive process. If there are items that meet your criteria, the archive proceeds and the AutoArchiving dialog box appears displaying a progress report on the archiving procedure. If there are no items that meet your criteria, nothing happens and you are returned to the folder from which you started.

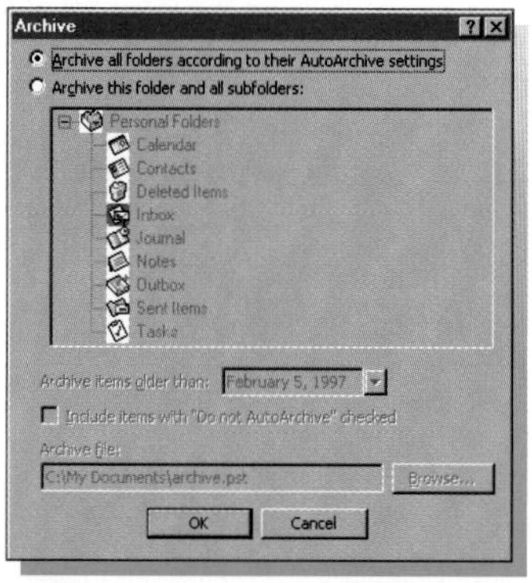

5 For those times when you just want to accelerate the AutoArchive process by forcing it rather than allowing it to wait for the next scheduled session, select the Archive All Folders According to Their AutoArchive Settings.

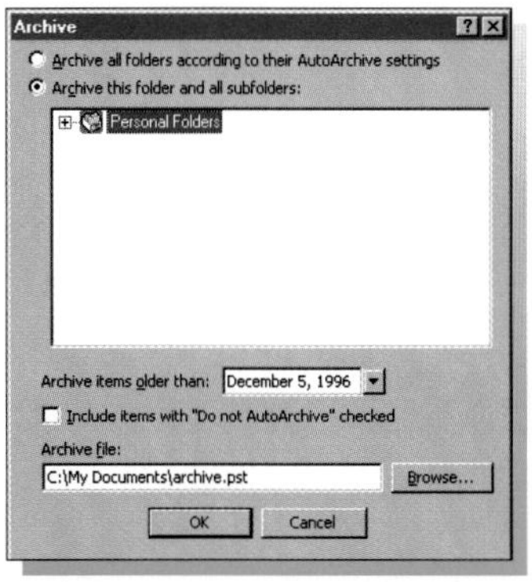

2 The Archive dialog box that opens offers you the option of archiving all folders or a single folder. The default setting is for an archive of all Personal folders using a single Older Than date that you specify. This results in a complete archiving of all folders based on the date you supply. It will override all folder-specific AutoArchive options you have entered in individual folder Property sheets.

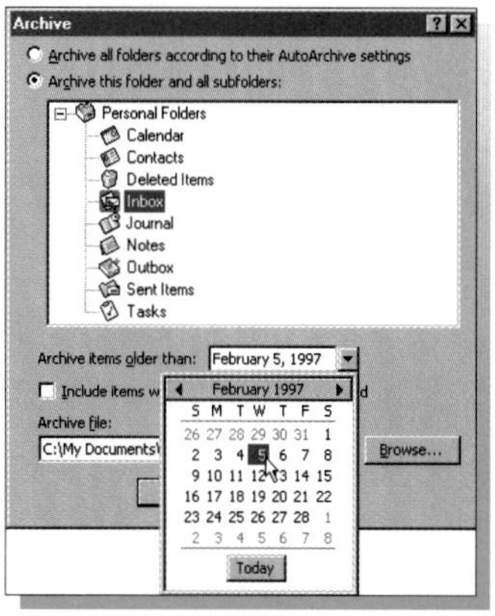

3 To perform a manual archive on a single folder, click the plus sign next to Personal Folders to expand the folder list and select the folder you want to archive. Move to the Archive Items Older Than field, and click the down arrow to open the drop-down calendar. Select the date upon which to base the aging condition.

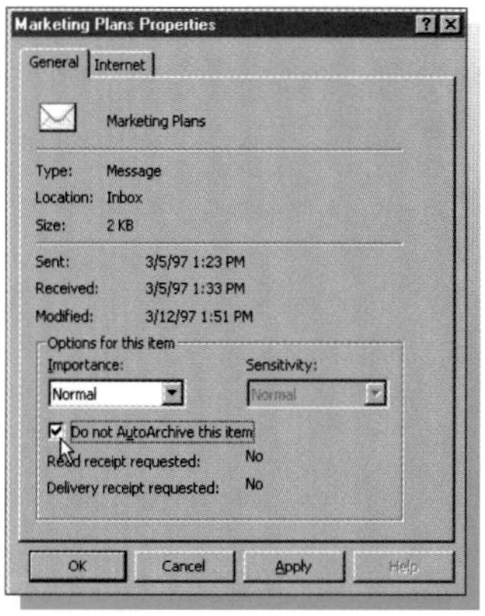

4 The next option, Do not AutoArchive This Item Checked, gives you the opportunity to archive even those items that are ignored by AutoArchive. You can set the properties of an individual item to ignore AutoArchive regardless of the item's age by opening the item and choosing File, Properties to open its Properties dialog box. Then enable the Do Not AutoArchive This Item choice by clicking it and placing a checkmark in the box. Click OK to return to the item, and click OK again to close the item.

How to Retrieve Archived Items

Storing items for posterity is great, but what happens if you need to access those items? Fortunately, Outlook provides a way to view and retrieve archived items. The basic procedure for bringing archived items back to life is to import them into their original folders (and there's an Import Wizard to help you).

There is, however, another way. You can create a set of folders for the archived items and put those folders on your Folder list. Then you just have to open the appropriate folder to see the archived items. The only catch to this system is that you have to go through a setup routine to create those folders. You must perform an archive process before you can create these Archive folders (the archiving process creates the Archive file you'll need to complete the configuration of the Archive folders).

This section covers that setup, and also explains how to import archived items in case you choose not to set up a second set of folders for archived items.

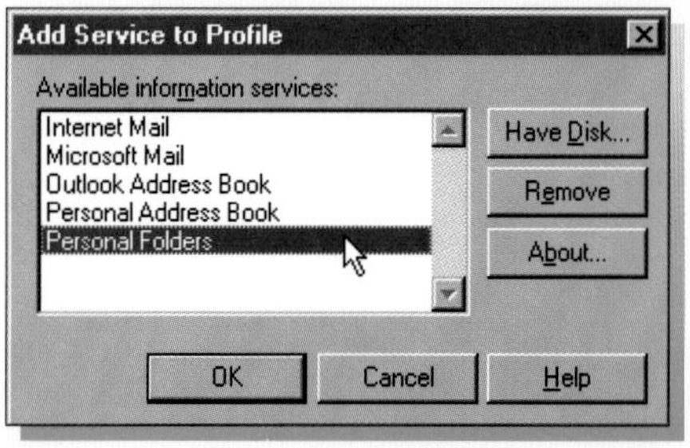

1 To set up a set of folders for archived items, choose Tools, Services to open the Services dialog box. Then click Add to open the Add Service to Profile dialog box and select Personal Folders.

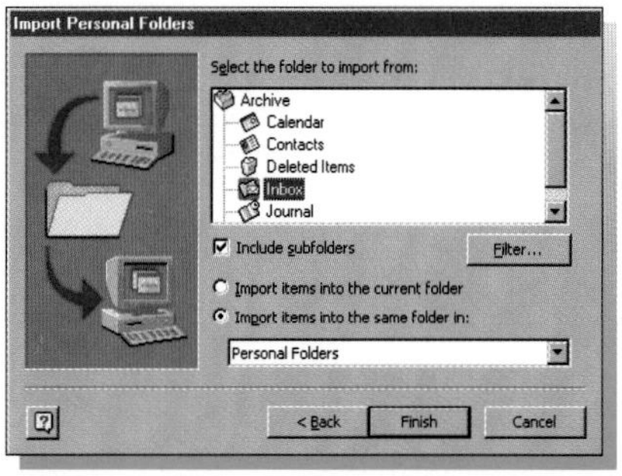

7 Select the Archive File folder to import from and the Personal Folders folder to import into, then click Finish to complete the import.

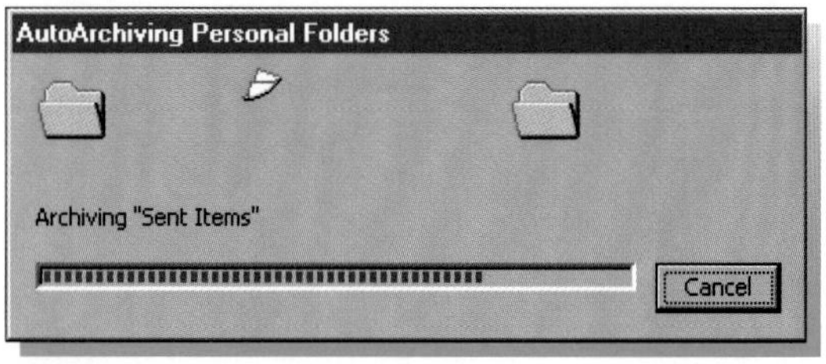

6 In the Import Personal Folders dialog box enter the path and name of the Archive file (or click browse to locate it, then double-click the file name). Set the duplicates option, and click Next.

FYI

- **If you want to import selected items from an Archive file rather than an entire folder, you can use the Filter option in the second Import Personal Folders dialog box of the Import and Export Wizard.**

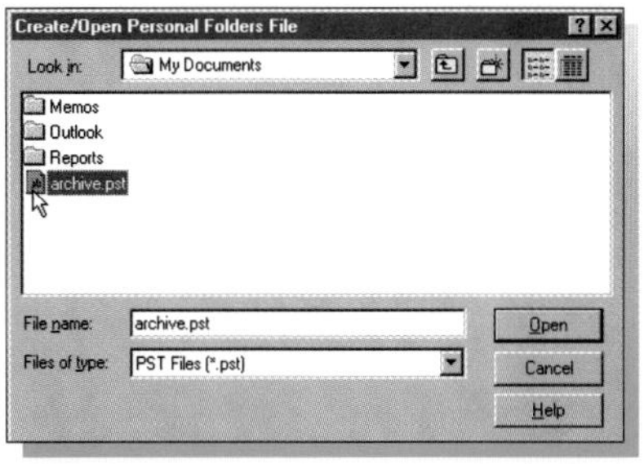

2 Click OK to open Create/Open Personal Folders File. Outlook displays your Windows Operating System folder, but your Archive file is probably not there. It's usually located in the My Documents directory of your hard drive, and is called archive.pst. Click the arrow next to the Look In box to move through your hard drive and locate the Archive file. When you locate it, highlight it and click Open.

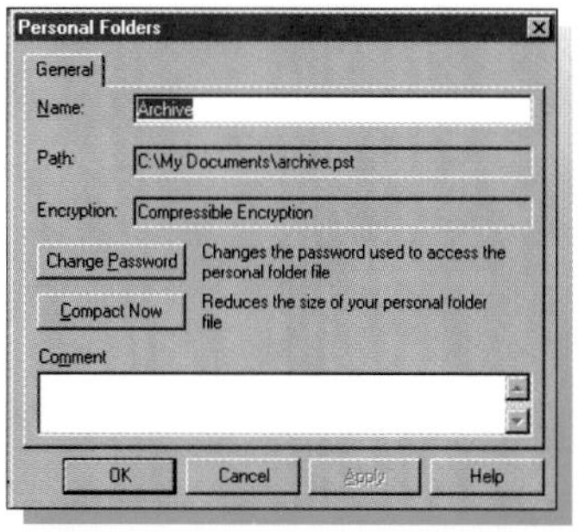

3 In the Personal Folders dialog box that opens, change the name from Personal Folders to Archive so you can easily distinguish it from your original Personal Folders. Then click OK to add the file as an information service. Click OK again to return to Outlook.

4 To view the archived items, open the Folder list, expand the Archive subfolders by clicking the plus sign next to Archive, and click a folder to view its contents. You can view, copy, move, or even edit the archived items.

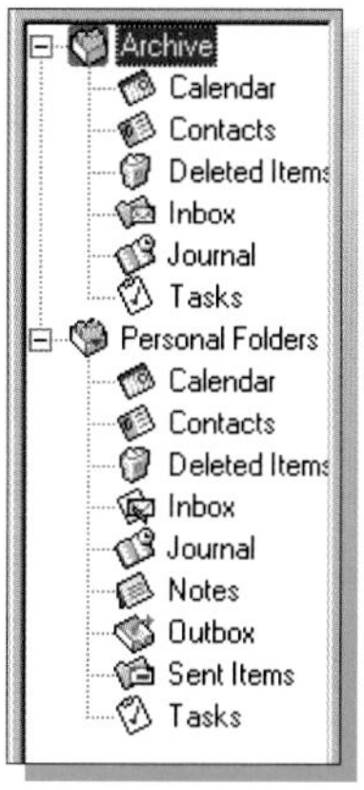

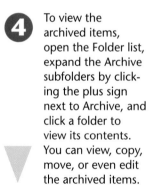

5 If you didn't create a set of folders for your archived items, you can import the archived file back into Outlook, returning a copy of the archived items to their original folder(s). Choose File, Import and Export from the menu bar. From the Import and Export Wizard dialog box select Import from a Personal Folder File (.pst), and click Next.

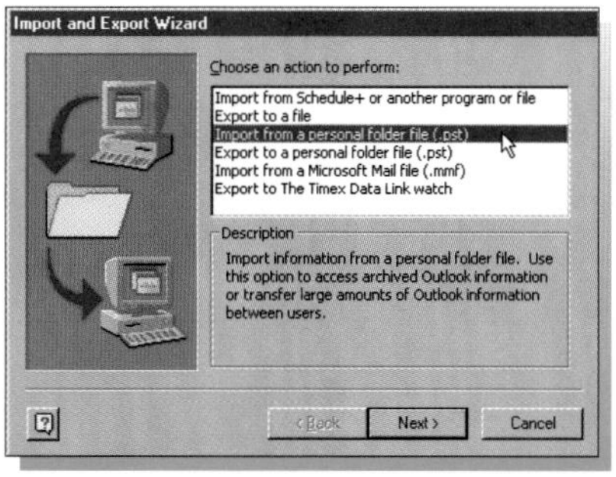

PROJECT 1

Follow the steps in this project to create an e-mail message of your own. In this exercise you'll put a new pen-pal into your Personal Address Book, and then send him or her an e-mail message.

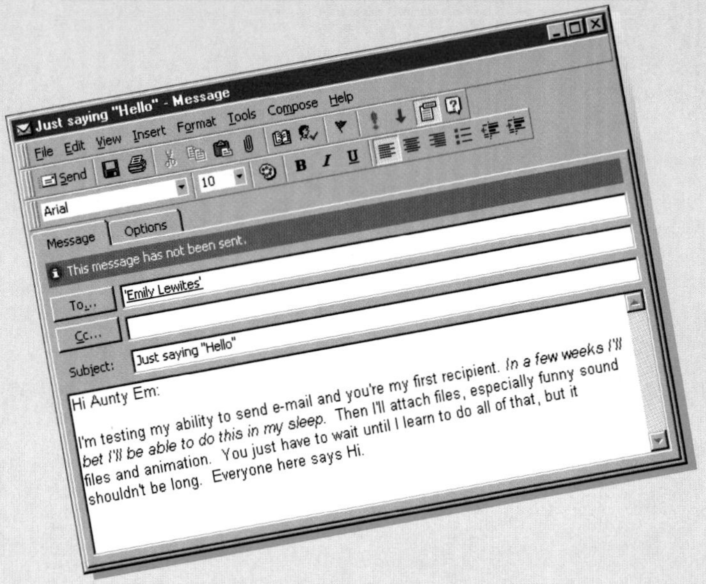

1

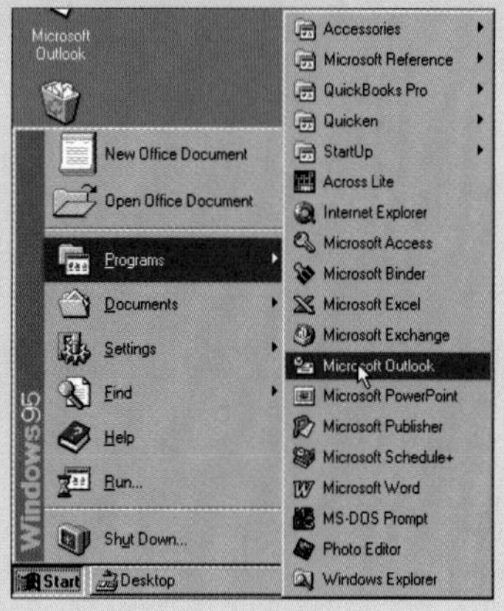

Click Start to open the Start menu, place your pointer on Programs, then click Microsoft Outlook. If you use Windows NT 3.51, open the program group that contains the Outlook program icon, then double-click the icon.

2

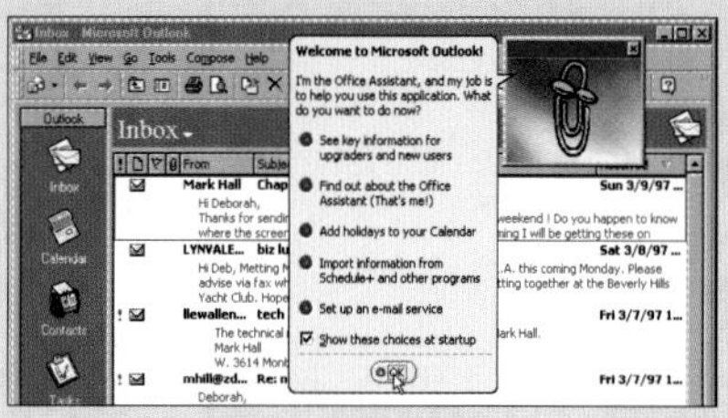

Outlook opens and displays your Inbox. The Office Assistant is sitting atop the window, showing you a list of help topics you might want to investigate. Get rid of the message by clicking OK.

3

Go to the toolbar and click the Address Book icon.

4

The Address Book opens and displays its entries. Click the New Entry icon. (First, make sure the Personal Address Book is active. If you are connected to an Exchange Server system, the Global Address book is probably displayed. Click the arrow to the right of the box named Show Names and select the Personal Address Book.)

5

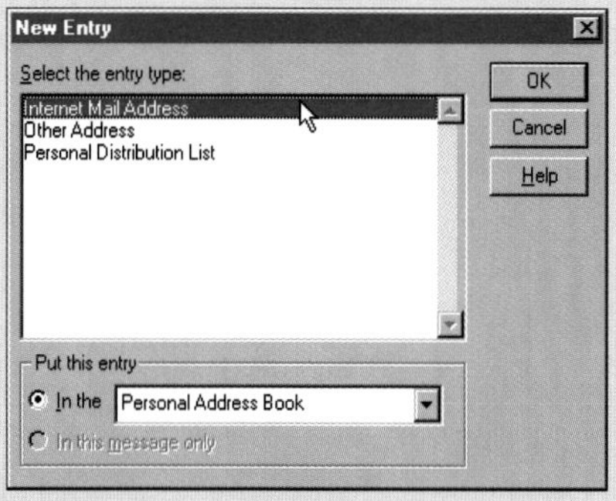

The New Entry dialog box displays. In this exercise, you're going to enter the e-mail address for a friend or business associate (okay, of course you can use a relative if you'd like) whom you contact via the Internet. Select Internet Mail Address and then click OK.

6

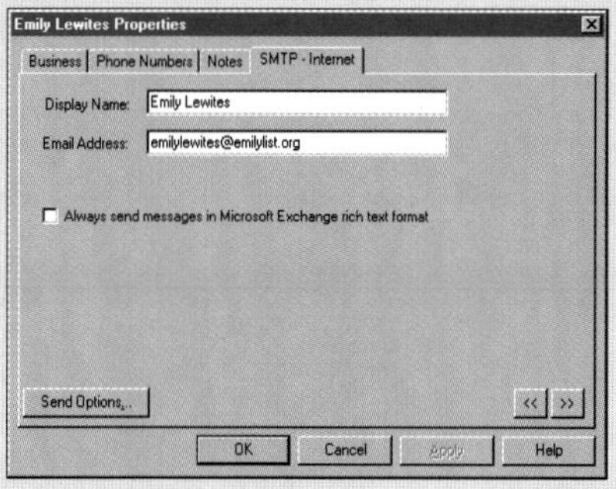

When the New Internet Mail Address Properties dialog box opens, enter a Display Name. This is the name that shows in your address book, it isn't the official e-mail address. If you don't know anybody who has an Internet address (hard to believe), use your own name and e-mail address (you can send mail to yourself, it works fine). Then press Tab and enter the e-mail address.

7

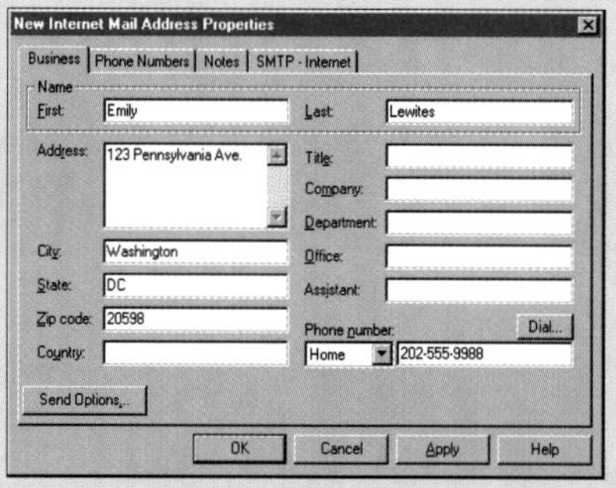

Click the Business tab and fill in as much information as you want to keep track of. Remember to change the entry in the First Name field because it automatically fills in the display name.

8

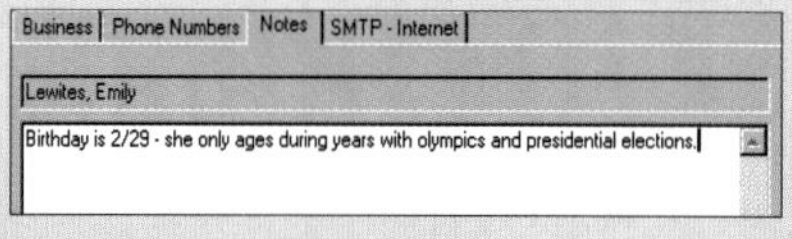

Use the Phone Numbers tab and the Notes tab to enter any additional information you think you might find useful.

9

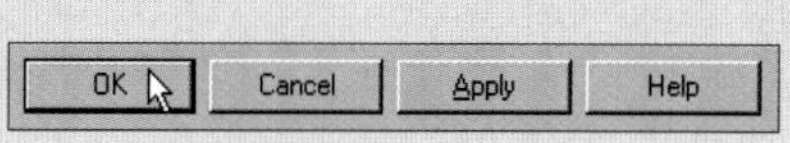

When you finish entering all the information, click OK.

10

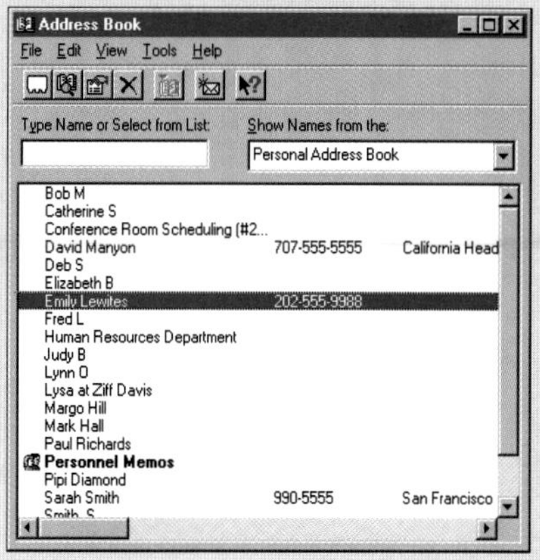

When you return to the Address Book, the new entry is there. Close the Address book.

Continue to next page

PROJECT 1

Continued from previous page

11

Click the New Message icon on the toolbar.

12

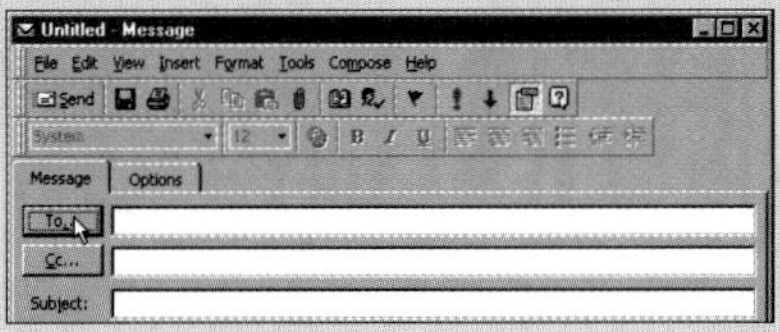

A blank Message form opens. Click the To button to begin addressing this message.

13

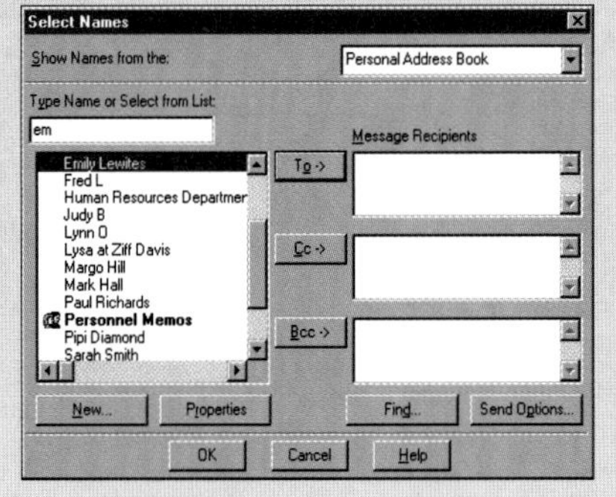

In the Select Names dialog box, find the entry for the person you just added to your address book. The quickest way to get to an entry is to begin typing characters in the Type Name box at the top of the dialog box.

14

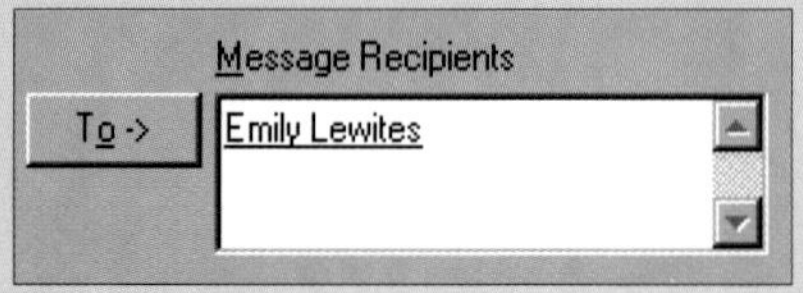

Double-click the entry, which moves it into the Message Recipients pane of the Select Names dialog box, indicating that this name is selected as a recipient. Click OK to return to the message form.

15

Move to the Subject field and enter a phrase that indicates what the contents of the message are.

16

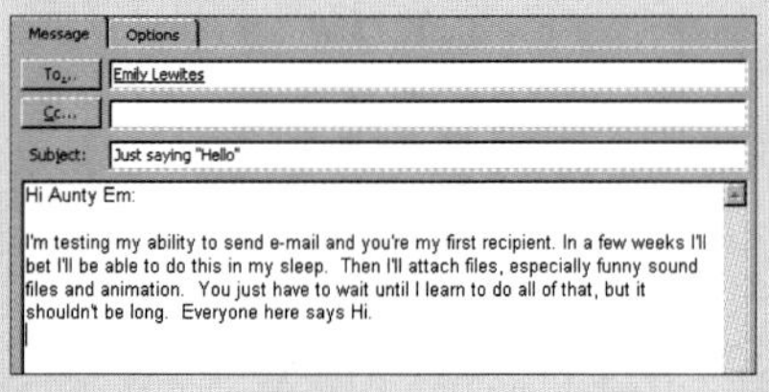

Move to the message text box and enter the message. For this exercise, enter the text you see here. Make sure your salutation is for the name of your recipient; it would be silly to say "Hi Aunty Em" if you're writing to a coworker named Phillip.

17

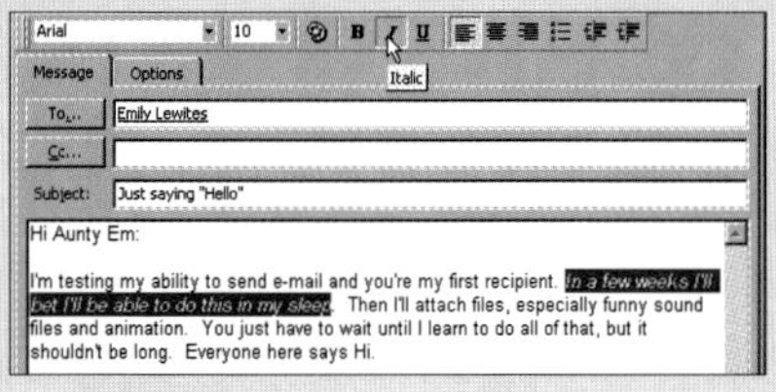

Select the sentence that starts with "In a few weeks." When it is highlighted, click the Italic button on the toolbar.

18

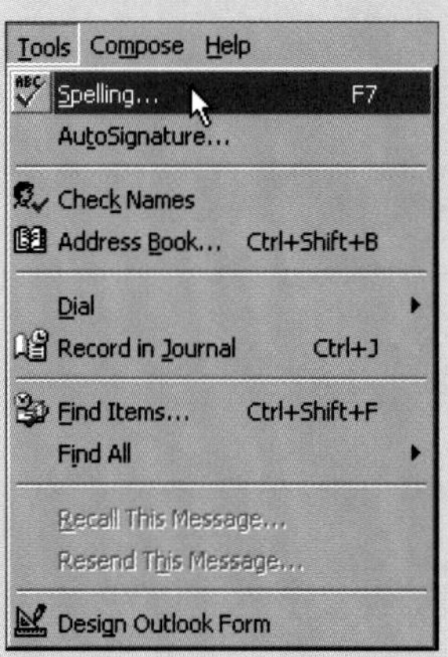

To avoid embarrassment, check the spelling by choosing Tools, Spelling.

19

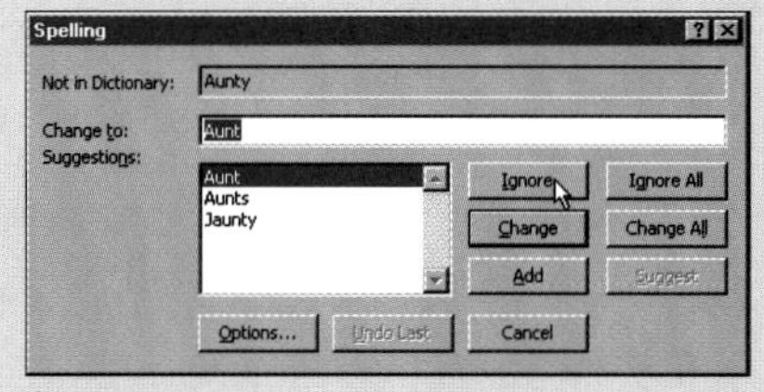

This spelling check didn't like Aunty and wants to change it to Aunt. Your spelling check will probably stop at the name you used (since it's not in the Outlook dictionary). Choose Ignore.

20

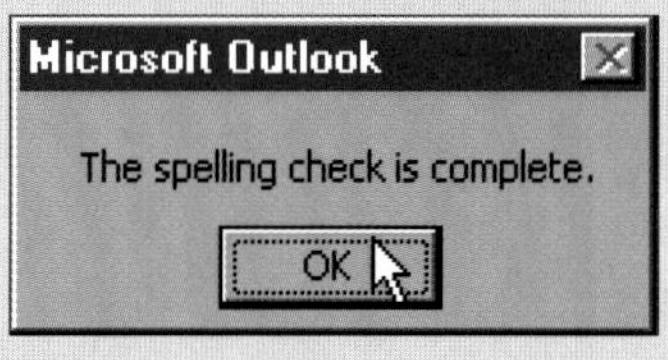

When Outlook announces the spelling check is complete, click OK.

21

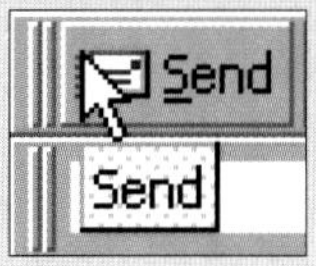

This message is ready to go. Click Send.

PROJECT 2

Sending messages, receiving messages, and managing all those messages are important skills. Now it's time to use those skills by doing some hands-on exercises that involve the things you've learned. You'll send an e-mail message with a file attached, open files that are attached to messages, and move a message into a folder you created.

1

To begin, click the Mail horizontal bar in the Outlook Bar to display the Mail icons on the toolbar.

2

Click the New Mail Message icon to begin composing a message.

3

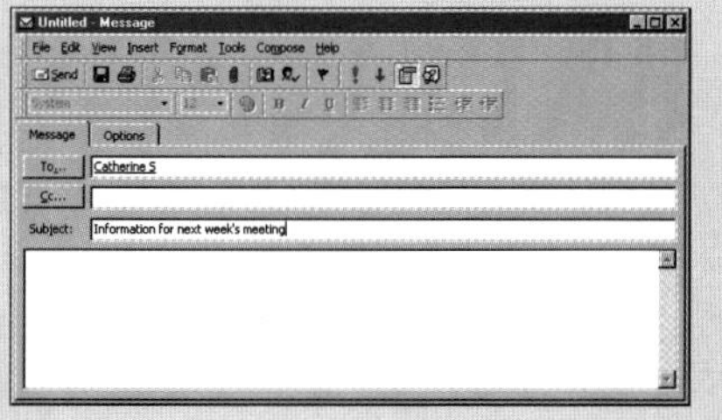

Fill out the header information, using your Personal Address Book to fill in the recipient name (pick a recipient who won't mind receiving a test message from you, or send this message to yourself by entering your own e-mail address in the To field). Then fill out the subject line, and indicate that you're attaching a file to this message.

4

Click the Insert File icon on the toolbar.

5

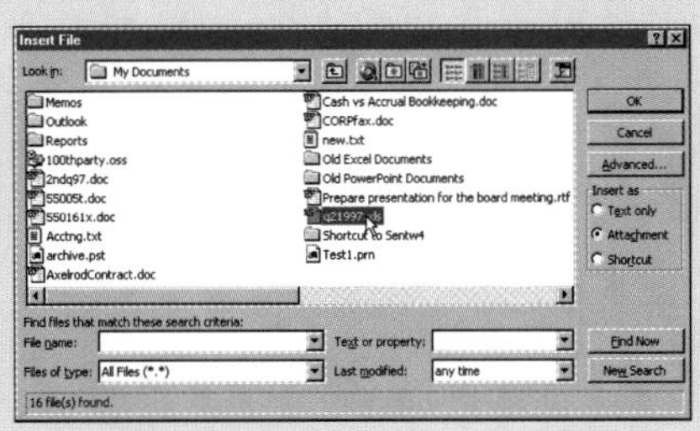

When the Insert File dialog box appears, choose the file you want to attach and click OK (or double-click the file). If the file is not in the folder that's displayed, use the icons on the toolbar to navigate through your hard drive to find the file you need.

6

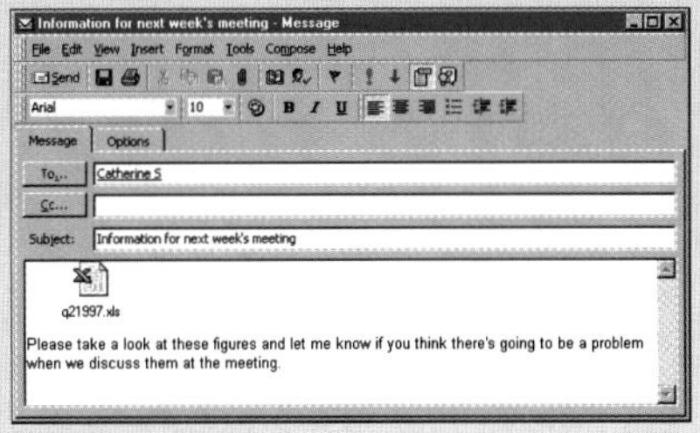

The attachment's icon appears in the message text box. You should add a note explaining why the file is attached.

7

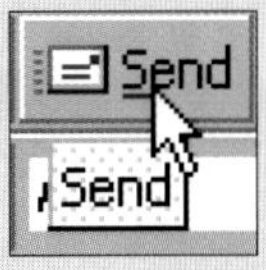

Press Send to ship the message and its attachment to the recipient.

8

Let's move on to handling received mail. Click the Inbox icon on the Outlook Bar to display the Inbox Information Viewer.

9

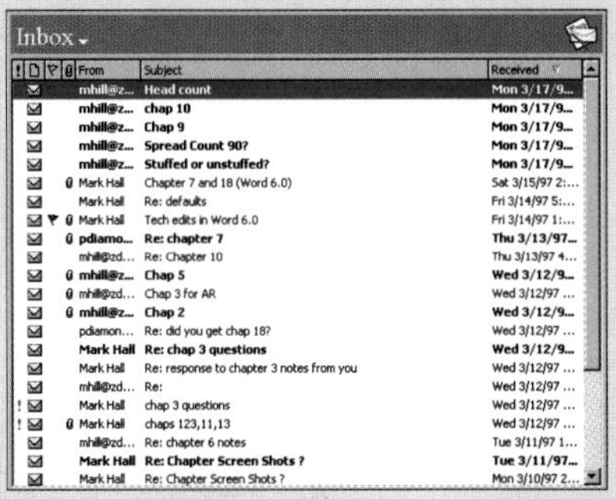

The list of messages can seem overwhelming. The first thing to do is handle the messages you haven't read yet. They're listed in bold so it's easy to tell them from the messages you've already read. However, it would be easier to find them if they were the only messages being displayed.

10

Click the arrow to the right of the Current View box on the toolbar and choose Unread Messages.

Continue to next page ☞

PROJECT 2

Continued from previous page

11

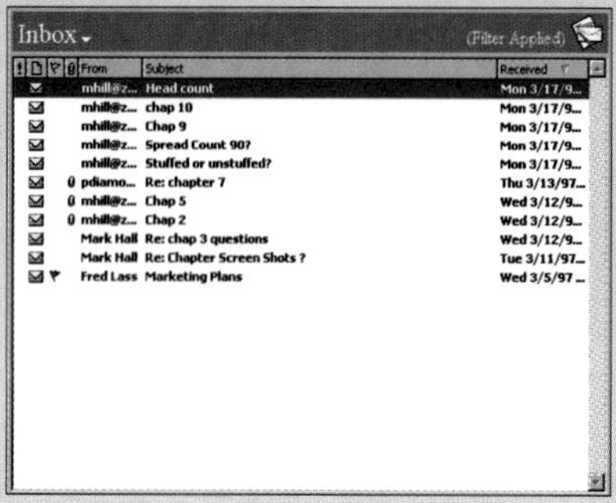

The message listing shows only your unread messages. Notice that the Inbox title bar has a note that indicates a filter has been applied. This view is built with a filter for unread messages.

12

Locate a message that is marked as having an attachment (a paper clip icon to the left of the listing).

13

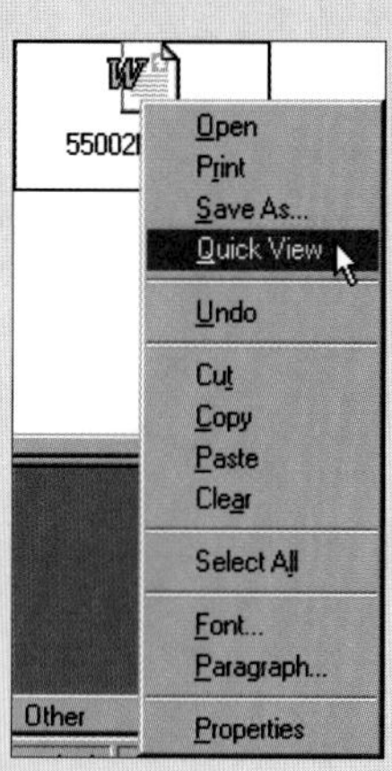

Double-click the listing to open the message. The attachment is represented by an icon with the file name below it. To peek inside to see what is in the message, right-click the icon and choose Quick View from the menu.

14

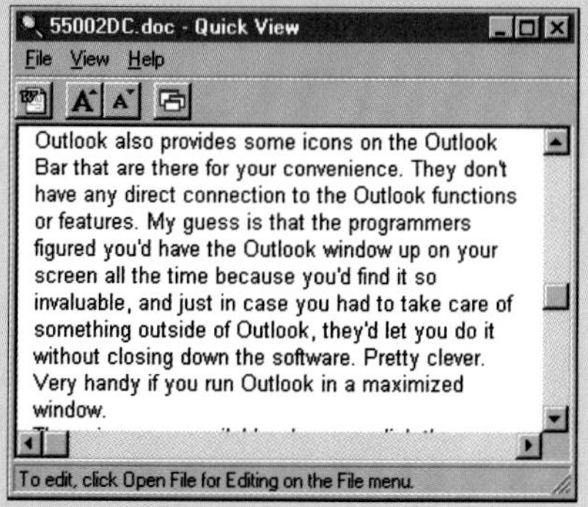

The Microsoft Windows Quick View program opens so you can see the data in the message.

15

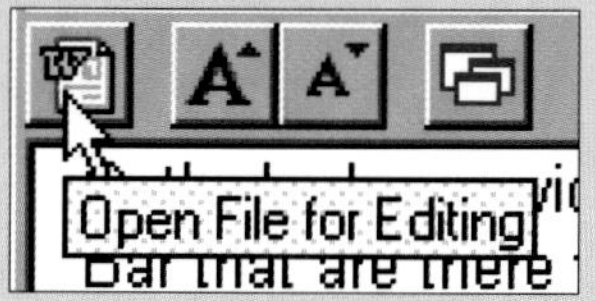

To open the file you must have a software program that can handle this file type, either the same program that created it (you can usually tell from the icon which software was used to create the file) or a program that can convert it and then handle it. To open the file from the Quick View program, click the Open File for Editing icon on the toolbar (you could also close Quick View and then double-click the attachment's icon).

16

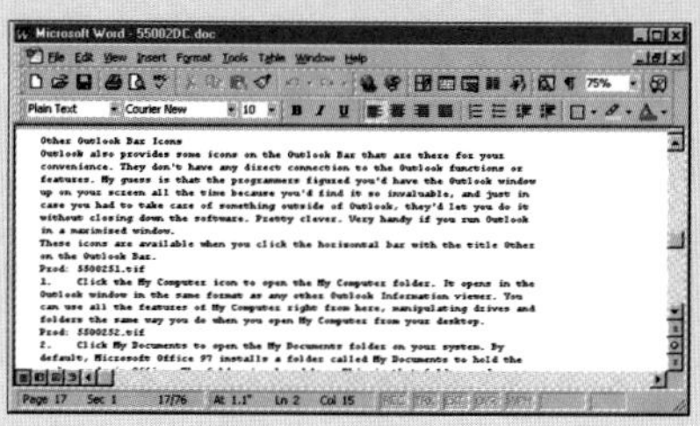

The associated software opens and the attachment file is displayed in the software window. You can edit it, save it, or print it using the software's tools. When you have finished working on the file, close the software and you are returned to the message.

17

Close the message. When the Inbox listing appears, the message is no longer listed because the current view contains only unread messages. Since we want to store this message in a folder connected to its project, we have to see it on the listing. From the Current View box on the toolbar, choose Messages.

18

The Inbox displays all the messages. Right-click the message you just read and choose Move to Folder from the menu.

19

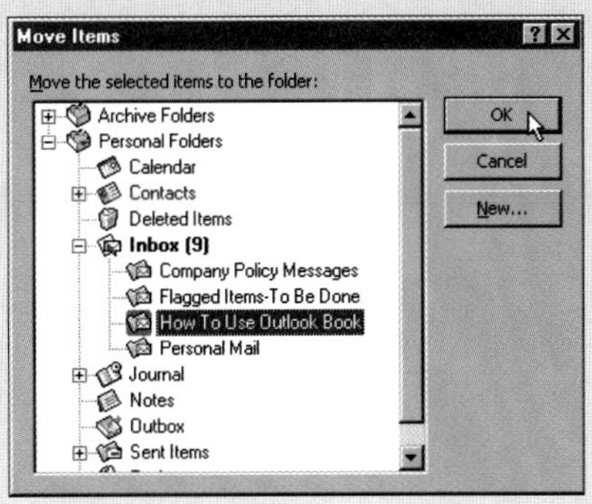

When the Move Items dialog box opens, select the folder you want to use as the container for this message, then click OK. Remember to click the plus sign (+) next to parent folders to expand them so you can see the subfolders you created.

PROJECT 3

It's time to put your new-found personal information management skills to work. A little practical application goes a long way in making the theory come to life.

In this exercise you'll create a new business contact, so grab your rolodex, or root around in your desk until you find one of those business cards you accepted, threw in a drawer, and immediately forgot. Once you create the new contact, you can apply what you've learned by sending an e-mail, autodialing the phone number, creating a task, and scheduling an appointment.

1

To start this exercise you are going to create a business contact, so switch to the Contacts folder by clicking the Contacts icon in the Outlook Bar.

2

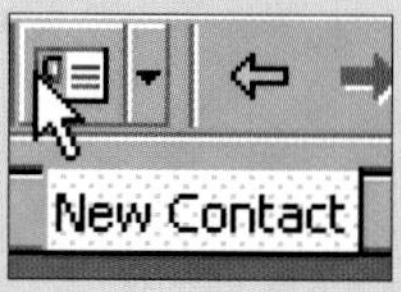

Now click the New Contact icon in the toolbar to open a blank Contact card.

3

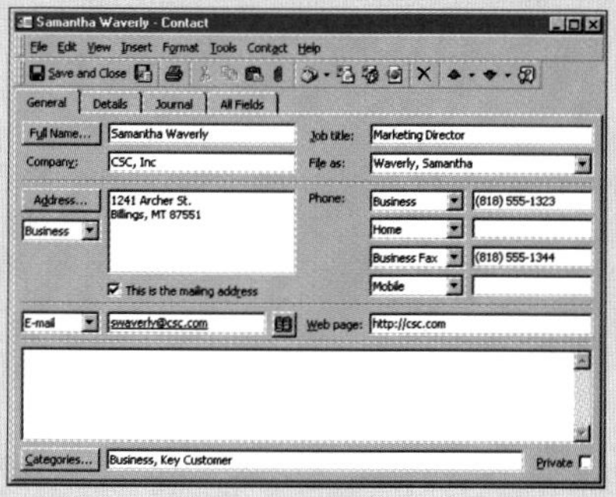

Begin entering the general contact information. Be sure to include all the information you'll need to conduct business with the individual.

4

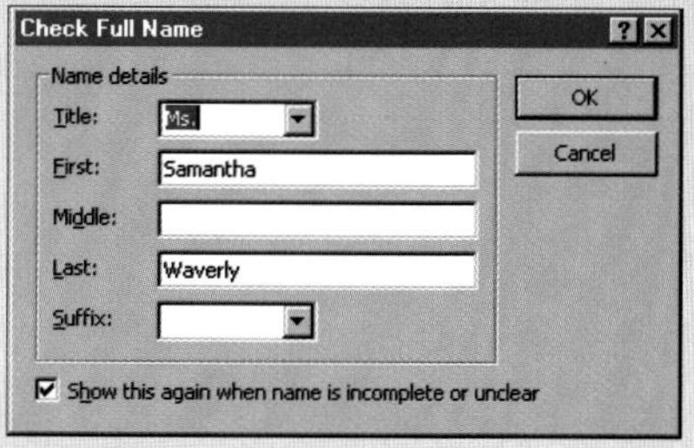

To add a title or suffix to the name, click the Full Name button to open the Check Full Name dialog box.

5

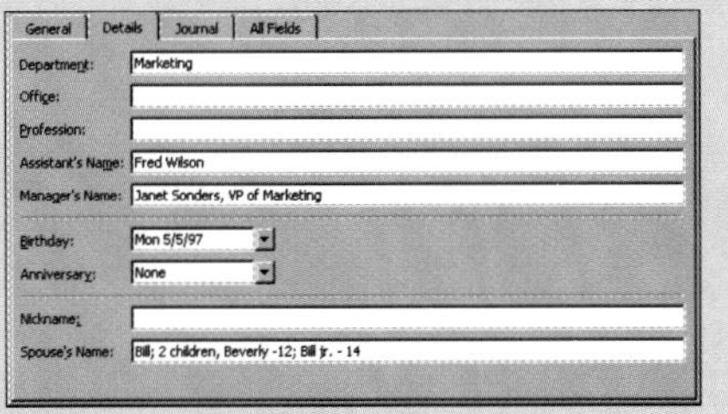

A little detailed and personal information can go a long way in establishing a closer business relationship. Click the Details tab of the Contact card, and fill in as much detailed information as you have.

6

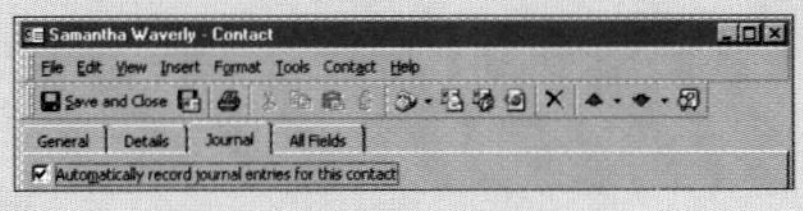

Click the Journal tab to open the Journal information card. Click the option called Automatically Record Journal Entries for This Contact. Keeping track of your interaction with business contacts is essential.

7

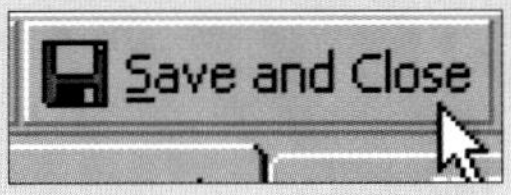

Click Save and Close to save the new contact and return to the Contacts information viewer.

8

Now that you've created a new contact let's send her an e-mail message. Highlight the new contact in the Contacts information viewer and click the New Message to Contact icon in the toolbar.

9

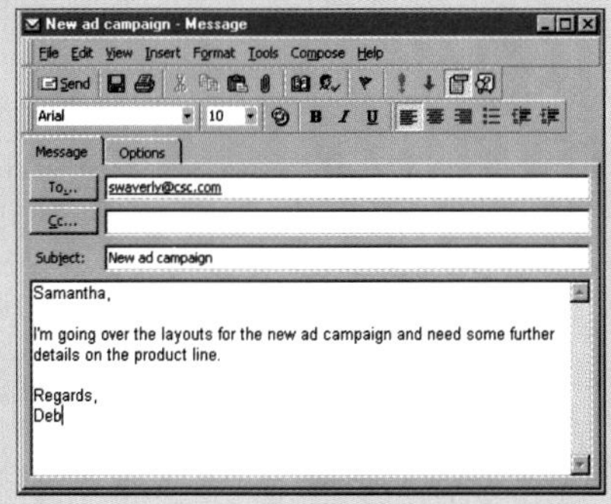

The new message card that opens has the contact's e-mail address in the To field. Fill in the subject and type a message.

10

Click the Send icon to dispatch your message.

11

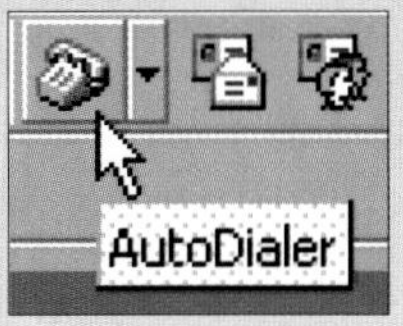

Perhaps you need a quick response to a question. No problem, just give the contact a call. Highlight the contact in the Contacts information viewer and click the AutoDialer icon in the toolbar.

12

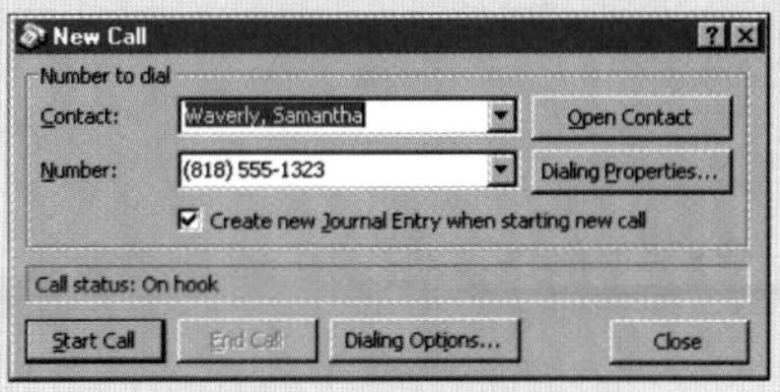

The New Call dialog box appears with the contact name and business phone number. Click Start Call to dial the number.

Continue to next page

PROJECT 3

Continued from previous page

13

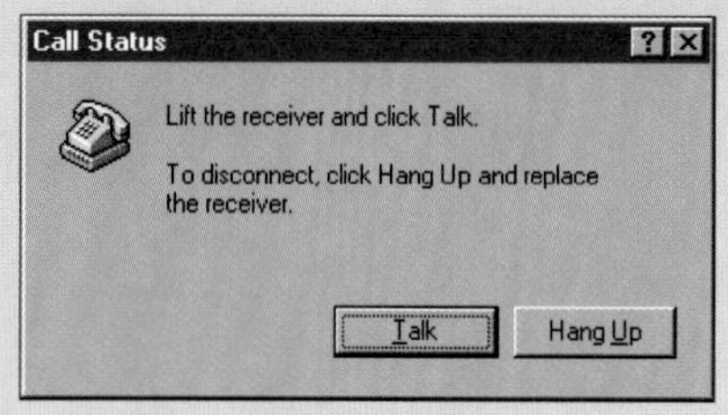

Once the number is dialed, the Call Status dialog box opens. Lift the telephone receiver and click Talk or click Hang Up to disconnect.

14

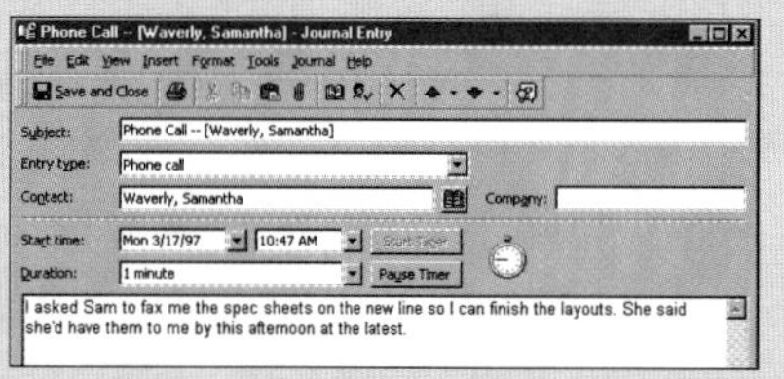

A new Journal Entry card opens so you can record the conversation. The basic information is automatically filled in, so the only thing you have to do is take notes. Click Save and Close when you're done.

15

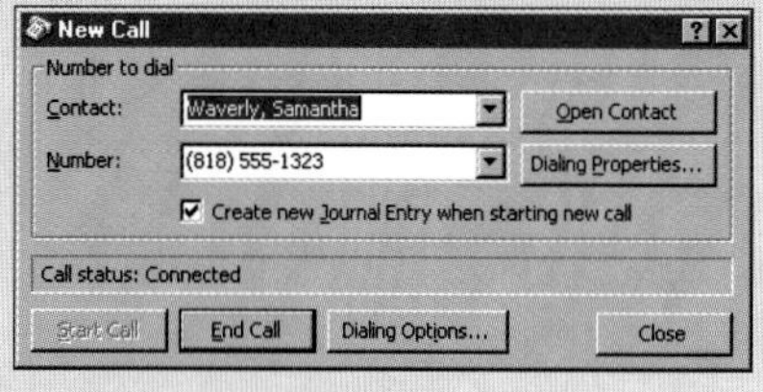

The Journal Entry closes and the New Call dialog box reappears. Click End Call to disconnect, then click Close to return to the Contacts information viewer.

16

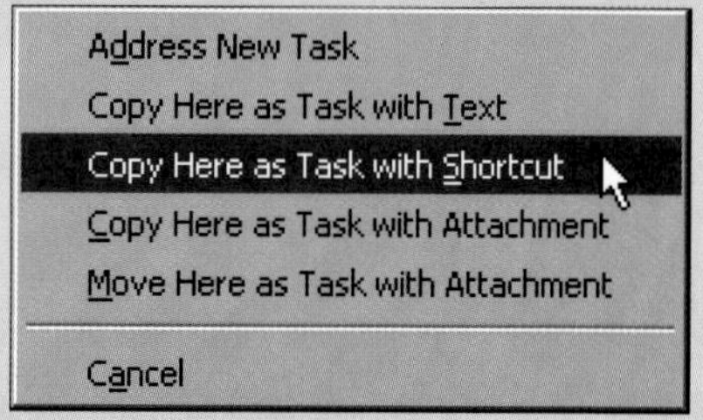

Set up a task that is related to this contact by selecting (highlighting) the Contact card. Then right-drag it to the Tasks icon in the Outlook Bar (that means press and hold down your right mouse button while you drag). When you release the mouse button, a menu appears. Choose Copy Here as Task with Shortcut to open a new Task card. Including a shortcut means that an icon representing the contact card is on the task form. This enables you to open the contact card anytime you are reviewing the task by just double-clicking the shortcut icon.

17

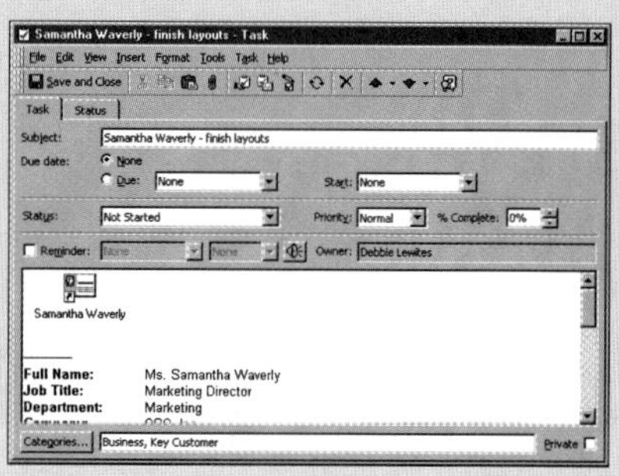

The new task card includes the contact name as the subject. Add a brief description of the task to the subject line.

18

Click the down arrow at the end of the Due field and select a due date from the drop-down calendar.

19

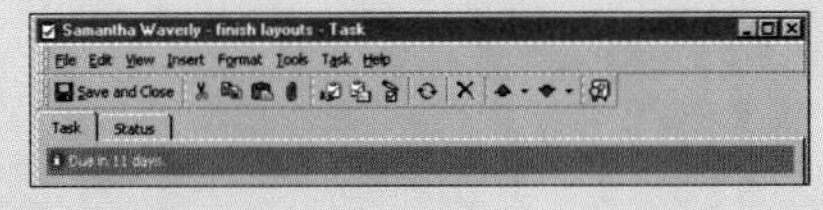

Note the appearance of the information banner between the Task tab and the Subject field, indicating the number of days until the task is due. Click Save and Close to return to the Contacts folder.

20

Now it's time to set up an appointment with the contact to discuss some final issues. Using your right mouse button, drag the Contact card to the Outlook Bar, and drop it on the Calendar icon.

21

From the pop-up menu choose Copy Here as Appointment with Shortcut.

22

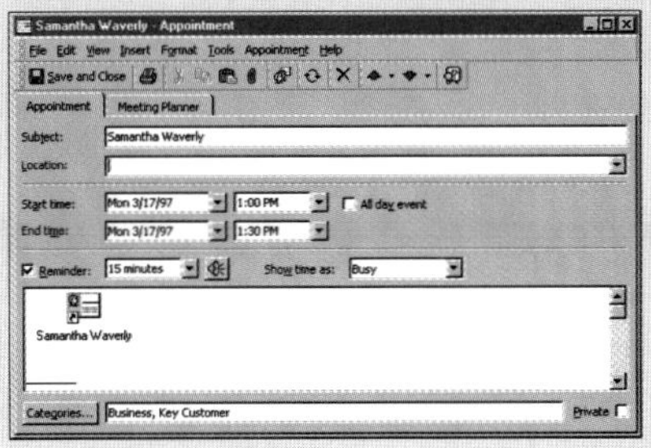

A new appointment card opens with the contact name as the Subject, and a shortcut to the contact in the notes section of the appointment card.

23

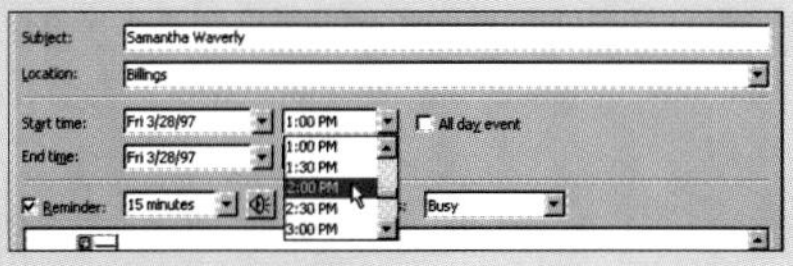

Enter the location of the meeting, then select a start date from the drop-down calendar in the Start time field. Move to the time field and click the down arrow and select a time from the drop-down list.

24

Set the End date and time for the appointment. Then move to the Reminder Time field. Click the down arrow and select the amount of time prior to the appointment you want the reminder to appear.

25

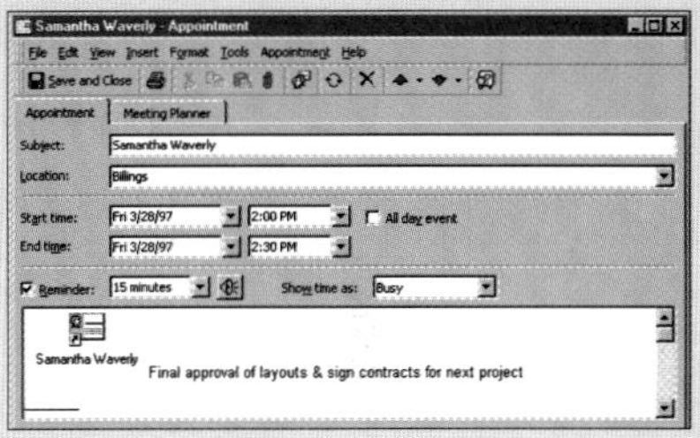

Add any notes you need in the text box below the reminder fields and click Save and Close to return to the Contacts folder.

INDEX